MW01120065

**Library of Congress Control Number: 2005931103**



*The author gratefully acknowledges the teachings and influence of Bible StudyFellowship, Charles Spurgeon, Oswald Chambers, Rick Warren, Dr. Bruce Wilkinson, Dr.Charles Stanley, Charles Swindoll, Max Lucado, Henry Blackaby, Chip Ingram, and others who the Lord has used to guide me in His Word., and into a greater understanding of His truth. It is not my intent to copy anyone, but I am sure that many of these truths I have appropriated have been from Scriptural understandings taught by some of these teachers.*

*ISBN: 0-9742612-7-0*
*Published by Homily Grits Publishing Co.*

# *Homily Grits 4*

## *"Snack food for the Soul"*

Other Books by Robert VanHoose

**Homily Grits** (2003)
**HomilyGrits 2** (2003)
**Homily Grits Daily Discipline of Applied Truth and Proactive Prayer** (2004)

Homily Grits Publishing Co.
Ocala, Florida
www.homilygrits.com
RVanHoose@homilygrits.com

## Dedication

This book is dedicated to my dear past and present Promise Keeper Brothers in the Lord who for over A Dozen years have encouraged and blessed me through our small group Bible studies.

## About the Author

It seems a stretch to go from business man, horseman, real estate developer, and lay church leader to a ministry of the Word, but this is the way God has worked it out in the life of Robert VanHoose.

In seeking to remain faithful and fruitful with the gifts God has given him, Bob developed a passion for writing Word based daily devotions that almost anyone can understand and identify with.

Bob's understanding of Scripture is based on a 50+ year walk with the Lord many years of which have been spent teaching and growing in the Word through study of the Bible and some of the great Bible Teachers of the past fifty years.

It has been gratifying to find that many pastors of many faiths are using "Homily Grits" for sermon ideas and illustrations.

These devotions have been a blesssing to soldiers in Iraq, several thousand prisoners throughout the United States, home schooling and religion class students as well as just plain believers and seekers trying to grow in and better understand the Word.

Bob and his wife Lorna (married in 1952) have been blessed with 6 children and 11 grandchildren who are the dividends of their golden years. Bob founded and ran Big Sandy Furniture stores in the tri-state area of Ky, W.Va, and Ohio in 1954. Big Sandy Superstores are now one of the 100 top furniture and appliance retailers in the United States.

Bob bred, exhibited , and promoted Arabian horses for some 40 years in Kentucky and Florida.

Bob takes very seriously James' admonishment that those who teach will be judged by God with greater strictness.,(James 3:1) and leans solely on His grace that these meditations will be pleasing in His sight.

There is a convenient Alphabetical Title Index located In the back of this book.

Please visit and tell your friends about www.homilygrits.com Thank You!

**Read 1 Corinthians 5:1-10, Psalm 84** **January 1**

## *Just Wait 'till I Get You Home!*

**"There are many rooms in my Father's home, and I am going to prepare a place for you. If this were not so, I would tell you plainly." John 14:2**

How many times have you heard or used this phrase in connection with misbehavior out in public, or where instant correction was not possible?

> *"How lovely is your dwelling place, O LORD Almighty. I long, yes, I faint with longing to enter the courts of the LORD."*
> *Psalm 84:1,2a NLT*

The fear of punishment has been a great tool for teaching children obedience and respect for parents for generations.

When we relate this phrase to Jesus' promises to us, it turns fear into courage, weakness into strength, and fills you with bright hope for tomorrow and great peace and joy for today.

All of the bliss and joy of sinless perfection in our eternal life in heaven gives all believers a lot to look forward to when we persevere in faith until Jesus gets us home.

When Jesus gets us home, we will live forever in the mansion He has prepared for us, rent, tax, and maintenance free.

When Jesus gets us home, we will receive new bodies that will never decay, die, or suffer illnesses of any kind.

When Jesus gets us home, there will be a homecoming reunion with loved ones, which can't even be fully imagined.

The idea of living in a world of total happiness and joy with no more sorrow, pain, suffering, and sin seems almost too good to be true, but we have the revelation of God through His Word and the resurrection of Jesus to prove that it is the destination of all believers.

> *"For we know that when this earthly tent we live in is taken down—when we die and leave these bodies—we will have a home in heaven."*
> *1 Corinthians 5:1a NLT*

When we have received this blessed promise by faith in the one who died to insure it, it gives us strength, joy, and peace through all of the problems of our lives on this earth.

The fear of death loses its sting when we think about all of the joys that await us in heaven.

**Father, help me to always keep my "eye on the prize" as I run the race of life on this earth. Amen.**

January 2 Read 1 Peter 2, Job 20:12-29

## *Leaving a Bad Taste*

**"How sweet are Your words to my taste, *Sweeter* than honey to my mouth!" Psalm 119:103**

This saying is still used by many to describe an unpleasant experience or defective product. Many broken relationships leave this kind of taste.

> ***"He enjoyed the taste of his wickedness, letting it melt under his tongue. He savored it, holding it long in his mouth. But suddenly, the food he has eaten turns sour within him, a poisonous venom in his stomach." Job 20:12-14 NLT***

.Rude and overbearing people often leave a bad taste when we think of them. A defective car or other product will often leave a bad taste that we will remember for a long time.

Many sins taste so sweet for a season but leave a bad taste of guilt that only the forgiveness of God through confession and faith in Jesus Christ will take away.

The sweet taste of gossip, revenge, winning an argument, stroking our own egos, etc., will usually end up leaving a "bad taste in the mouth".

A foul mouth that pours out the filth of the heart leaves a bad taste for those who hear it, but even more for those who let it fly from their mouths.

Many people have been turned off from Christ and His church because of the bad taste they have received at the hands of so called Christians.

Scripture clearly warns us against being a stumbling block to others.

*"Taste and see that the Lord is Good" (Psalm 34.8)* reminds us that God will never leave a bad taste in our mouth when we receive Jesus in our hearts and let the Holy Spirit live within us and guide us.

The blood of Jesus is the soul wash that removes the bad taste of sin and guilt and refreshes us with the sweetness of God's love. It will remove deceitfulness and evil and replace them with the taste tingling fruit of the Spirit.

> ***"As newborn babes, desire the pure milk of the word, that you may grow thereby, if indeed you have tasted that the Lord is gracious. 1 Peter 2:1***

Love, joy, peace, longsuffering, kindness, goodness, faithfulness, gentleness, and self-control have never been known to leave a bad taste in anyone's mouth.

**Father, let me wash out the bad tastes daily through the cleansing of confession, forgiveness, and repentance. Amen**

**Read Acts 2:22-28, Psalm 52** **January 3**

## *Celebrating the Real Presence*

**"For where two or three come together in my name, there am I with them." Matthew 18:20 NIV**

There are different understandings of Scripture among believers regarding the real presence of the body and blood of Jesus Christ in the bread and wine of communion.

> ***"I will praise You forever for what You have done; in Your name I will hope, for Your name is good. I will praise You in the presence of Your saints."***
> ***Psalm 52:9 NIV***

All too often lost sight of and less appropriated to our corporate worship is the real presence of Christ when we come together to worship in His name.

What a difference it makes when we gather for worship in anticipation of coming into the presence of our living Lord and Savior!

We all too often approach worship from a sense of duty instead of privilege. Our corporate worship can too easily become a habit instead of a highlight.

We often are influenced by the messenger instead of the message and want to be entertained instead of inspired. We too often fail in expecting to see Jesus with the excitement that the reality of His promise to be present should bring.

If we were invited to the White House for a visit with the president, how would we prepare? How excited would we be? How attentive would we be to every detail of the visit?

How much greater to be invited to visit Jesus Christ at church every time we go! What if we were as prepared, excited, and attentive to every detail as if we were going to the White House?

When we approach corporate worship with real excitement and expect Christ to show up as He has promised, we will not be disappointed.

> ***"You have made known to me the paths of life; You will fill me with joy in Your presence."***
> ***Acts 2:28 NIV***

Our corporate worship will rise to a new level of joy and intimacy with Christ.

**Father, by the power of the Holy Spirit, help me to come to church with a heart prepared and a mind focused on seeing Jesus. Amen.**

January 4 Read 1 Corinthians 1:4-9, Isaiah 28:16-29

# *Falling Short*

**"In the same way, wisdom is sweet to your soul. If you find it, you will have a bright future, and your hopes will not be cut short." Proverbs 24:14 NLT**

We all know a lot about falling short. Physically, no matter how tall we may be, we find ourselves climbing ladders or standing on our tip toes to reach a little bit higher.

> ***"For you have no place of refuge—the bed you have made is too short to lie on. The blankets are too narrow to cover you,"***
> ***Isaiah 28:20 NLT***

Relationally, we often fall short of the expectations of others or have others fall short of ours, which brings problems in marriages, jobs, sports and about every pursuit of life.

Financially, we often come up short in having the funds to cover our actual or perceived wants and needs.

Spiritually, we *"all fall short of the glory of God" (Romans 3:23b)* and are doomed unless we receive the saving grace of God through faith in Jesus Christ as Savior.

The rich young ruler fell short because he was too tall in riches of this world. King Agrippa was almost persuaded to become a Christian by the eloquence of Paul, but came up short.

The arms of God are never too short. He reaches out to receive all, and He pours out blessing upon blessing on both the just and the unjust. He is the giver of every good gift.

> ***"Even as the testimony of Christ was confirmed in you, so that you come short in no gift, eagerly waiting for the revelation of our Lord Jesus Christ,"***
> ***1 Corinthians 1:6, 7***

We also need to know that we can fall short of all the blessings God has for us because some of them are based on our conduct and cooperation with Him.

If our life on this earth is cut short, we dare not face an eternity separated from God because we fell short of receiving the wonderful free gift of salvation as a result of our preoccupation with anything that would make us miss the call.

**Father, stretch my strength with Yours that I might not fall short. Amen.**

# *Guard Rails for Glory*

**"The LORD is slow to anger and rich in unfailing love, forgiving every kind of sin and rebellion. Even so he does not leave sin unpunished, but he punishes the children for the sins of their parents to the third and fourth generations." Numbers 14:18**

God's moral laws are still on the books, and although no longer a matter of eternal life or death, they set boundaries for obedience that lead to the abundant life in Christ.

***"That they may set their hope in God, and not forget the works of God," Psalm 78:3***

When Jesus died on the cross for us, He paid the penalty for our sins, but His commandments continue to remind us of our sinfulness and need for a Savior. His commandments serve as guard rails to keep us living within the parameters of His will.

When Adam and Eve disobeyed the first guard rail God ever established, *("But the LORD God gave him this warning: 'You may freely eat any fruit in the garden except fruit from the tree of the knowledge of good and evil. If you eat of its fruit, you will surely die.'" Genesis 2:16*) they brought separation from God and all of its consequences into the world for them and for us.

If children are not brought up honoring their parents, they are robbed of the blessing "*that your days may be long, and that it may be well with you,*" (Deuteronomy 5:16) and they will grow up disobeying God.

***"But afterward there will be a quiet harvest of right living for those who are trained in this way." Hebrews 12:11b***

Thanks be to God that in His love and mercy, He came down to earth as a man, lived a perfect life to fulfill the law for us, and provided a means of escape from the curse of sin for us!

God has established guard rails for our good and for His glory. He gives us the power of the Holy Spirit to live within them. We are without excuse for not obeying.

**Father, thank you for loving me enough to give me guard rails for living a life fully pleasing to You. Amen.**

# *Living Below the Poverty Level*

**"Jesus replied, 'I am the bread of life. No one who comes to me will ever be hungry again. Those who believe in me will never thirst.'" John 6:35**

The government annually computes an income level that delineates the poverty level. Millions of Americans live below the line of material poverty.

> ***"He will rescue the poor when they cry to Him; He will help the oppressed, who have no one to defend them." Psalm 72:12 NLT***

Five or ten times as many Americans, including believers, live their lives below the spiritual poverty level.

Some people wander aimlessly through life looking for love and meaning in trash laden dumpsters of darkness and are doomed to living and dying in spiritual poverty.

Others receive Jesus Christ as Savior so that they can go to heaven when they die, but they never experience the joy of living in the richness of God's love on an everyday basis on this earth.

God loves us and receives us just the way we are, but He loves us too much to let us continue living in spiritual poverty. He wants us to grow into the fullness of His Son and to enjoy the intimacy of a personal relationship with Jesus, in which we become brothers and friends who experience the fullness of His love, His joy, His answered prayers, and His blessings reserved for those who abide in Him and His Word.

Just as the financially impoverished do not have the money to pay when the bills come due, the spiritually impoverished do not have the strength and power of the Holy Spirit to rejoice and persevere through troubles in the joy of the Lord.

> ***"You say, 'I am rich. I have everything I want. I don't need a thing!' And you don't realize that you are wretched and miserable and poor and blind and naked." Revelation 3:17 NLT***

The spiritually impoverished can not enjoy life to the fullest that comes only when we do the good works for which we were created.

We need a real war on the real poverty of the soul. Care to enlist?

**Father, let me never again suffer the woes of spiritual poverty. Amen.**

**Read John 17, Psalm 5** **January 7**

## *Sink Holes of Shattered Dreams*

**"For wisdom will enter your heart, and knowledge will fill you with joy." Proverbs 2:10 NLT**

Anyone who lives in Florida becomes well aware of sink holes. A whole city block sank in Winter Park, Florida, in the 1970's, and interstate highways, homes, and businesses continue to sink.

> ***But let all who take refuge in You rejoice; let them sing joyful praises forever. Protect them, so all who love Your name may be filled with joy."***
> ***Psalm 5:11 NLT***

One of the realities of life is that we will all at sometime, and many times often, experience the sink holes of shattered dreams.

Our make-believe dreams of living the perfect life with great friends, great spouses, perfect children, trouble-free relationships, great looks, great jobs, and great health sink under the pressure of living life in a sin-sick world.

The real question is not if, but when, our dreams get shattered, how do we respond? How do we fill these sink holes of life?

Many have turned to alcohol, drugs, or other destructive relationships or practices to take away the hurt and get their minds off of their shattered dreams. Some will try to fill the big hole of despair with anger at God and withdrawal into living joyless lives. Others will become offensive to cover up the hurt and vent their frustrations over shattered dreams.

The best defense for shattered dreams is to first realize that we are not living in a make-believe world but as imperfect people living in a sin-sick world inhabited by imperfect people.

Once we accept these realities, it is not hard to realize that we need a Savior, a deliverer, a comforter, and helper who can and will fill our sink holes with living water. He will give us the power and strength to persevere and prosper through our shattered dreams.

> ***"And now I am coming to you. I have told them many things while I was with them so they would be filled with my joy."***
> ***John 17:13 NLT***

**Father, thank you for giving me Your all-surpassing peace and all-sufficient grace for my sink holes of life. Amen.**

## *God's Moral Compass*

**"Thy Word is a lamp unto me feet and a light unto my path." Psalm 119:105**

History lessons seem to be a waste of time. Instead of learning from the past, the world continues to try to make man into God and repeats the moral decadence that put the children of God into captivity, which caused the fall of all the great empires and civilizations of the past.

***"Direct my steps by Your word, and let no iniquity have dominion over me." Psalm 119:133 NLT***

Even within Christ's church, we find the Word of God being ignored or twisted by so-called liberal theology, which chooses to ignore or put a spin on the Word of God that causes its edges to be dulled. Thus, God's truth becomes man's relative truth.

While it is true that Jesus Christ fulfilled the law and set us free from the bondage of sin, which the law could never do, the law remains our mirror, our guide, and our curb.

Even the Ten Commandments reduction into two commandments in no way minimizes the importance of God's law.

In fact, the two commandments to love God and to love others cover a number of sins not specifically mentioned in the Ten Commandments. They become an even more comprehensive means of convicting us of our sin, promoting righteousness, and curbing our sinfulness,

If we truly love God, we will not put any other gods above Him. We will not take His name in vain; we will honor our fathers and mothers. If we love others, we certainly will not steal, envy, bear false witness against them, or harm them.

***"Yes indeed, it is good when you truly obey our Lord's royal command found in the Scriptures: 'Love your neighbor as yourself.'" James 2:8 NLT***

By the power of the Holy Spirit, God has written the law on our hearts and has given us the freedom and the strength to obey them. We should never try to navigate the journey of life without God's moral compass.

**Father, guide me through this barren land. Amen.**

**Read Colossians 3:1-17, Psalm 100** **January 9**

# Job Satisfaction

**"For we are God's masterpiece. He has created us anew in Christ Jesus, so that we can do the good things he planned for us long ago." Ephesians 2:10 NLT**

We sometimes find ourselves in jobs or doing tasks that we absolutely hate, or at least feel totally unsatisfied in doing. God tells us to persevere through these situations and "work as unto the Lord," which will certainly help lighten the burden of such tasks.

> ***"Serve the LORD with gladness; Come before His presence with singing."***
> ***Psalm 100:2***

If we are fortunate, we will find ourselves in jobs that we enjoy so much we would do them for free. To have that job or task that you can't wait to get up in the morning and get to work is one of the great blessings of life and trophies of God's grace.

When we have this God-given passion for a particular occupation or profession, we generally also have a God-given talent and "sweet spot" for this endeavor.

We see what a difference finding this "sweet spot" makes in the lives of those around us. Teachers who have found their "sweet spot" in teaching bring a passion and excellence that impacts their students way beyond the classroom of school and into the classroom of life.

Preachers who have found their "sweet spot" in ministry will minister with such love and enthusiasm that their church will attract worshippers like flies to honey.

It is a real joy to see waitresses, doctors, mechanics, nurses, janitors, policemen—people in every walk of life who have found their "sweet spot."

It often takes a lot of different jobs along with prayer and a realistic assessment of our talents, abilities, and passions to find and enjoy our "sweet spot," but it is well worth the finding.

> ***"And whatever you do or say, let it be as a representative of the Lord Jesus, all the while giving thanks through Him to God the Father."***
> ***Colossians 3:17 NLT***

**Father, thank you for letting me know the joy of Your anointing in my job and my tasks. Amen.**

January 10 Read Ephesians 4:7-16 Psalm 84

# *Upward Mobility*

**"To know the love of Christ which passes knowledge; that you may be filled with all the fullness of God." Ephesians 3:19**

Upward mobility has been the defining characteristic of our culture for many years. Moving on up into higher and higher levels of prosperity, pleasure, and life styles has brought an excess of stress and problems into the lives of many people.

> ***"They will continue to grow stronger, and each of them will appear before God in Jerusalem."***
> ***Psalm 84:7 NLT***

Upward mobility has affected our cultures views on families and parenting. These higher and higher levels of prosperity become dependent on two pay checks instead of one. As a result, children are often influenced more by strangers than by parents.

The stress of always moving upward can take its toll. When we do not achieve our expectations or the expectations of others, we often become disillusioned and depressed, joining the ranks of the walking wounded who go through life withdrawn and defeated.

Moving on up in the knowledge and fullness of Christ should be the defining characteristic of every believer.

Receiving Jesus Christ as Savior is not the end but the beginning of our upward mobility. As the forever-forgiven and redeemed children of God and brothers and sisters of Christ, we are free to begin fulfilling the purposes for which we were created, one of which is growing into the fullness of Christ .

We are born again through saving faith, which is a living faith that should grow bigger and stronger every day of our lives. As we are continually being transformed into the image of Christ, we are continually "moving on up" in the fullness of our joy and peace and to a future that will exceed all expectations.

> ***"Till we all come to the unity of the faith and of the knowledge of the Son of God, to a perfect man, to the measure of the stature of the fullness of Christ;"***
> ***Ephesians 4:13***

**Father, by the power of your Spirit, help me to "move on up." Amen.**

Read Luke 12, Psalm 130 January 11

## *Cashing in on Your Connection*

**"So now we can rejoice in our wonderful new relationship with God—all because of what our Lord Jesus Christ has done for us in making us friends of God." Romans 5:11 NLT**

God knows all about the politicians, merchants, salesmen, and other self promoters who join churches to try to cash in on their connection with God. This does not mean that all these people do this. In fact, many people want to do business with fellow believers and have confidence in doing this.

> ***"O Israel, hope in the LORD; for with the LORD there is unfailing love and an overflowing supply of salvation."***
> ***Psalm 130:7 NLT***

God has provided many wonderful ways that we can cash in on our connection with Him that He not only approves but encourages.

We can cash in on our connection with God when we use the power of the Holy Spirit to stand firm and resist temptation.

We can cash in by receiving the robe of righteousness that covers all of our sins when we confess, repent, and receive Jesus Christ as our Savior.

We can cash in when we claim by faith all of the wonderful promises of God as they are revealed to us through His Word.

Perhaps best of all, we can cash in on our personal relationship with Jesus as our High Priest, to whom we can go with all confidence to the throne of grace confident that He will hear and answer our prayers according to God's perfect will and timing.

We can be confident that by virtue of our connection with the Son, our Father will supply all of our needs and provide His all-sufficient grace for any season of suffering or failure.

> ***"Yes, a person is a fool to store up earthly wealth but not have a rich relationship with God."***
> ***Luke 12:21 NLT***

We will never again have to face any situation alone when we have godly connections. These are connections we can take to the bank of blessings.

**Father, keep me plugged into my connection with You. Amen.**

# Lesson of the Jig Saw

**"God has given gifts to each of you from his great variety of spiritual gifts. Manage them well so that God's generosity can flow through you." 1 Peter 4:10 NLT**

> ***"Give unto the Lord the glory due to His name; worship the Lord in the beauty of holiness."***
> ***Psalm 29:2***

One of the best illustrations of different gifts is the example of the jig saw puzzle. Some have over 1,000 pieces, all different and all essential for completing the puzzle. Each piece is sized and shaped to fit a particular spot. No other piece can take its place.

God did not use a cookie cutter when He made us. We were custom built with different finger prints, voice prints, and DNA. There is not another person just like us anywhere.

Overlooking this fact can be one of the biggest mistakes we can make in raising children or in making career choices. (How many bad preachers and bad doctors are there who got into something they were not gifted for as a result of wanting to please their parents?)

Although God can and often does use ungifted people to accomplish His purposes in order to demonstrate His wonder-working power, churches are sometimes full of stressed out people damaging the cause of Christ by being asked to or volunteering to do things for which they are not gifted.

We have all probably heard singers who cannot sing, greeters who cannot greet, teachers who cannot teach, and preachers who cannot preach because they are trying to do something without the gift.

We dare not use our lack of gifts as an excuse for disobedience to the great commission or other areas of ministry. We need to learn to obey in a way that best utilizes our giftedness.

> ***"Now all of you together are Christ's body, and each one of you is a necessary part of it."***
> ***1 Corinthians 12:27 NLT***

God created and gifted us for good works before we were ever born. We just need to be available, obedient, and discerning in how to use our gifts in a way that edifies others and glorifies God

**Father, help me to find my fit in this puzzle of life. Amen.**

Read James 4, Psalm 119:7-16 January 13

# An Undivided Heart

**"The heart *is* deceitful above all *things,* and desperately wicked; who can know it?" Jeremiah 17:9**

A divided heart is probably one of the biggest problems with which even the most faithful of believers often struggles. As we live in this sin-corrupted world in corrupted flesh, the temptation to divide our loyalties and loves is always present.

> ***"I will praise You with uprightness of heart, when I learn Your righteous judgments. I will keep Your statutes" Psalm 119:7***

Satan often tries to deceive us into dividing our hearts. Sometimes it's between God and pride or ambition. Often it's between self, family and God. Sometimes it may be divided according to the day of the week.

The fact that God is a jealous God who will not tolerate His glory being usurped or shared with anyone is often overlooked to our peril.

Moses found this out when He tried to take joint credit with God in making water flow out of the rock and was banned from entering the promised land. Annanias and Sapphira held out a portion of the proceeds of their sale and were struck dead instantly.

We can and should take great joy and comfort in knowing that we have a God of longsuffering, love, compassion, grace, mercy, and forgiveness. But, we should never forget that we have a God who will not be mocked and who will not play second fiddle to anyone or any thing.

When we try to divide our heart's affections, we become double minded and an abomination to God.

God's umbrella of grace covers a lot of sins. He sent His Holy Spirit to guard our hearts. He gives us His peace to do the same.

> ***"Draw near to God and He will draw near to you. Cleanse your hands, you sinners; and purify your hearts, you double-minded." James 4:8***

**Father, give me an undivided heart where You are first in every area of my life. Amen.**

January 14 Read Luke 12:33-40, Psalm 98

## *Wrong Place at the Wrong Time*

**"Go back to what you heard and believed at first; hold to it firmly and turn to me again. Unless you do, I will come upon you suddenly, as unexpected as a thief." Revelation 3:3 NLT**

One of the most common explanations of disasters of all kinds is that he or she was in the wrong place at the wrong time. Those killed in the Twin Towers crashes were certainly in the wrong place at the wrong time.

> ***"For He is coming to 'udge the earth with righteousness He shall judge the world, he peoples with equity." Psalm 98:9***

Innocent victims of drive-by shootings, fatal car crashes, plane crashes, etc. have all been in the wrong place at the wrong time.

There are neighborhoods and troubled areas of most every city that people avoid because they don't want to be caught in the wrong place at the wrong time.

Life seems to be filled with blessings and problems that seem to be a matter of timing and position. Jobs are found and people are fired many times because of timing and position.

The question that we should continually ask ourselves is: are we where Jesus would have us be, doing what He would have us do, when He returns to claim His kingdom?

Dare we really be found indulging in gossip, pornography, pride, or any other activity that gives offense to God?

When we understand what it means to be temples of the Holy Spirit, we need to get serious about keeping our temple clean by daily washing of confession and repentance.

If we knew the president of the United States was coming to visit us tomorrow, we would do everything possible to be ready and be in the right place at the right time.

> ***"Therefore you also be ready, for the Son of Man is coming at an hour you do not expect." Luke 12:39***

How much more important to live in a way that we will be in the right place at the right time when Jesus returns!

**Father, let me always be found abiding in You. Amen.**

**Read 1 Thessalonians 4:1-12, Psalm 39** **January 15**

## *Have You Got a Hemi?*

**"Since we are receiving a kingdom that cannot be destroyed, let us be thankful and please God by worshiping Him with holy fear and awe. For our God is a consuming fire." Hebrews 12:28, 29 NLT**

> ***"My thoughts grew hot within me and began to burn, igniting a fire of words," Psalm 39:3 NLT***

The internal combustion engine was one of the key developments in the history of mankind. It opened the doors of transportation, commerce, industry, overall progress, and general prosperity.

Like it or not, we are all operating on internal combustion engines. Our performance on the speedway of life depends a great deal on the kind of fuel on which we are running.

We sometimes run fueled by outbursts of anger that rev our engines over the red line and leave us stranded in the pit of remorse with a harvest of bitterness. Prisons and hell are both full of anger-fueled people.

Lust can be a powerful fuel additive that offers fast take offs but usually causes serious crashes and many burned out engines.

> ***"For God did not call us to uncleanness, but in holiness. [8]Therefore he who rejects this does not reject man, but God, who has also given us His Holy Spirit." 1 Thessalonians 4:7, 8***

When we fill up with greed or envy, we burn with desire to get more and more and burn out the shut-off switch so that we never will have enough fuel to get where we think we want to go.

Pride is the worst fuel of all to burn in our chambers. It can never bear up under the demands of racing alone without a pit crew.

It is only when we burn the fuel of God's love that we can ever know the thrill of riding down victory lane with those who have maintained peak performance on the straight-aways and around the curves of this roadway of life.

The added power and strength we receive through the fire of the Holy Spirit burning within us is better than any "hemi" man could ever devise.

**Father, keep me fueled by the power of Your Spirit as I fill up at Your fountain of love, grace, and mercy. Amen.**

January 16 Read Matthew 25, Ecclesiastes 8:1-8

## *Expiration Dates*

**"Do you think that God will judge and condemn others for doing them and not judge you when you do them, too? Don't you realize how kind, tolerant, and patient God is with you? Or don't you care? Can't you see how kind He has been in giving you time to turn from your sin?" Romans 2:3, 4 NLT**

About every food product comes with an expiration date. We have expiration dates for insurance policies, rebate offers, sale prices, and all of our credit cards.

> ***"None of us can hold back our spirit from departing. None of us has the power to prevent the day of our death." Ecclesiastes 8:8a NLT***

These expiration dates should remind us that we all have an expiration date of life on this earth. We never know when, but we know for sure that it is going to happen.

Scripture repeatedly points out the importance of being ready. From the parable of the wedding garment to the parable of the oil in the virgins' lamps, we are taught to be ready.

God's wonderful offering of salvation to all who would call upon the name of Jesus and be saved has an expiration date. Although God wants all to be saved and gives us ample opportunity to receive His gift of salvation, we dare not refuse to open the door when Jesus comes knocking.

Scripture is full of the "almost persuaded" who couldn't pick up their cross and follow when called because they were too rich, too busy, or had other priorities.

> ***"Watch therefore, for you know neither the day nor the hour in which the Son of Man is coming." Matthew 25:13***

We see examples all around us of the evil prospering, the good dying young, and many mistaking the grace of God as a license to keep on sinning and disobeying Him.

Our expiration date means our time to believe and receive salvation also expires. Our opportunity to store up treasures in heaven will expire as well. We need to hold these truths tightly for our sake and for the sake of those we love.

**Father, help me to be ready for my expiration date. Amen.**

## *Are You Berean?*

**"And the people of Berea were more open minded than those in Thessalonica, and they listened eagerly to Paul's message. They searched the Scriptures day after day to check up on Paul and Silas, to see if they were really teaching the truth." Acts 17:11**

Those who seek after God with an open mind will never be disappointed if they seek in the Word of God.

> ***"But may all who search for You be filled with joy and gladness. May those who love Your salvation repeatedly shout, "The LORD is great!" Psalm 40:6 NLT***

Unfortunately, even a number of churches and pastors will often disappoint because they choose to ignore or misinterpret the clear teachings of Scripture in order to tailor Scripture to their tastes instead of God's truth.

Evidences of God can be seen as far as the naked eye can see. God's revelation of who He is, what He has done, and what He has promised to do are all available to anyone in order that He may be found by those who seek Him.

Not only may God be found, but *"He rewards those who seek Him" (Hebrews 11:6b).*

People who choose to ignore the reality of God and people who refuse to worship God in Spirit and in truth are all going to fall short of the salvation that God offers and wants to give to all.

Being open minded doesn't mean that it doesn't matter what you believe as long as you're sincere. It doesn't mean that commandments are really only suggestions or that truth is only relative.

> ***"And since you don't believe what he wrote, how will you believe what I say?" John 5:47***

The meaning of life and all of its glorious blessings can only be found in a right relationship with God through faith in Jesus Christ. This truth is validated when we appropriate the Berean mindset of searching Scriptures day after day, week after week, year after year.

**Father, give me a Berean mentality. Amen.**

January 18 Read Romans 2:5-11, Psalm 25

# *The Key*

**"Observe and obey all these words which I command you, that it may go well with you and your children after you forever, when you do *what is* good and right in the sight of the LORD your God." Deuteronomy 12:28**

Just as faith in Jesus Christ is the key to receiving eternal life, obedience is the key to the sanctified, abundant life in Christ.

> ***"The LORD leads with unfailing love and faithfulness all those who keep His covenant and obey His decrees."***
> ***Psalm 25:10 NLT***

Faith without obedience is like seed sown among the thorns and succumbs to the cares of this world. It is almost as bad as no faith at all.

It is an utterly amazing and deplorable thing that many will not receive Jesus Christ as Savior at all because they are not willing to give up what they perceive as pleasures and treasures while totally blind to the truth that God promises so much more in real pleasures and treasures. The old things pass away and are not even missed as all things become new in Christ.

We might well paraphrase 1 Corinthians 13 and substitute obedience for love and find out that without obedience we are just clanging symbols making "meaningless noise."

He not only sent us the Good Shepherd to lead us and lay down His life for us, but He also sent the Holy Spirit to guide us and give us the power to live the lives of obedience that growing into the fullness of Christ requires.

> ***"Eternal life is given to those who by patient continuance in doing good seek for glory, honor, and immortality. But to those who are self-seeking and do not obey the truth, but obey unrighteousness— indignation and wrath."***
> ***Romans 2:7, 8***

When we give up self control for Spirit control, we trade our corruptible nature for an incorruptible one and cover our weaknesses with God's strength. This is the key to unlocking the treasures of the abundant life.

**Father, help me to enjoy the blessings of obedience in every area of my life. Amen.**

**Read Ephesians 3:16-29, Psalm 29** **January 19**

# *Strength Coach*

**"And He said to me, "My grace is sufficient for you, for My strength is made perfect in weakness." 2 Corinthians 12:9**

> ***"The LORD gives His people strength. The LORD blesses them with peace."***
> ***Psalm 29:11 NLT***

Successful sports teams for years have been using strength coaches off season and on to keep athletes physically strong and performing at their peek.

This is actually not a bad way of looking at the Holy Spirit. He has been given to us by the lover of our soul to strengthen us in our obedience to God and to conform and perfect us into the image of Christ and His fullness.

We often are so full of ourselves and our abilities that we don't see the need for a strength coach. It's only when we find our strength failing that we can appreciate the all-sufficient grace and strength that God provides through the Holy Spirit that carries us through our weaknesses.

The Bible and real life is full of ordinary people who were given supernatural strength to do extraordinary things by the power of the Holy Spirit.

God's character-development program for believers often includes going through deep waters of doubt, depression, failure, pain and suffering that will make us realize that God's strength is made perfect in our weakness.

Strength coaches and the Holy Spirit both rely heavily on diet and vitamins as part of their training. Our spiritual vitamins of abiding in the Word, prayer, and fellowship with other believers are means of enhancing our strength and developing our muscles so that we can stand firmly while being faithful and fruitful as we live out our lives in the power of the Spirit.

> ***"I pray that from His glorious, unlimited resources He will give you mighty inner strength through His Holy Spirit."***
> ***Ephesians 3:16 NLT***

**Father, thank you for giving me my own personal strength coach. Amen.**

# *The Hall of Shame*

**"But now they desire a better, that is, a heavenly *country.* Therefore God is not ashamed to be called their God, for He has prepared a city for them." Hebrews 11:16 NLT**

In this politically correct, faith-bashing world in which we live, it is very easy to fall into the trap of being ashamed of Jesus.

> ***"Keep my soul, and deliver me;
> Let me not be ashamed, for I put my trust in You."
> Psalm 25:20***

When we dare mention anything about God's perspective or try to promote the truths of Christ, we are often ridiculed, shot down, and labeled as religious fanatics or extremists. Perhaps even worse, when we see God's glory being defiled by the conduct of religious leaders, congregations, denominations, and professing Christians, we become ashamed to be identified as Christians.

Our righteous indignation should never trigger self-righteous hypocritical glory when these things happen, but rather we should pray for forgiveness and restoration for those giving such offense to God.

*Our Lord said: "For whoever is ashamed of Me and My words in this adulterous and sinful generation, of him the Son of Man also will be ashamed when He comes in the glory of His Father with the holy angels" (Mark 8:38).*

The difference between being in God's hall of fame instead of His hall of shame may well be in living lives fully pleasing to God and fruitful in every good work.

> ***"May you always be filled with the fruit of your salvation—those good things that are produced in your life by Jesus Christ—for this will bring much glory and praise to God."
> Philippians 1:11***

God forgives and forgets our sins. However, He is going to remember our stewardship of the lives we have been given and not be ashamed to be called our God when fruits of righteousness remain after the wood, hay, and stubble of our lives is burned away.

**Father, let me never be ashamed of You and let me never give cause for You to be ashamed of me. Amen.**

**Read Luke 6:43-49, Psalm 101** **January 21**

# *False-Hearted Lovers*

**"For out of the heart come evil thoughts, murder, adultery, sexual immorality, theft, false testimony, slander." Matthew 15:19 NIV**

Satan started it all by pretending to be Adam and Eve's friend in the garden and leading them down the path of destruction for them and us.

> ***"No one who practices deceit will dwell in my house; no one who speaks falsely will stand in my presence." Psalm 101:7 NIV***

If you have not been jilted or dumped by one false-hearted lover in your relationships of life, you are a rarity.

Whether it's the politician professing a love for humanity and your best interests when he really cares nothing about any one or any thing except getting elected or the salesman who professes wanting to help you but who is really wanting you to help line his pockets, false-hearted lovers are all around us.

At work, at play, at school, at home, and even at church, we find false-hearted lovers professing one thing and doing another, including robbing others of their faith in people and sometimes even their faith in God.

There is probably no greater stumbling block than a false-hearted Christian. Whether a pastor, elder, or professing Christian, we must all be on guard against the deceitfulness of our hearts.

As bad as some false-hearted lovers are, none can hold a candle to the original. The evil one continues to pose as a friend dedicated to our happiness and well being while he is really dedicated to destroying us.

> ***"The good man brings good things out of the good stored up in his heart, and the evil man brings evil things out of the evil stored up in his heart. For out of the overflow of his heart his mouth speaks." Luke 6:45 NIV***

Even the new heart we received when we received Jesus as our Savior can still be corrupted by the sin of this world in which we live. We need to ask God to recreate this new heart and a right spirit within us as we confess and repent daily.

**Lord, deliver me from being and from being taken in by false-hearted lovers. Amen.**

**January 22** **Read Matthew 7, Psalm 9**

# *The Quest*

**"And without faith it is impossible to please God, because anyone who comes to Him must believe that He exists and that He rewards those who earnestly seek Him." Hebrews 11:6 NIV**

We are all constantly seeking something. Whether it is to satisfy a longing, relieve pain, achieve a goal, find approval, or acquire wealth, our lives are spent on a quest.

> ***"Those who know Your name will trust in You, for You, LORD , have never forsaken those who seek You." Psalm 9:10***

Seekers seem to have no problem in knowing where to look. The harder challenge is to know what to look for. Lifetimes are wasted and ruined in looking for the wrong things in the wrong places.

When we seek to fill our longing for security and satisfaction in the things of this world, we often get more than we bargained for. When we seek our security and satisfaction in other people, we are often disappointed. The "if" of "I would only be happy 'if'…" never seems to provide satisfaction in anything for very long.

When our quest is to seek first the kingdom of God and His righteousness, we find the security and satisfaction that only a right relationship with God can provide. The "if" becomes an "I" and the "would" becomes an "am".

The realization that I am happy because I have found the peace that surpasses all understanding in knowing that I am unconditionally loved, forever forgiven, and totally accepted in the eyes of God begins a transformation.

> ***"Ask and it will be given to you; seek and you will find; knock and the door will be opened to you." Matthew 7:7***

This transformation produces a motivation and quest to pursue the righteousness of Christ through which we become more like Him everyday in every area of our lives.

As God blesses our faithfulness and obedience (as He always does), we find that our needs and longings are satisfied far beyond what we had ever hoped for when we were seeking them apart from God.

**Lord, thank you for showing us what our quest should be and what peace and joy we will have in pursuing it. Amen.**

# *Tested and Approved*

**"In this you greatly rejoice, though now for a little while you may have had to suffer grief in all kinds of trials" 1 Peter 1:6 NIV**

Job has been a book of encouragement to believers for generation after generation. The example of one, who was dearly loved and approved by God, being subjected to such tragedy, pain, and suffering as a test of faith is something we might all take to heart when testing comes.

> ***"Shall we accept good from God, and not trouble? In all this, Job did not sin in what he said."***
> ***Job 2:10b NIV***

Whenever you get down and depressed, look at the restoration and reward of Job for His faithfulness, and you will receive encouragement and strength to persevere.

The perseverance of the Saints is a principle tenet of our faith and life in Christ. It is God's character-development course for spiritual fitness.

God brings or allows tests in order to inspect, detect, correct, and perfect our total faith and trust in Him. Also, He uses tests to reveal His strength and His faithfulness to us.

There is no way we can better experience God's strength than when ours fails and no better way to experience God's mercy than when we receive it. We cannot grow into the fullness of Christ without experiencing some of the pain and suffering He endured for our sake.

When trials come, we need to first judge ourselves. If our self judgment reveals no reasons for being chastened, we can be assured that God is at work conforming us into the fullness of Christ.

We must always remember that God never wastes a hurt, and that He sometimes even uses the hurts inflicted upon us by others for His working all things for our good and His glory.

> ***"Because you know that the testing of your faith develops perseverance,"***
> ***James 1:3 NIV***

**Father, thank you for Your promise that You will not give us trials without Your all-sufficient grace and more than adequate strength to persevere through them. Amen.**

January 24 Read 2 Thessalonians 3:1-5, Psalm 18

## *The Long Arm of the Law*

**"The eternal God is your refuge, and underneath are the everlasting arms. He will drive out your enemy before you, saying, 'Destroy him!'" Deuteronomy 33:27**

This expression has been around for ages referring to the ability of the law to not only capture and bring to justice but to reach into every area of our lives.

> ***"For who is God besides the LORD ? And who is the Rock except our God? It is God who arms me with strength and makes my way perfect."***
> ***Psalm 18:31, 32 NIV***

The long arm of God's law is still used as a mirror, a guide, and a curb. Unfortunately, some seem to think that they are saved by obeying the law. The law never saved anyone. It is like a prosecuting attorney that seeks to convict us of our sins and our need for a savior.

The long arms of God are arms of grace. No matter how far we fall, His everlasting arms of grace are underneath to save us. God makes it very plain in Scripture that His arms are not too short to reach out and rescue anyone.

God's arms of grace carry us when we cannot continue in our own strength. The Good Shepherd gathers us in His arms and carries us close to His heart.

God's arms of grace shelter us under His wings like an eagle protects her young.

God is our refuge and strength, our very present help in time of trouble. He is also our joy and our hope. He is our reason for living and our sustainer of life here, now, and forever.

> ***"But the Lord is faithful, and He will strengthen and protect you from the evil one."***
> ***2 Thessalonians 3:3 NIV***

When we learn to lean by faith on the everlasting arms of God's grace, we find the secret of true peace and contentment.

**Father, help me to lean more and more on You and less and less on myself that I might really know the joy of my salvation. Amen.**

**Read James 4:7-10, Jonah 2** **January 25**

# *Getting Back On*

**"Revive us so we can call on Your name once more. Turn us again to Yourself, O Lord God Almighty. Make Your face shine down upon us. Only then will we be saved. Psalm 80:18b, 19 NLT**

One of the basic rules of horseback riding is to get back on as soon as you fall off before fear sets in. Many people have lost the pleasure of riding horses forever because they didn't get back on.

> ***"I sank down to the very roots of the mountains. I was locked out of life and imprisoned in the land of the dead. But You, O Lord my God, have snatched me from the yawning jaws of death!" Jonah 2:6 NLT***

Another rule of thumb is that you have to fall off at least three times before you can become a good rider.

These principles can be applied to life and our relationship with God.

Although we have been set free from the bondage of sin and its power to destroy us, we need to understand that this does not make us invincible to it, and we are going to sin as we go through life coexisting with our corruptible flesh.

When we fall off the path of righteousness, we need to get right back on by confessing and repenting before our conscience becomes numb and our hearts hardened.

Scripture records the stumblings and fallings of many of God's elect. Jonah, Saul, Solomon, David, Peter and the other disciples validate the fact that back sliding has and can happen to anyone at any time.

The prodigal son and the heroes of the faith discovered that God is always willing to forgive and restore those who come back to Him with godly sorrow and true repentance.

> ***"When you bow down before the Lord and admit your dependence on Him, He will lift you up and give you honor." James 4:10 NLT***

What a great hymn "Back in the Saddle Again" can be when we get back on the mercy seat of grace that we can ride all the way home.

**Father, thank you for getting me "back in the saddle" when I sin. Amen.**

## *Getting High is Great!*

**"Though you have not seen Him, you love Him; and even though you do not see Him now, you believe in Him and are filled with an inexpressible and glorious joy." 1 Peter 1:8 NIV**

It is amazing that so many millions of people would spend their lives "getting high" on all the wrong things. From beer and other alcoholic beverages, to sniffing glue, smoking pot, or doing dope, many people seem to have a natural desire to "get high."

> ***"I was filled with delight day after day, rejoicing always in His presence, "***
> ***Proverbs 8:30 NIV***

Sometimes, it's just for the sheer perceived fun of it. Other times, it is an escape from the reality of failures, pressures, and traumas of life. Whatever the reason, getting high through controlled substances will lead to misery if continued.

We also find ourselves getting high on athletic, scholastic, artistic, or other performances and successes. This gives us high self esteem to cover our low view of ourselves and compensates for a lot of our weaknesses and failures.

The trouble with all of these artificial highs is that they will never last. They will require more and more of the substance or more and more of the performance and success and give less and less satisfaction.

Giving control of our minds and bodies to a pill or a potion and refusing to give control to the higher power who created us, loves us with an everlasting love, and gives us more than enough self esteem and significance is a "no brainer."

To spend so much time and money to "feel good" is idiotic when the highest high and greatest feeling in the world is available free of charge.

When we "get high" on Jesus, we are filled with the power of the Holy Spirit, and we are freed to soar in the heavens of hope and swim in the oceans of love. Our lives are filled with joy, peace, meaning, and purpose.

> ***"Do not get drunk on wine, which leads to debauchery. Instead, be filled with the Spirit."***
> ***Ephesians 5:18 NIV***

**Father, let me know the joy of "getting high" on You. Amen.**

## *Are you Covered?*

**"He who dwells in the shelter of the Most High will rest in the shadow of the Almighty." Psalm 91:1 NIV**

Health care coverage is a big concern for millions of people these days. It is virtually impossible to get through any serious accident or illness without bankruptcy if you are not well covered.

> ***"You forgave the iniquity of Your people and covered all their sins."***
> ***Psalm 85:2 NIV***

We are required to have coverage for other people and automobiles in most states. We search through our home owners policies to see if we are covered when trees blow down, our dog bites someone, etc.

Police work, warfare, and many sports are based on having some thing or some one covering us or backing us up.

The most important coverage anyone can have is the blood of Jesus. This coverage blots out our sins from God's book of our lives and adorns us with a spectacular wedding garment to wear at the royal banquet hall.

When we stand before the throne of God, he doesn't see us tarnished and eaten up by our sins, but He sees us as holy, innocent, and adorable brothers and sisters of Christ who have been fully covered by the righteousness of Christ.

You can't buy this kind of coverage from All State, Nation Wide, or any other insurance company. You can't earn it, regardless of how hard you might work. You can only receive it by faith when God's salesman comes calling you into a relationship with God through Jesus.

The death benefits of this coverage are so great; we can hardly wait to collect them. The good news is that we don't have to wait.

The minute we die to sin and become alive in Christ, we become beneficiaries of unconditional love, forever forgiveness, and total acceptance. We have automatic premium overdraft protection from the Holy Spirit who has come to live in us as our personal life assurance agent.

> ***"Blessed are they whose transgressions are forgiven, whose sins are covered."***
> ***Romans 4:7 NIV***

**Father, thank you for giving me the full coverage of Your grace, forgiveness and compassion. Amen.**

# *Behold!*

**"Then He who sat on the throne said, 'Behold, I make all things new.' And He said to me, 'Write, for these words are true and faithful.'" Revelation 21:5**

This nifty word is used almost 600 times in the King James versions of the Bible but is missing from most other translations. It often expresses a sense of wonder and most often means "look and see" with an extra emphasis.

***"Behold, God is my salvation, I will trust and not be afraid; for Yah, the LORD, is my strength and song; He also has become my salvation." Isaiah 12:2***

When we behold the wonders of God's creation all around us, we should never doubt that God does exist and that He made it all.

When we behold Jesus standing at the door and knocking to come into our hearts and receive Him by faith, we receive that new life in Him that washes us clean and sets us free. When we behold the amazing grace of God in the lives of His redeemed, we should never cease to remember that this grace is ours to claim and own by faith. *"Behold, now is the accepted time; behold, now is the day of salvation" (2 Corinthians 2:9.*

The joy of our amazement should grow into the joy of our confidence as we experience this sustaining, all-sufficient grace of God in our lives.

Our confidence will grow into the security of that all-surpassing peace that can only come from beholding the glory of the Lord as we live out lives beholding Christ.

We have the great privilege of witnessing to those around us as they behold our faith, our joy, and our peace as we become imitators of Christ during the on-going process of being transformed and conformed into His likeness.

***"Behold what manner of love the Father has bestowed on us, that we should be called children of God!" 1 John 3:1***

There is a day coming when God will behold us and see us clothed in the righteousness of Christ. There is a day coming when Jesus will behold the fruit of our lives and reward us accordingly. Are you ready to be "beheld"? **Father, help me to always behold You in every situation. Amen.**

**Read Philippians 4:4-13, Psalm 149** **January 29**

## *Are you Trigger Happy?*

**"My brethren, count it all joy when you fall into various trials, knowing that the testing of your faith produces patience." James 1:2**

One of the basics of addiction therapy is to identify the people, places, and things that trigger the need for the relief that the addictive substance or behavior provides.

> ***"Let the faithful rejoice in this honor. Let them sing for joy as they lie on their beds." Psalm 149:5 NLT***

We know that a headache or toothache will trigger a need or desire for an aspirin, Advil, or whatever will numb the pain.

When we are insecure in ourselves and our relationship with God, our need for self esteem triggers our seeking of the false security of a bottle, pill, or some sort of sexual gratification.

Guilt is one of the most powerful and destructive emotions for triggering the need for relief. Many will go through life trying to mask their pain through substance abuse without ever realizing that they have a Savior who came to earth to bear the pain of their guilt on a cross so that they may find the only true and lasting relief through believing this.

When we realize which people, places, and things trigger our anger, fear, lust, or other sinful reactions, we need to learn to avoid them or to recognize and overcome them with the supernatural power of the Holy Spirit who is alive and living in the hearts of all believers.

> ***"Be anxious for nothing, but in everything by prayer and supplication, with thanksgiving, let your requests be made known to God; and the peace of God, which surpasses all understanding, will guard your hearts and minds through Christ Jesus." Philippians 4:6***

There is no law against or limit to the joy of being "trigger happy" by rejoicing in the good times as well as the bad and letting the love of Christ reign in our hearts.

We cannot control many things. Bad things are going to happen to good people. However, we can always choose how we will respond to the triggers of life and choose to be "trigger happy".

**Father, thank you for giving me that peace that surpasses all understanding when I respond to life with joy and thanksgiving. Amen.**

 Read 1 Peter 1:3b-6, Psalm 91

# *Protective Grace*

**"Yet he was merciful and forgave their sins and didn't destroy them all. Many a time he held back his anger and did not unleash his fury!" Psalm 78:38 NLT**

Most believers know about the saving grace of God which reconciles us to Him through faith in Jesus Christ.

> ***"For He shall give His angels charge over you, to keep you in all your ways," Psalm 91:11***

We also need to be ever mindful and thankful for the ocean of sparing grace for which we seldom give God the thanks and Glory that He deserves.

The trauma of divorce, bondage of addiction, wandering aimlessly lost, heartbreak, pain, disaster, and tragedy are all around us. Sometimes a split second is all that saves us from a terrible wreck or from being in the wrong place at the wrong time.

When we see these calamities in the lives of others, we should get down on our knees and thank God for His sparing grace in not allowing these things to happen to us.

Our prayers ignite this sparing grace for ourselves and for others. We also have the Holy Spirit and Christ making intercession for sparing grace for us at the throne of God.

When we think of what it might be like to be born and brought up in some of the rest of the world, we should thank God for sparing us what those there have to live with every day of their life.

God is sovereign; He is in control of the universe and our lives. The fact that He not only has chosen to favor us with the unmerited gift of salvation but with unmerited favor and protection in so many areas of our life should keep us humble and filled with thanksgiving and praise to Him.

> ***"May you have more and more of God's special favor and wonderful peace." 1 Peter 3:2b NLT***

**Father, thank you for Your protection. Amen.**

# *The Joy of Sharing*

**"Instead, you must worship Christ as Lord of your life. And if you are asked about your Christian hope, always be ready to explain it." 1 Peter 3:15 NLT**

God has given us all a great desire for interacting with others through a community of interest.

> ***"Declare His glory among the nations, His wonders among all peoples."***
> ***Psalm 96:2***

Parents enjoy sharing the problems of parenting with other parents. Stock car enthusiasts love to talk about the races and drivers with other enthusiasts. Whatever vocational, recreational, civic, political, or vocational interests we have, we love to share these interests with others.

It is refreshing and encouraging to hear anyone share their interests about almost anything when they do it with passion and enthusiasm.

It may be part of our tribal instinct to come together to share and address common problems and pool resources in order to solve them.

Talk radio is prospering as people tune in to share or hear shared opinions and comments about practically everything under the sun. There is an internet chat room available to share thoughts about any subject.

If all of this is so true, why is it so hard to share our joy in the Lord and what He has done for us even with other believers? Why can't we talk about our relationship with God with the same passion and enthusiasm that we have when talking about the car we drive?

> ***"But sanctify the Lord God in your hearts, and always be ready to give a defense to everyone who asks you a reason for the hope that is in you, with meekness and fear."***
> ***1 Peter 3:15 NLT***

Why are we so adept at making cheap conversation about the weather or other things and so bashful when talking about our faith? The fear of rejection and ridicule loom large.

Failing to share what we consider a personal matter without realizing that we may be God's conduit of making faith in Jesus Christ a personal matter for someone else who desperately needs the Lord is a serious failing.

**Father, let me know the joy of sharing my faith with others. Amen.**

**February 1** **Read Matthew 23:1-12, Psalm 101**

# *Descending to Greatness*

**"But those who exalt themselves will be humbled, and those who humble themselves will be exalted." Matthew 23:12**

Hold it! What's this about descending? Our life's purpose is to be upwardly mobile, rising to the top, and ascending to greatness. It is contrary to human wisdom to even think of putting others first or bowing down.

> ***"I will not tolerate people who slander their neighbors. I will not endure conceit and pride."***
> ***Psalm 101:5 NLT***

If we believe the Bible, we must surely believe that we are to *"trust in the Lord with all our heart and lean not on our own understanding, and in all our ways acknowledge Him and He will direct our paths" (Proverbs 3:5).*

God directs our paths to obedience, holiness, and humility. When He calls us into a personal relationship with His Son, He begins to conform us into the image of Jesus.

We cannot be imitators of Christ without descending into servant hood. If *"And being found in appearance as a man, He humbled Himself and became obedient to the point of death, even the death of the cross"* (Philippians 2:8) was required of Jesus, it is also God's call to us.

The Scribes and Pharisees are not found in God's hall of fame, because of their pride and self righteousness.

The disciples had visions of grandeur about becoming movers and shakers in Jesus' earthly kingdom. They seem to have argued often about who was going to ascend to the highest of the high in the pecking order of God. Jesus wasted no time in telling them: *"If anyone desires to be first, he shall be last of all and servant of all" (Mark 9:35b).*

> ***"But he who is greatest among you shall be your servant."***
> ***Matthew 23:11***

Our new life in Christ was given to us when we humbly confessed our sins and need for a Savior. It is to be lived out in bowing down to serve others in love as our ministry of service.

**Father, help me to understand the difference between glorifying You and glorifying myself. Amen.**

**Read Hebrews 4:12-16, 1 Chronicles 28:9, 10** **February 2**

## *You're a Celebrity!*

**"I knew you before I formed you in your mother's womb. Before you were born, I set you apart and appointed you as my spokesman to the world." Jeremiah 1:5 NLT**

The dictionary defines celebrity as a well-known person. That being true, congratulations! You are a celebrity in the eyes of God!

> ***"For the LORD searches every heart and understands every motive behind the thoughts. If you seek him, he will be found by you; but if you forsake him, He will reject you forever."***
> **1 Chronicles 28:9 *b NIV***

You are very well known to the one who formed you in your mother's womb, who created you for good works that would glorify Him, who gifted you with whatever abilities and talents you have.

He hates and is hurt by our sins, but He still loves us sinners. He knows the worst about us, but chooses to believe the best. He chooses to do this not because of anything that we have done, but because of what His Son did for us on the cross of Calvary.

Our names are written in the celebrity book of life, where every good thing we do is recorded and every bad thing is erased from God's memory bank.

God forbid that we should respond to our celebrity status like the Scribes and Pharisees or by abusing God's grace as though we had a license to sin.

> ***"And there is no creature hidden from His sight, but all things are naked and open to the eyes of Him to whom we must give an account." Hebrews 4:13 NLT***

Isn't the God who knows us so well worth getting to know as well as we can through learning as much about Him as possible through His Word, prayer, and His presence in our life?

Shouldn't living for Him and His purposes be the high calling of our lives?

**Father, thank you for knowing me so well and still loving me so much. Amen.**

February 3 Read Hebrews 12:15-29, Psalm 58

# *Poisoned Water*

**"For I see that you are poisoned by bitterness and bound by iniquity." Acts 8:23**

As believers, we have a river of living water that will never run dry. Unfortunately, it can become so polluted by sin that we are afraid to drink it. When we persist in unrepented sins, we are dumping toxic waste into our river which will kill our joy and make us unable to bear fruits of righteousness.

> ***"They spit poison like deadly snakes; they are like cobras that refuse to listen," Psalm 58:4***

A few drops of gossip poison can kill relationships, break ties that should never be broken, and leave us with one of the hardest to clean stains of guilt.

The poison of unforgiveness is perhaps the greatest grace buster of all. When we let this get into our life blood, we shut ourselves off from God's ocean of love and forgiveness that we all need if we are going to live the abundant life God has promised us.

The poison of pride can muddy our water so badly that we can't get it running clear and pure without having it run through the filter of humiliation and hurt.

Although these poisons can cause a number of painful consequences and literally make us sick or miserable, they are not usually fatal unless they are symptoms of the poison that kills.

The poison of unbelief is the poison that will kill us and rob us of our right to be called the children of God. Unbelief will make it impossible to be reconciled to God and have paradise restored.

Unbelief dries up the river before it can even begin to flow through us. It relegates us into living in the desert of the damned, with no rain in sight.

> ***"Look after each other so that none of you will miss out on the special favor of God. Watch out that no bitter root of unbelief rises up among you, for whenever it springs up, many are corrupted by its poison." Hebrews 12:15 NLT***

**Father, by the power of Your Spirit, help me keep from polluting my river of living water. Amen.**

**Read Luke 14:18-24, Proverbs 24:10-22** **February 4**

## *Excuses, Excuses*

**"For since the creation of the world His invisible *attributes* are clearly seen, being understood by the things that are made, *even* His eternal power and Godhead, so that they are without excuse," Romans 1:20**

There is one "factory" that has been operating since the beginning of time at full capacity with no shut downs or work stoppages. Its products have been used throughout the world, and thanks to continuous upgrades and innovations, its products continue to be the all time best sellers. Welcome to the excuse factory!

> ***"Someone is watching you closely, you know - someone not impressed with weak excuses." Proverbs 24:12 MSG***

Adam invented this product when he said the woman made him do it, and to this day, blaming others has been the excuse of choice by zillions of people for zillions of mistakes and shortcomings.

Psychiatrists will blame parents for emotionally scarring us, spouses will blame each other for causing the divorce, and parents will blame teachers as the cause of their "little darlings'" misbehavior. We blame our bosses, our coaches, our neighbors, our pastors, and even our best friends.

Books have been written about the excuses given traffic cops as excuses for speeding. "Hurrying to get to a rest room" and "trying to get to a gas station before I run out of gas" are a couple of my favorites.

God says that we are without excuse for not knowing Him and entering into a saving relationship with Him by receiving Jesus Christ.

God does not want our excuses. He wants a broken spirit and a contrite heart. Only when we confess and take ownership of our sins, instead of trying to excuse them, can we find that forgiveness that brings salvation that gives us an excuse for heaven.

We need to remember that God's excuse window is closed, but His forgiveness counter is always open on the avenue of true sorrow and repentance.

> ***"Then they all began to beg off, one after another making excuses." Luke 14:18a MSG***

**Father, help me to quit hiding behind excuses and walk in the light of Your love. Amen.**

February 5 Read Romans 6:12-23, Psalm 4

# *Do You DUI!*

**"We know that we are children of God and that the world around us is under the power and control of the evil one." James 5:16 NLT**

> ***"Don't sin by letting anger gain control over you. Think about it overnight and remain silent."***
> ***Psalm 4:4 NLT***

Driving under the influence of alcohol is a crime and the cause of many deaths and much misery. As bad and offensive as this is, we all have a whole lot of DUI's to worry about that are maybe just as bad and often worse.

Driving under the influence of rage is an ever growing malady that may be causing more accidents and fatalities than alcohol. It is a scary thought that there are millions of armed, road maniacs driving the highways like time bombs ready to explode anytime at the slightest provocation or accident.

And then there is the matter of being driven under the influence of sin.

When we are driven by pride, we are setting ourselves up for a fall. God hates it, we hold on to it, and it is usually one of the last strongholds of our flesh to surrender to our new birth.

Lust can drive us to self destruct and often bring painful consequences to those we love most. We need to use our theology to control our biology in sexual matters and remember that we can lust for many other things.

When we become driven by revenge, jealousy, anger or hatred, we become all that we can be in our flesh, which is a far cry from being all that we can and should be.

The truth of the matter is that whenever we drive through life under the influence of our control, we are going to blow it. We need to get out of the driver's seat and be driven by the transforming power of the Holy Spirit.

> ***"Do not let sin control the way you live; do not give in to its lustful desires."***
> ***Romans 12:12 NLT***

When we are driven under the influence of the Holy Spirit, we are driven by longsuffering, patience, kindness, gentleness, love, and self control. We can live lives supercharged by the resurrection power of Jeus Christ . This is a DUI ticket we should all strive to get.

**Father, let me always be driven under the shelter of Your wings and the example of Your life. Amen**

Read Philippians 2:14-18, Deuteronomy 1:26-45 February 6

## *Don't Suck it Up!*

**"How can I account for this generation? The people have been like spoiled children whining to their parents." Matthew 11:16a NLT**

The history of God and His people is full of "joy suckers." The children of Israel were among the first, but surely not the last of whiners and complainers, who were never satisfied and never thankful.

> ***"When the LORD heard your complaining, He became very angry. So He solemnly swore, 'Not one of you from this entire wicked generation will live to see the good land I swore to your ancestors." Deuteronomy 1:34-35 NLT***

The scribes and Pharisees tried to undermine Jesus' miracles and ministry by complaining that He sat and ate with sinners.

A few years ago, a TV interviewer tried to suck the joy out of baseball star Pete Rose being allowed to be honored as one of the greatest baseball players of the century by bringing up his expulsion from baseball for gambling before a TV audience of millions.

Martha tried to suck up Mary's joy in Jesus' visit by complaining that she wouldn't help her.

We need to always remember that a critical spirit is not one of the fruits of the Spirit. We need to be aware of and avoid criticizing the failures and faults of others in order to make ourselves look and feel better by comparison.

In the family, in the church, and in the work place, a "joy sucker" can kill relationships, be a stumbling block to others, spread a malaise of despair, and destroy morale which makes a lot of company for their own misery.

> ***"In everything you do, stay away from complaining and arguing, so that no one can speak a word of blame against you." Philippians 2:14a NLT***

The next time a "joy sucker" comes trying to steal your joy, tell them that you took all your complaints and whining to the cross and exchanged them for the joy of the Lord.

**Father, deliver me from the "joy suckers" and never let me be one. Amen.**

February 7 Read James 1:2-18, Jeremiah 14:22

## *Living in the World of Make Believe*

**"But against all illusion and fantasy and empty talk there's always this rock foundation: fear God!" Ecclesiastes 5:7 MSG**

If we were to clock the hours spent in the make-believe world of TV, movies, video games, and internet, we would find that we and a number of others are spending a great deal of time living in a fantasy world of make believe.

> ***"They speak foolishness made up in their own lying hearts."***
> ***Jeremiah 14:22b NLT***

Belief runs the gamut from the reality of our faith in the ability of Jesus to save us and the reality that He is the truth, to the make believe of denial that we are sinners who need a Savior, that we have an addiction of any kind, or that God doesn't really mean what He says.

Some enter into a make-believe expectation of marriage where everything will be wonderful, and it will be full of bliss, free from conflict, and free from misunderstandings.

Others enter into a make-believe concept of religion, where if we pay our tithes, go to church, and don't sin too much, we will become wealthy, healthy, and wise with great marriages, perfect kids, beautiful homes and fast cars.

We often seem to prefer a make-believe God, who we can define by our view of who He is and should be, and we can do or believe anything as long as we're sincere.

We don't have a make-believe God! He has revealed His sovereignty, His majesty, His omniscience, His presence, and His heart. He came to earth to reveal Himself as the Word made flesh so that we don't have to make believe anything about Him, His love, or His will for us.

> ***"They can't make up their minds. They waver back and forth in everything they do."***
> ***James 1:8 NLT***

Is the reality of God and our personal relationship with Him lived out in believing the reality that Jesus is the Way, the Truth, and the Life?

**Father help me to get over my unbelief, and more importantly my make belief that is contradiction to your Word. Amen.**

Read Romans 8:37-39, Psalm 71 February 8

## *Overwhelming Love*

**"And the peace of God, which surpasses all understanding, will guard your hearts and minds through Christ Jesus." Philippians 4:7**

The amazing grace of God is often overwhelming. As we live out lives of faith abiding in Christ through His Word and in His presence, we see Him come to life in our lives and in the lives of those around us. We are filled with such peace, such joy, and such love that we can't contain it. We have to pass it on.

> ***"I will tell everyone about Your righteousness. All day long I will proclaim Your saving power, for I am overwhelmed by how much You have done for me."***
> ***Psalm 71:15 NLT***

It is overwhelming and at times incomprehensible that He has created fellowship with Him in a personal, living relationship that continues to grow and makes us fruitful in every area of our lives.

When the Holy Spirit moves from our head to our hearts, He often creates such a joy, such a passion, and such a thirst for God and His righteousness that we are literally "set on fire" for the Lord.

As great as this feeling is, we need to always be mindful that we can never let our faith be determined by our feelings.

Our feelings can change, but God's Word never changes. We suffer minor and major setbacks, but God's love for us never changes. Sometimes when we feel the worst, God is actually loving us even more than when we are feeling the best.

We are living in a war zone. There is an enemy of our souls out to overwhelm us if he can. He will bring feelings of depression, disappointment, anger, pride, envy, and lust to try to knock us off our mountain-top perch under the shelter of God's wings of faith.

> ***"No, despite all these things, overwhelming victory is ours through Christ, who loved us."***
> ***Romans 8:37 NLT***

As much as we can and should enjoy the feelings of overwhelming joy of our salvation, we need to be anchored deep in the faith of the truth of God's Word and His promises, rather than feelings that can and often will deceive us.

**Father, let my overwhelming joy be based on your truth instead of my feelings. Amen.**

February 9 Read Luke 15:11-24 , Psalm 85

# *God's Lemon Laws*

**"The LORD has taken away your judgments, He has cast out your enemy. The King of Israel, the LORD, *is* in your midst; you shall see disaster no more." Zephaniah 3:15**

The federal government and nearly every state have taken upon the task of protecting consumers against false advertising, defective and harmful products and services, and fraud.

> ***"Restore us, O God of our salvation, and cause Your anger toward us to cease." Psalm 85:4***

Unfortunately, they don't afford much protection from the billions of dollars spent advertising alcoholic beverages that fail to mention the frequent consequences such as driving fatalities, alcoholism, impaired judgment, and liver disease.

All of us at some time or another have bit into some of the lemons of life that promise pleasures that will not last, approval of others instead of the approval of God, and worship of people, pastimes, and possessions above the worship of God.

We have the greatest "consumer's bill of rights" ever written called "The Holy Bible." When we acknowledge our lemons, confess, and repent of them, we can find restitution and restoration.

We also have Jesus and the Holy Spirit as our consumer advocates who are not only guiding us by example and conscience, but also continually interceding for us at the throne of God to overcome the penalty for our lemons.

The believers bill of rights promises payment in full for every lemon we ever bite into and indemnifies and holds us harmless against the penalty of death when we call upon the name of the Lord for forgiveness with true sorrow.

> ***"And the son said to him, 'Father, I have sinned against heaven and in your sight, and am no longer worthy to be called your son.'" Luke 15:21 NLT***

What forbidden fruit have you bitten into lately that has turned out to be a lemon? Are you ready to apply for protection under God's bill of rights for believers?

**Father, thank you for the provisions of your lemon laws. Amen.**

**Read 1 Thessalonians 4, Psalm 65** **February 10**

## *God's Will for You*

**"But seek first the kingdom of God and His righteousness, and all these things shall be added to you." Matthew 6:33**

Holiness is not a popular concept. It makes us uncomfortable to think that our call to salvation in Christ is also a call to a lifelong pursuit of holiness in our lives.

> ***"What joy for those You choose to bring near, those who live in Your holy courts."***
> ***Psalm 65:4 NLT***

How humbling it is to realize that we have been sanctified and made holy in the sight of God the hour we first believed, yet we fail to live holy as unto the Lord.

When we realize that our first priority in life should be to seek God and His holiness so that our lives will reflect the glory of God and His love, we are making a big break through in understanding God's will for our lives. God will add everything else to us including holiness when our minds are fixed on Him.

Holiness is not piety and living in hypocritical glory. It is living out our faith in the joy of the Lord for the love He has showered upon us, by loving Him, loving others, and seeking to please Him in every area of our lives.

When our Christ-centered spiritual condition takes control of our self-centered human condition, we become free to live in freedom from bondage to our human condition and to live lives fully pleasing to God and fruitful in every good work.

When we grow into the fullness of Christ through growing in our personal relationship with Him, we get to know Him better and better through His Word. We will reflect His glory, love, and friendship, and we will experience more answered prayers and the incredible joy that comes from abiding in Him.

> ***"We urge you in the name of the Lord Jesus to live in a way that pleases God, as we have taught you."***
> ***1 Thessalonians 4:1b NLT***

**Father, by the power of Your Spirit help me to thirst after Your righteousness and holiness. Amen.**

 **Read Mark 2:1-12, Isaiah 47**

# *Paralyzing Sin*

**"What will you do in the day of punishment, and in the desolation *which* will come from afar? To whom will you flee for help? And where will you leave your glory?" Isaiah 10:3**

We all probably have close, personal knowledge of the paralyzing effect of strokes or muscular dystrophy on a loved one. To lose the use of an arm, a leg, or even our whole body is a fate suffered and endured by many in their prime or golden years of life.

> ***"Your 'wisdom' and 'knowledge' have caused you to turn away from me and claim, 'I am self-sufficient and not accountable to anyone!" Isaiah 47:10b NLT***

Unrepented sin causes a spiritual paralysis far worse than any physical paralysis caused by a stroke or other illness.

The paralyzing effects of sin include living separated from the blessings of obedience promised to all who call upon the name of the Lord and obey His commands.

Unforgiveness creates a root of bitterness that cripples our relationship with God and with others, whom we are commanded to forgive and to love. This also has harmful effects on physical health and is linked to cancer and many other diseases.

Guilt and shame will overwhelm and paralyze believers, making it virtually impossible for them to be the salt and the light that God has called us to be.

> ***"Is it easier to say to the paralyzed man, 'Your sins are forgiven' or 'Get up, pick up your mat, and walk?' I will prove that I, the Son of Man, have the authority on earth to forgive sins." Mark 2:9 NLT***

Pride, anger, envy, and lust are sins that not only cripple us but also cause great harm to those around us.

God will not be mocked. The more we sin against Him by disobeying or ignoring Him, the more devastating and severe our paralysis will be.

The difference between paralysis and power is in cleansing our consciences with God through confession, godly sorrow, and true repentance.

**Father, may I never let willful and unrepented sin make a cripple out of me. Amen.**

Read Ephesians 5:2-11, Psalm 80 February 12

# *Making God Smile*

**"May the LORD smile on you and be gracious to you. May the LORD show you his favor and give you His peace." Numbers 6:25 NLT**

> ***"GOD, God of the angel armies, come back! Smile your blessing smile: that will be our salvation."***
> ***Psalm 80:19 MSG***

The idea that we can cause God to smile is foreign to much of our thinking. The idea that a Sovereign, Majestic, Holy God could delight in us and that we could actually bring a smile to His face is a big stretch for many.

We can easily identify with making God angry and somehow think of piety as wearing a starched collar. It is hard for many to view God as a Father who is intimately involved in every aspect of the lives of His children.

As children, we can still remember doing things that made our parents smile. As parents and grandparents, we still smile at memories of some of the delightful things our children did that entertained or pleased us. If God delights in giving good gifts to His children, why is it so hard to realize that God delights in enjoying us?

If God is always there to comfort us in our sorrows and cry with us, why is it so hard to believe that He is also there to share our joy and rejoice with us?

We know that God was pleased with His servant Job. Noah *"found favor with the Lord" (Genesis 6:8 NLT).* He was so delighted with Abraham that He founded a great nation upon him. He took great delight in David, a man after His own heart. He proudly announced that He was very pleased with His own Son.

> ***"Try to find out what is pleasing to the Lord. Take no part in the worthless deeds of evil and darkness; instead, rebuke and expose them."***
> ***Ephesians 5:10 NLT***

We make God smile by our obedience. He inhabits the praises of His people. He is pleased with our prayers. He is pleased with our spiritual growth. He smiles biggest of all when we show our love to Him, reflect His love to others, and fulfill the purposes for which He created us.

**Father, may I bring smiles to You as I grow into the fullness of Your Son. Amen.**

February 13 Read 1 Corinthians 2:9-16, Psalm 50

# *The Awesomeness of God*

**"For now we see in a mirror, dimly, but then face to face. Now I know in part, but then I shall know just as I also am known."**

**1 Corinthians 9:13**

God has revealed His awesomeness to us in many ways. We see it in His creation. His sovereignty, majesty, omniscience, and presence are only partially comprehensible.

> ***"Let the heavens declare His righteousness, for God Himself is Judge."***
> ***Psalm 50:6***

His character is purer than 24 karat gold; His love, patience and mercy hold back the wrath of His righteous indignation over our sins.

To even imagine that a God so big and involved in everything going on in the universe 24 hours a day, 7 days a week, century after century,could at the same time be so personal and so alive in the heart of every believer exceeds our comprehension, but it is true.

To know the eye that is on the sparrow is also watching over us gives us a sense of security and peace that will see us through the deepest oceans of tears and valleys of disappointment and even death.

To know that we were created in the image of the Creator and ruler of the universe and to realize that we were created for His pleasure and His enjoyment as we fellowship with Him is awesome. This should give us a great desire to live our lives fully pleasing to Him.

To know God as our Father who loves us with an unconditional everlasting love and who has plans to bless us and give us a future and a hope should draw us even closer to Him.

> ***"Eye has not seen, nor ear heard, nor have entered into the heart of man the things which God has prepared for those who love Him."***
> ***1 Corinthians 2:9***

As awesome as we know God to be from our limited understanding, think about how great it's going to be when all things will be revealed when we meet Him face to face for an eternity of perfect bliss in heaven.

**Father, You truly are my awesome God. Blessed be your name forever and ever. Amen.**

Read Job 1:20-24, Deuteronomy 28:2-20 February 14

## *Divine Dividends*

**"For God is the one who gives seed to the farmer and then bread to eat. In the same way, he will give you many opportunities to do good, and he will produce a great harvest of generosity in you. Yes, you will be enriched so that you can give even more generously."**

**2 Corinthians 9:10,11a NLT**

There is a universal law of life that says you only get out of something what you put into it. We have all heard this axiom used in regard to clubs, hobbies, and other activities.

> ***"You will experience all these blessings if you obey the LORD your God."***
> ***Deuteronomy 28:2 NLT***

There are promises from God that we will always get more out of investing our time, talents, and treasures in obedience to Him. Unlike the stock market these divine dividends are guaranteed.

Although Paul is specifically talking about money in 2 Corinthians 9, we can expand this principle to our other areas of offerings.

When we invest our faith in Jesus Christ, we receive instant new life, everlasting eternal life, and divine dividends including the peace and security that only a right relationship with the Father through the Son can give.

When we invest our time in fulfilling the purposes for which God created us, we receive the overwhelming joy that only glorifying God can provide.

When we invest our talents to the glory of God and to His service, we receive the dividend of satisfaction in knowing that God is pleased when we honor Him.

We cannot out give, out serve, or out love God. When we give Him our all, we become plugged into the fount of blessings that will never run dry. In every case, He will return more and better than we can ever offer.

> ***"Live in such a way that God's love can bless you as you wait for the eternal life that our Lord Jesus Christ in his mercy is going to give you."***
> ***Jude 1:21 NLT***

**Father, help me to make wise investments in Your kingdom that I might reap the harvest of blessings You promise to all who invest in You. Amen.**

**February 15** **Read Psalm 119:27-37, Ecclesiastes 1**

# *Forever Blowing Bubbles*

**"Smoke, nothing but smoke. [That's what the Quester says.] There's nothing to anything—it's all smoke." Ecclesiastes 1:2 MSG**

There is a certain fascination about blowing bubbles. They can get so big and so beautiful before they pop.

> ***"Turn my eyes from worthless things, and give me life through your word."***
> ***Psalm 119:37 NLT***

Some people always seem to be blowing bubbles or perhaps "blowing smoke" in today's vernacular. They dream lofty dreams, build great expectations in themselves and others, but nothing seems to come to fruition.

As our sinful natures and the sin in this world become manifest in our lives, many of our bubbles of dreams and ambitions seem to pop and disappear into thin air.

We go looking for love and security in all the wrong places. We try to validate our worth by possessions, approval of peers, or the world's standards and often find, as Solomon did, the wisest man who ever lived, that all is vanity and that we are "chasing after the wind".

Many have to discover the futility of life apart from God before they realize that they need a Savior who can reconcile them with God and realize that the abundant, eternal life in Christ is real and not just a bunch of "smoke."

God created us for His pleasure and His purposes. He has made plans for each and everyone of us. *"'For I know the plans I have for you,' says the LORD. 'They are plans for good and not for disaster, to give you a future and a hope'" (Jeremiah 29:11 NLT).*

When our self-centered bubbles burst and we are ready to accept the reality that life is all about a personal relationship with a God who loves us unconditionally, forgives us forever, and accepts us just the way we are, we are ready to receive the salvation that fills our longing for a Savior who cannot fail and will never disappoint.

> ***"Fear God and keep His commandments, for this is man's all. For God will bring every work into judgment, including every secret thing, whether good or evil."***
> ***Ecclesiastes 12:13b-14 NLT***

**Father, help me to bubble over with trust in You. Amen.**

Read James 5:13-16, Psalm 92 February 16

# *The Mercy Seat of God*

**"The truth is, you can go directly to the Father and ask Him, and He will grant your request because you use My name. You haven't done this before. Ask, using My name, and you will receive, and you will have abundant joy." John 16:23b,24 NLT**

Whether sitting, standing, lying down, or kneeling…whether at home, or in a hospital, car, plane, or at church….all believers have a reserved seat at the mercy seat of God and access to His throne of grace through prayer.

> ***"To declare Your loving kindness in the morning, and Your faithfulness every night," Psalm 92:2***

There are prayers of adoration and praise, of confession and repentance, of thanksgiving, and of supplication for our needs and the needs of others.

Prayers cost us nothing, yet they cost Jesus everything, even His own life. It was only through the perfect, unblemished life of Jesus and His blood shed as the perfect sacrifice that rent the veil of the temple and allows us free access into the very presence of God through prayer.

Prayer will provide God's strength to cover our weaknesses, God's wisdom to light our path, and give peace to calm our troubled hearts.

God's mercy seat abounds in grace and forgiveness we don't deserve. There is nothing that God will not forgive when we ask with a broken spirit and contrite heart.

God loves to give good gifts to His children who ask. When we abide in Christ, we get more prayers answered because we pray more for things that honor and glorify God and less self centered and selfish.

There are millions of changed lives, saved souls, and blessings more abundant than we could ever dare ask or hope that testify to the truth that God honors the fervent prayers of the faithful.

There are millions of healings, saved marriages, provisions for every need, and even the granting of the desires of hearts that are the results of answered prayers at the mercy seat of God.

> ***"The earnest prayer of a righteous person has great power and wonderful results." James 5:16b NLT***

**Father, thank you for the sacred delight of experiencing answered prayers. Amen.**

# *Lenses*

**"For now we see in a mirror, dimly, but then face to face. Now I know in part, but then I shall know just as I also am known." 1 Corinthians 3:12**

How do you view life? What lenses are you seeing through?

> ***"But because I have done what is right, I will see You. When I awake, I will be fully satisfied, for I will see You face to face." Psalm 17:15 NLT***

Close up viewing often blinds us to the bigger picture of life. We can begin focusing on ourselves, our work, our treasures, and pleasures so closely that we can never see beyond.

Our telescopic lens is great for seeing the big picture of where we would like to go and who we would like to be, but it often leaves us clueless as to how to get there.

The lens of faith enables us to believe what we cannot see and allows us to claim all of the wonderful promises of God for our lives.

The lens of hope will allow us to view life with that Christian optimism that affirms our faith that we do have a future and a hope.

The lens of love helps us to see God clearly and to love Him dearly. It helps us to see others as Christ sees us and to respond to His love for us by loving others as we are commanded.

We sometimes need lens filters to blot out the besetting sins that cloud our vision and darken our understanding.

> ***"Yes, dear friends, we are already God's children, and we can't even imagine what we will be like when Christ returns. But we do know that when He comes we will be like Him, for we will see Him as He really is." 1 John 3:2 NLT***

We need the lens of optimism that will allow us to see glasses that are half full instead of half empty.

Perhaps most of all, we need to filter our views through the filter of holiness, without which we will never really see God.

**Father, thank you for opening my eyes to Your love. Help me to continually seek to see and live Your truth. Amen.**

**Read Colossians 1:1-23, 2 Samuel 22:20-53** **February 18**

# *It is About You!*

**"The steps of a *good* man are ordered by the LORD, and He delights in his way." Psalm 37:23**

Even though we are to become Christ centered and lead lives fully pleasing to Him, accomplishing the good works for which He created us, it is still all about us as far as God is concerned.

> ***"He led me to a place of safety; He rescued me because He delights in me."***
> ***2 Samuel 22:20***

Even though we are to put God first in every aspect of our lives, it is still about us and what we do with the life we have been given.

God has made us unique. Our DNA proves this. God made us for His purposes not ours. He gifted us and made us special. We are the "apple of his eye."

Our majestic, all-powerful, ever-present, all-knowing God is bigger than anything yet has the hairs on our head numbered. He created us for forever fellowship with Him and has demonstrated how much He loves us by letting His only begotten Son die so that we might live in relationship with Him forever.

We are the only creatures made in His own image. We are the only creatures with souls that can reflect the heart of God and His love.

God has made plans to bless, not harm, each and everyone of us. He has given us a future and a hope.

No one can live our life for us. No one can make the right connection with God for us. We can't even make it for ourselves. It is only through the power of the Holy Spirit that we can open the door when God comes knocking in the person of Jesus Christ.

> ***"As a result, He has brought you into the very presence of God, and you are holy and blameless as you stand before Him without a single fault."***
> ***Colossians 1:23***

We have been bought with a price. Our lives are no longer our own. We must lose self to find our new life where it's all about God and living in a growing personal faith relationship with Him.

**Father, keep me ever mindful that you created me for a personal relationship of life with You. Amen.**

# *Why Believe the Worst?*

**"This is a true saying, and everyone should believe it: Christ Jesus came into the world to save sinners—and I was the worst of them all." 1 Timothy 1:15 NLT**

The growing tendency to use negative campaigning in politics seems to be because people don't trust politicians and will gladly have their suspicions confirmed by believing the worst and ignoring the best that is said about them.

> ***"Only simpletons believe everything they are told! The prudent carefully consider their steps." Proverbs 14:15 NLT***

There seems to be a number of people who delight in the sins or alleged sins of pastors and religious leaders because it confirms a judgment that the church is full of hypocrites.

It is so easy for professing Christians to become stumbling blocks by letting their actions speak louder than words which encourage unbelievers to affirm their distrust and unbelief of God and Christians.

The thought that we will be judged by the same standards we use in judging others is sobering and should make us more loving and less prone to rush to judgment in believing the worst about others. We should never take pleasure in believing the worst about others.

Even when the facts are undeniable and the worst is true, we need to remember that God hates the sin but loves the sinner and commands us to do the same.

When we remember that our own goodness is "as filthy rags" when compared to the perfect goodness of God, we can believe the best which is that God forgives sinners, instead of the worst that we are so much better than others.

If we chose to believe the worst about Abraham, David, Peter, and Paul we could have no future and no hope. By believing the best about them, we are brought into friendship with the one who is always believing the best about us.

> ***"He will use every kind of wicked deception to fool those who are on their way to destruction because they refuse to believe the truth that would save them." 2 Thessalonians 2:10***

**Father, help me to think the best instead of the worst about people. Amen.**

**Read 2 Kings 2:19-22, Psalm 105:41-45** **February 20**

## *Dams on the River of Life*

**"Instead, I want to see a mighty flood of justice, a river of righteous living that will never run dry." Amos 5:24 NLT**

> ***"He opened up a rock, and water gushed out to form a river through the dry and barren land."***
> ***Psalm 105:41 NLT***

There is a river of living water that flows through the lives of all believers. This is the love of God that flows to us through the love of Christ and flows into others as we become conduits of His love in fulfilling both the great commandment and great commission.

This flow of living water often gets dammed up and reduced to a trickle when we block it at the source by quenching the Holy Spirit by not growing in God's Word, worshipping, praying, and fellowshipping with other believers.

We were created for a close and personal relationship with God through faith in Jesus Christ who is our wellspring of living water. When we ignore Him or fail to grow into our relationship with Him, we restrict the flow of His grace.

As we meander through life it is very easy to build dams that will quench the flow of living water through us and into the lives of others.

Dams of selfishness and self centeredness will leave us dried up and unable to give to others.

Dams of deliberate and willful sins will create a drought of faith that will reduce our river of life into a mere trickle.

Dams of unforgiveness will turn our living waters into polluted cesspools of bitterness, which will not only poison us but also those around us.

> ***"Thus says the LORD: 'I have healed this water; from it there shall be no more death or barrenness.'"***
> ***2 Kings 2:21b***

Dams of doubt will restrict the flow of joy in our lives and rob us of our peace.

Dams of disobedience will quench the flow of purpose and keep us from doing that for which we were created.

Worst of all, a dam of unbelief will doom us to getting mired into the quicksand of death from which we can never know the joy of eternal life.

**Lord, may Your river of life always flow freely through me. Amen.**

February 21 Read Ephesians 1:1-14, Psalm 19

## *Are You Orbiting the Son?*

**"But seek first the kingdom of God and His righteousness, and all these things shall be added to you." Matthew 6:33**

Many laws of the universe seem to carry over into the laws of life.

> ***"The heavens declare the glory of God, and the firmament shows His handiwork." Psalm 19:1***

Any change in the earth's orbit around the sun would result in the end of life on this planet. A few degrees closer and we fry; a few degrees further and we freeze. This one small speck in the universe would be no more.

Being the egocentric creatures that we are by nature, we often live and act as though the world revolves around us. We can easily be so self absorbed that we can never see the big picture.

Even if we get ourselves out of the picture, we often make our spouses, our children, our careers, or other pursuits the center of our universe, and our world revolves around them.

From God's perspective, anything that we put ahead of Him becomes an idol of our worship and robs God of the glory that is due Him. *("for you shall worship no other god, for the LORD, whose name is Jealous, is a jealous God" Exodus 34:14)*

It is only when we make Jesus the center of our universe and let our lives revolve around Him that we can ever know the fullness of His love, peace, forgiveness, and joy that is the birth right of every one who is born again through faith in Him.

When our love of our spouse models Christ's love for the Church, we have great marriages. When our love of children and others models Jesus' love, we have great families and great relationships. When our work is "done as unto the Lord," we achieve success and blessing as never before.

> ***"God's secret plan has now been revealed to us; it is a plan centered on Christ, designed long ago according to his good pleasure." Ephesians 1:1***

These are just a few of the "all things" that will be added to us when we live our lives revolved around the Son!

**Father, by the power of Your Spirit, let my life be centered in You. Amen.**

# *Soul Bait*

**"Now then, we are ambassadors for Christ, as though God were pleading through us: we implore *you* on Christ's behalf, be reconciled to God." 2 Corinthians 5:20**

When you think about it, we are really the bait instead of the angler when it comes to being fishers of men.

> ***"Light shines on the godly, and joy on those who do right."***
> ***Psalm 97:4 NLT***

Just as bugs are drawn to the light and animals are drawn to traps baited with appealing food, we humans are motivated by many baits that can trap us and hold us captive to a large number of sins and abominations.

We get baited by lust, pride, envy, anger and other temptations that catch us and put us into the frying pan before we even realize it.

When it comes to winning souls for Christ, we are actually called to be the "bait" by which the Holy Spirit unleashes the power through which all are called into a saving relationship with God through faith in Jesus Christ.

Scripture makes it very clear that *"no one can say that Jesus is Lord except by the Holy Spirit" (1 Corinthians 12:3 b).* It is only by this power that anyone can be brought into the family of God.

We are called to be the light of the world, living lives that reflect the light of God's love that attracts others. We are told to love others as Christ has loved us. We are told to always be ready to give an answer for the hope that is within us and to proclaim the Good News throughout our world.

This is all that we can do. We can't work faith in the heart of anyone or make anyone believe. God may use us as one of the "bites" that people sometimes nibble on before they finally become convinced of their sinfulness and their need for a Savior, or He may use us as the final "bait" through which the Holy Spirit can reel in the "fish."

> ***With lustful desire as their bait, they lure back into sin those who have just escaped from such wicked living."***
> ***2 Peter 2:18b NLT***

**Father, keep me in Your tackle box as one of Your prized lures for fishing for souls. Amen.**

February 23 Read James 1, Psalm 105:1-22

# *Look for the Silver Lining!*

**"So be truly glad! There is wonderful joy ahead, even though it is necessary for you to endure many trials for a while." 1 Peter 1:6 NLT**

> ***"Until the time came to fulfill His word, the LORD tested Joseph's character."***

This old song from the 1920's gives some great advice for today. When we look at circumstances from God's perspective, we find consolation and strength for persevering through the storms of life.

Knowing that sunshine follows the rain helps us through the clouds of darkness and despair that often accompany the inevitable problems of life in a sin-sick world.

Whether as a consequence of our sins or the by products of the sin that abounds all around us, we have been fore warned by Christ, who said, "In this world, you will have troubles."

Like the little boy shoveling manure out of the stall figuring that there had to be a pony in there somewhere, we need to dig deep to look for the silver lining accompanying our cloud.

It may be that God is disciplining us in order to conform us to the image of Christ. It may be that God is equipping us to comfort and strengthen others when they face the same problems.

We learn from Scripture that God's character-development program for us will often include faith-building opportunities disguised as failures or troubles.

God not only tells us to rejoice in tribulation, and to count it all joy when we have troubles, but He also gives examples in the lives of Joseph, Job, Peter, Paul, and others to show *"that all things work together for good to those who love God, to those who are the called according to His purpose" (Romans 8:28).*

> ***"Dear brothers and sisters, whenever trouble comes your way, let it be an opportunity for joy." James 1:1 NLT***

As believers, we are privileged to know that we have an all-powerful God who loves us with an everlasting love, who can turn what others mean for evil into good, and who wants the very best for us. This is the real silver lining that accompanies every cloud of life.

**Father, help me to find the silver lining in the clouds of life. Amen.**

**Read John 7:37-38, Jeremiah 2:1-13** **February 24**

## *Soak it Up!*

**"Whosoever drinketh of the water that I shall give him shall never thirst. But the water that I shall give him will become in him a fountain of water springing up into everlasting life."John 4:14**

One of the greatest gifts God gives to every believer is a fountain of living water that will never run dry. No matter how often and how much we drink of it, it will never run dry.

> ***"For my people have done two evil things: They have forsaken me—the fountain of living water. And they have dug for themselves cracked cisterns that can hold no water at all!" Jeremiah 2:13 NLT***

The wellspring of our own personal fountain is the Holy Spirit, who comes to keep us filled with the love, grace, and mercy of God that is sufficient for our every need.

How can we not be content when we have this spring of joy, peace, and consolation? How can we be lonely when we have a friend who sticks closer than a brother?

When we are filled with the blessed assurance of our eternal life in heaven, we can go through the cares and troubles of this world without the despair of the one who has no hope.

Worry and depression cannot stick against the flow of knowing that Christ in us is our hope of glory. How can we worry when we have our security in knowing that God has promised to work all things for our good?

All of the thirsts from the lusts of the flesh, the approval of the world, and the temptations of satan will be washed away and replaced by the fullness of Christ which will cause us to thirst for His righteousness and to get closer to Him.

> ***"If you believe in me, come and drink! For the Scriptures declare that rivers of living water will flow out from within." John 7:38 NLT***

As we come to the water and stand by His side, we will find a fuller enjoyment of His love and in loving others. Our only thirst will be to drink more and more of Jesus from this well that will never run dry.

**Father, fill my cup to overflowing with the living water of Your love. Amen.**

February 25 Read Revelation 22:1-5, Isaiah 66:12, 13

# *The River of Life*

**"He who believes in Me, as the Scripture has said, out of his heart will flow rivers of living water." John 7:38 NLT**

Our lives can be somewhat likened to a river. We start out as just a couple of drops of liquid and grow into a stream, a tributary, and finally, a full-fledged river flowing to our final destination.

> ***"Behold, I will extend peace to her like a river, and the glory of the Gentiles like a flowing stream."***
>
> ***Isaiah 66:12***

Along the way, we become rivers of living water when the Holy Spirit indwells us and pours living waters into us.

Our waters often become polluted by run offs of sin which rob us of our purity and clarity. As we move downstream, we never know exactly what is around the next bend in the river.

We often get churned up and muddy as we flow through storms of disappointment and failure.

Stagnation sometimes sets in when droughts of doubt and dams of indifference restrict our flow.

As we meander through the rocks of rebellion and over falls of tribulation, our living waters become filtered by the amazing grace of God that allows us to become rivers of healing and viaducts of love through a very sin-parched land.

As we persevere, God filters out all of our impurities and makes us pure water of life, crystal clear, and life-giving sources for irrigating the choice vineyards of God's fruitfulness.

> ***"And he showed me a pure river of water of life, clear as crystal, proceeding from the throne of God and of the Lamb."***
>
> ***Revelation 22:1***

Just as a river flows into and becomes a part of the power and majesty of the sea, so will we flow into God's ocean of love, joy and peace that awaits all who receive Jesus Christ as Savior.

**Father, supply my river of life with Your daily shower of manna that I might never run dry. Amen.**

Read 2 Corinthians 9:5-15, Psalm 119:129-140 February 26

## *The Only Test God Allows*

**"Bring all the tithes into the storehouse, that there may be food in My house, and try Me now in this," says the LORD of hosts, "If I will not open for you the windows of heaven and pour out for you *such* blessing that *there will* not *be room* enough *to receive it.*" Malachi 3:10**

Scripture makes it very clear that we are not to test God. The scribes and Pharisees tried it several times and were rebuked and reminded that we are not to test God.

> ***"Give me an eagerness for your decrees; do not inflict me with love for money!" Psalm 119:36 NLT***

Annanias and Sapphira tested God by withholding some of the proceeds from the sale of their property and died. Some tested God's patience and were bitten by poisonous snakes and died. God allowed Job to be tested by every imaginable trial to prove his faith.

God is continually at work testing us. He tests our hearts, our faithfulness, our obedience, our righteousness, and our character, so that we can be conformed to the image of Christ.

Jesus will test the stewardship of our lives when all of the wood, hay, and stubble of vain pursuits are burned away, and only the good works we did which God had chosen for us before we were born and the fruit of our lives that glorified God will remain.

It is very interesting to note that God not only allows, but He commands that we test Him in the area of giving to Him. He specifically promises blessings so abundant that we will not be able to receive them all.

Just as if we had the faith of a mustard seed, we could move mountains; if we had the faith to test God as He commanded, we would be healed of greed and able to receive the overflowing cup of blessings He promises to all who obey this command.

> ***"Yes, you will be enriched so that you can give even more generously. And when we take your gifts to those who need them, they will break out in thanksgiving to God." 2 Corinthians 9:11 NLT***

**Father, give me the faith to give God the only test He allows. Amen.**

February 27 Read Romans 8:6-13, Psalm 18

# *Collision Avoidance Systems*

**"Unfailing love and faithfulness cover sin; evil is avoided by fear of the LORD." Proverbs 16:6 NLT**

> ***"He is a shield for all who look to Him for protection." Psalm 18:30b NLT***

Federal Aviation Administration records show over a hundred "mid-air collision near misses" each year. All planes now carry collision avoidance equipment to warn of impending crashes with other planes, mountains, or other objects and to give instructions on how to avoid them.

Millions of dollars are being spent on research to design a workable collision avoidance system on automobiles. Many new cars come with a warning system that sound the alarm when you are about to back into something.

God has designed a collision-avoidance system for every believer. He sends the Holy Spirit to help us avoid the pitfalls of hell by calling us to faith in Jesus Christ.

When we receive Jesus Christ as our Savior, we also receive the indwelling presence of the Holy Spirit to guide us into all truth and to help us avoid the collisions with the sins lurking all around us.

The Holy Spirit is continually making intercession for us according to the will of God that we might avoid the collisions caused by the weakness of our flesh and find His way of escaping the temptations that beset us.

When we are filled with the fruit of the Spirit, our love, joy, peace, longsuffering, kindness, goodness, faithfulness, gentleness, and self-control will help us avoid many collisions that might otherwise damage our relationship with God and with others.

God's collision-avoidance system will use our conscience, our prayers, His Word, or the concern of fellow believers to warn us of impending collisions. We need to pray for the spiritual discernment to hear the warnings and follow the instructions to "pull up," "turn," "fight," "flee," etc.

> ***"For if you keep on following it, you will perish, but if through the power of the Holy Spirit you turn from it and its evil deeds, you will live." Romans 8:13 NLT***

**Father, help me to obey the warnings of Your collision-avoidance system. Amen.**

**Read Matthew 15:1-16, Isaiah 29:13-27** **February 28**

## *Are You Conformed?*

**"And do not be conformed to this world, but be transformed by the renewing of your mind, that you may prove what *is* that good and acceptable and perfect will of God." Romans 12:2**

Scripture tells us that we are to spend a lifetime being conformed into the image of Christ.

> ***"They honor me with their lips, but their hearts are far away. And their worship of me amounts to nothing more than human laws learned by rote." Isaiah 29:13b NLT***

In response to God's great love in Christ, we should respond in love to Him and to become more and more like Him as we grow in our knowledge of Him through His Word and submit more and more to the power of the Holy Spirit living within us.

Being conformed can be a very slippery slope for many. It is very easy to be conformed to the image of the world and let the world's standards of success, pleasure, and accomplishment determine our conformation.

There is often a great danger of becoming conformed to religion rather than to Christ. Traditions often dictate what we should wear and how we should worship. The denominational walls are still standing and keeping the conformists to a particular denomination in and keeping many people who need the Lord out.

The great commission often seems to have been placed on the back burner as well-meaning, but often misguided, zealots make defending traditions more important than seeking and saving the lost.

The centrality of the Gospel is the defining confirmation of the faith of every Christian. It's really a matter of Who you know rather than what you know. All of the religious knowledge of the day did not save the Scribes and Pharisees, and it will not save you.

> ***"They are blind guides leading the blind, and if one blind person guides another, they will both fall into a ditch." Matthew 15:14 NLT***

Having faith that Jesus Christ died to earn your salvation on the cross at Calvary and having Him in our hearts as Savior and Lord is the confirmation of our conformation that counts.

**Father, by the power of Your Spirit, let me become more Christ-like in every area of my life. Amen.**

February 29 Read 2 Corinthians 4, Isaiah 43

# *It's So Good to Know!*

**"When you go through deep waters and great trouble, I will be with you. When you go through rivers of difficulty, you will not drown! When you walk through the fire of oppression, you will not be burned up; the flames will not consume you." Isaiah 43:2 NLT**

If we have never wandered aimlessly lost, we should thank God that we have been spared the futility of a life apart from God. If we have known the feeling of being lost, we should thank God that He has put us on the right path through this barren wilderness of sin.

> ***"For I am about to do a brand-new thing. See, I have already begun! Do you not see it? I will make a pathway through the wilderness for my people to come home."***
> ***Isaiah 43:19a NLT***

Jesus Christ came to earth to light the way for us to come home to God and to enjoy reconciliation and restoration with Him. We find a new life in Him.

No one is spared troubles and difficulties in this life. Trouble is just an illness or a circumstance, phone call, temptation, or sin away as long as we are living in this world.

This is why it's so good to know that in Jesus, we have a Savior who has overcome the world! Not only has He overcome the world, He has overcome death and now lives forever. Because Jesus lives, we can go through the deep waters without drowning and life's fires without burning.

Our fears and doubts are replaced by the confidence of knowing that God does work all things for our good and His glory, that a means of escape will be provided for every temptation, and that nothing can ever separate us from the love of God that is ours through faith in Jesus Christ.

> ***"For our present troubles are quite small and won't last very long. Yet they produce for us an immeasurably great glory that will last forever."***
> ***2 Corinthians 4:17 NLT***

Knowing that God is for us and our very present help in time of trouble should give us the strength and encouragement we need to get through the deep waters and fiery trials of life ever mindful of the prize that awaits on the other side.

**Father, thank you for the assurance of Your presence and protection during the trials of life. Amen.**

**Read 1 Corinthians 2:9-17, Psalm 119:17-24** **March 1**

## *Let's Make a Deal!*

**"So also Christ died only once as a sacrifice to take away the sins of many people. He will come again but not to deal with our sins again. This time he will bring salvation to all those who are eagerly waiting for him." Hebrews 9:28 NLT**

This TV game show featured the decision to trade your winnings for whatever was behind Door 1, 2, or 3. You often got something much better, and just as often got something worthless.

> ***"Deal bountifully with Your servant, that I may live and keep Your word." Psalm 119:17***

Some seem to think that they are playing "Let's Make a Deal" in the game of life.

The prodigal son traded his inheritance for a pottage of pleasure that ended up with him eating pig slop to stay alive.

Some will trade their character for popularity, their love of God for love of pleasure or possessions and end up getting short changed.

Satan tried to play "Let's Make a Deal" with Jesus in offering all of the kingdoms and glory of the world if He would bow down and worship him.

We sometimes consciously or subconsciously try to make deals with God; if He will do something we want, we will do something He wants, as though we have something to bargain with.

If we make a deal with the devil, we can expect only to get burned. The pleasures promised will soon turn to brass, and we will find that we have not only been deceived, but often disconnected from God in the process.

When God is the dealer "Let's Make a Deal" becomes a game worth playing. He never deals off the bottom of the deck of deception.

> ***"Eye has not seen, nor ear heard, nor have entered into the heart of man the things which God has prepared for those who love Him." 1 Corinthians 2:9***

When we ante up with faith, God deals a full house of blessings beyond anything we can dare hope for. We have the peace and joy of the present, and the bright hope for tomorrow in heaven.

**Father, thank you for dealing me the gift of salvation and all its benefits. Amen.**

March 2 Read Jude 1, Psalm 34

# *Does it Really Matter?*

**"Enjoy life, but stay within God's guidelines. God will hold us accountable for everything we do, and who wants to explain ungodliness to a holy God on the day of judgment?" Ecclesiastes 11:9 NLT**

Since we have God's forgiveness for every sin we have ever committed or will ever commit when we confess and repent, why should we worry about judgment day?

> ***"For God carefully watches the way people live; He sees everything they do."***
> ***Psalm 34:21***

As believers, we are going to stand before God covered with the righteousness of Christ and be welcomed into heaven with great rejoicing from all the Saints who have gone on before. This is the gift of God given to all who by faith have received Jesus Christ as Savior.

If this is true, and it is, why should we worry about explaining our ungodliness to a holy God?

What about those who call upon the name of the Lord, and He knows them not? When does grace become abused instead of used to free us to respond to God's wonderful gift of salvation by living lives pleasing to Him and fruitful in every good work?

Can it be, like James says: "faith without works is dead"? Can it be that when we are truly saved, we will want to bear the fruits of righteousness for a righteous God who has loved us with such great love?

Can it be that if we do not have godly sorrow when we are ungodly we might well question the validity of our faith?

> ***"Live in such a way that God's love can bless you as you wait for the eternal life that our Lord Jesus Christ in His mercy is going to give you."***
> ***Jude 1:19 NLT***

We can deceive others and even ourselves, but we cannot deceive God who knows the heart of all.

The baggage of ungodliness is certainly not something we should want to take on our journey home.

**Father, by the power of Your Spirit, help me to be a godly person. Amen.**

# *Higher Levels*

**"Don't ever let anyone call you 'rabbi,' for you have only one teacher, and all of you are on the same level as brothers and sisters." Matthew 23:8 NLT**

There are levels for about everything based on education, experience, performance, and ability. We have entry level wages for starting jobs in almost every field. As your experience increases and your ability is proven, you get more pay and more responsibility.

> ***"Teach us to make the most of our time, so that we may grow in wisdom." Psalm 90:12 NLT***

You enter the armed forces at the entry level of private, and you rise through the ranks as your experience and performance increases and your ability is proven.

The kingdom of God works the same way in many respects. The entry level for everyone is receiving the gift of salvation through faith in Jesus Christ. Everyone who calls upon the name of the Lord shall be saved. We are instantly made righteous in the sight of God, all our sins are forgiven, and we are assured of eternal life in heaven when we die.

In the meantime, we have a life to live on this earth. The quality of our life on this earth and even our life in heaven will often be determined by the levels of education we receive in God's Word, the experiences we have and how we respond to them, and how well we use the abilities God has given us in accomplishing the purposes for which He created us.

While Jesus Christ's performance is what assures us of getting to heaven, the parable of the minas and many other scriptures clearly indicate that other rewards await those who achieve a higher level of service and measuring up to God's standards in the conduct of their lives.

We all need to continually examine our hearts and our actions to make sure that we are growing into the fullness of Christ and living at higher and higher levels of excellence in glorifying Him by being good stewards of the lives we have been given.

> ***"To know the love of Christ which passes knowledge, that you may be filled with all the fullness of God." Ephesians 3:19***

**Father, help me to live on a higher level. Amen.**

# *Spiritual Sensitivity*

**"To those who are perishing we are a fearful smell of death and doom. But to those who are being saved we are a life-giving perfume. And who is adequate for such a task as this?" 2 Corinthians 2:16 NLT**

Spiritual discernment may be the most important of all the spiritual disciplines. When we develop sensitivity to the presence of God working in, around, and through us, we open the doors to spiritual wisdom and discernment that will take our lives in Christ to new heights, and in the healing, comforting, and strengthening touches of God, we find indescribable joy and are often overwhelmed by these blessings.

***"Blessed are the people who know the joyful sound!" Psalm 89:15***

When we seek after God, we will begin to see that He is alive and at work in every aspect of our lives and the lives of those around us. When our eyes are focused on Jesus, the author and perfecter of our faith, we will see where He wants us to join Him and as we walk by faith, our sight will become clearer and clearer.

When we learn to listen to that small still voice of the Holy Spirit living within us or to God's voice speaking as we read or listen to His Word, we are better able to discern the will of God for how we should live our lives and please Him.

Scripture tells us to taste and see that the Lord is good. We should learn to smell the roses of God's grace blooming all around us.

All of the knowledge in the world will not help us unless we can move it from our head to our heart. As we grow in spiritual sensitivity, we become more and more conformed into the image of Christ which is the highest purpose for every believer.

***"No eye has seen, no ear has heard, and no mind has imagined what God has prepared for those who love him." 1 Corinthians 2:9b***

**Father help me to develop my spiritual sensitivity that I might grow into the fullness of Your Son. Amen.**

**Read Galatians 6, Isaiah 53:1-11** **March 5**

# God Bears All

**"Give your burdens to the LORD, and He will take care of you. He will not permit the godly to slip and fall." Psalm 55:22 NLT**

> ***"And because of what he has experienced, my righteous servant will make it possible for many to be counted righteous, for he will bear all their sins."***
> ***Isaiah 53:11b NLT***

God's kindness in bearing with us and for us the penalty for our sins, our wanderings, and all of our other imperfections is a reminder that we need to be more forbearing and patient with others. God doesn't love us because of these things but in spite of them, and we need to love others in spite of their short comings.

God's bearing of all of our burdens is one of the greatest gifts we have ever been given. He replaces our worries with peace, our sorrows with joy, and our desperation with hope. He can carry all that we are willing to place upon Him.

With God the loads of fear, doubt, and guilt are lightened by the all-sufficient grace of God who will bear whatever burden we are not able to bear in our own strength.

God bears all so that we are free to bear all for which He created us. The only bearing we need to pursue is the fruit of the Spirit, the fruits of righteousness, and the fruits of good works that are ours for the bearing as we bear witness to the truth of God's love and transforming power by the lives we lead.

> ***"When he sees all that is accomplished by his anguish, he will be satisfied. And because of what he has experienced, my righteous servant will make it possible for many to be counted righteous, for he will bear all their sins."***
> ***Galatians 6:17***

Before God can bear all for us, we need to bare all before Him. We need to bare our shame, guilt, and sorrow for our sins so that He can become the heavy-weight lifter of our lives.

**Father, thank you for bearing the burden of all my sins, and for loving me in spite of them. Amen.**

# *Are You Enjoying God?*

**"For who can eat or enjoy anything apart from Him? God gives wisdom, knowledge, and joy to those who please Him." Ecclesiastes 2:25a NLT**

We were not only created to glorify God, but also to enjoy Him! The joy of the Lord should be our hope, our strength, our peace, our comfort, and our purpose.

> ***"Here is what I have seen: It is good and fitting for one to eat and drink, and to enjoy the good of all his labor in which he toils under the sun all the days of his life which God gives him; for it is his heritage."***
> ***Ecclesiastes 5:18 NLT***

Apart from God there can be no true joy. We can find pleasures, riches, and applause without Him and apart from Him, but never the peace that comes from filling that special longing that God has placed in the heart of everyone.

When we go through life seeking to fill that longing that only God can fill with the desires of the flesh and allures of the world, we are ultimately going to be very disappointed.

We learn to enjoy God by getting to know Him through His Son. We experience joy of the Lord through fellowship with and abiding in Christ, who said: *"These things I have spoken to you, that My joy may remain in you, and that your joy may be full." (John 15:11)*

There is no greater joy than receiving that peace that surpasses all understanding. This peace makes us continually aware of God's love and the love of others as we live out our lives under the shelter of His wings and seek to bring God joy by glorifying Him in accomplishing the tasks for which he gifted and created us.

God did not create us to live out our lives in fear or trembling of His wrath but rather to live them in the fullness of His joy as we grow into the fullness of Christ. He delights in us, and we should always delight in Him and find great joy in doing the things that please Him. This is exactly what Jesus did and this is what we should strive to do.

> ***"We are writing these things so that our joy will be complete."***
> ***1 John 1:5 NLT***

**Father, may I live in the fullness of Your joy. Amen.**

Read Matthew 6:19-21, Malachi 3:10-18 March 7

## *The First National Bank of Heaven*

**"In that day He will be your sure foundation, providing a rich store of salvation, wisdom, and knowledge. The fear of the LORD is the key to this treasure." Isaiah 33:6 NLT**

It's good to know that you have a full service bank with branches in every city and country throughout the world.

> ***"And try me now in this," says the LORD of hosts, "if I will not open for you the windows of heaven and pour out for you such blessing that there will not be room enough to receive it."***
> ***Malachi 3:10b NLT***

You open your account at this bank, by depositing your faith and trust in Jesus as your Savior and receiving His righteousness in the sight of God.

Just as other banks seem to have a branch on every corner, the First National Bank of Heaven has a convenient location near you. It is generally open for business every day and offers many benefits for customers.

When you invest your time on Sunday mornings, you make a deposit into your checking account and can withdraw as much grace as you need all week long with overdraft protection.

When you invest your talents during the week in helping others and using them to glorify God and help build up His kingdom, you will start drawing interest of joy.

When you start investing your treasures in obedience to the great commandment and great commission, you start receiving dividends that will overwhelm you, and you get automatic greed protection.

> ***"Store your treasures in heaven, where they will never become moth-eaten or rusty and where they will be safe from thieves."***
> ***Matthew 6:20 NLT***

The loan department offers a wide range of services. You can borrow strength when you find that you don't have enough to meet a pressing need. You can borrow comfort when yours is running low. Your loan officer is on duty 24 hours a day, 7 days a week, and is only a prayer away.

Your savings account is guaranteed and insured against loss of any kind. Are you ready for the benefits of full service banking at the First National Bank of Heaven?

**Father, come be my full service banker. Amen.**

# *Hope is Never Hopeless*

**"Now may the God of hope fill you with all joy and peace in believing, that you may abound in hope by the power of the Holy Spirit. Romans 15:13" NLT**

A lot of bad things seem to happen to an awful lot of good people. The reality of living in a sin-sick world with a lot of pain and suffering all around often becomes true "relative truth" for believers.

> ***"But as for me, I know that my Redeemer lives, and that He will stand upon the earth at last."***
> ***Job 19:25 NLT***

The thought that becoming imitators of Christ is also a call to the suffering of Christ is not a happy thought.

Sometimes it seems that the roses have all disappeared from our garden of life and that only thorns remain. Loved ones die and expectations never seem to be met. We suffer failure, rejection, disappointment, illness, betrayal, and any number of other disasters.

When it seems that all hope is gone, we need to remember that hope is never hopeless and that we are never helpless because Jesus is alive. and living in us through the indwelling of the Holy Spirit.

Jesus knew that we would go through mountains of sorrow and valleys of tears on our journey of life. This is why He sent the Holy Spirit to be our comforter, counselor, our advocate and our strength and to fill us with hope when it seems that all hope is gone.

> ***"Through Christ you have come to trust in God. And because God raised Christ from the dead and gave Him great glory, your faith and hope can be placed confidently in God."***
> ***1 Peter 1:21 NLT***

We must never live as one without hope. The same blessed assurance and hope that sustained Job and Paul through all of their sufferings is the birthright of everyone who has received the new birth in Christ. Our hope is never hopeless!

**Father, let me never forget that my hope is never hopeless. Amen.**

Read 2 Corinthians 9:9-14, Psalm 92 March 9

# *Are You One of Those Lepers?*

**"So Jesus answered and said, "Were there not ten cleansed? But where are the nine? Were there not any found who returned to give glory to God except this foreigner?" Luke 17:7**

There seem to be a lot of "lepers" in the world. In the hustle and bustle of life, we all probably are not as mindful of thanking people as we should be.

> ***"It is good to give thanks to the LORD, to sing praises to the Most High."***
> ***Psalm 92.1 NLT***

I have personally been amazed at the number of people who fail to acknowledge and say thanks for wedding or graduation gifts and in some cases very generous responses to pleas for help. We really not only should thank givers, but we should also thank God who is blessing us through them.

We are often better tippers to waitresses than we are tithers to God. People will meticulously calculate 15 percent at a restaurant, but wouldn't dream of figuring how much 10 percent is at church.

How often do we take our wonderful gift of salvation for granted and fail to thank God as we should? How often do we fail to give thanks for the price that God paid for us?

When we forget to thank people for gifts, courtesies, or random acts of kindness or love, we certainly don't do much to encourage them in their generosity.

When we fail to praise and give thanks to God for all of His many gifts and kindnesses to us, we miss out on the joy of having God inhabit our praises and accept them as an offering pleasing to Him.

> ***"And they will pray for you with deep affection because of the wonderful grace of God shown through you."***
> ***2 Corinthians 9:14 NLT***

Without giving thanks to God, we easily begin to take God's favor and blessings for granted. Without giving the courtesy of a "thank you" to others we might find that we have closed the pipe line of blessings from them in the future.

**Father, let me never forget to give thanks to You and to others. Amen.**

# *Prevailing Prayer*

**"If you abide in Me, and My words abide in you, you will ask what you desire, and it shall be done for you. By this My Father is glorified, that you bear much fruit; so you will be My disciples." John 15:7, 8**

There is overwhelming joy in prevailing prayer! Whether it brings healing, protection, restoration, repentance, or a closer relationship with the Lord, nothing affirms us more than prayers answered in the affirmative.

> ***"I love the LORD because he hears and answers my prayers." Psalm 116:1***

What are prayers that prevail? Scripture tells us that praise, faith, fervency, personal holiness, persistence, fasting, and asking for things that will glorify God have a lot to do with how prevailing our prayers will be. We also know that praying subject to the will of God is important.

Scripture also tells us that unforgiveness, unconfessed and unrepented sins, and selfish prayers are not likely to prevail. Prayers that are not in keeping with the express will and commandments of God will not be answered affirmatively.

The Lord's prayer is not actually a prayer to be prayed, but a model for how we should pray. We praise God by acknowledging Him as Heavenly father and King of Kings and asking that His will be done. We ask Him for needs He has promised to supply (food, forgiveness, protection from temptation, deliverance from evil, and reaffirmation of God's sovereignty).

The more we become conformed to the image of Christ by abiding in His Word, the more likely we are to pray with His mind set. It becomes harder and harder to pray prayers contrary to the character and mind set of Christ.

God is not Santa Claus, and He certainly is not Scrooge. He wants to answer our prayers. We just have to learn to ask for the right things with the right mind set.

> ***"The eyes of the Lord watch over those who do right, and His ears are open to their prayers." 1 Peter 3:12 NLT***

**Father, thank you for the overwhelming joy of answered prayers, and the confidence and encouragement this gives me. Amen.**

**Read Matthew 18:21-35, Psalm 32** **March 11**

# *Prisons of the Soul*

**"If you forgive those who sin against you, your heavenly Father will forgive you. But if you refuse to forgive others, your Father will not forgive your sins." Matthew 6:14, 15 NLT**

One of the cruelest and most abusive taskmasters anyone can have is unforgiveness. It wrecks relationships with others and with God and is a clinically-proven cause of many physical and emotional illnesses.

> ***"Yes, what joy for those whose record the LORD has cleared of sin, whose lives are lived in complete honesty!"***
> ***Psalm 32:2 NLT***

The destroyer of our soul will often use unforgiveness to separate us from the lover of our soul, and the consequences can have eternal significance.

When we drink of the bitter root of unforgiveness, we allow ourselves to be held captive by anger and resentment and allow them to rob us of our joy, our peace, and our purpose.

Many times the people that we are bearing grudges against aren't even aware of the offense. This adds insult to our perceived injury. Whether a person knows or not, either way we are allowing whoever and whatever we cannot forgive to fester and lock us up in a maximum insecurity prison.

No matter what the offense or who committed it, it can never be as great as the price Jesus paid to earn forgiveness for us.

When we are honest with ourselves, we realize how much forgiveness we have already received and how much we are going to continue to need as we co-exist with sin in a sinful world. It is a "no-brainer" to forget that the condition for receiving the mercy and forgiveness we need is to give it.

> ***"Shouldn't you have mercy on your fellow servant, just as I had mercy on you?"***
> ***Matthew 18:33 NLT***

Even if we can not forgive for the sake of the offender, we must realize that for our own spiritual, emotional, and physical well being, we must forgive if we are going to stay out of the prison of unforgiveness.

**Father, help me to guard my heart that I not fall into bondage to unforgiveness. Amen.**

# Loop Holes

**"Fear of the LORD is a life-giving fountain; it offers escape from the snares of death." Proverbs 14:27 NLT**

Many lawyers make a lot of money finding loop holes in order to evade taxes, to get around regulations, to get evidence ruled inadmissible, or to get even murder cases thrown out of court.

> ***"Those who know Your name trust in You, for You, O LORD, have never abandoned anyone who searches for You."***
> ***Psalm 9:6***

Since most laws are actually written by lawyers, it gives cause to wonder whether the loopholes are written ahead of time, or just found by a smarter lawyer. Law books and case records will show exceptions or loopholes for practically every rule and regulation.

There seems to be a lawyer mentality within many bodies of believers. The concept of love has been perverted into a loop hole for doing, saying, or being about anything one wants.

Eve thought she had found a loop hole in disobeying God by partaking of fruit of the tree and thought she would become all knowing just like God by eating it.

God's abominations are often tolerated through a misconception of what love being the fulfillment of the law means. We try to justify disobeying God on the basis that God wants us to be happy, it's not hurting anyone, and that we are not to judge.

> ***"Who shall bring a charge against God's elect? It is God who justifies."***
> ***Romans 8:33***

In His mercy, God has provided us all with a loop hole for avoiding the death penalty that God decreed as the wages for sin. Actually, He came as a substitute for us and to pay the death penalty we earned.

This loop hole was never intended or meant to be a license to disobey but a means of escape from bondage to sin and freedom to live lives fully pleasing to God in appreciation for the pardon that we have been given.

We should never abuse the grace of God by looking for loop holes to get out of obeying God in any area of our lives.

**Father, thank you for giving me a life saving loop hole. Amen.**

# *The Best Help*

**"Are you called to help others? Do it with all the strength and energy that God supplies. Then God will be given glory in everything through Jesus Christ" 1 Peter 4:11 NLT**

I had a cousin who a contractor once offered to do a job for $50 an hour if my cousin would help and for $25 an hour if he would stay away! We all can think of instances where people trying to be helpful have actually been anything but.

> ***"It is poor judgment to co-sign a friend's note, to become responsible for a neighbor's debts." Proverbs 17:18***

It is often easy to overlook that sometimes the best help we can give in a situation is no help at all. Even though our motives are good, we can hinder instead of help by our misguided efforts. God is in control and better knows how to help in any given situation.

In the area of raising children, we often hinder their maturity and independence by trying to be too helpful. When we take their side in problems at school, we are often hurting instead of helping.

When we try to help people by bailing them out of their financial problems without addressing the underlying problems, we often are just enablers who are offering no real help. Loaning often ends up in a loss of both the loan and the friend.

> ***"We can rejoice, too, when we run into problems and trials, for we know that they are good for us— they help us learn to endure." Romans 5:3 NLT***

Families have spent fortunes and gone into debt big time trying to help their loved ones through addictions and other consequences and have actually been enablers rather than helpers.

This in no way means that we should not always try to help others. Helping others in need is perhaps the most important characteristic of being imitators of Christ. It does mean that we should pray for spiritual wisdom and discernment to know what is helpful and what is hurtful and to realize that "tough love" is often the kindest love we can give.

**Father, let my mistakes be on the side of love, but give me the wisdom to discern the difference between help and hindrance. Amen.**

March 14 Read Ephesians 5:15-20, Micah 7:18-20

# *Stumbling is not Fatal*

**"The steps of the godly are directed by the LORD. He delights in every detail of their lives. Though they stumble, they will not fall, for the LORD holds them by the hand." Psalm 37:23, 24**

It's so good to know that we have a God who created us for His pleasure as well as for His purposes. He takes no delight in the revelry of the ungodly and will see that they all get their just desserts in His own good time.

> ***"Where is another God like You, who pardons the sins of the survivors among his people? You cannot stay angry with Your people forever, because You delight in showing mercy." Micah 7:18 NLT***

When He says, "vengeance is mine," we need to realize that He is much better at avenging than we are, and when people sin against us, they are also sinning against God who commands that others love us and cause us no harm. Scripture affirms that the sins of the guilty shall not go unpunished.

One of the greatest benefits of our salvation is that we become one of God's sacred delights. He walks with us and talks with us, and He tells us that we are His own.

He cleans us up and dresses us up in robes of righteousness more majestic than robes of royalty. When we received Jesus Christ as our Savior, we became reconciled to God with all of the privileges of children of the most High and Holy Father.

He even comes to live in our hearts as the Holy Spirit, sharing in our joys, comforting us in our sorrows, and providing all of the grace and strength we need as we live out our lives in a growing love relationship with Him because He delights in every detail of our lives.

> ***"Then you will sing psalms and hymns and spiritual songs among yourselves, making music to the Lord in your hearts." Ephesians 5:19 NLT***

Best of all, like any good father, He holds us by His hand so that when we stumble, we will not fall.

**Father, thank you for the blessed assurance I have in You and Your promises. Amen.**

**Read Psalm 105:39-45, John 6:32-58** **March 15**

## *Read, Mark, and Inwardly Digest*

**"Then he added, "Son of man, let all my words sink deep into your own heart first. Listen to them carefully for yourself" Ezekiel 3:10 NLT**

The Word of God is sharper than even a double-edge sword. It can penetrate even the thickest of armor and toughest of skins when God draws one to it by the power of the Holy Spirit.

> ***"The people asked, and He brought quail, and satisfied them with the bread of heaven." Psalm 105:40 NLT***

When Jesus talks about being the bread of life, we need to remember that He was the Word made flesh and came to feed us that food for the soul that satisfies, nourishes, and sustains our eternal life that is ours in Him.

While we can live physically on regular bread and water, we cannot live spiritually without feeding upon the Word of God on a regular basis.

Without keeping our sword of the Spirit sharpened by feeding on the Word, we can easily let the cares of this world, the desires of our flesh, or the temptations of the devil rob us of the nourishment that satisfies our longing for that unquenchable joy and peace that is ours when we abide in the Word.

God's Word is so rich we can't always comprehend everything that it says on the first go round. Often we will discover something new in the same passage we have read many times before, because it sometimes takes many repetitions for the Word to sink deep in our hearts, and sometimes the experiences of life give new perspectives and give new meaning to the Words that we read.

> ***"This is the bread which came down from heaven—not as your fathers ate the manna and are dead. He who eats this bread will live forever." John 6:58 NLT***

That "light unto our path and lamp unto our feet" that is the living Word of God is the only food that will satisfy the real hunger of our souls.

**Father, by the power of the Holy Sprit, let me digest your Word that it becomes a way of life for me. Amen.**

# *Obedience Trials*

**"Now if you will obey me and keep my covenant, you will be my own special treasure from among all the nations of the earth; for all the earth belongs to me." Exodus 19:5 NLT**

Obedience trials for dogs are a very popular and enjoyable sport for literally hundreds of thousands of people. Trophies are awarded, champions crowned, and competition levels run the gamut from local, state, and regional to national levels.

> ***"Reverence for the LORD is the foundation of true wisdom. The rewards of wisdom come to all who obey Him. Praise His name forever." Psalm 111:10 NLT***

The American Kennel Club's purpose statement starts with: "To demonstrate the usefulness of the purebred dog as a companion to man and not merely the dog's ability to follow specified routines in the obedience ring." (This might not be a bad statement to paraphrase. Just substitute person for dog!)

Obedience that comes from a heart filled with gratitude over what God has done for us puts a different perspective on obedience.

When our heart is right, we obey not because we have to, but because we want to. Obedience to the great commandment and the great commission become odes to joy. We become useful companions to God, fully pleasing and fruitful in every good work.

Down through the ages, God's covenants with His people have been obedience trials promising great blessings for those who do what God commanded. The blessings of obedience to God still abound.

> ***"So now we can tell who are children of God and who are children of the devil. Anyone who does not obey God's commands and does not love other Christians does not belong to God." 1 John 3:10 NLT***

**Father, help me to enjoy the blessings of obedience and living in a close relationship with You. Amen.**

**Read Romans 13:8-14, Psalm 119:165-176** **March 17**

## *What's Getting in Your Way?*

**"The righteous will move onward and forward, and those with pure hearts will become stronger and stronger." Job 17:9 NLT**

Our call to salvation is also a call to grow into the fullness of Christ. When we receive salvation by the grace of God through faith in Jesus, we are as saved and forgiven as we will ever be. We become righteous in God's sight because he sees us clothed in the righteousness of Christ.

> ***"Stand ready to help me, for I have chosen to follow Your commandments."***
> ***Psalm 119:173 NLT***

God loves us too much to let us keep this righteousness a secret. When we become brothers or sisters and joint heirs with Christ, God sends the Holy Spirit to come live within us in order that the world might see evidence that we are being conformed into the image of Christ.

Although nothing can separate us from the love of God that is ours by faith in Jesus, we do face obstacles that can get in the way of our being all that God would have us be in our lives in Christ.

Pride often gets in our way of becoming imitators of Christ. An unforgiving heart, the idolatry of making anything more important than our faith, and the self-centered pursuit of pleasure, possessions, and the approval of others can be very real and present obstacles blocking our way towards spiritual maturity and holiness.

God foresaw all of these potential problems that would stunt our growth. In His love and mercy He has provided a full set of armor and provides the wonder-working power of the Holy Spirit to empower us to move these obstacles out of our way.

> ***"Get rid of your evil deeds. Shed them like dirty clothes. Clothe yourselves with the armor of right living, as those who live in the light."***
> ***Romans 13:12b NLT***

Is this a good time to take inventory of your life and to identify and seek God's help in removing the obstacles holding you back?

**Father, help me to remove the things getting in the way of my relationship with You. Amen.**

March 18 Read Matthew 7:7-11, Genesis 32:22-32

## *Will You Wrestle For It?*

**"And in his strength he struggled with God. Yes, he struggled with the Angel and prevailed; he wept, and sought favor from Him." Hosea 12:2-3b,4**

The account of Jacob wrestling with God is one of the most remarkable incidents recorded in Scripture.

> ***"Then the man said, 'Let me go, for the day breaks,' but Jacob panted, 'I will not let you go unless you bless me.'" Genesis 32:26***

We all wrestle with our consciences on a regular basis. We need to wrestle even more with God in prayer. The fact that Jacob wrestled with God and won should encourage us all to heed Paul's words to *"pray without ceasing" (1 Thessalonians 5:17).*

James tells us *"The earnest prayer of a righteous person has great power and wonderful results"* (*James 5:16b NLT)* and goes on to tell how God answered Elijah's earnest prayer to stop the rain and then start it again.

We cannot pray earnestly with unconfessed and unrepented sins on our conscience or unbelief or unforgiveness in our hearts and expect God to answer our prayers.

Jesus tells us, *"But if you stay joined to me and my words remain in you, you may ask any request you like, and it will be granted!" (John 15:7).* When we abide in the Word, we get to know the mind of Christ, and we will find ourselves praying unselfish prayers that honor and glorify God and that are within the parameters of His will. Is there any reason to believe that He will not grant them as He says He will?

> ***"If you then, being evil, know how to give good gifts to your children, how much more will your Father who is in heaven give good things to those who ask Him!" Matthew 7:11***

When we wrestle with God in prayer, with earnestness and confidence, and subject to His good and gracious will, we too can win our blessings just as Jacob did.

**Father, by the power of Your Spirit, help me to pray the unselfish prayers that honor and glorify You. Amen.**

**Read Luke 16:8-13, Isaiah 40** **March 19**

# *Not a Bad Seat in the House*

**"For God *is* not unjust to forget your work and labor of love which you have shown toward His name, *in that* you have ministered to the saints, and do minister." Hebrews 6:10**

The great new sports stadiums and arenas are marvels of engineering and design. People are able to see, hear, and enjoy the action from even the highest and furthest away seats.

> ***"Yes, the Sovereign LORD is coming in all His glorious power. He will rule with awesome strength. See, He brings His reward with Him as He comes."***
> ***Isaiah 40:10 NLT***

When we arrive at our heavenly destination by the unmerited mercy of God through faith in Jesus Christ, there will be no bad seats. Everything about heaven will be wonderful.

Heaven is not a reward, but a free gift given to anyone who calls upon the name of the Lord to be saved. In order to get there, we have to have had all our sins washed away by the blood of Jesus. We will all be clothed with the righteousness of Christ and be warmly welcomed as co-heirs with Him. There will be no more sin or sorrow, no more pain or illness, and no more tears.

But we do need to realize that there are rewards in heaven that we earn by doing the will of the Father here on earth. These rewards will be given at the "resurrection of the just" when all of the "wood, hay, and straw" of our lives are burned away and only the things done to glorify God and fulfill the purposes He planned for us before we were ever born remain.

> ***"I tell you, use your worldly resources to benefit others and make friends. In this way, your generosity stores up a reward for you in heaven."***
> ***Luke 16:9 NLT***

What these rewards will be is not clear, but Scripture makes it abundantly clear that we will be rewarded as we respond to God's love by living to please Him not for what He is going to do but for what He has already done for us through Christ.

**Father, thank you for my confirmed reservations to heaven, and for the joy of knowing that You will remember any good thing that I have done to glorify You here on earth. Amen.**

## *Burden or Blessing*

**"But he said to her, 'You speak as one of the foolish women speaks. Shall we indeed accept good from God, and shall we not accept adversity?'" Job 2:9**

There are many blessings disguised as burdens. It's often a matter of perspective. When we look at life from our own self-centered perspective, it's very easy to feel burdened by the expectations and demands placed upon us.

> ***"Let all those who seek You rejoice and be glad in You; let such as love Your salvation say continually, 'The LORD be magnified!'"***
> ***Psalm 40:16***

Taking care of an elderly parent, giving to a beggar, loving the unlovable, tithing, and giving to more worthwhile causes than we can support all can weigh heavily upon us unless we view them with thanksgiving as opportunities for blessings.

We can find a lot of strength and comfort from looking at life from God's perspective and learning how God was able to turn so many terrible burdens and circumstances into so many wonderful blessings.

Joseph was a blessing to his owner, fellow prisoners, Pharaoh, and eventually his whole family. God turned burdens into blessings. Daniel was enslaved, yet God turned these burdens into blessings. Paul was beaten, imprisoned, falsely accused, and suffered a severe physical "thorn in the flesh," yet God was able to turn all of these burdens into blessings for Paul and for us today.

Dale and Roy Rogers discovered the joy of raising a Downs Syndrome child. Joni Erickson Tada is a living testimony to how God continues to turn burdens into blessings.

> ***"So don't get tired of doing what is good. Don't get discouraged and give up, for we will reap a harvest of blessing at the appropriate time."***
> ***Galatians 6:9 NLT***

When we accept the sovereignty of God and receive the supernatural power to "Count it all Joy," we can find blessings instead of curses in even the worst of situations.

**Father, help me to find the silver lining of blessings often wrapped as burdens. Amen.**

**Read 1 Corinthians 3, Psalm 116** **March 21**

# *What Will Remain?*

**"Store your treasures in heaven, where they will never become moth-eaten or rusty and where they will be safe from thieves. Wherever your treasure is, there your heart and thoughts will also be." Matthew 6:20,21 NLT**

The reality of judgment day should give us all cause to ponder. We will go to stand before the righteous judge clothed in the righteousness of Christ which we received as a free gift by faith, but we still must give an account of the stewardship of our lives.

> ***"What shall I render to the LORD for all His benefits toward me?" Psalm 116:12***

The big car we drove, the money we made, the trophies we won, and all of the achievements that the world uses to define success are going to burn away like wood, hay, and stubble.

The hours spent in the vast wasteland of movies and TV will not win any accolades from God. The hours spent comforting those who mourn, visiting the sick and those in prison, raising godly children, and making disciples are the things that God promises to reward.

The dollars spent on the toys of life and selfish pursuits are not going to fill any storehouses in heaven. Feeding the hungry, clothing the poor, and being generous with God on every occasion is how we send our treasures ahead.

The squandering of the talents God has given to glorify ourselves instead of using them as a witness and sacrifice of praise to the Lord short circuits God's plans for us to be fruitful in good works that glorify Him and allow Him to achieve His purposes through us.

> ***"If anyone's work which he has built on it endures, he will receive a reward. If anyone's work is burned, he will suffer loss; but he himself will be saved, yet so as through fire." 1 Corinthians 3:14, 15***

Could there really be anything sweeter than hearing "well done" from the one who did it all for us? Isn't it time to start thinking about the future and bearing some fruit of righteousness that will remain after the straw has been burned away?

**Father help me to better use my time, talents, and treasures to serve and glorify You while there is still time. Amen.**

# Doing Life God's Way

**"'For I know the plans I have for you,' says the LORD. 'They are plans for good and not for disaster, to give you a future and a hope.'" Jeremiah 29:11**

We all have barriers of sin to overcome if we are to live life God's way.

> ***"There is a way that seems right to a man, but its end is the way of death." Proverbs 14:2***

The barrier of pride keeps us from admitting that we are sinners in need of a Savior.

The barrier of self centeredness tells us that life is about us and satisfying our desires for pleasure, purpose, approval of others, and satisfaction in buying into the ways of the world.

The barrier of unbelief lets the truth of God's revelations go into one ear and out the other without taking root in our minds, hearts and souls.

Complacency is a barrier that stunts our growth and calls us to fall far short of the plans and purposes that God has for us.

Jesus has clearly revealed himself as the Way, the Truth, and the Life. We do not have to be rocket scientists to realize that if we would do life God's way, we need to learn to do what Jesus did.

Jesus exchanged pride for humility. He sought His father's will in all things and submitted to it in perfect obedience. Jesus frequently went into a spiritual retreat of prayer and fasting seeking divine guidance and strength for knowing and doing the will of God. He never doubted, was never complacent, and never rested on His accomplishments.

> ***"And you will know how good and pleasing and perfect His will really is." Romans 12:2b NLT***

God knew from the history of mankind that we would never be able to "do life" His way on our own. This is why He sent the Comforter, the Holy Spirit, to give us the strength and the power and to fill us with the "wisdom from on high" in order that we might grow into the fullness of Christ and live life in the fullness of His joy and His love.

Jesus came that the sin barriers might come down and that we may rise up in the newness of life He died to give all who believe.

**Father, give me the desire and the strength to live a life fully pleasing to You and fruitful in every good work. Amen.**

**Read Ephesians 3:8-20, Psalm 107** **March 23**

# *Who Can Fill Your Every Longing?*

**"For whoever finds me finds life and wins approval from the LORD." Proverbs 8:35**

Every child born of woman is born with needs and longings. We need the basics of food and water to sustain our lives. We need shelter from the elements and provision for our physical and emotional needs.

> ***"For He satisfies the longing soul, and fills the hungry soul with goodness." Psalm 107:9***

Beyond the needs, God has placed a longing for Him in the heart of every person. Primitive cultures have expressed this longing for God in every imaginable way. They have worshipped the sun, the moon, nature, animals, and every type of idol in trying to satisfy this inbred longing for God.

All of these longings for God seem to have been manifested by trying to appease God through sacrificial rituals or making graven images to worship.

In today's supposedly advanced civilization and enlightened culture this longing for God seems to manifest itself in trying to satisfy this longing for significance and security by worshipping idols of power, applause, possessions, and pleasure with often disastrous results.

We do not have the excuse of the sun and moon worshippers who had no revelation of the Word to guide them.

God has plainly spoken through the prophets and through the life, death, and resurrection of Jesus Christ that Jesus is the only one who can fill the longing of our hearts for real significance and security.

> ***"To know the love of Christ which passes knowledge, that you may be filled with all the fullness of God." Ephesians 3:19***

Jesus is the Way, the Truth, and the Life. He has come to fill that inborn longing for God with unquenchable joy and peace that surpasses all human understanding. There is no fullness apart from a right relationship with God through faith in Jesus Christ.

**Father, fill me with Your Spirit that my heart's longing might be satisfied in You. Amen.**

March 24 Read Ephesians 3, Psalm 103

# *You Deserve a Break Today?*

**"We are all infected and impure with sin. When we proudly display our righteous deeds, we find they are but filthy rags." Isaiah 64:6**

Where did you ever get the idea that you deserve a break today? McDonalds certainly didn't get this slogan from Scripture, so where does it come from?

> ***"He has not punished us for all our sins, nor does He deal with us as we deserve."***
> ***Psalm 103:10 NLT***

We look down at welfare rights organizations lobbying for more benefits as though they deserve them while we often feel we deserve more.

Although we sometimes have a problem loving our neighbors as ourselves, we certainly don't have a problem loving ourselves to the extent that we think that life is all about us, and we deserve to enjoy the good things of life because we have earned them by our performance.

As believers, we often fall into the trap of thinking we deserve all of the good breaks of life and none of the bad because of our good conduct.

The truth is that our righteous conduct is as filthy rags according to God's standards of righteousness and holiness. We have all sinned and will continue to sin and fall short of the righteousness of God as we live out our lives in this earthly, fleshly body that was corrupted by the curse of sin which we inherited.

We need to be very careful about asking for what we deserve. The scribes and Pharisees were among the brightest and the best and devoted their lives to fulfilling every jot and tittle of the law. Our Lord reserved his severest criticism for them and called them hypocrites.

> ***"Just think! Though I did nothing to deserve it, and though I am the least deserving Christian there is, I was chosen for this special joy of telling the Gentiles about the endless treasures available to them in Christ."***
> ***Ephesians 3:8 NLT***

The one who got the break was the sinner who cried out, "Lord have mercy on me!"

Grace and mercy are all about God giving us not what we deserve, because of who we are and what we have done, but because of who Jesus Christ is, and what He did for us.

**Father, please don't give me what I deserve. In Your mercy and because of what Jesus Christ did, give me Your grace. Amen.**

**Read Matthew 25:14-30. Deuteronomy 28:1-14** **March 25**

# *Principles of Investing*

**"He will give you all you need from day to day if you make the Kingdom of God your primary concern." Luke 12:31 NLT**

Putting money to work by investing is the bed rock of capitalism and the key to economic prosperity. Investors get a return and growth on their money, companies get the financial resources to expand, build their businesses, and "trickle down" jobs and prosperity to employees who can then become investors themselves.

> ***"And all these blessings shall come upon you and overtake you, because you obey the voice of the LORD your God." Deuteronomy 28:2 NLT***

Investing is also the bed rock of building up the kingdom of God. God invests in us by giving us a life to fulfill the purposes for which He created us. He gives us the "working capital" of time, talents, and treasures and expects a return on His investment.

As God's investment in us begins to bear fruit, it "trickles down" from us to others as we invest in them. When parents invest the time required to bring children up in the nurture and admonition of the Lord and model Christian virtues, they are promised covenant blessings for their children.

When we invest our time, talents, and treasures in obedience to the great commandment and great commission, we build up a portfolio of wealth where it will give a great return now and continue to grow in value forever.

The storehouse of blessings promised to those who obey is open for us to receive and enjoy in this life.

We can only imagine what the heavenly rewards awaiting those who receive our Lord's "well done" on judgment day will be when we arrive at our heavenly home which we receive as a free gift of God's grace. One thing is certain. Investing our time, talents and treasures in being fruitful in every good work is a real "blue chip" investment.

> ***"He called together his servants and gave them money to invest for him while he was gone." Matthew 25:14b NLT***

**Father, help me to invest my life in the things that matter to You. Amen.**

# *Don't Worry Humpty*

**"Though he falls, he shall not be utterly cast down; for the LORD upholds *him with* His hand." Psalm 37:24**

Have you ever felt like Humpty Dumpty, who fell off the wall? Has it seemed that "all the king's horses and all the king's men" couldn't put Humpty together again?

> ***"The LORD upholds all who fall, and raises up all who are bowed down." Psalm 145:14 NLT***

Some children fall so many times in learning to walk that they keep crawling far too long. Those who continue to get up and try again will learn to walk much sooner.

The falls of life come in many shapes and sizes. We suffer failures in jobs, relationships, health, and finances.

Sometimes the falls pile up so painfully and seemingly so endlessly we feel that nothing can ever restore the brokenness that we are experiencing.

Thanks be to God, we don't have to depend on all the king's horses and all the king's men to put us back together again. We have "Almighty God, Everlasting Father," as our very present help in time of trouble.

God is not only our refuge where we can find shelter and protection from the falls of life, but He is also our strength who will enable us to get up when our own power fails. We must always remember that failure is never final with God!

The trials of Job, Joseph, David, and Peter attest to the fact that God can restore and put back together the pieces of any brokenness.

The pain, suffering, and death of our Lord Jesus Christ allowed God to manifest His power to work all things to His glory.

> ***"My brethren, count it all joy when you fall into various trials, knowing that the testing of your faith produces patience." James 1:2***

Jesus came to make all things new again. He made the blind to see, the lame to walk, the lepers to be cleansed, and the dead to rise.

He is alive and well, sitting at the right hand of the Father continually interceding for us as the Holy Spirit fills us with the resurrection power to get up and persevere over the falls of life.

**Father, help me to always get up when I stumble and fall. Amen.**

**Read James 2:17-26, Psalm 106** **March 27**

## *A Little Dab'll Do Ya*

**"I have come to call sinners to turn from their sins, not to spend My time with those who think they are already good enough." Luke 5:32**

Brylcreem was the original hair gel for men and probably the best-selling hair product of the 30's and 40's thanks to this catchy slogan.

> ***"Who can list the glorious miracles of the LORD? Who can ever praise him half enough?" Psalm 106:2 NLT***

Some people seem to have this thinking about religion. A little dab might be alright, but don't get to loving Jesus too much, or people might think you're a fanatic!

Maybe just enough faith and church attendance to keep the door to the pearly gates open, just enough tithes to keep us on the books so we can be buried in the church cemetery, or just enough prayer to remind God of our wish list are the "little dabs" that define the carnal Christian.

Our Lord had little use for the religious leaders of His day who were great dabblers but really "white-washed tombs" and hypocrites.

True Christianity is not a religion, but a personal relationship with the only Son of the all-powerful, all-knowing, ever-present, eternal God the Father who lives in the hearts of all true believers through the indwelling presence of the Holy Spirit.

The "little dab" of faith that calls us into a saving relationship is a seed that once planted grows us into the fullness of Christ that we may be one with Him and submit to His Lordship in every area of our lives.

That "little dab" turns into a fountain of living water that will never run dry and fills us to overflowing with the love of Christ so that we may be conduits of His love and proclaim the Good News of His love to others.

> ***"So you see, it isn't enough just to have faith. Faith that doesn't show itself by good deeds is no faith at all—it is dead and useless." James 2:17 NLT***

As this relationship satisfies our every longing, it also creates a desire for more and more of the love, grace, and mercy of God. We should never be satisfied with a "little dab" when God's wants us to have it all.

**Father, help me to quit "dabbling" and to start growing into the fullness of my destiny in You in every area of my life. Amen.**

## *Playing With Fire*

**"And God is faithful. He will keep the temptation from becoming so strong that you can't stand up against it. When you are tempted, He will show you a way out so that you will not give in to it." Corinthians 10:13b NLT**

The road to moral meltdown is paved with the false bravado of the pride of invincibility. "It can never happen to me"…"I can quit anytime I want"…"I can control it"…"just one more"..."I don't have a problem" - these are just a few of the "famous last words" of addicts, substance abusers, and commandment breakers as they fall into the bondage of addiction or other sins.

> ***"Above all else, guard your heart, for it affects everything you do." Proverbs 4:23 NLT***

The often used illustration of the frog in the kettle that is oblivious to the heat gradually building up and dies without even being aware of any danger is a good illustration of how we can get burned when playing with fire.

God's advice for avoiding sin is to guard our hearts, flee temptation, and resist the devil.

We guard our hearts by not allowing any sinful thought room to take root and grow and by avoiding corrupting "junk food" that is coming at us from every direction through TV, movies, and the internet.

When temptation comes, as it does and is going to do, if we flee before it can take root and hold us captive, we can find the way of escape that God has promised to provide.

When we resist the devil with the full set of armor God provides, he is the one who will give up and flee.

The only fire we can play with without getting burned is the flame of the Holy Spirit, fueled by the Word of God, warming our hearts with the love of God and generating the power to live lives pleasing to God and free from bondage to any besetting sin.

> ***"Those who indulge in sexual sin, who are idol worshipers, adulterers, male prostitutes, homosexuals, thieves, greedy people, drunkards, abusers, and swindlers—none of these will have a share in the Kingdom of God." 1 Corinthians 6:9b NLT***

**Father, protect me from getting "sin burnt." Amen.**

Read 1 Peter 1:1-9, Psalm 91 March 29

## When the Rubber Meets the Road

**"But for those who are righteous, the path is not steep and rough. You are a God of justice, and You smooth out the road ahead of them." Isaiah 26:7**

Defective tires have been identified as the cause of literally thousands of accidents and deaths over the years, in spite of the fact that improved technology has produced tires that last longer, go faster, ride smoother, handle better, and are safer than ever.

> ***"For he orders His angels to protect you wherever you go, they will hold you with their hands to keep you from striking your foot on a stone."***
> ***Psalm 91:11, 12 NLT***

Many assume that their tire warranties cover many things that aren't covered and find out that tire failures due to abuse, cuts, road hazards, faulty alignment, failure to maintain proper air pressure, etc. are usually not covered by warranties.

The tires that we travel on through the journey of life are also subject to a number of things that may not alter our ultimate destination as believers but certainly affect the quality and joy of our journey.

When we hit a pot hole of relational, financial, physical, or emotional problems, we often get our wheels knocked out of alignment and suffer excessive tread wear.

When we forsake the assembling of ourselves together and abiding in the Word, we find ourselves trying to run under inflated tires the friction of which causes excessive heat and abnormal wear.

When we find ourselves beset by some reoccurring or unrepented sin, we will find how it feels trying to control a car during a high speed blow out.

> ***"There is wonderful joy ahead, even though it is necessary for you to endure many trials for a while."***
> ***1 Peter 1:6 NLT***

Although we only get one set of tires per life, the Good News is that they come with a puncture repair kit called grace and a lifetime warranty called faith.

Have you checked your tires lately?

**Father, keep me pumped with the power of Your Spirit and aligned with the balance of obedience as my rubber meets the road. Amen.**

March 30 Read John 12:21-25, Psalm 22

# *The Best Beach Diet*

**"Later that same day, Jesus left the house and went down to the shore, where an immense crowd soon gathered. He got into a boat, where He sat and taught as the people listened on the shore." Matthew 13:1,2 NLT**

I am a great fan of the now famous South Beach Diet. I lost 21 pounds in 30 days.

> ***"The poor will eat and be satisfied. All who seek the LORD will praise Him. Their hearts will rejoice with everlasting joy." Psalm 22:26 NLT***

As good as this diet is for the overweight, it can't begin to compare with the Galilee Beach Diet. It was on the Beach of Galilee where Jesus called Peter, Andrew, James, and John. It was here that He taught some of His greatest truths to the crowds on the beach.

Best of all, it was just up the hill from this beach that Jesus gave us all the recipe for blessings. It was here that He taught us: *"God blesses those who realize their need for Him, for the Kingdom of Heaven is given to them. God blesses those who mourn, for they will be comforted. God blesses those who are gentle and lowly, for the whole earth will belong to them. God blesses those who are hungry and thirsty for justice, for they will receive it in full. God blesses those who are merciful, for they will be shown mercy. God blesses those whose hearts are pure, for they will see God. God blesses those who work for peace, for they will be called the children of God. God blesses those who are persecuted because they live for God, for the Kingdom of Heaven is theirs. God blesses you when you are mocked and persecuted and lied about because you are my followers. Be happy about it! Be very glad! For a great reward awaits you in heaven. And remember, the ancient prophets were persecuted, too." (Matthew 5:3-12 NLT)*

> ***"'Now come and have some breakfast!' Jesus said. And no one dared ask Him if he really was the Lord because they were sure of it." John 21:12 NLT***

When we diet on the good food from the good seed, we will get rid of a great deal of our excess baggage of sin, despair, and depression.

**Father, help me to feed on all the healthy, life-giving food of Your Word. You are truly my "Bread of Life." Amen.**

**Read 1 Peter 1:13-25, 2 Chronicles 6:14-40** **March 31**

# *The Chickens Have Come Home to Roost*

**"You can't whitewash your sins and get by with it; you find mercy by admitting and leaving them." Proverbs 28:13 MSG**

Some people seem to get away with everything, while we can't seem to get away with anything. No matter how it may seem, the truth is that there is a payback for good or bad conduct.

> ***"Then hear from heaven, and act, and judge Your servants, bringing retribution on the wicked by bringing his way on his own head, and justifying the righteous by giving him according to his righteousness."***
>
> ***2 Chronicles 6:23***

Although God has set us free from the dominion and penalty of sin and forgiven every sin we have ever committed or will commit, sooner or later there are consequences.

If we would ever learn to count the cost of sinning not only to ourselves but to those we love, we would soon learn to flee and just not go there.

If we ever stopped to think about what our sins cost Jesus, we would not so easily be beset by sins or treat them so lightly.

How many homes have been broken up as a consequence of sin? How many people are dying from AIDS because of sin? How many birth defects and on-going health problems are encountered because of alcohol and substance abuse?

Prisons throughout the world are filled to overflowing as a stark testimony to the consequences of sin.

Confession and godly sorrow is wonderful, but without true repentance, they offer no relief. On a brighter note, the seeds of love, kindness, and compassion also come home to roost.

> ***"So think clearly and exercise self-control. Look forward to the special blessings that will come to you at the return of Jesus Christ."***
>
> ***1 Peter 1:13 NLT***

When we become filled with the love, kindness, and grace of God and start investing this love in those around us, we will take great delight and experience overwhelming joy when these investments start paying instead of costing.

Which chickens have come home to roost in your heart?

**Father, in the power of the Holy Spirit, help me to sew the good seeds that come back as blessings. Amen.**

April 1 Read Matthew 11:25-30, Psalm 38

## *Careful with Those Back Packs*

**"Cast your burden on the LORD, and He shall sustain you; He shall never permit the righteous to be moved." Psalm 55:22**

"Back Pack Safety America" is a national program born out of the increasing concern over injuries to children caused by improper use of or too heavily laden back packs.

> ***"For my iniquities have gone over my head; like a heavy burden they are too heavy for me."***
> ***Psalm 38:4***

Up to one half of the millions of children wearing back packs will at some time or another experience some sort of back pain or strain.

On the spiritual and emotional level the injuries caused by improperly used or too heavily laden back packs will cause some sort of pain or strain on just about every one born of woman.

The burden of guilt can be a real crippler. If left to fester, it can grow and do damage in every area of our life.

Unforgiveness is another heavy burden that is like a boomerang that will do more harm than the actual cause of the unforgiveness.

The burden of failure is always painful and if not handled properly, can do far more damage and cause much more grief than it should.

The consequences of willful, deliberate, and unrepented sins often bring painful consequences not only to the sinner, but to those who love the sinner most.

Experts have determined that a child should never carry a back pack weighing more than 15% of total weight of child. God says that He has sent His Son to be our burden bearer so that we no longer have to go through life weighted down.

When we put on the yoke of obedience and cast our burdens upon the Lord, we find that unquenchable joy and all-surpassing peace that comes only when our burdens are lifted by the one by whose stripes we were healed.

> ***"For My yoke is easy and My burden is light."***
> ***Matthew 11:30***

**Father, help me to cast my burdens on You through daily confession and repentance. Amen.**

**Read 1 Corinthians 3, Proverbs 20** **April 2**

# *Whose Standards?*

**"Repent now every one of his evil ways and his evil doings, and dwell in the land that the LORD has given to you and your fathers forever and ever." Jeremiah 25:5 NLT**

The Supreme Court has ruled that obscenity will be defined by the prevailing standards of a community.

> ***"The LORD despises double standards of every kind." Proverbs 20:10 NLT***

As more and more people fall away from faith and trust in God, God's standards continue to fall by the wayside, and our country and communities sink deeper into the mire of carnality and the standards of depraved men replace the standards of God.

The National Institute of Standards and Technology has been established to develop and promote measurement, standards, and technology to enhance productivity, facilitate trade, and improve the quality of life. It is a shame that there are no longer governmental standards based on God's standards to achieve the same purposes.

The fact that our government is no longer guided by God's standards is hard to realize and accept.

We bemoan the removal of God and prayer from our schools, currency and government. We are sick at heart over the mantle of respectability being legislated for things that God calls abominations, but the reality is that this is the reality of life in Americ a at the start of the 21st century.

> ***"Stop fooling yourselves. If you think you are wise by this world's standards, you will have to become a fool so you can become wise by God's standards." 1 Corinthians 3:18 NLT***

We need to go beyond bemoaning and being sick at heart. We need to start electing federal judges for regular terms instead of having them appointed to life-time terms with no accountability.

We need to bring back God's standards by bringing our people back to God through revival and renewal that will bring a return to His precepts. Most importantly of all, we must resolve, *"But as for me and my house, we will serve the LORD"(Joshua 24:15b).*

**Father, let world-wide renewal and revival begin with me. Amen.**

 **Read Acts 17:26-31, Psalm 71**

# *Abounding Boundaries*

**"How can a young person stay pure? By obeying your word and following its rules." Psalm 119:9 NLT**

Boundaries have been a fact of life since the beginning of time. We have boundaries of space, boundaries of land and sea, and territorial boundaries for continents, countries, states, counties, streets, right down to lots.

> ***"My mouth shall tell of Your righteousness and Your salvation all the day, for I do not know their limits."***
> ***Psalm 71:15***

In families, churches, vocations, and organizations of all kinds, territorial rights and limits seem to be strived for and fought over, and it seems a basic instinct of man to guard and defend his territory and set boundaries and limits which may not be trespassed.

All good parents set boundaries within which their children can be nourished and allowed to grow and develop. When no boundaries are set and enforced, children grow up like wild seed, rebellious against their parents and against God, and many are lost forever.

In His love, God has always established boundaries for His children for their good and His glory. The only boundary in paradise was the tree of the knowledge of good and evil, and when this was violated, evil came into the world. All have been under its curse ever since.

Abounding sins have been covered by abounding grace and the promise of paradise has been restored for all who receive Jesus Christ as their personal Savior by faith.

When God reconciles our hearts to Him, He implants the power of the Holy Spirit into us and enlarges our hearts into the fullness of Christ until moment by moment, day by day, year by year, there is no boundary of sin separating us. Once again, we shall walk with Him, talk with Him, and enjoy the perfect joy and bliss of eternal life in paradise restored.

> ***"From one man He created all the nations throughout the whole earth. He decided beforehand which should rise and fall, and he determined their boundaries."***
> ***Acts 17:6***

**Father, thank you for giving me rules to show me the way. Amen.**

\

Read Matthew 25:21-29, Deuteronomy 28 April 4

## *Are You Making Money?*

**"Beloved, I pray that you may prosper in all things and be in health, just as your soul prospers." 3 John 1:2**

In the old days, people used to sell themselves into slavery to pay off debts. Today, many find themselves working the biggest part of their time for some Detroit or Japanese automaker, a mortgage company, or a Visa or Master Card bank. Easy credit is easy to be taken in and very hard to get out.

> ***"The LORD will send rain at the proper time from His rich treasury in the heavens to bless all the work you do. You will lend to many nations, but you will never need to borrow from them." Deuteronomy 28:7 NLT***

No one takes time to remind you that interest charges go on 24 hours a day, 7 days a week, and 52 weeks a year. No one bothers to warn you that the deeper in debt you get, the more vulnerable you become to higher interest rates as you become a higher credit risk.

In this age of instant gratification, easy credit, and defining our significance by the car we drive, the neighborhood we live in, and the clothes we wear, many people are not only not making a living; they are losing money every week by spending more than they take in.

How can God trust us with more when we cannot be good stewards of little? How can we expect God to supply our wants in addition to our needs when our "wanters" get out of whack and get us going into debt for things that we don't really need and things that we can't really afford?

> ***"The master said, 'Well done, my good and faithful servant. You have been faithful in handling this small amount, so now I will give you many more responsibilities. Let's celebrate together!'" Matthew 25:21 NLT***

Our God is not a stingy God. He lavishes blessing upon blessing upon even the worst of us but reserves some blessings for those who are generous to Him as proof that He is first in their hearts and obedient to His commands regarding managing what He gives them well.

**Father, guide me into Your truth regarding managing well the financial resources You provide for me. Amen.**

April 5 Read Romans 6, Psalm 68:28-35

## *The Power to Be Your Best*

**"And now I will send the Holy Spirit, just as my Father promised. But stay here in the city until the Holy Spirit comes and fills you with power from heaven." Luke 24:49 NLT**

Apple computers brought a whole lot of good things to life and were leaders in the Cultural Revolution affecting almost every area of life over the past 25 years.

> ***"God is awesome in His sanctuary. The God of Israel gives power and strength to His people." Psalm 68:35 NLT***

The power of today's computers to process and store unlimited amounts of information and data, and to control robots, airplanes, and traffic lights, etc. is amazing.

While computers may well provide a lot of power for learning, manufacturing, healing, and communicating, they do not give anyone the power to be their best.

God has ordained that we can only become our best through the transforming power of the Holy Spirit who gives us the power to become sons and co-heirs through faith in His Son, Jesus Christ as our Savior.

While a dramatic change takes place and we are made holy spiritually in God's sight the minute we receive Jesus as our Savior, the process of being made holy in the flesh is the on-going, never ceasing, work of the Holy Spirit - Christ in us who will do whatever it takes to conform us into the image of Christ.

Our character development often involves a lot of pain, suffering, and chastising as the battle between our flesh and our spirit rages, and we press on toward the prize which has already been won for us by Jesus on the Cross at Calvary.

> ***"And just as Christ was raised from the dead by the glorious power of the Father, now we also may live new lives." Romans 6:4 NLT***

We don't win all the battles, but, thanks be to God, we have won the war by the power of the indwelling presence of the Holy Spirit.

This is the real power that God gives us to be our best!

**Father, thank you for giving me the power to be my best for You. Help me to stay close to the source through abiding in You and Your Word. Amen.**

**Read Mark 7:6-8, Isaiah 57:8-13** **April 6**

# *No Substitutions!*

**"There is a way *that seems* right to a man, but its end *is* the way of death." Proverbs 16:25**

Many restaurants have specials that allow no substitutions. Car makers offer a package of options only available as a package with no substitutions. If even restaurants and car makers can establish this rule, does it make any sense at all to think that God allows substitutions?

> ***"Behind closed doors, you have set up your idols and worship them instead of Me." Isaiah 57:8 NLT***

We all have a free will to receive or reject God's grace, mercy, and new life in Christ. The problem is that we often want to exercise our free will and our intellect in substituting our perceptions for God's truth.

We want to receive assurance of eternal life, but we don't want to choose obedience to the new manager of our new life in Christ.

Many have the tendency to choose and believe that God wants everyone to be prosperous and healthy in spite of the fact that most of the disciples were neither. (If the apostle Paul's prayers for healing were not granted, what makes us think that all of ours will be?)

Many seem to have the mistaken idea that sincerity can be substituted for obedience, that love can be substituted for truth, and that what belongs to us is more important than to whom we belong.

When we try to substitute tolerance, respectability, and enlightenment for what God calls sin, we become grace "junkies" who turn the commandments into suggestions and become carnal Christians.

> ***"For you ignore God's specific laws and substitute your own traditions." Mark 7:8 NLT***

We need to know that God hates sin but loves sinners, and we are called to do the same. As sinners saved by grace, we need to renounce sin and flee from it. We are to live lives fully pleasing to God and fruitful in every good work.

The only substitutes God has ever allowed was the lamb provided as a substitute for Abraham's son and Jesus as the substitute atonement for our sins.

**Father, help me know that You are the God who says what He means and means what He says and live accordingly. Amen.**

April 7 Read Hebrews 12, Isaiah 52:1-10

## *Why Settle for Less Than God's Best*

**"For the LORD sees clearly what a man does, examining every path he takes. An evil man is held captive by his own sins; they are ropes that catch and hold him. He will die for lack of self-control; he will be lost because of his incredible folly." Proverbs 5:21-23 NLT**

The pursuit of what the world perceives as success and pleasure finds many settling for less than the best that God wants for them.

> ***"For thus says the LORD: 'You have sold yourselves for nothing, And you shall be redeemed without money.'" Isaiah 52:3***

True success consists of enjoying the true peace and joy that cannot be found apart from a close personal relationship with God through Jesus Christ.

When we sell out our godly character to the basic sexual urges of the flesh, we are settling for less than God's best. The consequences of disease, guilt or pregnancy, are all obstacles to enjoying God's best in the purity of not only the physical but also the spiritual union that God wants for us.

When we sell out control of our minds and conduct to a mind-altering pill, powder, or beverage, we are settling for bondage to a lesser God that is out to destroy us and rob us of our rich inheritance that is God's best for us.

When we sell out to peer pressure or seeking the approval of the wrong crowd and wrong people, we are robbing God of His glory and putting others ahead of God.

> ***"Look after each other so that none of you will miss out on the special favor of God." Hebrews 12:15 NLT***

When we pursue the folly of a self-centered life controlled by our own pride and egos, we are setting for far less than God's best, reserved for those who are transformed and conformed into the image of Christ by the Holy Spirit.

**Father, help me seek Your best instead of settling for less in any area of my life. Amen.**

Read Ephesians 5:1-14, Deuteronomy 6:1-18 April 8

## *Politically Correct or Scripturally Sound*

**"Later, He turned the cities of Sodom and Gomorrah into heaps of ashes and swept them off the face of the earth. He made them an example of what will happen to ungodly people." 2 Peter 2:6 NLT**

As God is taken out of schools and court rooms, His truth becomes replaced by man's spin called relative truth. God's side appears to be losing in the war for the hearts of man.

> ***"Do what is right and good in the LORD'S sight, so all will go well with you. Then you will enter and occupy the good land that the LORD solemnly promised to give your ancestors." Deuteronomy 6:18 NLT***

Who would ever have thought that Christians would become a minority in this country? Who would ever have thought that a vocal minority would gain control of the courts and media and make God's abominations politically correct and government protected?

We have homosexuality, same-sex marriages, murder of the unborn, and destruction of traditional family values promoted as politically correct values. Even within many churches, anyone who dares quote Scripture to show what God thinks about such moral corruptness is shouted down and labeled a religious fanatic.

We no longer have government under the authority of God but under the yoke of secular humanism which has made man god, sin non-existent, and hedonism the life style of choice for the enlightened.

If people do not believe in God, they are not going to believe in His law. They are going to pursue self-centered gratification and fulfillment regardless of the consequences for themselves and for others.

> ***"Don't be fooled by those who try to excuse these sins, for the terrible anger of God comes upon all those who disobey Him." Ephesians 5:6 NLT***

Regaining the territory for God can only be done through Spiritual means because only God can change hearts. We must have a "great awakening" of repentance and turning to God among unbelievers that they might come back "under God" as individuals, a nation, and a world.

**Father, bring revival into the hearts of men, and let it begin with me. Amen.**

April 9 Read Revelation 21:1-8, Isaiah 53:1-11

# *The Good of Good Friday*

**"I have been crucified with Christ; it is no longer I who live, but Christ lives in me; and the *life* which I now live in the flesh I live by faith in the Son of God, who loved me and gave Himself for me." Galatians 2:20**

We are overcome with great sadness on Good Friday when we are reminded of what our Lord went through for us.

> ***"But he was wounded and crushed for our sins. He was beaten that we might have peace. He was whipped, and we were healed."***
> ***Isaiah 53:5 NLT***

When we realize that He was suffering because of our sins, our grief becomes almost unbearable.

The good of Good Friday is that the death of Jesus Christ on the cross brought salvation and reconciliation with God forever and ever for all who would call upon the name of the Lord and be saved.

When Jesus said, "It is finished," He was pronouncing completion of the purpose for which he came to earth. He became the "good tidings of great joy." He became our Savior! Jesus died on the cross to be the perfect, unblemished offering to make atonement for our sin.

What joy and comfort there is in realizing that God not only came to die so that we would not have to but came to give us every spiritual blessing along with His special favor and mighty power.

> ***"And he also said, 'It is finished! I am the Alpha and Omega-the Beginning and the End. To all who are thirsty I will give the springs of the water of life without charge!'"***
> ***Revelation 21:6 NLT***

The crucifixion of Christ on Good Friday should be a constant reminder that, as believers, we have been crucified with Christ and become dead to sin and alive in Christ by the resurrection power of the Holy Spirit. May the good of Good Friday carry over into living lives fully pleasing to God and fruitful in every good work in every area of our lives every day of our lives on earth.

**Father, may the sorrow of Your crucifixion on Good Friday give way to the joy of my salvation that You died to give me. Amen.**

**Read Hebrews 5:7-14, Psalm 119:60-68** **April 10**

# *Come to the Source*

**"All praise to the God and Father of our Lord Jesus Christ. He is the source of every mercy and the God who comforts us." 2 Corinthians 1:3 NLT**

We are continually looking for sources for everything. Newspaper reporters love to talk about "unidentified sources." The source of a lot of gossip is hard to track down.

> ***"You are good, and the source of good; train me in your goodness." Psalm 119:68 MSG***

Doctors are always searching for the source of our infection or illness. The internet has become a great source of information on products, services, and anything else of interest.

Elisha performed his first miracle by going to the source. *"Then he went out to the source of the water, and cast in the salt there, and said, 'Thus says the LORD: 'I have healed this water; from it there shall be no more death or barrenness'" (Kings 2:21).*

This is a good illustration of what happens to us when we go to the source and receive the living water of salvation. The blood of Jesus that was shed for us on the cross of Calvary washes away our sin and there is no more death.

Jesus is so much more than the source of our salvation. He is the source of every blessing. He is the source of our joy, our peace, our strength, and our love.

While the world seeks security and significance in power, possessions, and pleasure, the Light of the World calls us into the brightness of a new life of peace with God and eternal life for the present and future. He wants to be our source for the true happiness that can never be found apart from Him.

> ***"In this way, God qualified Him as a perfect High Priest and He became the source of eternal salvation for all those who obey Him." Hebrews 5:9 NLT***

**Father, teach me to acknowledge You as the source of every blessing. Amen.**

## *Have You Had Your Shower?*

**"And I will send showers, showers of blessings, which will come just when they are needed." Ezekiel 34:26 NLT**

Showers seem to have taken over as the bathing of choice for more people. Whether they are quicker, do a better job, or are more enjoyable depends on whom you ask.

> ***"The LORD is good to everyone. He showers compassion on all his creation." Psalm 145:9 NLT***

God sends daily showers of blessings, sometimes disguising them as major problems when He really wants to get our attention.

In supplying His grace sufficient for our every need, God sometimes sends or allows the consequences of our sins to bring showers of pain and suffering, disappointment and failure, and tears and mourning as He continues to mold and conform us into the image of Christ.

As God develops our character, *"We can rejoice, too, when we run into problems and trials, for we know that they are good for us—they help us learn to endure. And endurance develops strength of character in us, and character strengthens our confident expectation of salvation" (Romans 5:3).*

Sometimes we find ourselves in storms of anger, doubt, and fear as torrents of temptations and sins seem bent on washing us away and taking all of our assurance and hope with them. We need to remember that these things do not come from God but from the evil one who is out to destroy us and our faith through any means possible.

> ***"All who are victorious will inherit all these blessings, and I will be their God, and they will be my children." Revelation 21:7 NLT***

God showers His blessings on both the just and the unjust but reserves the greatest blessings for those who are blessable because of their faith and obedience.

**Father, rain down your blessings upon me. Amen.**

**Read 2 Peter 1, Psalm 18** **April 12**

## *Designated Driver*

**"And God, in his mighty power, will protect you until you receive this salvation, because you are trusting him" 1 Peter 1:5**

Designated drivers have saved a lot of lives and a lot of problems for those who drink too much and become too drunk to drive a car.

> ***"The LORD is my rock, my fortress, and my savior; my God is my rock, in whom I find protection."***
> ***Psalm 18:2 NLT***

We all need a designated driver sometimes when we become too possessed by possessions, power, pride, lust or any other mind or conduct altering worry or sin.

God knows us better than we know ourselves. In providing for our needs, he gives us the indwelling presence of the Holy Spirit to be our designated driver through the muck and the mire, the land mines and potholes, and the bruises and detours on our journey through this life.

The Holy Spirit will convict us of our sin and our need for a Savior. He will guide us into all truth. As we get to know Christ better through getting to know His Word better we will receive the power to live a godly life full of the goodness and glory of God.

> ***"As we know Jesus better, his divine power gives us everything we need for living a godly life. He has called us to receive his own glory and goodness!"***
> ***2 Peter 1:3 NLT***

As we turn over control of our lives to God, we receive the strength and power of the Holy Sprit to live Iruitful lives fully pleasing to God and in the sufficiency of His grace

When we become Spirit driven instead of self driven, we become dead to sin and alive in Christ. We receive our own personal chauffeur. We receive a designated driver who has been given with a guarantee that He will take us safely to our destination.

**Father, Let me become Spirit driven that I might reach my heavenly home safely. Amen**

April 13 Read Ephesians 4:21-31, Proverbs 12

## *Wonder Salve*

**"But for you who fear my name, the Sun of Righteousness will rise with healing in His wings." Malachi 4:2 NLT**

Saymon's Salve has been a staple in our medicine cabinet for over 50 years. My wife probably learned about it from her mother, so it has probably been used in our family for a hundred years.

> ***"Some people make cutting remarks, but the words of the wise bring healing." Proverbs 12:18***

The prescription for about any minor cut or bruise, especially painful hang nails, was always a liberal application of Saymon's Salve covered by a band aid. When the salve was applied, the soreness and wound soon disappeared, and everything was fine. The only requirement was that you apply it to the hurt.

God's Word is a whole lot like salve. When scriptural truth is applied to any hurt or bruise, it can diminish the pain and often work miraculous healing of the mind, body, and soul of those who apply it and cover it with a bandage of faith. We just need to know where to find it in the medicine cabinet- a/k/a The Holy Bible.

We can learn to find the salve for salvation rooted in John 3:16. We can find the salve for sanctification rooted in Matthew 5. The balm for healing sin can be found in Psalm 51. The salve for relational healing can be found in Matthew 18.

Jesus applied great truth and prescriptions for living in the many parables that people could easily understand. When we understand and appropriate these truths into our lives, we find ourselves experiencing unquenchable joy and all-surpassing peace.

> ***"Get rid of all bitterness, rage, anger, harsh words, and slander, as well as all types of malicious behavior." Ephesians 4:31 NLT***

Many of us can still remember the kisses that our parents applied to our hurts, which somehow made them better. The kisses of God's love, grace, and mercy that can make anything better and bearable are all to be found in the great medicine cabinet that is the Word of God.

**Father, thank you for the salve of Your amazing grace. Amen.**

**Read Luke 2:49-52, Psalm 11** **April 14**

## *Taking Care of Business*

**"So he called ten of his servants, delivered to them ten minas, and said to them, 'Do business till I come.'" Luke 19:13**

We have been given our lives to do business for the Lord. We were created for God's pleasure and glory and to do the good works He planned for us before we were even born.

> ***"GOD's business is putting things right; He loves getting the lines straight," Psalm 11:7 MSG***

We who believe in Jesus Christ have been given eternal life as a free gift by the grace of God without any conditions of doing any good works, because a gift cannot be earned.

If both of these statements which Scripture after Scripture makes the truth of which abundantly clear, how do we reconcile the apparent conflict? 1 Corinthians 3:13-16 tells us: "*But there is going to come a time of testing at the judgment day to see what kind of work each builder has done. Everyone's work will be put through the fire to see whether or not it keeps its value. If the work survives the fire, that builder will receive a reward. But if the work is burned up, the builder will suffer great loss. The builders themselves will be saved, but like someone escaping through a wall of flames.*"

Salvation is not a reward but our Savior's "*well done, thou good and faithful servant*" is going to be music to the ear of every believer who has taken care of God's business and fulfilled His purposes.

When we fall in love with Jesus because of His love for us, we can know no greater joy than having the privilege of loving Him by serving and glorifying Him to the highest level of our gifting in this life and in the life to come.

> ***"And He said to them, 'Why did you seek Me? Did you not know that I must be about My Father's business?'" Luke 2:49***

When we give our utmost for His highest purposes here, we are going to be rewarded by serving His highest purposes in heaven. This should make us all want to make taking care of God's business our number one priority.

**Father, let the stewardship of every area of my life reflect my response to Your love and Your call. Amen.**

**April 15** **Read Ephesians 3:14-21, Job 11:5-20**

# *Deeper than the Ocean*

**"Deeper and deeper I sink into the mire; I can't find a foothold to stand on. I am in deep water, and the floods overwhelm me." Psalm 69:2 NLT**

We all have or will experience the frustration of getting in "over our heads." Whether it's debt, relationships, competition, or temptation, we sometimes find that we sink instead of swim.

***"Can you search out the deep things of God? Can you find out the limits of the Almighty? They are higher than heaven—what can you do? Deeper than Sheol—what can you know? Their measure is longer than the earth and broader than the sea." Job 11:7-9***

Usually, the sin of pride precedes our sinking. We fail to heed Paul's warning, *"Don't think highly of yourself, but fear what could happen" (Romans 20:11b).*

We ride the waves of easy credit and keep up appearances until we become overwhelmed and sink in an ocean of unpaid bills, foreclosures, and repossessions.

We try soaring with the eagles of a faster crowd and get taken to the cleaners and hung out to dry before we realize that we are in over our heads. We try competing beyond our level of training, ability, or expertise to find that we can't compete, much less win.

When temptations come, we flirt with them and allow them an opening to realize only too late that the toe hold we have allowed has become a foothold that swallows us.

It's so good to know that no matter how deep we have sunk, or how overwhelmed we are, God's love is deeper, His power is greater, and that He can lift us up and save us from drowning even after we have failed so miserably and gotten in over our heads so deeply.

***"And may you have the power to understand, as all God's people should, how wide, how long, how high, and how deep His love really is. Ephesians 3:18 NLT***

Sometimes we have to sink to the depths in order to see and appreciate how high and how great the grace of God really is.

**Father, teach me how to swim and stay afloat in the river of life. Amen.**

**Read Hebrews 12:18-29, Psalm 48** **April 16**

## *Head for the Mountains*

**"So he took me in spirit to a great, high mountain, and he showed me the holy city, Jerusalem, descending out of heaven from God." Revelation 21:10 NLT**

The mountains of life have nothing to do with this line from a beer commercial; although if we were to believe the never-ceasing, constant barrage of beer commercials, we could be deceived to believe that good times and fulfillment of life could be found in a particular brand of beer.

> ***"Beautiful in elevation, the joy of the whole earth, is Mount Zion on the sides of the north, the city of the great King." Psalm 48:2***

There are good mountains and bad mountains looming in the lives of everyone.

We have mountains of fear, doubt, debt, bitterness, illness, guilt, shame, and grief that sometimes seem so overwhelming we don't even have the heart to try to climb or move them.

The consequences of some sins are so great that they can cause mountains of despair that make us just want to crawl into a hole and die.

The resurrection power of our risen Lord can move or remove these mountains. This power is ours to claim and harness through faith in Jesus Christ, whose strength is made perfect in our weakness and whose grace is sufficient for all our needs, including the ability to move or climb these mountains.

There are also mountains of incredible joy and unquenchable peace that should be the destination of every believer. We climb these mountains by learning to abide in Christ by abiding in His Word and growing into the fullness of His friendship and love.

> ***"No, you have come to Mount Zion, to the city of the living God, the heavenly Jerusalem, and to thousands of angels in joyful assembly. Hebrews 12:22 NLT***

These are the mountains we should all be heading for and training to climb through the disciplines of discipleship that make us true followers and imitators of Christ.

**Father, help me to become a mountain climber! Amen.**

 Read Revelation 7: 14-17, Psalm 72

# *Flow Through Me*

**"The LORD will guide you continually, and satisfy your soul in drought, and strengthen your bones; you shall be like a watered garden, and like a spring of water, whose waters do not fail." Isaiah 58:11**

Water is a basic necessity of our physical life. We can't live without it. Living water is a basic necessity of our spiritual life. We can't live the abundant life in Christ without it.

> ***"He shall come down like rain upon the grass before mowing, like showers that water the earth." Psalm 72:6***

Only living water can quench our thirst for righteousness and fellowship with God. The living water of baptism cleanses us from sin. The living water of healing heals the mind, body, and spirit as nothing else can.

The living water of tears and of pain and suffering nourishes our faith and causes it to grow strong. The incredible joy of the Lord and His amazing grace brings forth the living water of tears of joy.

There are scriptural references to waters of wrath, death, justice, and blessings.

When we experience the new birth by receiving Jesus Christ as Savior and Lord, the fountain of living water comes to indwell us and flow through us. The "fount of every blessing" fills our cisterns to overflowing so that we can bless others.

> ***"For the Lamb who is in the midst of the throne will shepherd them and lead them to living fountains of waters. And God will wipe away every tear from their eyes." Revelation 7:17***

In order to keep the living waters from becoming stagnant and dammed up, we need to need to keep our pump primed and the water way free of the debris of selfishness and sin by daily washing through prayer and repentance and by passing on God's love to others.

**Father, keep me filled with Your living water and let it flow through me that I may be a conduit of Your love to others. Amen.**

Read Philippians 2: 3-11, Psalm 16 April 18

## *"We Bring Good Things to Life"*

**"Every good gift and every perfect gift is from above, and comes down from the Father of lights, with whom there is no variation or shadow of turning." James 1:17**

Sorry, GE, but only God can "bring good things to life!" You do make some good products that make life a whole lot easier for millions of people, but the really good things come to life only in Christ.

> ***"All the good things I have are from you," Psalm 16:2 NLT***

When God brings His new covenant of grace to life in the hearts of all who receive Jesus as their Savior and Lord, He brings really good things to life.

He brings forever forgiveness, total acceptance, and freedom from condemnation. He brings the resurrection power that raised Jesus from the dead to empower us to live in the freedom from bondage to sin and in the incredible joy of the Lord.

As we grow in Christ through growing in the Word, we bring good things to life for ourselves and others. Our relationships improve as we season our actions and reactions with grace.

We find ourselves wanting to obey God and live lives fully pleasing to Him, instead of feeling that we have to in order to win His favor.

We find a new life of peace and joy and a supernatural power of living in the peace and joy of the Lord through the most difficult of circumstances and misfortunes.

We enjoy the wonderful friendship with Christ that comes through obedience to the Father, which Christ models for us. We receive the Holy Spirit as a 24-hour-a-day advocate, making intercession for needs we don't even know we have.

Best of all, our faith in Christ brings the good life in heaven where we will live forever in perfect bliss with no more pain, no more tears, and no more sorrow.

> ***"May you always be filled with the fruit of your salvation—those good things that are produced in your life by Jesus Christ—for this will bring much glory and praise to God." Philippians 2:11 NLT***

**Father, thank you for bringing the really good things of life for me in Christ. Amen.**

April 19 — Read Mark 9:33-37, Psalm 18

## *Bringing up the Rear*

**"Take My yoke upon you and learn from Me, for I am gentle and lowly in heart, and you will find rest for your souls. For My yoke *is* easy and My burden is light." Matthew 11:29**

We hear a lot about the front line troops that charge into battle and lead the way to victory. We give little thought to the importance of the rear guard. In addition to stopping or discouraging desertion or retreat of the front-line troops, the rear guard also protects the army from attacks from the rear, and often organizes the cleaning up of the messes and spoils of battle. There is no disgrace in being members of the rear guard.

> ***"For You will save the humble people,<br>But will bring down haughty looks."<br>Psalm 18:29***

The Kingdom of God is built by Christian soldiers of the cross, many who serve as foot soldiers in the rear guard.

A mighty preacher of the Word might be used by God to give the lost God's call to salvation, while others might be more effective at discipling through teaching the Word or at evangelizing by being sermons in shoes through the lives they lead and the examples they set.

Guarding the back door so that none of the sheep stray or that no wolves in sheep's clothing come in is often harder than bringing others into a relationship with God through faith in Jesus Christ.

In God's army, the greatest must become the least, and true humility is the crown of glory. We can only find our new lives by losing our old. We can only be a good leader by being a good follower. We can only advance to the front by coming up from the rear.

> ***"Anyone who wants to be the first must take last place and be the servant of everyone else."<br>Mark 9:35***

As co-workers for Christ, it's the quality of our faith relationship that allows us to be faithful to carrying out the purposes for which we were created. There are no insignificant ones. There is enough of God's Grace and glory to crown the faithful from front to rear.

**Father, use me wherever and however You choose for my good and Your glory. Amen.**

Read Galatians 6:7-10 April 20

# *Las Vegas Religion*

**"He will bring the people of the world to judgment. He will convict the ungodly of all the evil things they have done in rebellion and of all the insults that godless sinners have spoken against Him." Jude 1:15 NLT**

It is interesting that even the Las Vegas visitors and convention bureau prides itself on being the city where "anything goes." They forget to mention that almost any money you bring to the casinos goes from your pockets to theirs sooner than later.

> ***"He shall judge the world in righteousness, and He shall administer judgment for the peoples in uprightness." Psalm 9:8***

The casinos are filled with people who actually think that they can beat the dealer. The fact that these casinos continue to prosper and grow because they pick the customers clean doesn't seem to sink into the thinking of most people.

Many seem to think they can beat the dealer in the game of life. As they seek to "eat, drink, and be merry" and totally reject, mock, and ignore God, they think that "anything goes" that will make them happy, wealthy, and wise and bring them pleasure.

As believers, we come to know the God of the Universe, the almighty, all-knowing, ever-present, and eternal God who holds all the cards. He equips everyone with the "wild card" of freedom of the will which allows freedom of choice to believe or reject and to receive or forfeit the winning of eternal life through receiving the free gift of salvation through faith in Jesus Christ.

The "anything goes" pursuit of hedonism, relative truth, and instant gratification at the expense of others often seems to be a winning hand until the time comes when we will all have to "ante up" with an accounting of the lives we were given and how well we accomplished the purposes for which we were created. This is where the real winners can cash in their chips.

> ***"Do not be deceived, God is not mocked; for whatever a man sows, that he will also reap." Galatians 6:7 NLT***

**Father, help me to live so that my account will be filled with the fruits of righteousness on judgment day. Amen.**

April 21 Read Romans 8:31-39, Job Chapters 38-42:1-6

## *Wheel of Fortune*

**"For My thoughts *are* not your thoughts, nor *are* your ways My ways," says the LORD. For as the heavens are higher than the earth, so are My ways higher than your ways, and My thoughts than your thoughts." Isaiah 55:8, 9**

The providence of an all-powerful, all-knowing, ever-present God is beyond human understanding, but it is real.

> ***"I know that You can do everything, and that no purpose of Yours can be withheld from You." Job 42:2***

Some prefer to liken their lives to a giant roulette wheel where the ball bounces, and we land either at the right place or the wrong place at the right time or wrong time.

The fact that we often short circuit God's plans for us as a consequence of willful disobedience or unbelief is not too hard to understand.

The fact that God allows bad things to happen to good people seems much harder to understand, until we consider what happened to God's only Son, who was the best person ever born of woman.

Scripture after Scripture attests to the sovereignty of God. God has the supernatural power to turn what others mean for evil into good. He often works in the most mysterious of ways, His wonders to perform.

When we make God our "wheel of fortune" by receiving Jesus Christ as not only our Savior but as the Lord and model for our life, we receive the blessed assurance that no matter which way the cookie crumbles, no matter where the chips fall, God is working all things for our good and His glory.

> ***"And I am convinced that nothing can ever separate us from His love. Death can't, and life can't. The angels can't, and the demons can't. Our fears for today, our worries about tomorrow, and even the powers of hell can't keep God's love away." Romans 8:38 NLT***

We should daily thank God that He loves us too much to allow us to stay the way we were when He found us, wandering aimlessly lost, and adopted us as His own sons and daughters.

He comes to live within us to conform us into the likeness of His Son through chipping away at the imperfections and impurities in our lives. These chips need to fall.

**Father, thank you for making me a winner in the game of life. Amen.**

Read 2 Peter 3:10-17, Psalm 101 April 22

## *The Slippery Slope*

**"People with integrity have firm footing, but those who follow crooked paths will slip and fall." Proverbs 10:9 NLT**

There is a slippery slope to sin. The fall is often painful and the consequences severe.

> ***"I will set nothing wicked before my eyes; I hate the work of those who fall away,"***
> ***Psalm 101:3***

When we fall into deception and deceit, we lose all credibility, and no one will believe us or trust us when our lies come to light.

When we fall into gossip and backbiting, we often cause irreparable harm to relationships and reputations.

When we fall into self promotion and self praise, we set ourselves up for the fall that inevitably follows pride. The sins of jealousy, envy, anger, and lust also have a downside that lead to consequences of strife, guilt, and shame.

David's slip into lust led to murder and the consequences of a still born child, rebellious children, and the anguish of shame and guilt that only God could forgive.

When we slip into the sin of unforgiveness, we risk falling into the ranks of the unforgiven, because Scripture makes it very clear that we cannot receive forgiveness without forgiving.

When we slip into the sin of unbelief, we fall into the downward spiral of despair that awaits all who refuse to believe in the Lord Jesus Christ and be saved.

> ***"You therefore, beloved, since you know this beforehand, beware lest you also fall from your own steadfastness, being led away with the error of the wicked,"***
> ***2 Peter 3:8***

The character of God has been modeled by the character of Jesus, who came to earth to show us how to live out the great commandment and great commission. When we live lives of integrity built on this firm foundation, we will enter into the joy of the Lord not only in this life but in the eternal life to come. We may sometimes slip, but we will never fall into the valley of the doomed.

**Father, by the power of Your Spirit, help me to walk with the firm footing of a right relationship with You. Amen.**

# *Is God's Glory Safe With You?*

**"The eyes of your understanding being enlightened; that you may know what is the hope of His calling, what are the riches of the glory of His inheritance in the saints." Ephesians 1:18**

We were created for God's glory, not for our own or for anyone else's. We are called to glorify God by giving Him the praise and honor due Him. We are commanded to love the Lord with all our heart, all our soul, and all our strength (Deuteronomy 6:5).

***"You who fear the LORD, praise Him! All you descendants of Jacob, glorify Him," Psalm 22:3***

The degree to which we love God is reflected by the degree to which we obey Him in loving others and reflecting the character of His Son, in whom He was well pleased.

God has chosen to manifest His glory through us by creating us for purposes that He planned for us before we were ever born. *"For we are His workmanship, created in Christ Jesus for good works, which God prepared beforehand that we should walk in them" (Ephesians 2:10).*

When we place any thing or any person above God, we are robbing God of His glory. What or who do we treasure most?

When we waste or bury our talents in self-satisfying pursuits instead of using them to glorify God, we are not being faithful to our calling.

When others God brings across our path of life cannot see the glory of the Lord shining through us by the way we live and love, we are not being faithful to our calling.

God has given us our lives as a sacred trust and repository of His grace and His glory through which He reaches others. We can fail to use it and lose it like the unfaithful steward who buried his talents in the ground, or we can be faithful in safekeeping the glory of God by obeying Him and His commandments and commission.

***"And all Mine are Yours, and Yours are Mine, and I am glorified in them." John 17:5***

Are you going to receive the Lord's "well done"?

**Father, You have bought me with the blood of Your Son and claimed me as Your very own. Make me faithful to Your calling in every area of my life. Amen.**

Read Philippians 4:4-13, Psalm 18 April 24

## *Living Beyond Your Means*

**"And He said to me, 'My grace is sufficient for you, for My strength is made perfect in weakness.'" 2 Corinthians 12:9 NLT**

Most of us have had the experience of living beyond our means financially and often found out what a severe master bondage to debt can be. Those easy payments can become not so easy when they pile up and exceed our capacity.

> ***"The LORD is my rock and my fortress and my deliverer; my God, my strength, in whom I will trust; my shield and the horn of my salvation, my stronghold." Psalm 18:2 NLT***

Too many of us, too many times, try to live beyond our means spiritually in that we try to deal with the problems of life in our own strength instead of tapping into the strength of the Sovereign God who loves us with an everlasting love and who wants His very best for us.

Gods call to all who are heavy laden to come unto Him and put on the yoke of obedience to Him gives a promise that He will not only give us His grace, sufficient for our every need, but also His strength.

No matter what the circumstance, we can choose to live beyond our means to cope by focusing on ourselves and the circumstance or by focusing on God's providential purposes and power to use the worst of our circumstances for the best of His purposes for us and those we love.

God uses circumstances to inspect, correct, protect, and perfect us as He conforms us to be more like His Son. Even the consequences of sins, although painful, can and will be used by God for accomplishing His purposes for us.

> ***"For I can do everything with the help of Christ who gives me the strength I need." Philippians 4:13 NLT***

When we quit striving to live in our strength and begin living in the strength of "Christ in us–our hope of glory," we are going to find the strength that Paul found through the beatings, imprisonments, and disasters that he went through and learned to "count it all joy."

**Father, help me to live beyond my weaknesses and in the security, peace and joy of Your strength. Amen.**

# *Are You Ready?*

**"Destruction is certain for those who say that evil is good and good is evil; that dark is light and light is dark; that bitter is sweet and sweet is bitter." Isaiah 5:20**

There is a war raging throughout the world. The powers of darkness and forces of evil are assaulting Christ and His Church from within and without.

> ***"Come to me with your ears wide open. Listen, for the life of your soul is at stake." Isaiah 55:3 NLT***

The minds of men are being poisoned by enlightened thinking and liberating lifestyles that end in bondage, misery, darkness, and despair.

It all starts with the denial that man is sinful, and that sexual immorality is not sin but "Victorian prudishness." There are no moral absolutes. Everything is relative. The end justifies the means.

We are called to worship the intellect of man and to deny the existence and sovereignty of God. God's Word is dismissed as irrelevant and untrue. Those who dare to believe the Bible are facing ridicule and scorn more and more.

AIDS, undermining of the family and family values, corruption, cruelty, and compromise are just a few of the fruits of victory for this new age of enlightenment and idolatry. When we seek to become all that we can be apart from God, we become all that we shouldn't be and are doomed for eternal death and destruction.

The good news is that we don't have to succumb and be casualties in this raging spiritual warfare that is spreading like wildfire. We have a mighty fortress in our God, who is our Shield and Defender, and who has provided His full armor for our protection and our victory.

> ***"He will use every kind of wicked deception to fool those who are on their way to destruction because they refuse to believe the truth that would save them." 2 Thessalonians 2:10 NLT***

Before God's patience wears out, we had better let His Son and the salvation He brings into our lives before the certain destruction comes.

**Father, let me rejoice in the victory over destruction that You won for me on the cross at Calvary. Amen.**

**Read 1 Corinthians 6:1-17, Psalm 17** **April 26**

# *You Don't Have to Go*

**"Flee also youthful lusts; but pursue righteousness, faith, love, peace with those who call on the Lord out of a pure heart." 1 Timothy 2:22**

The guilt, shame, and hurtful consequences of our sins for ourselves and for others can be virtually eliminated if we just choose to heed the biblical admonishment to flee.

> ***"But because I have done what is right, I will see you. When I awake, I will be fully satisfied, for I will see you face to face."***
> ***Psalm 17:15 NLT***

We are told to flee sexual immorality, idolatry, trouble makers, bad influences, love of money, etc. When the enticement to sin comes, we can refuse to go.

We do not have to argue. We don't have to dance to the tune of our peers. We don't have to give in to the lusts of our flesh or the enticements of the world. We can just say no!

We need to say no and goodbye to acquaintances that try to lead us astray. We need to avoid the bars, TV programs, movies, and internet sites that trigger thoughts that lead to sins if we choose to go there.

Instead of pursuing these destructive pursuits, we are exhorted to *"pursue righteousness, godliness, faith, love, patience, gentleness" (1 Timothy 6:11).*

God tells us *"resist the devil and he will flee from you" (James 4:7).* We don't have to go where Jesus wouldn't go and do what Jesus wouldn't do.

God has given us the Holy Spirit and the full armor with which to stand. He has promised that He will allow no temptation to come without providing a means of escape.

Our freedom to "just say no" and to choose "not to go there" is the blood bought gift of God who loved us enough to come and live the perfect life that we could never live, die so that we would never have to, and come to live in us so that we could have the power to live the fruitful lives of freedom that he died on the cross to earn for us.

> ***"God is faithful, who will not allow you to be tempted beyond what you are able,"***
> ***1 Corinthians 10:13b***

**Father, give me the strength to resist, and the resolve to "not go there" when temptation comes. Amen.**

April 27 Read Isaiah 49:8-26, Galatians 5

# True Freedom

**"God makes homes for the homeless, leads prisoners to freedom, but leaves rebels to rot in hell." Psalm 68:6 MSG**

What does freedom mean? During the revolutionary war, it meant being free from the tyranny and control of the King of England. To a slave, it meant being set free from the ownership and control of an earthly master. To the addict, it means being free from bondage and dependency upon drugs or some other controlling substance.

> ***"Through you I am saying to the prisoners of darkness, 'Come out! I am giving you your freedom!'"***
> ***Isaiah 43:9 NLT***

To the ACLU and apparently many of our federal judges, freedom does not mean freedom of religion but freedom from religion and the moral responsibility that it encompasses.

To the believer, true freedom is the realization that sin has no more dominion over us. It no longer has the power to destroy us and our relationship with God through faith in Jesus Christ.

Because we know that there is no longer any condemnation by God for those who are in Christ, we are able to grow into the fullness of Christ by no longer being slaves to sin but slaves to Christ.

As long as we offer ourselves to God and walk in His freedom, we will never use our freedom to sell ourselves back into slavery to sin. We are free to do whatever we want to do, because when we submit to the control of the Holy Spirit in our lives, we will want to live lives pleasing to God and be fruitful in every good work.

Freedom sometimes takes a lot of getting used to. Although we are freed from the control of sin when the Holy Spirit calls us to faith in Christ, we often revert to our flesh mode as we grow in spiritual maturity. We need the daily cleansing of confession, repentance, and the transforming power of the Holy Spirit to keep us living in the freedom that was purchased for us on the cross.

> ***"Stand fast therefore in the liberty by which Christ has made us free, and do not be entangled again with a yoke of bondage."***
> ***Galatians 5:1***

**Father, help me to enjoy the joy that comes from living in the freedom I have received to honor and glorify You. Amen.**

## *Going Public*

**"Today I am giving you the choice between a blessing and a curse! You will be blessed if you obey the commands of the LORD your God that I am giving you today." Deuteronomy 11:26, 27 NLT**

Small companies that grow into big ones usually go public by selling stock to raise money for further expansion or to accumulate wealth for the owners and employees.

> ***"For they brag about their evil desires; they praise the greedy and curse the LORD." Psalm 10:3 NLT***

Many people are enjoying the benefits of having invested in companies like Microsoft and Yahoo when they first went public and have watched the value of their stock increase.

There seems to be a lot of going public with what God says is sinful and not enough going public about what God tells us to go public.

Public immorality is at an all time high. People who indulge in what God calls abominations are going public demanding respectability and rights previously reserved for those who seek to abide by God's standard of conduct and morality.

An aggressive vocal minority has gotten a lot of power and control over the courts who are now taking control of our country by rewriting laws instead of enforcing them, because they have lifetime appointments and no accountability at all to the majority who are supposed to be in control.

The situation in many instances has gotten so bad that those who dare go public with their Christian beliefs, that represent the values and beliefs of a vast majority, are persecuted, ridiculed, and shouted down by the vocal minority.

Unless more and more Christians live out the great commandment and obey the great commission by going public with their faith and letting God work through them to change values and conduct by changing hearts, the history of God's chosen ones falling into captivity and bondage to pagans is going to repeat itself.

> ***"Do not be deceived, God is not mocked; for whatever a man sows, that he will also reap." Galatians 6:7***

**Father, give me the strength and courage to go public with my faith and help me to uphold Your standards. Amen.**

# *Safety Valves*

**"And don't sin by letting anger gain control over you. Don't let the sun go down while you are still angry, for anger gives a mighty foothold to the Devil." Ephesians 4:26**

All boilers and pressure cookers are equipped with safety valves to prevent explosions from building up too much pressure.

> ***"Don't sin by letting anger gain control over you. Think about it overnight and remain silent." Psalm 4:4 NLT***

We all need safety valves in dealing with excess anger that can lead to harmful explosions.

Some vent their angers and frustrations by taking them out on their children, family, friends, team mates, employees, etc. Most problems with abuse spring from faulty safety valves.

There are books and courses on anger management that offer suggestions for expressing, suppressing, and calming anger.

Expressing anger in an assertive but non-aggressive manner is one of the best ways to deal with it, because this prevents a lot of problems caused when anger is suppressed and builds up within and causes all sorts of physical and emotional problems.

Suppressing anger and then redirecting it by focusing on something positive works for some people. Calming anger may be as simple as counting to ten before responding or by letting anger subside before responding to any provocation.

God dealt with His anger over the fall and disobedience of man by sending His Son to suffer the wrath of God on behalf of us all so that we will never have to bear the brunt of His anger forever.

> ***"For God sent Jesus to take the punishment for our sins and to satisfy God's anger against us." Romans 3:24***

Jesus Christ turned God's anger into God's grace and took away all eternal condemnation and eternal punishment for those who receive this marvelous grace by faith. Jesus is the ultimate safety valve!

**Father, thank you for giving me relief from Your anger through faith in Jesus Christ. Amen.**

Read Acts 2:37-40, Psalm 78 April 30

## The Highest Calling

**"Now therefore, if you will indeed obey My voice and keep My covenant, then you shall be a special treasure to Me above all people; for all the earth *is* Mine." Exodus 19:5**

The world is in crisis! At home and abroad, within the church and without, many children are out of control and growing up into adults controlled mainly by baser instincts and bad character traits.

> ***"That the generation to come might know them, the children who would be born, that they may arise and declare them to their children."***
> ***Psalm 78:6***

Among the many causes advanced as the reason for this sad state of affairs, the best case can be made for the failure of parents to fulfill their responsibilities to obey the great commandment and the great commission by teaching them and modeling them for their children.

If a child is not brought up in the nurture and admonition of the Lord, if they are not brought up to honor and obey their parents, they are not going to grow up obeying God. When we do not obey God, we disqualify ourselves from receiving the many blessings of obedience.

In most instances when covenants are broken by parents, the blessings promised to their children and children's children are lost. We are letting our children be raised by TV and taught the world's views and values that lead to destruction rather than raising them in the nurture and admonition of the Lord and all of His blessings.

Permissiveness never leads to real happiness. Boundaries are not meant to restrict but rather to inspire and instruct in seeking the righteousness of God and appropriating all of the incredible peace and true joy that this promises.

> ***"For the promise is to you and to your children, and to all who are afar off, as many as the Lord our God will call."***
> ***Acts 2:37-40***

When we stand before God and give an account of what we have done with the life we have been given, we dare not face the consequences of not having been obedient to the explicit commands regarding loving and discipling the children that have been entrusted to our care.

**Father help me to keep the circle unbroken by passing on the covenants of faith and obedience to my children. Amen.**

## *Rubbing the Wrong Way*

**"If you have anything against someone, forgive—only then will your heavenly Father be inclined to also wipe your slate clean of sins." Mark 11:22 MSG**

Most things rubbed the wrong way create friction. We often hear about someone who "rubs me the wrong way." Many people are offended or rubbed the wrong way by conduct, attitudes, or personality traits of others.

> ***"I'll rub their faces in the dirt of their rebellion and make them face the music, but I'll never throw them out, never abandon or disown them." Psalm 89:32 MSG***

Jesus certainly rubbed the religious leaders and teachers of the day the wrong way when He exposed their hypocrisy and self righteousness, and He was persecuted and killed when He revealed Himself as God.

Preachers often rub hearers the wrong way when they bring up sins about which they don't want to be reminded.

We all get rubbed the wrong way in order to become convicted of our sinfulness and either respond by acknowledging, confessing, repenting, and receiving salvation or by hardening our hearts and denying our need for a Savior.

Some people seem to take delight in "rubbing it in" when someone makes a mistake. Partisan basketball fans are especially good at "rubbing it in" when an opposing player misses a free throw or shoots an "air ball."

> ***"Fortunate those whose crimes are carted off, whose sins are wiped clean from the slate. Fortunate the person against whom the Lord does not keep score." Romans 4:7 MSG***

"Rubbing in" is often a manifestation of pride or anger that indicates no forgiveness or grace. Given all of the grace and mercy we need and have received from God, we need to "rub out" sins and transgressions of others as God has "rubbed out" ours and remembers them no more.

**Father, when others rub me the wrong way, help me to "rub it out" instead of "rubbing it in." Amen.**

## *Shine Christian Shine!*

**"Those who are wise will shine as bright as the sky, and those who turn many to righteousness will shine like stars forever." Daniel 12:3**

This De Beers diamond slogan has been around for a long time, but diamonds have been around a lot longer. They have been treasured down through the ages and are still today's most popular token of choice for expressing undying love.

> ***"No longer will you need the sun or moon to give you light, for the LORD your God will be your everlasting light, and He will be your glory." Isaiah 60:19***

Like people, diamonds all come with flaws. There is no such thing as a perfect diamond or a perfect person (except for the perfect righteousness of Christ with which God views us by faith).

Diamonds in the rough are just shiny rocks often encrusted by the carbon from which they were formed. They take a lot of cutting and finishing to bring out their full brilliance and beauty.

Diamond cutting is a skilled art with little room for error. A faulty facet cuts down the clarity and brilliance. A faulty cut can result in the diamond being broken and made smaller and of less value. It takes light for diamonds to reflect in order to show their brilliance.

If you think about it, we are all diamonds in the rough. We are born encrusted by sin and need a lot of cutting and finishing to bring out our best. We certainly can never reflect the brilliance of the Son without the light of our salvation which we receive through faith in Him.

When we place ourselves in the hands of the master diamond cutter, He will chip away at our rough edges, and cut many beautiful facets so that we will shine brighter than the stars as we begin to reflect the love of God to others in fulfilling both the great commandment and great commission.

> ***"For it is the God who commanded light to shine out of darkness, who has shone in our hearts to give the light of the knowledge of the glory of God in the face of Jesus Christ." 1 Corinthians 4:6 NLT***

Like diamonds, we will shine forever.

**Father, let Your Son shine through me. Amen.**

# *Better or Better Off?*

**"For all have sinned and fall short of the glory of God, being justified freely by His grace through the redemption that is in Christ Jesus," Romans 3:23, 24**

Christians often get a bad rap for being self righteous and thinking they are better than others. The Pharisees were so thankful that they were without sin like the others. Many religious leaders were upset because Jesus ate with and ministered to the unrighteous.

> ***"My mouth shall tell of Your righteousness and Your salvation all the day," Psalm 71:15***

While it is true that those who claim the name of Christ should show some evidence of their faith by their conduct and bearing the fruits of the Spirit produced within them, we dare not fall into the trap of thinking that we are more righteous and better than others because of our conduct.

The Bible makes it perfectly clear that there is none righteous, no not one, that "all have sinned and fall short of the glory of God," and that "our righteousness is as filthy rags."

The difference between the good and the bad is not always in conduct, but in position. As believers, we become members of the family of God, brothers and sisters, and joint heirs with Christ in the inheritance of eternal life.

When we stumble and fall into sin, as we all do, believers are just a whole lot better off with forever forgiveness and the perfect goodness and righteousness of Christ in God's sight when we confess and repent.

Being better off means we have experienced a new birth and transforming power to live free from condemnation and free to become better and better people as we grow in holiness and into fullness of Christ.

> ***"He saved us, not because of the good things we did, but because of his mercy." Titus 3:5a NLT***

Aren't you glad that you're better off? Don't you wish that everyone was?

**Father, let me never become self righteous, but ever mindful of being Christ righteous because of my faith in Him. Amen.**

**Read Luke 12:42-48, Psalm 132** **May 4**

# *Missed Opportunities*

**"I will make them and the places all around My hill a blessing; and I will cause showers to come down in their season; there shall be showers of blessing." Ezekiel 34:26**

God showered down manna from heaven daily to feed the children of Israel. They had to use it or lose it because it could not be hoarded, stored, or saved.

> ***"I'll shower blessings on the pilgrims who come here," Psalm 132:15 MSG***

God sends us showers of blessings daily including the opportunities to be blessed by being a blessing to others. We have to use or lose these opportunities because many of them must be taken advantage of or lost when they are offered.

Self centeredness is probably our biggest "blessing buster." We all too often are so preoccupied in our own agenda that we miss out on many of God's "divine appointments for blessings."

Jesus stands at the door and knocks offering His wonderful gift of eternal life, and people are so engrossed in themselves that they don't even hear the knock and miss out on the real opportunity of this lifetime.

We miss out on opportunities to share our faith because we are not prepared to "give an account of the hope that is within us" when we get the opportunity and don't even realize it until it has passed.

We often hoard the material, relational, physical, and gift abundance that God has given us so that we can be generous on all occasions and fail to meet His expectations for those to whom He gives and expects much.

> ***"Much is required from those to whom much is given, and much more is required from those to whom much more is given." Luke 12:48b NLT***

There are showers of blessatunities to pass on by reflecting God's love through random acts of kindness, mercy, forgiveness, patience, generosity, and service to others every day of our lives. We need to soak them up and wring them out to those God places in our paths or hearts each day.

**Father help me to always remember that You have blessed me so that I can be a blessing to others. Amen.**

f

# *Who's Your Co-signer?*

**"My child, if you co-sign a loan for a friend or guarantee the debt of someone you hardly know—if you have trapped yourself by your agreement and are caught by what you said—quick, get out of it if you possibly can! You have placed yourself at your friend's mercy." Proverbs 6:1**

Credit is extended on the basis of character, capacity, permanence, and reputation for paying bills on time. A deficiency in any of these areas may result in a low credit score that might cause your credit to be turned down.

> ***"God's reputation is twenty-four carat gold, with a lifetime guarantee." Psalm 19:9 MSG***

Using someone else's credit to establish ours is at least as old as the Old Testament.

Many of us have had a co-signor to help get our credit established. Frankly, I don't know how I would have survived the early days of my business if my father-in-law had not graciously co-signed a note for me.

As a general rule, co-signing is a bad practice to get involved in, often leading to strained relations and loss of friendship with those you tried to help by co-signing.

Given our propensity for sin, none of us could ever qualify for opening an account with God on the basis of character. Our capacity for paying God back for his tender mercy and loving kindness is nil.

God knew this and has dealt with it by giving us a co-signer.

As believers, we have the greatest co-signer of all – the Holy Spirit! He is given to us as a "guarantee" that Jesus death on the cross paid our sin debt in full, and that we can live in the eternal security of knowing that nothing can ever separate us from the love of God that is ours by faith in Christ.

> ***"The Spirit is God's guarantee that He will give us everything He promised and that He has purchased us to be His own people." Ephesians 1:14 NLT***

**Father, thank you for giving a co-signer who guarantees that my righteousness account has been guaranteed. Amen.**

**Read Ephesians 6:16-18, Psalm 3** **May 6**

# *How's Your Fire Wall?*

**"He grants a treasure of good sense to the godly. He is their shield, protecting those who walk with integrity." Proverbs 2:7 NLT**

Fire walls for computers have become a big business. This special software is designed to put up a barrier between hackers and your hard drive, blocking access to sensitive files, financial records, and personal data.

> ***"But You, O LORD, are a shield for me,"***
> ***Psalm 3:3***

Fire walls can filter out unwanted intrusions to your privacy and help protect credit card fraud and identity theft.

Long before computers, buildings had fire walls designed to stop the spread of fires, and forests had fire walls consisting of clearings to keep fires from spreading beyond.

The world, our flesh, and satan are continually seeking to intrude into our lives, undermine our faith, cause us to compromise our conduct, and steal our wonderful identity as the children of God.

God knew full well that this was going to happen. In His love, He sent the Holy Spirit to take up residence within us to serve as a fire wall to put out the brush fires of temptation, continually intercede on our behalf, and to equip us with the full armor of God so that we might stand firm through all these intrusions.

In a sense, Jesus is our ultimate fire wall. We come under the shelter of His wings, are separated from our sins, and are rescued from the torment of hell's fire in eternity.

> ***"In every battle you will need faith as your shield to stop the fiery arrows aimed at you by satan."***
> ***Ephesians 6:16 NLT***

Although this firewall was very costly, it is now available as a free gift to all who would call upon the name of the Lord Jesus Christ to be saved.

Don't put off another day of receiving it or of using it, if you have already received it.

**Father, thank you for surrounding me with the firewall of Your love which offers me daily comfort and strength to stand. Amen.**

May 7 Read Romans 8:29-39, Psalm 146

# Upside Down

**"These who have turned the world upside down have come here too." Acts 17:6**

Unless you're talking pineapple upside down cake, upside down just doesn't work. Ships can't sail, planes can't fly, and cars can't run upside down. Poor turtles were never made to live upside down.

> ***"But the way of the wicked He turns upside down." Psalm 146:9***

We were made for fellowship and friendship with God, but the world and our flesh has turned this upside down. We are living self-centered lives standing on our heads, instead of on the wonderful promises of God.

God sent His only Son into the world to turn it right side up and re-establish fellowship and friendship with Him. When we find ourselves hopelessly lost and drifting through life upside down and call upon the name of the Lord to be saved, something wonderful happens.

The Holy Spirit of God comes to live within us, transforming us from darkness into light through the resurrection power of the risen Lord.

We are not only set right side up for sailing through life with the imputed righteousness of Christ, but we are given a life preserver to keep us safe when we find ourselves blown off course by trials and temptations that might temporarily turn us upside down occasionally.

We can find ourselves taking on a lot of water, being blown about by many a conflict and many a doubt, but we have God's promises and the testimony of the Holy Spirit living within us that He will never let us drown.

We can seek all the security we want in fortune, fame, and power, but the only real security is the peace that comes with knowing that because of Jesus Christ, God loves us unconditionally, forgives us for everything forever, accepts us just as we are, and that we are secure. Our lives have meaning and significance in Christ.

> ***"And having chosen them, He called them to come to Him. And He gave them right standing with Himself, and He promised them His glory." Romans 8:30 NLT***

**Father, help me to learn how to use my life preserver by reading Your life-saving manual. Amen.**

Read Luke 16:1-14, Psalm 37

May 8

## *Your "Golden Parachute"*

**"In that day, He will be your sure foundation, providing a rich store of salvation, wisdom, and knowledge. The fear of the LORD is the key to this treasure." Isaiah 33:6 NLT**

Corporate CEO's seemed to have learned a lesson from Luke 16. When corporate CEO's bail out, they have what is called a "golden parachute" of sometimes millions of dollars to cushion their fall. They have certainly been shrewd in planning for their financial future and have an everlasting life of luxury while on this earth.

> ***"Though he fall, he shall not be utterly cast down; for the LORD upholds him with His hand." Psalm 37:24***

Hopefully, most of us have packed a "golden parachute" to provide for our financial needs after our paychecks stop, and our stored benefits start.

It is a really good idea to pack a chute full of savings to handle the expectable and unexpected financial emergencies that we seem to fall upon. Whether an expensive car, home repair, doctor bill, or braces for the kids' teeth, having the funds to cover is a positive result of planning ahead.

The really big "golden parachute" is the one God packed for us in sending Jesus Christ to die on the cross to cushion our fall from death into life eternal. We put it on by faith and should never try to fly through life without it.

God repacks and repacks this parachute as we go through the jump school of life and practice falling through many "trials, toils, and snares" cushioned by His amazing grace, divine strength, and protection as we persevere, preparing ourselves for the "big jump."

If we are really wise, we will take heed and store up treasures in heaven by taking care of our Father's business with our time, talents, and resources, which should be used to accomplish the purposes for which we were placed here on earth.

> ***"I tell you, use your worldly resources to benefit others and make friends. In this way, your generosity stores up a reward for you in heaven." Luke 16:9 NLT***

**Father, when I fall, let me wear Your golden parachute which You issue to all Your faithful ones. Amen.**

# Business Plan

**"'For I know the plans I have for you,' says the LORD. 'They are plans for good and not for disaster, to give you a future and a hope.'" Jeremiah 29:11**

The old axiom in business: "never plan to fail, but don't fail to plan" is good advice for life. Failure to plan can bring disaster in every area of life. It is undoubtedly one of the leading causes of failure.

> ***"Commit your work to the LORD, and then your plans will succeed."***
> ***Proverbs 16:3 NLT***

Successful businesses today run on business plans. It is hard for a business to borrow money or sell stock without one written out in detail.

Many growing churches appropriate a model plan that includes things that have been successful in other churches for raising money, evangelizing, Vacation Bible Schools, and many other activities.

There is a difference between worry and planning. In fact, thoughtful planning can eliminate a lot of worries.

No one would think of building a house without a plan. No one should think of building a life without a plan if they want to live a happy and fulfilling life.

God has given us detailed plans for living a life worth living. Seek first the kingdom of God and His righteousness should be the foundation for any plan for the abundant life. Good planning should always include counting the cost. We should never fail to count the cost of living in sinful rebellion against God.

> ***"This 'foolish' plan of God is far wiser than the wisest of human plans, and God's weakness is far stronger than the greatest of human strength."***
> ***1 Corinthians 1:25 NLT***

**Father, help me always remember that You created me for good works before I was even born. Help me to discover and accomplish them by living a life fully pleasing to You. Amen.**

Read Philippians 2, Psalm 26 May 10

## *Attitude Adjustment*

**"May God, who gives this patience and encouragement, help you live in complete harmony with each other—each with the attitude of Christ Jesus toward the other." Romans 15:5 NLT**

There is nothing like counting your blessings for adjusting your attitude. The garbage of life will continually take its toll if we let it get us down by dwelling on the negatives of life. We can control our attitude An "attitude of gratitude" is a great place to start.

***"Examine me, O LORD, and prove me; try my mind and my heart."***
***Psalm 26:2***

We all need constant attitude adjustment, although not as found in booze or other mind- altering substances.

In sports, careers, and every day life, we run across many people with bad attitudes that have a negative effect on others around them.

The life-transforming power of the resurrection that is ours to claim by faith when we are born again should be our catalyst for our attitude adjustment.

This new birth should not only make us live life differently, but should give us a new attitude for doing things God's way. The fact that Jesus Christ did everything necessary for our salvation means that we don't have to do anything to earn this free gift, but it should make us want to do everything pleasing to Him in response to what He has done for us.

We know from Scripture that God is pleased with a broken spirit and contrite heart that gives us the gracious and becoming humility modeled by Jesus. We receive the power to live lives fully pleasing to God and fruitful in every good work. We live with an attitude of joy and peace in the Lord.

If you need to adjust your attitude to conform to the reality of Christ living in you, try starting an hour a day delighting in meditating, growing, and abiding in Christ through studying His Word and celebrating His love through prayer and praise.

***"Your attitude should be the same that Christ Jesus had."***
***Philippians 2:5 NLT***

**Father, by the power of Your Spirit help me to adjust my attitude so that I will live wanting to please You in every area of my life. Amen.**

# *Where's Your Delight?*

**"Delight yourself also in the LORD, and He shall give you the desires of your heart." Psalm 37:4**

In spite of many who would have you believe otherwise, true religion overflows with happiness and joy. There are no delights like sacred delights.

> ***"Then you will delight yourself in the Almighty and look up to God." Job 22:26a NLT***

David, the "man after God's own heart," was full of delight in the Lord. Throughout the Psalms, David talks about His delight in the law of the Lord. David acknowledged God as *"the source of all my joy" (Psalm 43:4 NLT).*

Jesus promised that we would be overflowing with joy when we obey Him and remain in His love.

Paul extols the joy of forgiveness, the joy of faith, the peace and joy of the Holy Spirit, the joy of God's presence, the special joy of witnessing, joy in spite of disappointments and hardship, joy in the love of others, the joy of the great future we have in heaven, and exhorts us always to be full of joy in the Lord.

Jesus condemned the "grace busters" of the law and the hypocrisy of going through the motions of joyless religiosity. The idea that holiness and delight are united in true faith is foreign to many who view religion as anything but a pleasure.

The blessings of the unity of faith and joy are the hallmarks of every true believer. They are driven by the response of delighting in doing the things that please God and being the ambassadors of Christ in thankfulness and joy for the love that God has showered upon them in the gift of salvation through saving faith in Jesus Christ.

> ***"Love each other with genuine affection, and take delight in honoring each other." Romans 12:10 NLT***

If your delight is not in the Lord, you are missing out on the overflowing blessedness and the true joy of your salvation which is the birthright of all who have been born again.

**Father, help me to experience the source of true delight. Amen.**

Read Galatians 5, Psalm 68 May 12

# *Prisoners of the Past*

**"He has sent me to bind up the brokenhearted, to proclaim freedom for the captives and release from darkness for the prisoners," Isaiah 61:1b NIV**

Hopefully, we have all learned and grown from our past experiences. Experience is one of our best teachers in every area of our lives.

> ***"God places the lonely in families; He sets the prisoners free and gives them joy."***
> ***Psalm 68:5***

We cannot really appreciate so many of the blessings of life until we experience their absence. It is so easy to take good health for granted until we get sick. We don't appreciate having a job nearly as much unless we have lost one.

God gives us experiences to grow us, not to stunt us. He is going to do whatever it takes to convict us of our sinfulness and need for a Savior. He is then going to begin the life-long process of conforming us to the image of His Son and equipping us for ministries of comforting, faith sharing, giving, and encouraging others.

Sometimes satan uses our guilt, failures, and humiliations of the past to imprison us and rob us of our great present and future.

Sometimes it is easier to accept God's forgiveness than to accept our own. Dwelling on our past experiences of sin, failure, rejection, and mistakes leads to living a life of defeat and bondage.

Jesus Christ came to set us free from this bondage. He forgives every sin we have ever committed or will ever commit. He supplies His all-sufficient grace to help us turn our backs on the failures of yesterday and to use them as learning experiences and building blocks for living victorious lives in the present and future.

> ***"Stand fast therefore in the liberty by which Christ has made us free, and do not be entangled again with a yoke of bondage."***
> ***Galatians 5:1***

The lives of Abraham, David, Gideon, Peter, and Paul are just a few of the Biblical examples of the truth of God's power not only to save but to transform, restore, and use even the worst of sinners with the greatest of sins on their record. He wants to do the same for us.

**Father, help me to turn my back on the sins of yesterday and go forward in the sureness of Your forgiveness. Amen.**

# *Are You A Seven?*

**"Thus the heavens and the earth and all the host of them, were finished. And on the seventh day God ended His work which He had done." Genesis 2:1**

Man seems to favor a scale from 1 to 10 or multiples thereof in rating everything from progress to perfection. Tasks are 20, 30, and 50 percent completed until they are 100 percent complete. Women seem to be rated on a scale of 1 to 10 by men, and men seem to be rated by women on the same scale. Many surveys and questionnaires ask us to rate something on a scale of 1 to 10.

***"Seven times a day I praise You, because of Your righteous judgments." Psalm 119:164***

Biblically speaking, the number 7 symbolizes completeness and perfection. Starting with creation which was completed and perfected in seven days, both the Old and New Testament contain over 300 references to the number 7 and multiples thereof.

The 7-day week, 7-day feasts and offerings, 7-day march around Jericho, 7-year cancellation of debt, 7-day rest for man and 7-year rest for the land are just a few of the "significant sevens" of the Old Testament.

In the New Testament, the 7 churches mentioned in Revelation probably symbolizes all or the complete number of churches; 70 times 7 symbolizes the limitless forgiveness we are to extend. Seven "men of good reputation" were chosen to be overseers of the business of the early church.

If 7 represents completeness, how do you rate yourself in your commitment to Christ? You have all of Christ in you thanks to the indwelling of the Holy Spirit. The question is, how much of you does God have?

On a scale of 1 to 7, how much of your time, talents, and treasures do you own, and how much does God own? How much are you trusting in God and how much are you trusting in yourself? How complete and how fulfilling is your relationship with God? What would it take to make it a 7?

***"And he who overcomes, and keeps My works until the end, to him I will give power over the nations—" Revelation 2:25***

**Father, give me the will to totally surrender my all to You. Amen.**

Read Acts 9:1-31, Proverbs 2 May 14

## *How Many to Change a Light Bulb?*

**"Beware lest anyone cheat you through philosophy and empty deceit, according to the tradition of men, according to the basic principles of the world, and not according to Christ. Colossians 2:8**

This old joke with the classic answer of "change?" is often used to poke good-natured fun at the traditionalists who cling to the past and would seem to allow their churches to close rather than change anything.

> ***"When wisdom enters your heart, and knowledge is pleasant to your soul, discretion will preserve you; understanding will keep you." Proverbs 2:10, 11***

Sadly, a lot of people are seeing this happen in churches that are dying out all over the country because they will not change their traditions to relate to today's life.

The new birth that takes place in the heart and soul of someone who receives Jesus Christ as Savior is often evidenced by radical change.

Today's Scripture account of Paul's Damascus road experience is a perfect example of radical change. Zaccheus's change not only involved repentance but also restitution and a pledge to holiness.

When we receive Jesus, we receive the Holy Spirit in our hearts who brings the strength and power of the resurrection to effect radical changes in our hearts and also in our conduct. The Holy Spirit not only catches us much like we catch fish, but He begins the process of cleaning us like fish.

We not only become clean in God's sight the minute we receive Christ and His righteousness by faith, but we start getting cleaned and made more Christ-like daily as we confess, repent, and receive the all-sufficient grace and strength of God to "live lives fully pleasing to God and fruitful in every good work."

> ***"Saul stayed with the believers in Damascus for a few days, and immediately he began preaching about Jesus in the synagogues," saying, 'He is indeed the Son of God!'" Acts 9:20 NLT***

We should all give serious thought to the change that our coming to faith in Christ has made in our lives and the way we are living. Even the casual acquaintance or friend should see this difference as we reflect the love of God and our response to the love of God with faith in action.

**Father, help me to be changed into the image of Christ. Amen**

 **Read Revelation 14:12-20, Psalm 139**

# *Why Are We "Hangin' Around"?*

**"For all who enter into God's rest will find rest from their labors, just as God rested after creating the world." Hebrews 4:10 NLT**

Have you ever wondered why the Lord doesn't just take us home to all of the joys of heaven when we receive Him as Savior? We could all escape a lot of heartache, pain, and suffering if we could just get a "fast track to glory" by going to be with the Lord as soon as we receive the wonderful gift of salvation.

> ***"You chart the path ahead of me and tell me where to stop and rest. Every moment you know where I am." Psalm 139:3 NLT***

The answer is that it's not about us. It's all about God, who created us for His pleasure and His purposes. God wants to live in, with, and through us that we might be examples of His love and grace to others and that others may come to know the joy of His salvation as we live out the great commandment and great commission.

As good as it is going to be when we are finally with Him in the eternal bliss of heaven, there is great joy and great blessing in living useful, holy lives to "the praise of the glory of His grace" here on earth.

All the time, we are promised in eternity to rest from our labors we perform for God on this earth. In the meantime we should be about our Father's business of being the salt and light of the world as we grow into the fullness of Christ as we become conformed to His image day by day and year by year by the power of His Holy Spirit living within us.

We can be sure that God loves us dearly. We can be sure that He is not going to keep us out of paradise one minute longer than is absolutely necessary.

If we are still breathing, we can be sure that God is still at work accomplishing His perfect will and good pleasure through us. Even the way we die might be the way God uses to bring eternal life to someone else.

> ***"Yes, says the Spirit, they are blessed indeed, for they will rest from all their toils and trials; for their good deeds follow them!" Revelation 14:13b NLT***

**Father, let me be faithful in accomplishing the purposes for which You created me as long as I live on this earth. Amen.**

**Read 1 John 5, Psalm 115** **May 16**

# *Win, Win, Win!*

**"The Lord hath done great things for us, whereof we are glad." Psalm 126:3**

Great things happen when we enter into a close and personal relationship with Jesus Christ.

> ***"The LORD remembers us; He will surely bless us."***
> ***Psalm 115:12 NLT***

First of all God is glorified. There is rejoicing in heaven when we receive Jesus as our Savior and enter into that relationship with God for which we were created.

Second, we are blessed. We receive that peace that surpasses all understanding and the joy and friendship of the Lord, as well as the love of other brothers and sisters in Christ.

Third, the unsaved will be drawn into a relationship with God as they see His love and His fruit manifest in us and ask us why we are so happy or notice the change in our lives in some other way.

Best of all, we receive confirmed reservations to the winners' circle of everlasting life reserved for those who have their sins washed away by the blood of the lamb.

We receive instant perfection in the eyes of God who sees us robed in the righteousness and perfection of Christ. We receive the indwelling presence of the Holy Spirit who begins the life-long work of perfecting us into the image of Christ.

With all of these benefits waiting for those who come to faith in Christ, why, oh why, do so many choose to go through life as losers?

For the most part, losers buy into the lie of the world, the flesh, or the devil that there is happiness to be found apart from God. They are deceived into believing that they can be winners in their own strength, or that they can find happiness in a toy, pill, bottle, immoral relationship, or practice. Scripture says, *"There is a way that seems right to a man, but its end is the way of death" (Proverbs 14:12).*

> ***"And the ones who win this battle against the world are the ones who believe that Jesus is the Son of God."***
> ***1 John 5:5 NLT***

**Father, thank you for being with me all the way to the finish line and into the winners' circle. Amen.**

May 17 Read Romans 10:14-21, Psalm 67

## *Do You Believe in Out Sourcing?*

**"And then He told them, 'Go into all the world and preach the Good News to everyone, everywhere.'" Mark 16:15**

The ongoing debate over out sourcing American jobs overseas seems to raise more questions than answers. Honest people seem to have strong and honest differences of opinion over this practice, and the arguments are going to become more heated and examples more compelling as time goes by.

> ***"My God will send forth His unfailing love and faithfulness." Psalm 57:3b NLT***

There has never been any question of outsourcing the Good News of Jesus Christ throughout the world. Today's commercial out sourcers have taken a page out of the book of many evangelism outreach ministries.

Instead of exporting missionaries, it has often proven much more effective to export equippers who will train native believers to proclaim the Good News and spread the gospel in their own countries and own languages.

In some instances, it has proven more effective to bring foreign Christians to this country for training and equipping as missionaries in their own countries.

Just like the love of God, the Gospel is one treasure that we should seek to give away. The truth of God's love flows from a limitless and unending stream of living water that will never go dry.

In some instances, there seems to be a preoccupation with out sourcing at the expense of domestic missions. We can fall into the trap of taking a world view of spreading the gospel instead of concentrating on the opportunities of the neighborhoods and communities we live in which abound with people who need the Lord.

> ***"How beautiful are the feet of those who preach the gospel of peace, bring glad tidings of good things!" Romans 10:15b***

It's really a scary thought that some jobs of evangelizing America are being out sourced to believers in other countries who are being sent to this mission field from abroad.

**Father, let the boundaries of my mission field start in my own neighborhood. Amen.**

Read 1 John 4:7-11, Psalm 103 May 18

## What's the Use?

**"So don't get tired of doing what is good. Don't get discouraged and give up, for we will reap a harvest of blessing at the appropriate time. Whenever we have the opportunity, we should do good to everyone, especially to our Christian brothers and sisters." Galatians 6:9**

If you have ever been discouraged or disappointed by well doing, welcome to the club. Sometimes it seems that nobody cares or appreciates our best efforts, or, even worse, someone returns our kindness with ridicule or disappointment.

> ***"He has not punished us for all our sins, nor does He deal with us as we deserve." Psalm 103:10 NLT***

There is a special vulnerability connected with trying to help those who are hard to help. Whether trying to help a cranky senior, dysfunctional addict, rebellious teenager, or someone with pressing financial problems, we often end up disappointed, betrayed, and vowing never again to get involved.

When we pray for the mind of Christ, we need to understand that we are seeking to have the heart that will allow us to respond to others as Christ responds to us. If anyone had cause to be disappointed or discouraged by the conduct of another, think about all of the times we have disappointed Him, and be thankful that He never gives up on us and will never abandon us.

We should do good to others not because they are deserving or appreciative, but because Christ has been so good to us that we respond to His love by loving and helping others.

> ***"Beloved, if God so loved us, we also ought to love one another." 1 John 4:11***

When we realize that God cares and that whatever we do out of love for Him will never go unnoticed or unrewarded in due time, we can handle the disappointments that often come from doing good to others with the same grace with which Christ handles it when we disappoint Him.

**Father, help me keep from becoming weary in well doing. Amen.**

# *Hows your "ology" quotient?*

**"I was one of the most religious Jews of my own age, and I tried as hard as possible to follow all the old traditions of my religion." Galatians 1:14**

A lot of people seem to get their "ology's" mixed up. Methodology is not theology, but practice or tradition often seems to get confused with truth in a lot of churches and among a lot of Christians.

> ***"Sing to the LORD a new song. Sing His praises in the assembly of the faithful." Psalm 149:1b***

Before the Bible was available, Martin Luther spread the gospel by using it as lyrics sung to tunes of the popular bar songs of the day. This was his methodology of teaching theology.

Prior to World War II, there was great resistance among Lutherans in America to publish a hymnal in English instead of German, which is a good example of methodology taking precedence over theology. The Catholic celebration of the mass in Latin long after Latin became a dead language is another example of methodology getting in the way of theology.

Many churches today are dying out daily while others are growing in the same areas, many times because of the failure of tradition bound churches to change their methodology to make it relevant in today's world.

> ***"Don't let anyone lead you astray with empty philosophy and high-sounding nonsense that come from human thinking and from the evil powers of this world," Colossians 2:8***

The theology of divine truth should never change, because our God is a changeless God. The methodology of applying and celebrating divine truth must change with the environment of the times if the body of Christ is to continue to be the salt and the light of the world.

The traditions of the past can be appreciated and respected but should never be worshipped. We should never let the methodology of the scribes and Pharisees overshadow the theology of divine truth.

**Father, give me wisdom and spiritual discernment to know the difference between theology and methodology. Amen.**

**Read Romans 8, Psalm 10** **May 20**

# *Watch Out For Your Nature*

**"All of us used to live that way, following the passions and desires of our evil nature. We were born with an evil nature, and we were under God's anger just like everyone else." Ephesians 2:3**

When we don't believe in God, we don't believe that what He says is wrong is truly wrong, and we are free to wallow in the worst that our sinful natures can come up with.

> ***"They say to themselves, 'nothing bad will ever happen to us! We will be free of trouble forever!'" Psalm 10:6***

We can pursue all of the pleasures of the flesh, the approval of the world, and the influences of the devil. Without God, we answer the call of nature to live much like wild animals roaming through the jungle of life living on basic instincts.

Without God, we become our own gods and make our own judgments concerning approving or participating in things God specifically forbids, such as homosexuality, same-sex marriages, killing unborn babies, living together apart from marriage, and living the lie of relative truth.

When God sets us free from bondage to our sinful nature through giving us a new life in Christ He gives us a very sensitive instrument to gauge our conduct and our thinking. It's called a conscience.

Our conscience kicks in to convict us of our sinfulness and our need for a savior. The Holy Spirit who comes to live inside of us when we receive Jesus Christ as our Savior continues to develop our consciences to guide our paths and to keep us living in the freedom from sin that Christ died to give us.

> ***"That's why those who are still under the control of their sinful nature can never please God." Romans 8:8 NLT***

When we are abiding in Christ, we have the green light of a clear conscience that fills us with the peace and joy of the Lord which is what the abundant life is all about.

This conscience is designed to send out warnings to override the control of the calls of our sinful nature and give us the strength to overcome them. The more we grow into the fullness of Christ, the more strength we will receive to live a life fully pleasing to God.

**Father, keep my conscience clear that I may know the overflowing joy of peace in You. Amen.**

## *No Exemptions*

**"So He became their Savior. In all their affliction He was afflicted, And the Angel of His Presence saved them; in His love and in His pity He redeemed them; and He bore them and carried them." Isaiah 63:9**

David, "a man after God's own heart", was not exempt.

> ***"For you will rescue me from my troubles," Psalm 54:7aNLT***

Job, about whom God said, *"Have you noticed my servant Job? He is the finest man in all the earth—a man of complete integrity. He fears God and will have nothing to do with evil," (Job 1:8b NLT) was not exempt*

Jesus Christ, Son of God, Savior of the World, was not exempt. He was "*a man of sorrows, acquainted with grief." (Isaiah 53:3*)

It is not a question of if, but only when troubles will come. Troubles complete the trinity of three certainties– death, taxes, and troubles.

While none of us are immune to troubles, there is comfort in knowing that we can live through, above, and beyond them. Our Lord told us, *"In the world you will have troubles, but be of good cheer, I have overcome the world" (John 16:33b).*

The resurrection of Jesus is the proof that Jesus has overcome the world. And because He lives, we can face the troubles of today and tomorrow with the confidence that we too shall overcome this world and all of the pain and suffering it often brings.

The power that raised Christ from the dead is alive within us to claim by faith not to exempt us from trials and tribulations but to supply us with the strength and grace to endure and grow stronger through them.

> ***"For our light affliction, which is but for a moment, is working for us a far more exceeding and eternal weight of glory," 2 Corinthians 4:17***

We do have the one big exemption that we should never forget. We have received exemption from eternal death and received the blessed assurance of eternal life by faith in Jesus Christ as our Savior.

**Father, thank you for giving me the big exemption. Amen.**

**Read Mark 12:28-34, Psalm 60** **May 22**

## *How do You Smell Success?*

**"And walk in love, as Christ also has loved us and given Himself for us, an offering and a sacrifice to God for a sweet-smelling aroma." Ephesians 5:2**

Sweet smells do not necessarily come in perfume bottles and are often by-products of something else. One smell only lasts a few days, but it can cost up to $700 a month for 5 years. If someone could bottle and sell this perfume, they would make a fortune. In case you haven't figured the answer to this riddle, I am talking about that unique new car smell!

> ***"What I want instead is your true thanks to God; I want you to fulfill your vows to the Most High."***
> ***Psalm 50:14 NLT***

The Lord *"smelled a soothing aroma" (Genesis 8:21)* in the burnt offering of Noah. Sacrifices and burnt offerings were referred to as "fragrances of sweet aromas" throughout the Old Testament.

The immoral woman's anointing of Jesus with expensive perfume was not a sweet aroma because it was perfume, but because it was a gift of worship from the heart.

It's probably a good thing that no one has yet invented "smell a vision." With the stench of immorality, perversion, and wickedness filling the channels, we couldn't stand the smell.

Even the sweet smell of success can turn foul if it leads to pride and self centeredness.

> ***"And I know it is important to love Him with all my heart and all my understanding and all my strength, and to love my neighbors as myself. This is more important than to offer all of the burnt offerings and sacrifices required in the law."***
> ***Mark 12:33 NLT***

Today's sweetest aroma to God is the living sacrifice of thanksgiving and praise in lives lived out in obedience to the great commandment and the great commission, lives that respond in love to the one who first loved us.

Our Lord Jesus Christ was perhaps the most expensive perfume ever made. It cost Him His life to make a sweet-smelling aroma of sacrifice to God which covers the stench of our sins and gives us the sweet smell of righteousness in God's sight.

**Father, let my life have a sweet aroma of love for You. Amen.**

May 23 Read Hebrews 12:1-12, Psalm 19

## *Run Your Own Race!*

**"I have fought the good fight, I have finished the race, I have kept the faith. Finally, there is laid up for me the crown of righteousness, which the Lord, the righteous Judge, will give to me on that Day, and not to me only but also to all who have loved His appearing." 2 Timothy 4:7**

Most marathons not only give a trophy to the one who finishes first but often give a certificate of accomplishment to all who compete in and finish the race.

> *"It rejoices like a athlete eager to run the race."*
> *Psalm 19:5b NLT*

The good news of the Gospel is that we are all winners in Jesus Christ and receive our crown of righteousness just by participating by faith in His life, death, and resurrection.

The race of life on this earth begins when we receive Jesus Christ as Savior and ends when we cross the finish line and receive our victor's crown and eternal life from our Lord.

In the time in between, we are commanded not only to be disciples, but to make them, not only to follow Christ, but to imitate Him, and not to confuse self righteousness with Christ righteousness.

Because God has bought us with the blood of His only Son and does not want any of us to perish, he regenerates us into a new life under the power of the Holy Spirit, and He will see us safely through the pitfalls of sin, death, and destruction when our hearts and minds are fixed on him.

Each of us must run our own race of faith. No one can run our race for us, and we certainly cannot run someone else's race. Although we can and should be concerned about the ungodly, hell-bent race of destruction being run by others, we should never let this concern become self-righteous condemnation but rather persistent and fervent prayer to the only one who can work faith in the hearts of the unsaved and unregenerate.

> *"And let us run with endurance the race that God has set before us."*
> *Hebrews 12:1b NLT*

**Father, help me to run in the power that only a right relationship with You can provide. Amen.**

Read Galatians 5, Psalm 32 May 24

## *Need a Governor?*

**"Keep me from deliberate sins! Don't let them control me. Then I will be free of guilt and innocent of great sin." Psalm 19:13**

Governors not only head governments, but they are also devises that limit speeds on automobiles, motors, and engines that keep them from running too fast, burning out, or breaking down.

> ***"Do not be like a senseless horse or mule that needs a bit and bridle to keep it under control." Psalm 32:9 NLT***

They used to be in a lot of taxis, rental cars, and trucks. They are used in most power generators. They can be dangerous if you are trying to pass another car.

God has equipped every one of us with a governor. He is called the Holy Spirit, and He has been installed within us in order to guide us into all truth, pray for us constantly, recall all things to our remembrance, and to guarantee our safe arrival to our heavenly home.

When we are living on the fast lane and out of control, He will flip our guilt switch and use our conscience to bring us to a screeching halt and back into the Father's loving arms through confession and repentance.

If this doesn't work, He will do whatever else it takes to lovingly discipline us and bring us back under control. He makes the way of the transgressor very hard so that we will not want to exceed our safe operating speed.

> ***"But when the Holy Spirit controls our lives, He will produce this kind of fruit in us: love, joy, peace, patience, kindness, goodness, faithfulness, gentleness, and self-control. Here there is no conflict with the law." Galatians 5:22, 23 NLT***

Rather than look upon the limits that God sets through His law and His instructions as barriers, we should look upon them more as guide posts for enjoying all of the blessings that accompany obedience to Him and living in a close personal relationship with His son.

**Father, thank you for loving me enough to discipline me so that I not live out of control and out of fellowship with You. Amen.**

# *Where's Your Confidence?*

**"Do not throw away this confident trust in the Lord, no matter what happens. Remember the great reward it brings you! Patient endurance is what you need now, so you will continue to do God's will. Then you will receive all that He has promised." Hebrews 10:35, 36 NLT**

"Looking out for number one," "I did it my way," "Lord, it's hard to be humble when you're perfect in every way," might be good book or song titles, but they are bad theology for those who are hoping to see God.

> ***"The Lord will perfect that which concerneth me." Psalm 138:8***

As admirable as self reliance and the understanding that there is "no free lunch" are as character traits, they make trusting God's grace alone for salvation very difficult.

As great as self confidence is, it can't begin to compare to God confidence when it comes to eternity. Why in the world would anyone want to depend on what they have done or have resolved to do, instead of what the Lord has done and will do?

When we base our assurance of eternal life in heaven on our goodness and what we have done, we rob God of the glory that rightly belongs to Him as author and perfector of our faith.

Moses tried to claim some of God's glory for himself (Numbers 20:10-12) and was banned from entrance into the promised land. The devout and religious scribes and Pharisees dedicated their lives to keeping God's law and traditions, yet our Lord called them "white washed tombstones," "brood of vipers," and hypocrites.

> ***"We are confident of all this because of our great trust in God through Christ." 1 Corinthians 3:4 NLT***

May God forbid that we ever make light of the grace of God alone as our hope of glory or ever abuse the grace of God by living in willful disobedience to Him.

**Father, thank you that You covered me with the perfection of Your Son and His robe of righteousness that covers me. Amen.**

**Read Ephesians 4:17-31, Psalm 37** **May 26**

## *A Reminder at Every Intersection*

**"The secret *things belong* to the LORD our God, but those *things which are* revealed *belong* to us and to our children forever, that *we* may do all the words of this law." Deuteronomy 29:29**

Traffic lights and signs are an essential part of traffic safety all over the world. In addition to telling when to stop and when to go, they advise caution and warn of bridges being "slippery when wet," of lanes ending, and even dead end roads.

> ***"Stop your anger! Turn from your rage! Do not envy others—it only leads to harm." Psalm 37:8 NLT***

The knowledge, wisdom, and discernment to know when to stop, go, and when to proceed with caution in living life are essential qualities for getting through the many "dangers, toils, and snares" that lie before us and that will allow us to live life at its best.

Recognizing opportunities and pursuing them until something says stop has led to a lot of success in business and professions for millions of people. In the choice of a mate, failing to heed the go, stop, and caution signs is one of the biggest reasons divorce is rampant.

Scripture after Scripture stresses the importance of teaching our children the "rules of the road" so that they will not depart from them.

The commands on what to do are "go" signs that lead to enjoying the abundant life and the "future and the hope" that God wants for all of His children. There are no stop signs when it comes to loving God and loving others, and there are no limits on being filled with the Spirit.

> ***"With the Lord's authority let me say this: Live no longer as the ungodly do, for they are hopelessly confused." Ephesians 4:17 NLT***

The admonitions or the "stop" signs are not given to make us miserable but to let us enjoy the blessings of living in the peace and joy of the Lord. Not to lie, cheat, murder, steal, bear false witness, lust, envy, or otherwise harm our neighbors are just a few of the obvious "stop" signs or boundaries God has posted for the good of everyone.

God has even given us a "traffic cop" to teach and remind us of the "stop," "go," and "caution" signs of life. Are we paying attention?

**Father, help me to heed Your signals on the highway of life. Amen.**

 Read Philippians 4:6-9 Proverbs 4

# *The Flip Side*

**"Be on guard. Stand true to what you believe. Be courageous. Be strong. And everything you do must be done with love."**

**1 Corinthians 16:13 NLT**

In the old days of phonograph records you got only two songs – one on each side of the record. The best sellers were hits, and another usually nondescript song was included on the "flip side".

> ***"Above all else, guard your heart, for it affects everything you do."***
> ***Proverbs 4:23 NLT***

As believers, we often seem to have a "flip side." Who we are when we think nobody is looking is often a "flip side" that should be a cause for grave concern.

If we were to go out and ask our co-workers, class mates, play mates, fellow church members, and others with whom we have had associations or experiences, which side of our record of life would be revealed?

Oh would someone the gift give us to see ourselves as others see us! Our self image is often so different from the image we project to others, our talk is often so different from our walk; it's as though we are perceived as several different people depending on whom you ask and the circumstances involved.

Some advanced automatic record players of the old days were able to flip the record over and play the flip side.

Sometimes our flesh or the world tends to turn us over and let our "flip side" play out in ways that impugn our testimony, make us stumbling blocks, and give us the characteristics of hypocrites that we all despise.

Scripture tells us that it's what's inside that counts. *"A good man out of the good treasure of his heart brings forth good, and an evil man out of the evil treasure of his heart brings forth evil" (Luke 6:45a).*

> ***"His peace will guard your hearts and minds as you live in Christ Jesus."***
> ***Philippians 4:7b NLT***

The more our faith moves from our head to our heart, the more our "flip side" resembles our best side, and the more everyone will see us as the person recognized as an ambassador of Christ.

**Father, give me the strength of Your Spirit to be conformed without any shading into Christ's image inside out and outside in. Amen.**

Read James 1, Psalm 92 May 28

## *The Growth Pill Called Pain*

**"He cuts off every branch that doesn't produce fruit, and He prunes the branches that do bear fruit so they will produce even more." John 15:2**

Whether in plants, churches, or people, there is one universal growth principal of nature and of God that we all need to know. It is called pruning.

> ***"But the godly will flourish like palm trees and grow strong like the cedars of Lebanon." Psalm 92:12 NLT***

Any gardener or plant husbandry expert will tell you that you get bigger and better fruits or flowers by regularly pruning excess branches so that all of the nutrients from the soil, water, and air will be channeled into fewer branches.

Every church or body of believers is a living organism that will wither on the vine and eventually die out if all of the distractions and excess baggage of human agendas and self-centered motives are not cut out so that all of the talents and resources can be focused on the great commandment and the great commission.

In the journey of life of every believer, God's recipe for growing into the fullness of Christ will always include pruning. Before we can be "fruitful in every good work for which we were created," there are many excess branches that need to be trimmed or cut off so that we will be healthy and bear good fruit in abundance.

We believers need to understand and respond to the failures, disappointments, and heartaches of life with the joy of knowing that God is using them to develop our character as He conforms us into the image of Christ.

> ***"So let it grow, for when your endurance is fully developed, you will be strong in character and ready for anything." James 1:4 NLT***

Only the supernatural grace of God working through the power of the Holy Spirit can give us the grace and the peace to "count it all joy."

If our trouble is not a consequence of sin, we can be assured that it is God's character-building program at work within us, and we can have the joy and the peace that surpasses all understanding even in times of trouble.

**Father, give me the grace to "count it all joy." Amen.**

# *Are You Amply Wired?*

**"Though I am surrounded by troubles, You will preserve me against the anger of my enemies. You will clench your fist against my angry enemies! Your power will save me." Psalm 138:7 NLT**

Having ample electrical circuits has become an ever-increasing problem, especially for older houses built before the days of air conditioning, electric water heaters, heat pumps, etc.

> ***"You are their glorious strength. Our power is based on Your favor. yes, our protection comes from the LORD," Psalm 89:17 NLT***

Many older homes still have four or five circuits with old-fashioned fuses that often burn out and throw a room or house into total darkness.

Houses now come with 200 to 500 amp services in order to meet the demands of all the electrical appliances and fixtures.

People living in today's sin-sick, stress-filled world also have a problem in handling the overloads of life. Some psychiatrists use a 300 amp stress index limit for people's ability to cope with the traumas of life.

Divorce, death of a loved one, health issues, financial, and relational problems head the list of disasters that can pile up and cause a physical or emotional burnout or breakdown when the combination reaches or exceeds a score of 300.

Today's believers need to develop the character of the early martyrs who endured through the trials and tests of life by persevering and growing into the fullness of Christ through it all.

> ***"So humble yourselves under the mighty power of God, and in His good time He will honor you." 1 Peter 5:6 NLT***

It is only through growing into His fullness that we can really know that God's grace is all sufficient, that His strength is made perfect in our weaknesses, and that He does work all things to the good.

Just as a bigger electrical service increases our power capacity, a bigger faith honed and sharpened by persevering in the faith through the storms of life increases our comfort zone and capacity for living joyously and victoriously in today's world.

**Father, keep the power of the Holy Spirit flowing so that I don't have a short circuit or blow a fuse on my journey of life. Amen.**

**Read Hebrews 12:13-29, Psalm 1** **May 30**

## *Rand McNally Don't Publish This Map*

**"Stay on the path that the LORD your God has commanded you to follow. Then you will live long and prosperous lives in the land you are about to enter and occupy." Deuteronomy 5:33**

A road atlas is a handy thing to have when traveling, and I believe far superior to some of the computer print outs that seem to get me mixed up at times. It sure beats stopping to ask for directions which are often confusing and often wrong.

> ***"For the LORD watches over the path of the godly, but the path of the wicked leads to destruction." Psalm 1:6***

The road of life can often be a nightmare to travel, especially without a map. There are detours, bridges out, dead ends, breaks in pavement, and even mine fields that can cause major problems for the uninformed and unsuspecting traveler.

Before we can plan a route, we need to have a destination or some idea of where we are going.

Some set their sights on happiness as defined by the world's standards and go down paths that lead only to misery and suffering. Some choose short cuts that will cut short any hope of reaching their destination all in one piece.

Scripture tells us, "*There is a way that seems right to a man, but its end is the way of death" (Proverbs 14:12).* If we go through life flying by the "seat of our pants," navigating by relative truth, and doing whatever feels good, we can be sure that our ultimate destination will be the "lake of fire."

God sent His only Son to show the way and give us a light and a path to glory and the destination of eternal life. He tells us how to be blessed and how to be accursed.

> ***"Mark out a straight path for your feet." Hebrews 12:13a: NLT***

He tells us the secret of real joy and real happiness that can never be achieved apart from Him. Oh that we might pay attention to Him and the truth and the way He teaches that leads to eternal life to its fullest for now and forever.

**Father, help me to follow Jesus along the paths of righteousness until I am safely home. Amen.**

# Our Worst Enemy

**"For we do not wrestle against flesh and blood, but against principalities, against powers, against the rulers of the darkness of this age, against spiritual *hosts* of wickedness in the heavenly places."** ***Ephesians 6:12***

"I wouldn't wish this even on my worst enemy" is a familiar saying to many. "He's his own worst enemy" is a much more common and much truer statement.

> ***"They wear pride like a jeweled necklace," Psalm 73:6 NLT***

When we think of enemies, we automatically start thinking about people we have been or are in conflict with, people who have harmed or offended us in some way, or people who we perceive to be evil. During war, the enemy is the soldiers and forces of the opposing country or faction.

When St. Paul speaks of "principalities and powers of darkness" and "spiritual hosts of wickedness in heavenly places," he is pointing out that there are demons under the control of satan who are out to defeat Christ's church and to turn us away from Him and back to sin.

When we think of enemies, we need to think of the enemies lurking within us that are always a very real and present danger. Our own flesh, the world, and satan are at work to bring us down to the depths of depression, defeat, and despair so that we might be tempted to "curse God and die."

To refuse to acknowledge and believe in the existence of these enemies is a sure recipe for disaster. The pride of the flesh has caused more people to fall short of the salvation and love of God than anything. Pride always has and always will lead to a fall.

Pride will keep us from acknowledging that we need a Savior. It will keep us from admitting our sins and from forgiving others. It will lead to adopting the idolatry of the world in worshipping self, money, fame, applause, and pleasure. It is most often the devil's weapon of choice against us.

> ***"God resists the proud, but gives grace to the humble." 1 Peter 5:5***

**Father, help me to recognize my greatest enemy, and to claim You as my sure defense. Amen.**

**Read Romans 8:28-39, Psalm 51** **June 1**

# *Not Only*

**"Do not throw away this confident trust in the Lord, no matter what happens. Remember the great reward it brings you! Patient endurance is what you need now, so you will continue to do God's will. Then you will receive all that he has promised." Hebrews 35, 36 NLT**

This is hard for many people to comprehend, but God not only promises that He will never leave nor forsake us but also promises that if we are truly His, we will never forsake Him.

***"The sacrifices of God are a broken spirit, a broken and a contrite heart- these, O God, You will not despise."***
***Psalm 51:19***

When we receive Jesus Christ as our Savior, we also receive the fullness of the Holy Spirit as a guarantee that *"He who has begun a good work in you will complete it until the day of Jesus Christ" (Philippians 1:6).*

Jesus said, *"My sheep hear My voice, and I know them, and they follow Me. And I give them eternal life, and they shall never perish; neither shall anyone snatch them out of My hand" (John 10:27).*

We may stumble and fall and succumb to the temptations of the flesh and of the devil from time to time, but if we are truly saved, we can be sure that God will never allow us to perish by forsaking Him.

If we persist in intentional and deliberate sins, we at some point have to ask whether we were truly saved. We know from Scripture that all who call Jesus Lord are not saved.

One of the most hurtful darts of satan is the one making us doubt our salvation when we sin. As long as we have godly sorrow and the cleansing of confession and repentance, we can be sure that we are saved and that God loves us, forgives us, and accepts us, not because of our sins, but in spite of them– not on what we did or didn't do but on what Christ did for us.

***"And I am convinced that nothing can ever separate us from His love. Death can't, and life can't. The angels can't, and the demons can't. Our fears for today, our worries about tomorrow, and even the powers of hell can't keep God's love away."***
***Romans 8:38 NLT***

**Father, let me know the security of Your love. Amen.**

# *The Believers R & R's*

**"Don't try to avoid responsibility by saying you didn't know about it. For God knows all hearts, and He sees you. He keeps watch over your soul, and He knows you knew!" Proverbs 24:12 NLT**

We hear a lot more about rights than about responsibilities these days. We have civil rights, women's rights, welfare rights, arms rights, property rights, etc.

> ***For you have heard my vows, O God. You have given me an inheritance reserved for those who fear Your name."***
> ***Psalm 61:5 NLT***

Seldom do we hear about any kind of responsibility coming with rights. As long as we maintain the self-centered, self-interest focus of the world and the flesh, we are not going to worry about being responsible.

As believers, we have tremendous rights covenanted by God. We have the right to live free from bondage of any kind, the right to live transformed lives to their fullest, and the right to be called the children of God.

We have not been given the right to be free from the penalty of sin in order to sin more but to sin less. We have not been given freedom from want in order to want more, but in order to give more. We have not been given the freedom to bear arms in order to murder others but to protect ourselves. A woman's right to choose should never be construed as the right to kill.

> ***"If your gift is to encourage others, do it! If you have money, share it generously. If God has given you leadership ability, take the responsibility seriously."***
> ***Romans 12:8 NLT***

When "me, me, me" is replaced by "He, He, He," something wonderful happens. Our rights become privileges to be used and enjoyed in the ways that God intended as we live out lives of stewardship and accountability to God for the way we use everything that He has given us.

Our rights become His rights, as He bought us with the price of His dear Son. Our responsibility becomes to respond to His love with our love lived out in a life where we do all the good works for which He ordained for us before we were even born.

**Father, keep me ever mindful of the responsibility I have to be a good steward of all that You have given me. Amen.**

Read Colossians 1:12-23, Psalm 105 June 3

# *Plan Ahead*

**"But I punish the children for the sins of their parents to the third and fourth generations. But I lavish My love on those who love Me and obey My commands, even for a thousand generations." Exodus 20:5 NLT**

In our self-centered, self-seeking world, we too often fail to give any thought to the influence of our lives on succeeding generations.

> ***"And He remembers, remembers His Covenant— for a thousand generations. He's been as good as His word."***
> ***Psalm 105:8 MSG***

When we think of an inheritance we generally think of some money, heirlooms, or property that a parent or close relative leave us when they die.

We provide for these gifts by writing wills. We can even write wills leaving our vital organs for medical science or for transplant to others.

We often never think of or pay much attention to the consequences of our sins on unborn generations.

As a nation, we are leaving a national debt that will burden generations to come and an environment that has been scarred and polluted in many ways.

Millions are dooming unborn generations to the ravages of birth defects caused by substance abuse, addictions, and promiscuous sexual activity.

As parents, we are too often breaking the covenants of God by disobedience and sin and thus cutting off future generations from covenant blessings.

> ***"Always thanking the Father, who has enabled you to share the inheritance that belongs to God's holy people, who live in the light."***
> ***Colossians 1:12-21 NLT***

Instead of teaching a child the way of walking in the Lord, we are by example teaching the way of walking in the flesh and in the ways of the world, and succeeding generations will pay the price.

**Father, help me to be aware of my responsibility to unborn generations to come so that they do not get shut off from your glorious promises. Amen**

June 4 Read Romans 12:9-31, Psalm 24

## *Show and Tell*

**"Woe to you, scribes and Pharisees, hypocrites! For you are like whitewashed tombs which indeed appear beautiful outwardly, but inside are full of dead men's bones and all uncleanness." Matthew 23:27**

There is often a wide gap between what we say and what we do. Children are often told "don't do as I do, do as I say," when they question things like why do I have to go to Sunday school when you don't go to church, or what's wrong with me having casual sex when you have a live-in boyfriend or girlfriend?

***"He who has clean hands and a pure heart," Psalm 24:4***

Our Lord, who is love personified, seems to have reserved His greatest anger and distaste for the scribes and Pharisees who taught the law and gave outward obedience to it but whose hearts were corrupt and full of hypocrisy.

"White washed tombstones," "serpents, brood of vipers," and blind were some of the words used by our Lord in confronting and exposing hypocrites. One of the definitions of hypocrite in Greek is actor.

We are all actors at some time or another. Often, we even deceive ourselves.

When people start talking about what great Christians they are, it is often a good time to be wary. Real Christianity is not nearly as much about talking the talk as it is about walking the walk.

When we show God's love to others by the way we treat others, when we show God's joy by being cheerful, His mercy by being merciful, and His forgiveness by forgiving, we don't need to talk about what great Christians we are. Our actions will show it.

***"Don't just pretend that you love others. Really love them. Hate what is wrong. Stand on the side of the good." Romans 12:9***

**Father, guard my heart against deceit and hypocrisy. Let my life show the genuineness of my love for You, and the reality of Your presence living within me. Amen.**

Read Hebrews 13, Psalm 73 June 5

# The Gong Show

**"Through the LORD's mercies we are not consumed, because His compassions fail not." Lamentations 3:22 NLT**

There was a short-lived TV show in the 70's where contestants would be allowed to perform until getting "gonged" and cut off at anytime. Most of the contestants were pretty terrible and deserved to get the gong, but it was actually kind of cruel to try to entertain us at the expense of the inept performances of others.

> ***"My health may fail, and my spirit may grow weak, but God remains the strength of my heart; He is mine forever." Psalm 73:26***

In many ways, life in this world is kind of like the gong show. Some of our loftiest dreams and highest ambitions often get "gonged."

Athletic abilities some times get gonged by injury. Dreams of becoming a doctor or an astronaut often get gonged by the lack of money for training, lack of ability, or lack of talent.

Some marriages end up with one partner getting gonged by the other for any number of reasons.

All of us have or will have experienced the gong of failure in some manner or another during the course of our lives. We may get gonged financially, relationally, physically, or mentally sometimes in spite of our best efforts, often as consequences of our worst efforts.

Many times we get gonged by circumstances over which we have absolutely no control.

The good news is that these gongs are not fatal, that God can (and often does) turn what we perceive to be bad to good. His promises to never forsake us, to supply our every need, and to provide His all-sufficient grace to cover our weaknesses and failures are promises that can never be gonged.

He promises to gong the devil himself and cause him to flee when we stand firm and resist with the full armor of God.

> ***"That is why we can say with confidence, 'The Lord is my helper, so I will not be afraid. What can mere mortals do to me?'" Hebrews 13:6 NLT***

**Father, thank you for teaching, strengthening, and drawing me closer to You through the "gongs" of my life. Amen.**

# *Sweeter Than Honey*

**"They are sweeter than honey, even honey dripping from the comb. They are a warning to those who hear them; there is great reward for those who obey them." Psalm 19:10b, 11 NLT**

The great reward for those who keep the commandments is not eternal life. Heaven is a free gift earned for us on the cross of Calvary by the perfect sacrifice of Jesus Christ for our sins.

> ***"How sweet are Your words to my taste; they are sweeter than honey." Psalm 119:103***

According to verse 8 of Psalm 19, we are given great joy as a reward for obedience.

Simply put, when we do the right thing, we experience the joy of the Lord. Real joy is guilt-free joy, and we can only live guilt free through obedience to the laws of life that God has ordained for our good.

*"For I know the plans I have for you, declares the LORD, plans to prosper you and not to harm you, plans to give you hope and a future" (Jeremiah 29:11).*

Faith is the key to pleasing God and enjoying the fullness of His delight in us. *"But without faith it is impossible to please Him, for he who comes to God must believe that He is, and that He is a rewarder of those who diligently seek Him" (Hebrews 11:6).*

When our conduct fails to measure up to God's standards, we must have faith in the fact that He will forgive when we come to Him with a broken spirit and contrite heart confessing and turning away from our sins.

God knew that we would never be able to achieve the perfection that His justice requires. This is why He sent us a Savior so that He could forgive us all our sins and the Holy Spirit so that we can have the strength to cover our weaknesses and live lives of obedience.

> ***"Live a life filled with love for others, following the example of Christ." Ephesians 5:2 NLT***

We all need to constantly ask ourselves: "What do I need to do to enjoy the great rewards of obedience?"

**Father, help me to find the real joy of living within the boundaries of Your will. Amen.**

**Read Romans 6 Psalm 44** **June 7**

# *Emergency Power Source*

**"For the Kingdom of God is not just fancy talk; it is living by God's power." 1 Corinthians 4:20 NLT**

> ***"It was by Your mighty power that they succeeded; it was because You favored them and smiled on them:" Psalm 44:3 NLT***

Portable power generators sell like popcorn before every impending hurricane. Hospitals, airports, and many other buildings and businesses spend billions installing emergency power generators to use in case of primary power failure.

As good as these alternatives may be in providing emergency back up power, they can't begin to compare with the emergency power source believers have in the resurrection power of God.

This resurrection power comes with the indwelling presence of the Holy Spirit and has never been known to fail. This power turned defeated and dejected disciples into the transformers of the world as God gave them the power to preach, witness, perform miracles, and spread the Gospel throughout the known world. They were able to consider it all joy to suffer persecution and martyrdom for the cause of Christ.

As great as this power is for emergencies, it was never intended to be merely a back up source to our own strength and reason. It has been given as a basic, everyday, always available, primary source of empowerment for living out our lives growing into the fullness of Christ.

The power that brought us into saving faith is the power that will keep us there. It is that "very present help in time of trouble," our "bridge over troubled waters," that will transform us into the likeness of Christ by the renewing of our minds.

> ***"And just as Christ was raised from the dead by the glorious power of the Father, now we also may live new lives." Romans 6:4b NLT***

Our power source needs constant refueling from the Word of God, prayer, and the fellowship of other believers in order to have sufficient reserve power during peak demands. Are you "plugged in"?

**Father, thank you for giving me the faith to appropriate the power of your presence and the truth of your promises into my every day life. Amen.**

# *Believe What You Know!*

**"But as for me, I know that my Redeemer lives, and that He will stand upon the earth at last. And after my body has decayed, yet in my body I will see God! I will see Him for myself. Yes, I will see Him with my own eyes." Job 19:25-27 NLT**

Someone once said, "If you don't know what you stand for, you're liable to fall for anything." If your faith is not backed by knowing the inerrant truth of God's Word, it is very easy to fall prey to the wolves in sheep's clothing who seek to mislead with false or half-truths that attempt to rob you of your joy and cause you to doubt your salvation in Christ.

> ***"I know the LORD is always with me. I will not be shaken, for He is right beside me." Psalm 16:8 NLT***

As you believe more of what you know an amazing thing happens. You also begin to know who you believe better and can say with Paul, *"For I know whom I have believed and am persuaded that He is able to keep what I have committed to Him until that Day" (1 Timothy 1:12b).*

We often become penitent and receive Christ as our Savior long before we become proficient in our knowledge of Him. The essence of our new life in Christ is to get to know Him better, day by day, week by week, and year by year so that we might grow into His fullness.

We do this by abiding in Him through His Word, prayer, and through fellowship with other believers.

> ***"Since you don't know who I am, you don't know who my Father is. If you knew me, then you would know my Father, too." John 8:19b NLT***

As we get to know Jesus better, we learn to see Him more in the lives of other people through circumstances and by experiencing His love, His grace, and especially His peace more and more.

There is no greater joy than knowing Christ in His fullness as we grow in Him.

**Father, thank You for working belief in my heart by the power of Your Spirit. Help me to know what I know and what I believe more everyday. Amen.**

Read Ephesians 6:11-18, Psalm 38 June 9

# *Have You Ever Been to "Big D"*

Dallas is big, but it's not even close to being one of the really "big D's."

> ***"Those who seek my hurt speak of destruction and plan deception all the day long." Psalm 38:12***

The darts of Satan are the really big D's. They often have more deadly poison than the pygmies' blow gun darts.

Satan's favorite darts of deception, denial, doubt, and defeat can stun, stop, and absolutely wreck families, lives and relationships.

We underestimate, ignore or dismiss satanic power at our own peril. Although the war has been won, the battles rage on and the principalities and powers of evil are committed to continue inflicting as much damage as possible.

Eve was the first victim of satan's deception, and everyone ever since has and will be, at some time or another, deceived by the master of deceit.

Usually the evil one sends denial along with deceit, making us blind to the truth and easy prey when we are attacked at our weakest moments in our most vulnerable areas.

Doubt is probably one of the cruelest and most destructive ploys used within the body of Christ and without. To have people thinking they are not healed because they don't have enough faith or that they are not saved if they do not have some of the extraordinary gifts are two of the cruelest doubts satan uses to create in the hearts of believers.

> ***"Put on the whole armor of God that you may be able to stand against the wiles of the devil." Ephesians 6:11 NLT***

When doubt makes us wonder if we are really saved or if God really loves us, we fall into despair and distress that robs us of our peace and joy.

Praise God that, in His love, He has given us a protector and the armor we need to withstand all of these "big D's."

Truth, righteousness, salvation, the shield of faith, and the sword of the Spirit will help us win the battles. We need to put these on with the rest of our clothes daily.

**Father, keep me aware of the real and present danger that satan is real and seeking to destroy me. Amen.**

June 10 Read John 8:43-47, Psalm 68

## *Children of a Lesser God*

**"Behold what manner of love the Father has bestowed on us, that we should be called children of God!" 1 John 3:1**

Why, oh why, would anyone choose anything less than the best? When Jesus stands at the door and knocks, why, oh why, do we choose to remain children of lesser gods?

> ***"A father of the fatherless, a defender of widows, is God in His holy habitation." Psalm 68:3***

Like new born kittens, we are also born blind, but unfortunately, ours is a spiritual blindness that keeps us in darkness with a genetic defect called sin. Unlike the kitten, whose eyes will open naturally, our spiritual eyes can only be opened by the supernatural work of God through His Holy Spirit. Until we choose to open that door of faith when Jesus knocks, we are doomed to live as children of darkness.

Unless we become the sons and daughters of God that we were created to be in Christ, we will spend meaningless lives worshipping at the throne of Baal, living self-centered lives driven by the idolatry of worshipping the lesser gods of pleasure, possessions, power, envy, anger, or pride.

If we choose to remain worshippers of a lesser god, we are going to miss out on the true pleasures, possessions, and powers that only worshipping the one true God can give.

Only when we abide in faith under the shadow of the wings of the real living God, can we enjoy the true pleasure of life in its fullness. Only when Jesus Christ becomes alive in our hearts can we possess the real treasures of love, joy, and peace. Only when the Holy Spirit brings the power of the resurrection into our lives can we find the power for living victoriously in a sin-sick world surrounded by darkness and evil.

> ***"He who is of God hears God's words; therefore you do not hear, because you are not of God." John 8:48***

Is there any area of your life where you are choosing to worship less than the best?

**Father, thank you for opening my eyes to the wonders of Your love, the riches of Your grace and the joy of knowing the one true God. Amen.**

Read Galatians 4:23-33, Psalm 66 June 11

## *Fulfillment Centers*

**"You who by orders from heaven have now heard for yourselves—through the Holy Spirit—the message of those prophecies fulfilled. Do you realize how fortunate you are? 1 Peter 1:10 MSG**

Fulfillment centers are a billion-dollar business. Most of our rebate applications go to rebate fulfillment centers. About everything we order on an 800 line or the internet are shipped from fulfillment centers. My experience with a lot of rebate fulfillment centers is that they seem to do everything possible to keep from paying that rebate.

> ***"We went through fire and through water; But You brought us out to rich fulfillment." Psalm 66:12***

Isn't it good to know that we have a God who established the ultimate fulfillment center in Jesus Christ? Think about it! Jesus came to fulfill prophecies made centuries before, to fulfill the law, to bring reconciliation with God by faith, and to fulfill our deepest needs and yearnings for real security, significance, and peace of mind.

When we make Jesus the center of our lives, we become totally fulfilled in Him. God has reserved a special place in the hearts of all whom He fills with the indwelling presence of the Holy Spirit when we receive Jesus as our Lord and Savior.

We find all of our needs fulfilled. We find grace sufficient for our every need. We become filled with incredible joy in the love of the Lord. We receive the resurrection power that makes God's strength perfect in our weakness.

Best of all, we experience the love of God that is the perfect fulfillment of the law. We not only receive it; we are commanded to give it both to God and to our fellow man by giving our time, talents, and resources to the glory of God and the up building of His kingdom. Have you been fulfilled?

> ***"But the son of the freeborn wife was born as God's own fulfillment of His promise." Galatians 4:23b NLT***

**Jesus, thank you for fulfilling the law for me so that I can be fulfilled by faith in You. Amen.**

June 12 Read 2 Corinthians 5, Psalm 90

## *Perfect Timing*

**"There is a time for everything, a season for every activity under heaven." Ecclesiastes 3:1 NLT**

> ***"Teach us to make the most of our time, so that we may grow in wisdom."***
> ***Psalm 90:12 NLT***

God is timeless and eternal, and we will be also when we get to heaven. Meanwhile, we live lives greatly controlled by time and due dates.

April 15 looms big for some people every year. Other tax due dates, insurance and license renewal dates, and homework assignments loom large for others.

Only God keeps perfect time as He keeps time with perfect timing. Unfortunately, we are not privy to all of the higher thoughts and higher ways of God. This leads us to make a lot of false assumptions regarding God's timing.

We are often surprised, perplexed, frustrated, and disappointed with God's timing because it does not mesh with our perspectives.

The call to salvation is a due date we don't want to miss. The penalties for late filing can be painful and severe. God is going to do everything possible to bring us in a faith relationship with Him through His Son, and the longer we put it off, the more severe the consequences in most cases.

We thank God that He is longsuffering, patient, and full of mercy and compassion. It is a mistake to presume that He is going to let us go past due forever.

There are days of repentance, good works, loving others, and spreading the Gospel, and we too often let these due dates come and go without a thought.

> ***"We grow weary in our present bodies, and we long for the day when we will put on our heavenly bodies like new clothing."***
> ***2 Corinthians 5:2 NLT***

The due date for our arrival in heaven is the date that seldom has any extensions or grace periods. We may want to go early to avoid troubles or for other selfish reasons. It is best to trust in the "perfect timing" of God and to let Him say of our pain and suffering, "It is enough."

**Father, keep me ever mindful of Your perfect timing. Amen.**

Read Jude 1:21-25, Psalm 84

June 13

## *Federal Withholding Taxes*

**"I tell you, use your worldly resources to benefit others and make friends. In this way, your generosity stores up a reward for you in heaven." Luke 16:9 NLT**

The genius who started the withholding of income and payroll taxes in 1943 deserves a spot in the bureaucratic hall of fame, if there is one. Before this bright idea came along during World War II, people just blithely ignored filing returns and paying taxes. This innovation revolutionized our government.

> ***"The LORD will give grace and glory; no good thing will He withhold from those who walk uprightly." Psalm 84:11 NLT***

Although God will not withhold any good thing from those who do right, Scripture is very clear that He does withhold some rewards until we get to heaven. He says that those who pray in public, and those who do good works in public in order to get praise from men are going to get only that. However, those who do these things in secret will get rewards from God.

We could learn a lot about storing up treasures in heaven from the governments payroll deduction idea. Instead of putting it into the bank or spending it on, wood, hay, and stubble that has no lasting value, we should think about making regular deposits of our time, talents, and treasures into God's bank account. This will assure that we don't get overcome by greed or destroyed by selfishness.

We should never give to get or get the idea that we can earn our way to heaven. Heaven is a free gift that we cannot buy or earn. We receive eternal life by God's grace. We should always give in gratitude for this marvelous gift God has given us.

> ***"Live in such a way that God's love can bless you as you wait for the eternal life that our Lord Jesus Christ in His mercy is going to give you." Jude 1:21 NLT***

The rewards that God promises when we give has nothing to do with where we are going, but may have a lot to do with what we will be doing when we get there. How much is in your heavenly withholding account?

**Father, may my heart yearn to hear Your "well done," and may my offerings of my life be acceptable to You. Amen.**

# *Is God a Legalist?*

**"The thief comes only to steal and kill and destroy; I have come that they may have life, and have it to the full. I am the Good Shepherd. The Good Shepherd lays down his life for the sheep." John 10:10, 11**

Where does anyone get the idea that God is a kill joy? Nothing could be further from the truth. Rather than rob us of joy and pleasure, God's moral code is designed to lead us to know joy to the fullest.

***"Those who are wise will take all this to heart; they will see in our history the faithful love of the LORD." Psalm 107:43 NLT***

In the area of sexuality, university studies show that people who live out their sexuality God's way report 39% higher sexual enjoyment, far fewer divorces, and far fewer problems with adultery, disease, and guilt.

When it comes to enjoying life to its fullest, Jesus reminds us that He is the way, the truth, and the life. Financial wealth has no real value apart from a close personal relationship with Jesus Christ. Jesus said, "*Yes, a person is a fool to store up earthly wealth but not have a rich relationship with God" (Luke 12:21 NLT).*

If we parents, being evil, try to protect our children by setting limits for them, how much more does our Heavenly Father protect us by providing us with a moral code designed to help us live life to the fullest God's way.

***"But if you keep looking steadily into God's perfect law—the law that sets you free—and if you do what it says and don't forget what you heard, then God will bless you for doing it." James 1:25 NLT***

God blesses us when we are meek, humble, and pure in heart, when we thirst after righteousness, and when we are peacemakers.

Would a kill joy come to earth as a man, live a perfect life, and suffer the torments of hell in order that we might escape the torments of hell?

**Father, thank you for loving me enough to not only die for me but to show me how to live life to the fullest in Your peace and joy. Amen.**

# *Quit Your Bellyaching!*

**"Is that grounds for complaining that God is unfair? Not so fast, please. God told Moses, "I'm in charge of mercy. I'm in charge of compassion. Romans 9:14 MSG**

Complaining and murmuring seem to be a given in the flesh of fallen man. When our comfort zones get squeezed, our whining and righteous indignation too often pours out.

> ***"Then all the people began weeping aloud, and they cried all night. Their voices rose in a great chorus of complaint against Moses and Aaron." Numbers 14:1 NLT***

How could God be so unfair? How could God be so cruel? How can this possibly be working for my good? Many other similar questions distract and send us down depression avenue to the big pity party at heart break hotel.

Discipline and what we perceive to be personal disasters are always painful at the time. Even though we may know how God tells us to respond to them, it is easy to be overwhelmed and overcome by doubt and despair.

God would not have sent us the Comforter if we were not going to need comfort. We cannot share in God's joy unless we share in His sorrow. We are never going to suffer anything as bad as He suffered. When we rejoice in our suffering, the comfort of the Holy Spirit comes to ease our pain, encourage us with our hope that is in Christ, and remind us of the wonderful promises of God that we know that He is going to keep.

The valleys of tears provide the moisture for the mountains of joy that will follow. We can be sure that one of these days, we will be able to look back and see how God has turned evil into good, doubt into confidence, and worry into peace.

> ***"In everything you do, stay away from complaining and arguing, so that no one can speak a word of blame against you." Philippians 2:14 NLT***

The idea that rejoicing is the proper response to problems is beyond human reason. This is why God reminded us that His ways are higher than our ways. We need to always remember that "Father knows best!"

**Father, help me to seek Your perspective and Your purposes under the piles of garbage and hurts of life. Amen.**

# *Remedial Math*

**"Will a man rob God? Yet you have robbed Me! But you say, 'In what way have we robbed You?'" Malachi 3:8**

It is absolutely amazing at how precise some people get in tipping a waitress 15 percent. Some pull out their calculators to get the exact amount. I believe it true to say that most everyone feels like they have to tip.

***"May He remember all your gifts and look favorably on your burnt offerings." Psalm 20:3 NLT***

This brings up the question of how precise we are in "tipping" God. Do we use the same calculation? Is our standard 10 or 15 percent or more like the national average of less than 2%? (I heard someone say that they tithed by throwing all their money in the air and letting God keep what He wanted, and he took what fell back down.)

Of all the areas of life where God most often gets stiff armed, giving is probably at the top of the list for most.

"'T*ry Me now in this,' says the* L*ORD of hosts, 'If I will not open for you the windows of heaven and pour out for you such blessing That there will not be room enough to receive it. And I will rebuke the devourer for your sakes, So that he will not destroy the fruit of your ground, nor shall the vine fail to bear fruit for you in the field,'" (Malachi 10b-11).*

Any abundance we have comes from God "so that we can be generous on all occasions." God doesn't honor any gifts given grudgingly. God loves a cheerful giver!

***"Now I want you to excel also in this gracious ministry of giving. I am not saying you must do it, even though the other churches are eager to do it. This is one way to prove your love is real." 2 Corinthians 8:7b, 8 NLT***

Do we really want to test God and receive the same percentage of grace and mercy that is expressed in the percentage of our giving to Him? God doesn't need our money; He wants our hearts. Our joy, generosity, and giving is the bell weather of how much of our heart God has.

Is it time for a little refresher course in tithing?

**Father, no matter how hard we might try, we can never out give you! Help me to practice first fruit giving to You. Amen.**

Read John 17, Psalm 9

June 17

## *What You Don't Know Won't Hurt You*

**"By humility and the fear of the LORD are riches and honor and life." Proverbs 22:4**

Whoever made up this saying obviously was not thinking straight. Not knowing that electricity can kill you can kill you. Not knowing that fire can burn you can cause you to get burned.

> ***"And those who know Your name will put their trust in You;"***
> ***Psalm 9:10***

Not knowing that something is against the law can land you in jail, as ignorance of the law is no excuse. God gave us the law to teach us the difference between right and wrong and to convict us of our sinfulness and need for a Savior.

Our favor with God is dependent upon knowing that He exists and that He is a rewarder of those who seek Him. These rewards include the gift of salvation and eternal life. The blessings of obedience are dependent upon our knowing what God requires of us.

To know God is to love Him and to live in the light of His love. Not to know Him is to live in darkness and without hope of anything beyond the "sweet tarts" of sin that might seem pleasant for a moment, but that will eventually turn bitter and end in death.

Knowing that we have a future and a hope that it is fulfilled in a personal relationship with a living, personal Savior lightens the darkness, overcomes fears and doubts, and gives us Jesus' joy, His friendship, and His love.

Knowing what Jesus did allows us to know what He would do in any given situation and gives us guidance for our lives as we seek to become imitators of Christ.

> ***"And this is eternal life, that they may know You, the only true God, and Jesus Christ whom You have sent."***
> ***John 17:3***

Knowing the fear of the Lord is only the beginning. Knowing the heart of the Lord should be the ultimate goal of every believer. There is really no bliss in the ignorance of not knowing God.

**Father, help me to be diligent in Your Word so that I may know You better. Amen.**

June 18 Read Romans 12, Psalm 116:12-19

## *Does God Deserve Our Leftovers?*

**"It is possible to give freely and become more wealthy, but those who are stingy will lose everything." Proverbs 11:24**

I believe that it was Chuck Swindoll who told the story of a little old lady who donated her used tea bags to be sent to a missionary. Before we start feeling that hypocritical glory about how good we are because at least we gave something better than that, we had best think about what leftovers we are giving God.

> ***"What can I offer the LORD for all He has done for me?" Psalm 116:12***

In the area of finances, are we giving first fruits or leftovers? Are we like the man who threw all his money in the air and told God to take what He wanted and he would keep the rest? Do we realize that every thing we have is on loan from God, and He has given specific instructions on how we are to manage our money? Do we really want to take a chance on being called robbers by God?

How about the stewardship of our time? God has put us on earth to do the things He planned for us before we were even born. We are told to manage until He returns. What portion of the hours, days, weeks, months, or years God gives us do we give to serving Him and being fruitful in good works? Does our time in ministry and in the Word indicate that God is number one in our lives and in our hearts?

What God-given talents do we hide or hoard that God could use to build up His kingdom and receive as an acceptable sacrifice?

> ***"And so, dear brothers and sisters, I plead with you to give your bodies to God. Let them be a living and holy sacrifice—the kind He will accept. When you think of what He has done for you, is this too much to ask?" Romans 12:1 NLT***

We would never even think of serving leftovers at a banquet for anyone. Unlike the little old lady with the tea bags, we need to be ever mindful of to whom we are giving, serving, and living for. God is always looking at our hearts for evidence that He is number one in them, with no other gods or priorities before Him.

**Father, in the power of Your Spirit, help me to give You the first and the best in every area of my life. Amen.**

**Read Matthew 25, Psalm 83** **June 19**

# *Positive, But Not Presumptive*

**"Therefore, brethren, be even more diligent to make your call and election sure, for if you do these things you will never stumble." 2 Peter 1:10**

> ***"That they may know that You, whose name alone is the LORD, are the Most High over all the earth." Psalm 83:18***

What a joy to know– not hope or think– that our Redeemer lives! John 20 tells us that the Bible has been written so that we may know that we have eternal life in Christ.

This is the blessed assurance that gives hope when things seem hopeless, perseverance through pain and suffering, and joy even through sorrow.

Knowing that our Redeemer lives is knowing that peace that surpasses all understanding and knowing that we have a future and a bright hope for the future that Jesus has gone to prepare for us. Knowing that our Redeemer lives is knowing that His promises are sure, that He will do what He says He will do, and that He has never broken a promise.

On the other hand, we need to be sure that we are not presumptuous in assuming that we know that our Redeemer lives. We need to have the evidence of a new birth to validate the sureness of our hope. We need to know our Redeemer and what He did, so we can know God through Him.

Scripture clearly tells us that faith without evidence of works is dead. If our Redeemer lives, He is living within us through the Holy Spirit giving us a new heart and a new passion to live lives fully pleasing to Him.

We need to read Matthew 25 very carefully. It gives us guidelines for separating obedient followers from pretenders and presumers. Just as Scripture tells us that not everyone who calls Jesus Lord is saved, it also makes it very clear that obedience has rewards that have nothing to do with our destination but a lot to do with what we are going to be doing when we get there.

> ***"But he answered and said, assuredly, I say to you, I do not know you." Matthew 25:12***

We are all works in progress. Let's progress in growing into the fullness of Christ, and always remember that we will know we are Christians by our love.

**Father, just as I know that You live, I know that I have a long way to go in living in You to the fullest. Help me live in You more by the power of the Holy Spirit living within me. Amen.**

# Just A Little Bit More

**"O God, I beg two favors from You before I die. First, help me never to tell a lie. Second, give me neither poverty nor riches! Give me just enough to satisfy my needs. For if I grow rich, I may deny You and say, 'Who is the LORD?' And if I am too poor, I may steal and thus insult God's holy name." Proverbs 30:7-9 NLT**

To the greedy, how much is enough is always "just a little bit more." Even the ungreedy often have a difficult time distinguishing between wants and needs.

> ***"Greed causes fighting; trusting the LORD leads to prosperity."***
> ***Proverbs 28:25 NLT***

We live in a consumer-driven economy that is based on creating a demand and then supplying that demand, and everything is made to look and sound so appealing.

Whether the world or the devil is doing the tempting, it is hard to resist the promise of the beer ads for fun and adventure, the car ads for the hemi, or for more power, more of everything, shampoo for beautiful hair, etc. All we have to do is discard our old and try the new and improved.

Satan will often plant seeds of dissatisfaction with our jobs and even our marriages to get us looking for "just a little bit more" happiness.

Sometimes we are so focused on seeking "just a little bit more" that we have it made and don't even know it until we mess up and realize too late how good we really had it.

> ***"Then the Lord said to him, 'You Pharisees are so careful to clean the outside of the cup and the dish, but inside you are still filthy—full of greed and wickedness!'"***
> ***Luke 11:39 NLT***

Generosity is one of the best antidotes for greed that has ever been invented. It also opens up the flood gates of God's blessings with which He wants to bless us.

What we really need to understand is that our worth and wealth is not based on what we have but on Who we have. We can always be greedy for "just a little bit more" of Jesus!

**Father, help me to be like Paul and learn to be content and filled with Your peace and joy, no matter what my worldly circumstances. Amen.**

**Read 1 Corinthians 1 Psalm 111** **June 21**

# *The Other Priceless Gift*

**"For the LORD grants wisdom! From His mouth come knowledge and understanding. He grants a treasure of good sense to the godly. He is their shield, protecting those who walk with integrity." Proverbs 2:6, 7 NLT**

Eternal life is the greatest gift ever given. King Solomon asked for the next greatest gift and so should we.

> ***"The fear of the LORD is the beginning of wisdom;" Psalm 111:10***

When we add knowledge and common sense to judgment, insight, and discernment, we begin to approach wisdom. When we get diligent in seeking God's will and are obedient to His Word, we will acquire the gift of wisdom.

When we try to replace the wisdom of God with the wisdom of man, we are asking for trouble, because true wisdom is spiritual discernment of God through learning truth by getting to know truth.

Jesus said that He was not only the way and the life, but He was the truth. Jesus was the truth of God made manifest so that it could be revealed to all who would seek. You don't have to be a nuclear physicist to realize that the more you know Jesus, the more you will know truth.

The more you know Jesus, the more you will know what He did so that you can better know what He would do in any given situation. Jesus said that He did only what His Father told Him to do. Just as He modeled perfection in everything else, Jesus modeled perfect obedience even unto death.

It is very easy to buy into the religion of secular humanism being taught in our schools and especially in our supposedly great universities, where the wisdom of man is exalted and the wisdom of God is dismissed as meaningless fables.

> ***"For it is written, 'I will destroy the wisdom of the wise, and bring to nothing the understanding of the prudent.'" 1 Corinthians 1:19***

As man becomes wise in his own conceit, the fact that there is no wisdom apart from God becomes abundantly clear. May we all seek wisdom the only place where it can be found— in God's Word!

**Father, let me be like Solomon in asking for Your wisdom in coping with the issues of life. Amen.**

# Let's Get Naked!

**"And they were both naked, the man and his wife, and were not ashamed. Genesis 2:25 NLT "Then the eyes of both of them were opened, and they knew that they were naked, and they sewed fig leaves together and made themselves coverings." Genesis 3:67 NLT**

The idea of standing naked before God is both terrifying and comforting, but we all need to be aware of the fact that this is the way we live before Him.

***"I could ask the darkness to hide me and the light around me to become night—but even in darkness I cannot hide from You." Psalm 139:11,12a NLT***

We can hide from others and even from ourselves, but nothing is hidden from our all-knowing, ever-present God. This is a terrifying thought at times because it takes away our hiding places and secret Strong holds of sin.

It is only when we realize our nakedness before God that we can fully appreciate what it means to be covered with the righteousness of Christ. This is much better than the fig leaves with which Adam and Eve tried to cover their nakedness!

The blessing of standing naked before God is that we don't have to try to put up a false front or try to impress Him. We are free to expose our weaknesses before God and to trust Him to help us overcome them with His strength.

Pretense and pride take a beating and the joy of our salvation is refreshed and renewed as we ponder anew what the Almighty has done for us in Christ. We are freed to stand naked and unashamed before God because the blood of Jesus has washed away all our guilt and shame, and we stand totally forgiven and totally acceptable in the sight of God.

***"We are made right in God's sight when we trust in Jesus Christ to take away our sins." Romans 3:22 NLT***

**Father, sometimes I can't even bear to look into a mirror because of my sins. Thank you that You see the righteousness of Christ when You look at me. Amen.**

Read 1 John 5, Psalm 119:105-112 June 23

## *You've Got Mail!*

**"My purpose in writing is to encourage you and assure you that the grace of God is with you no matter what happens."1 Peter 5:12b NLT**

> ***"Your word is a lamp for my feet and a light for my path."***
> ***Psalm 119:105 NLT***

Millions of people around the world have been greeted by the distinctive voice on AOL announcing that they have mail. E-mail, good and bad, is truly one of the great innovations of the last quarter of the 20th century. From Morse's telegraph to Bell's telephone to Marconi's radio, e-mail has evolved as one of the great communication inventions of all time.

Millions of people throughout the world are communicating instantly with others throughout the world every minute of every day.

Prior to the marvels of the electronic age, letters had been the means of one-on-one communication for centuries. Scripture records many letters in the Old Testament.

Today, we are the beneficiaries of some of the greatest mail ever sent– the Gospel of Luke; Acts of the Apostles written by Luke; the Letters of Paul to various churches and to Timothy and Titus; and the letters of James, Peter, and John.

This mail contains not only the good news of salvation but the history and record of the establishment of a new covenant of grace through the blood of Jesus Christ.

As our mail says in 2 Timothy 23:16, 17, "*All Scripture is inspired by God and is useful to teach us what is true and to make us realize what is wrong in our lives. It straightens us out and teaches us to do what is right. It is God's way of preparing us in every way, fully equipped for every good thing God wants us to do.*"

> ***"I write this to you who believe in the Son of God, so that you may know you have eternal life."***
> ***1 John 5:13 NLT***

This is mail we dare not fail to open, mail we dare not fail to read. People have died in delivering it and preserving it so that we can be enlightened, encouraged, and strengthened. Don't miss this mail call!

**Father, thank you for Your Word found in the letters of the Bible. Help me to feed on it, digest it, and appropriate Your truths. Amen.**

# *The Blame Game*

**"In all of this, Job did not sin by blaming God." Job 1:22 NLT**

Blaming God is one of the favorite darts of the devil to undermine our faith and rob us of our peace and joy in the Lord.

> ***"People are born for trouble as predictably as sparks fly upward from a fire."***
> ***Job 5:7 NLT***

Whether it is the outcome of the false expectations generated by "name it and claim it" or the prosperity gospel, or whether we somehow think that God promises us a rose garden, we all know people who are alienated from God because of their anger over His letting a loved one die or a reversal of fortune happen.

We need to remember that Scripture continually reminds us that in this world we will have trouble. God is not the one who causes trouble or wishes trouble for anyone. Trouble is the consequences of the sin that came into the world due to the fall of Adam.

When we choose to blame God, we will start a downward spiral in our relationship with Him that will give rise to seeds of bitterness and resentment in our hearts that we don't need or want.

Rather than blame God when troubles come, we need to seek Him. Scripture tells us, "*And we know that God causes everything to work together for the good of those who love God and are called according to his purpose for them" (Romans 8:28 NLT).*

When we seek God's perspective when troubles that are not the consequences of our sins come, we can claim by faith His promises and be assured that they have come for our good and God's glory. God is sovereign and in control. He can even turn the evil that we do into good.

> ***"I have told you these things, so that in me you may have peace. In this world you will have trouble. But take heart! I have overcome the world."***
> ***John 16:33 NIV***

Instead of blame, we need to respond with shame, confession, and repentance when it's our fault and praise, thanksgiving, and trust when we run into trouble.

**Father, keep me from falling into the trap of blaming You for my misfortunes, and help me to become stronger in You through them. Amen.**

**Read Psalm 116, Isaiah 53** **June 25**

# Out of the Darkness

**"This is so you can show others the goodness of God, for He called you out of the darkness into His wonderful light." 1 Peter 12:9b**

What has been the darkest and most painful moment or period of your life? Thinking about this can bring back some painful memories for all of us and is a good way to begin thinking of the most painful moment in the life of our Savior.

> ***"Death had its hands around my throat; the terrors of the grave overtook me. I saw only trouble and sorrow."***
> ***Psalm 116:3 NLT***

Nothing that we have ever suffered can ever begin to compare with what our Lord suffered. Betrayal, rejection, mockery, ridicule, torture, humiliation, and crucifixion were all part of the cup of suffering.

As terrible as all these things were, they could not begin to compare with the perfect, innocent, and Holy Lamb of God dying and suffering separation from God in the depths of hell.

The "Good News" is that He arose from death and brought the light of perfect love in all its brilliance and resurrection power for eternal life into the lives of all believers.

This supreme example of turning the darkness of despair into the marvelous light of our salvation and hope of glory should give us all cause to "ponder anew what the Almighty can do" and has done for each and every one of us.

> ***"He is despised and rejected by men, a Man of sorrows and acquainted with grief."***
> ***Isaiah 53:3 NLT***

As we go through the hills and valleys of life there is great hope and great comfort in knowing that our Lord has gone through much worse than we will ever have to go through, and no matter how deep the valley nor how dark the despair, He is there with us to sustain us by His grace, strengthen us with His power, and comfort us with His love.

**Father, thank you for being the solid rock on which I can stand and be sure that there is light at the end of any tunnel through which I must travel. Amen.**

# *Don't Get Tired of This!*

**"So don't get tired of doing what is good. Don't get discouraged and give up, for we will reap a harvest of blessing at the appropriate time." Galatians 6:8**

It is easy to fall into the chasm of boredom and futility. Sometimes, no matter how hard we try, nobody seems to notice or care. Other times, we get so focused on ourselves; we just can't see anything else. Other times we just get plain bored of "doing church."

> ***"You have given me greater joy than those who have abundant harvests of grain and wine."***
> ***Psalm 4:7 NLT***

There is often a wide gap between doing and being, and until we close this gap, we are never going to be fully content. Christ in us is not only our hope of glory but is the fount of every blessing. *"The eyes of the LORD search the whole earth in order to strengthen those whose hearts are fully committed to Him" (2 Chronicles 16:8a NLT).*

When Christ rules in our hearts, compulsion goes out and joy moves in. We not only experience joy in giving our tithes but joy in every area of our lives. We don't have to do anything, but we want to do everything that Jesus has shown and told us to do.

We find greater joy on the job because we learn to "work as unto the Lord." We find joy in loving and serving others and find that our own needs and desires are satisfied so much more through this than when we sought to satisfy them from a self-centered perspective.

> ***"Then you will not become spiritually dull and indifferent. Instead, you will follow the example of those who are going to inherit God's promises because of their faith and patience."***
> ***Hebrews 6:12 NLT***

When the Spirit of our living God is ruling in our hearts, instead of asking "What's the use?" we find the sacred delight of "being used" for the purposes for which God planned for us before we were even born.

**Father, help me to keep my eye on the prize and find my joy through abiding in You so that You will abide in me. Amen.**

# *Truth or Tradition*

**"But the time is coming and is already here when true worshipers will worship the Father in spirit and in truth. The Father is looking for anyone who will worship Him that way." John 4:23, 24 NLT**

Tradition is a wonderful thing, unless it gets in the way of truth. There is a certain comfort about knowing that the rituals of the past are continuing century after century as aids to worship and praise God.

> ***"Teach me Your ways, O LORD, that I may live according to your truth! Grant me purity of heart," Psalm 86:11 NLT***

The problem is that too often tradition becomes the main thing, and God's great commandment and great commission become secondary.

Many churches are disappearing because they have lost their future by losing their young people who have too often been unintentionally taught that God is boring and that faith is irrelevant.

The idea that the church is the dispenser of Grace seems too often emphasized over the importance of a personal relationship with Jesus Christ. Worshipping in the Spirit seems to get quenched rather than encouraged as "canned" responses and "canned" prayers are read instead of said.

God's truths are eternal, and they never change. People's sin problems and need for a savior never change from one generation to the next. What does change is the means of most effectively reaching people for the cause of Christ.

We need a relevant proclamation of the Gospel to dispel the myths of what is being taught as relative truth today. We need to use every viable resource available to lead others into the way, the life, and the truth that can only be found in Jesus Christ.

> ***"You must display a new nature because you are a new person, created in God's likeness—righteous, holy, and true." Ephesians 4:24***

**Father, by the power of Your Spirit, help me to worship You in spirit and in truth. Amen.**

June 28 Read Romans 8:31-39, Psalm 103

## *No Matter What!*

**"We are made right in God's sight when we trust in Jesus Christ to take away our sins. And we all can be saved in this same way, no matter who we are or what we have done." Romans 3:22 NLT**

We love to equate sins on a sliding scale. Different folks seem to use different scales. For some, sexual immorality is the worst. For others addictions to alcohol or drugs are the worst. Some are so heavy laden with the guilt of sins so terrible that they feel if they were ever found out, they would die of shame.

> ***"He forgives your sins—every one. He heals your diseases—every one."***
> ***Psalm 103:3 MSG***

There are some things we really need to know about sins and sinners. First of all, we need to know that there is nothing except the sin against the Holy Spirit by rejecting Him when He calls that God has not or will not forgive when we confess and truly repent.

The God who forgave David for adultery and murder, Peter for cowardice and denial, Moses for pride, and Paul for persecuting and killing Christians is the God who forgives every sin you have ever committed or will ever commit, when you confess and repent.

God seems to be much more eager to forgive the publicans and sinners than the high and the mighty, but He will forgive all, no matter whom!

The only requirements for God's forgiveness are: (1) believing that He will forgive for the sake of Jesus who died on the cross to earn our forgiveness; (2) come to God in the humility of brokenness and godly sorrow for our sins; (3) resolve that by the power of God living in us that we will turn away from our sins in true repentance; (4) forgiving others as we have been forgiven.

> ***"Who dares accuse us whom God has chosen for His own? Will God? No! He is the one who has given us right standing with Himself."***
> ***Romans 8:33 NLT***

We don't need to dwell on how bad we are but rather joy in how good God is, and how great His mercy is to us, no matter who or what!

**Father, have mercy on me a sinner saved by grace. Amen.**

# *Spiritual Elephantiasis*

**"I, even I, am he who blots out your transgressions, for my own sake, and remembers your sins no more." Isaiah 43:25 NIV**

Anyone who ever saw the old movie *Elephant Man* will remember the pathetic, gross disfiguration that this disease brings. What you visualize when you think of the outward symptoms of this disease is not a bad way to think of the far more serious inward symptoms of spiritual elephantiasis, which is far more prevalent and does much more damage.

> ***"As far as the east is from the west, so far has He removed our transgressions from us."***
> ***Psalm 111:12 NLT***

Spiritual elephantiasis is the crippling disease of the heart brought on by refusing to forget as well as forgive the past. We have all heard someone say, "I will forgive but will never forget," which, in effect, means that they have not really forgiven.

Years and years after an incident or offense, the offended one can recall and recount every vivid detail as if it just happened yesterday. In a fit of anger, we often throw up someone's mistakes and offenses of the past as a means of proving how right we are and how wrong they were.

We all need to strive to be imitators of Christ, who forgave even those who never even asked, and to be more like God, who "remembers our sins no more."

Hard as it may be to understand, when we fail to forgive and forget, we are the ones who suffer the most. A lot of people who hurt us will never even know that they offended. When we let hurts and wrongs fester, they grow into roots of bitterness and guilt that can cause emotional, spiritual, and even physical problems that can cripple.

> ***"Then Jesus said, 'Father, forgive them, for they do not know what they do.'"***
> ***Luke 23:34***

Elephants may be good to help Republicans remember how to vote, but we should never want to be like them when it comes to forgetting, except when it comes to remembering the good.

**Father, give me a forgiving heart so that I can receive all of the forgiveness that I will always need. Amen.**

# *Permission Granted*

**"And do not grieve the Holy Spirit of God, by whom you were sealed for the day of redemption. Let all bitterness, wrath, anger, clamor, and evil speaking be put away from you, with all malice." Ephesians 4:30, 31 NLT**

We seem to need a lot of permissions to live in a very permissive society. While about any moral lapse or scandalous conduct is condoned by a very permissive society, we are made to dance through hoops trying to get permission to build a house, drive a car, to own a gun, etc.

> ***"Offer proper sacrifices, and trust in the LORD." Psalm 4:5 NLT***

I have gotten into trouble sometimes thinking it is easier to get forgiveness than permission, especially from bureaucrats. I think that many people have the same problem in living their lives against the will of a just and holy God.

In His love, God chose to give us a free will and the opportunity to make choices. Before we were set free from bondage to sin by receiving Jesus Christ as our Savior, we had no choice but to live out our bondage to the sin of the flesh. This is why so many people in the world live their lives for all the wrong things and all the wrong reasons.

Once we received the new birth in Christ, we became dead to sin and alive in Him. We no longer have an excuse for our sins because we are no longer in bondage to them. It is only our failure to give the Holy Spirit permission to control every area of our life that keeps us from growing into the fullness of Christ and being all that God would have us be in Him.

> ***"But the fruit of the Spirit is love, joy, peace, longsuffering, kindness, goodness, faithfulness, gentleness, self-control. Against such there is no law." Galatians 5:22***

When we get our own self-centered and prideful flesh out of the way and let God be God, Christ in us becomes our hope of glory, our joy, and our salvation. We won't have to get a permit to carry the full armor of God or to produce the fruit of the Spirit.

**Father, help me to daily give You permission to take control of my life through the indwelling strength and power of Your Spirit. Amen.**

**Read 2 Corinthians 13:5-10, Psalm 105** **July 1**

# *Checkups and Inspections*

**"Because you have obeyed my command to persevere, I will protect you from the great time of testing that will come upon the whole world to test those who belong to this world." Revelation 3:10 NLT**

We live in an age of check ups and testing. Everything from the cars we drive to the meat we eat are checked and rechecked. Preventative maintenance has become a big business.

> ***"Search for the LORD and for His strength and keep on searching." Psalm 105:4***

Doctors keep us coming in regularly to check our eyes, our cholesterol, our weight, and monitor all sorts of things through various tests.

If believers monitored their spiritual health as well as they monitor their physical health and the health of their automobiles, boats, and other toys, this world would be a much better place.

The salvation is just the beginning of our new life in Christ. Spiritual maturity is custom designed by God to grow us into the fullness of Christ.

God is continually monitoring our minds and hearts and is pleased when they are "stayed on Him." He is continually inspecting our fruit to see that it is not corrupted by the drought of doubt or the worms of worry.

God knows exactly how to "take us down a notch" when our pride gets too obnoxious to Him. He knows exactly how to heal our hurts when people and circumstances disappoint us.

We monitor our spiritual health by judging ourselves. When we know we have fallen short of the glory of God and confess and repent, we eliminate the need for God to have to chasten us.

> ***"Examine yourselves to see if your faith is really genuine. Test yourselves. If you cannot tell that Jesus Christ is among you, it means you have failed the test." 2 Corinthians 13:5 NLT***

How are we doing in our fruit garden compared to a year ago? How much better do we know God through Jesus than we did a year ago? How much stronger is our faith than a year ago? What sins have we overcome by grace of God? What do we need to work on?

**Father, cover my weaknesses with Your strength and let me daily maintain and grow in my relationship with You. Amen.**

July 2 Read Romans 8:1-18, Psalm 119:41-48

# *The Statue of Liberty*

**"He has sent Me to heal the brokenhearted, to proclaim liberty to the captives and recovery of sight to the blind, to set at liberty those who are oppressed; to proclaim the acceptable year of the LORD." Luke 4:18b**

The Statue of Liberty was given by the people of France as a symbol of their friendship that was established during the American Revolution. Over the past 100+ years it has become a symbol of freedom and democracy for the millions who have entered this country seeking a new and better life.

> ***"And I will walk at liberty, for I seek Your precepts." Psalm 119:45***

As believers, we have a statue of Liberty that is embodied in the Cross. Whether we wear it, bear it, kneel down to it, or just carry it in our hearts, we need to be ever mindful of the freedom and liberty that it represents, and the price that was paid.

Jesus' death on the cross at Calvary set us free from all condemnation and bondage to sin and set us free from our death penalty for the wages of sin. When we receive Jesus Christ as Savior we become empowered to overcome sin and live in total freedom from bondage to it.

The liberty of our new life in Christ gives us liberty to live lives fully pleasing to Him and fruitful in every good work. This liberty makes us want to do the things that please Christ instead of feeling like we have to do them. It changes not only our conduct, but also our motives.

We no longer have to lead lives of trying to appease God, but rather have the privilege of leading lives that please God through his empowerment.

The freedom that we enjoy as Americans did not and does not come cheap. Thousands upon thousands have died to gain it and maintain it over the centuries. Unfortunately it becomes more and more abused and used as a license to promote evil and abominations.

> ***"There is therefore now no condemnation to those who are in Christ Jesus." Romans 8:1***

God's grace cost us nothing, but cost His Son everything. We dare not abuse it and use it as a license for sinning. **Father, let your cross be my statue of liberty for celebrating my freedom and liberty in Christ. Amen.**

**Read Romans 8, Psalm 119:40-45** **July 3**

## *The Emancipation Proclamation*

**"Therefore if the Son makes you free, you shall be free indeed." John 8:36**

*"And by virtue of the power and for the purpose aforesaid, I do order and declare that all persons held as slaves within said designated States and parts of States are, and henceforward shall be, free;" (Abraham Lincoln, September 22, 1862)*

Actual and spiritual slaves sometimes both have the same trouble. They cannot handle freedom.

> ***"I will walk in freedom,for I have devoted myself to Your commandments." Psalm 119:45 NLT***

When Lincoln abolished slavery and declared all slaves free, many just stayed where they were and as they were. Often prisoners commit crimes to get back into prison because they cannot handle their freedom on the outside.

Before we get all puffed up with condemnation and wondering how anyone could be so dumb, we need to take a look at our own lives.

Why do we live lives so often in bondage to the will of our flesh instead of lives of freedom controlled by the Spirit of God that is in us?

St. Paul struggled mightily with this same problem. *"But I see another law in my members, warring against the law of my mind, and bringing me into captivity to the law of sin which is in my members. O wretched man that I am! Who will deliver me from this body of death?" (Romans 7:23)*

Thank God for Romans 8 which teaches us that the resurrection power of God is ours to claim by faith. We no longer have to live in bondage to sin of any kind.

The war has been won by Christ's death on the cross. The battle for the control of our will goes on. No matter how many skirmishes we might lose, how many satanic darts hit us, we can stand firm and live victoriously not in our own strength, but in the supernatural strength of the resurrection power of Christ living in us, which is our hope of Glory.

> ***"For the power of the life-giving Spirit has freed you through Christ Jesus from the power of sin that leads to death." Romans 8:2 NLT***

When we appropriate this truth by faith, we fill find that we are free, indeed!

**Father, give me your power of the Holy Spirit to live in the freedom Your Son died to give me. Amen.**

July 4 Read 2 Corinthians 3:7-18, Psalm 119:45-50

# *Ultimate Freedom*

**"Keep me from deliberate sins! Don't let them control me.Then I will be free of guilt and innocent of great sin." Psalm 19:13 NLT**

> ***"I will walk in freedom,for I have devoted myself to Your commandments."***
> ***Psalm 119:45 NLT***

Many have died to give us freedom of speech, freedom from unreasonable search and seizure, freedom of religion, and other inalienable rights guaranteed by the US Constitution.

We strive to live in freedom from poverty, stress, disease, failure and other undesirable circumstances.Inmates yearn for freedom. Many children yearn for freedom from parental control.

Jesus Christ died on the cross to set us free from the bondage of sin. Whether we are in bondage to alcohol or other substances, sexual sins, or other bad habits, we can seek the freedom given by God, which will make us free, indeed.

A lot of us seem to have a problem appropriating our freedom by faith and living in our freedom by the power of the Holy Spirit. Like the children of Israel before us, we just can't seem to handle freedom very well.

We too often get caught up in pursuing wealth, pleasure, and happiness as defined by the world instead of God, and fall back into bondage.

The freedom of choosing how to respond to the circumstances of life is the ultimate freedom, and our peace, security, and happiness may well depend on the choices we make.

Our lives are filled with circumstances beyond our control as we experience the growing pains of God's character development program. The ultimate freedom is choosing to respond as Jesus would respond in any given situation. This is not only the ultimate freedom, but the ultimate test as to how well we have been conformed into the image of Christ.

> ***"Now, the Lord is the Spirit, and wherever the Spirit of the Lord is, He gives freedom."***
> ***1 Corinthians 3:17 NLT***

**Father, Give me the strength to respond with faith, hope, and love to the circumstances of life. Amen.**

Read Colossians 1:21-29, Proverbs 9:9-12 July 5

# *The All You Care to Eat Buffets*

**"And Jesus said to them, "I am the bread of life. He who comes to Me shall never hunger, and he who believes in Me shall never thirst." John 6:35**

I don't know about you, but I always over eat at those all you can eat buffets. It's always the worst on cruise ships. All the food looks and tastes so good, you fill your plate on the first goodies you see and seldom have room for the real goodies further down the line.

> ***"Wisdom has built her spacious house with seven pillars. She has prepared a great banquet, mixed the wines, and set the table." Proverbs 9:4***

Satan offers an all you can eat buffet in order to tempt us in every area of life.

The prodigal son had all of the pleasure he could stand until his inheritance ran out and he had to start slopping hogs in order to survive.

Some kids just can't wait to get out on their own where the controls are gone and they can have all of what the TV advertisements have touted as the good things in life. Thank God that He is long suffering, patient, and kind, and will bring most of them back to some sense of moderation and normalcy before their day of reckoning comes.

God has the best "all you can eat" buffet on the planet. He fills and refills the hunger in our soul. He satisfies, and yet keeps us wanting more and more.

As we feed at "God's buffet" we come into the presence of God, and we receive His love, friendship, encouragement, and strength. Best of all, we receive the heart of Jesus and become like Him.

> ***"To them God willed to make known what are the riches of the glory of this mystery among the Gentiles: which is Christ in you, the hope of glory" Colossians 1:27 NLT***

We can always eat our fill at the unlimited buffet of grace. The tab has been paid and there is plenty for all.

**Father, grant your daily supply of all the manna I can eat. Amen.**

## *The Annual Pass*

**"Don't be misled. Remember that you can't ignore God and get away with it. You will always reap what you sow!" Galatians 6:7**

Some of the great theme parks are discovering that selling annual passes, good for one whole year, are a real bonanza for business. They know that it is not going to cost them anymore because they have to stay open anyhow, that you will probably spend money on refreshments and parking, and even bring friends who don't have passes.

> ***"Because of your unfailing love, I can enter your house; with deepest awe I will worship at Your Temple."***
> ***Psalm 5:7 NLT***

There is cause to wonder if they might have gotten this idea from some nominal Christians who think they have an annual pass from God which only requires meeting with Him in His church on an annual basis of either Easter or Christmas.

When we rationalize and say that we don't have to go to Church to be saved, we are absolutely right. When we are really saved, we will want to go to celebrate our joy in the Lord and to Love God and one another.

Our faith is a living faith that needs to flourish and grow as we become more like Christ day by day. It needs not only the nourishment of the daily manna of prayer and abiding in the Word, but also the encouragement and fellowship of other believers that only comes from being plugged into the power source of regular authentic, corporate worship.

> ***"But since you are like lukewarm water, I will spit you out of my mouth!"***
> ***Revelation 3:16***

Although true faith can never die, it can suffer from debilitating malnutrition that no once a year pass can ever cure. Jesus Christ died to give us a lifetime pass for this life with a pass over into eternal life in heaven. We need to start acting like "frequent flyers."

**Father, let me feast not only daily, but weekly when I come to praise you and encourage and be encouraged by other Saints. Amen.**

Read 1 Corinthians 6, Psalm 116 July 7

## *Was I Worth It?*

**"You see, at just the right time, when we were still powerless, Christ died for the ungodly. Very rarely will anyone die for a righteous man, though fora good man someone might possibly dare to die. But God demonstrates his own love for us in this: While we were still sinners, Christ died for us." Romans 5:6-8 NIV**

"Saving Private Ryan" was one of the most brutal movies ever made before "The Passion of Christ" came to the screen. The opening scene showed Private Ryan in the sunset of life, with his wife, children, and grandchildren visiting the grave of Captain Miller who had died finding and saving him during World War II. Captain Miller often said and felt: "this guy had better be worth it" as he saw men dying all around him, and ultimately he himself in "Saving Private Ryan."

> ***"I will offer to You the sacrifice of thanksgiving, and will call upon the name of the LORD." Psalm 116:17 NLT***

Anyone who has ever seen or will ever see "The Passion of Christ" will have the price of the pain and suffering Christ bore for us embedded in their minds as never before, and will be moved "try to be worth it" by living a life fully pleasing to God.

When we stand before God at the great white throne of judgment and give account of the stewardship of the life He died to give us, his "well done, thou good and faithful servant", is the only validation that we will ever get affirming that we have lived a life pleasing to Him.

The truth is that no, we certainly were not worth dying for, and it was only by the grace of God that He loved us enough to come buy us eternal life by his blood.

The question that we all need to ponder is how we can respond to this "greater love" and priceless gift of eternal life that we have received.

Should we not, at the very minimum, strive to live a life fully pleasing to God that might make him at least feel that he didn't die in vain?

> ***"You do not belong to yourself, for God bought you with a high price. So you must honor God with your body." 1 Corinthians 6:20 NLT***

**Father, help me to always remember what I cost Your Son, and that I can never be worthy, but should always be thankful. Amen.**

July 8 Read Romans 8, Psalm 19

## *Give it Up!*

**"That's why those who are still under the control of their sinful nature can never please God." Romans 8:8 NLT**

Self will is one of the hardest possessions to give up that we will ever own. All of our pride, aspirations, and secular objectives are generated by our self will.

> ***"Keep me from deliberate sins! Don't let them control me.Then I will be free of guilt and innocent of great sin."***
> ***Psalm 19:13 NLT***

Self will is what got mankind into trouble with God in the first place. If Eve had just exercised a little self control instead of self will the world wouldn't be in the shape it's in today.

How many prayers have we prayed asking that God's will be done, while actually meaning our will be done? How many times have we sought to justify our will or our agenda by trying to pass it off as the will of God?

The best antidote for destructive self will is abiding and seeking God's will. Abiding will give us the very heart of God, and when we have that, we begin thinking His thoughts, become more sensitive to His leadings, and more centered on Christ and less on ourselves.

When we pray with Christ's heart, it's amazing at how many more of of our prayers are answered. This is because our prayers are Christ-centered, unselfish prayers that will glorify God and therefore are in accordance with God's will. Through this we learn and believe more and more that He really will do anything we ask that is in accordance with His will.

When we replace self will with God's will, our whole attitude changes. Instead of responding defensively and in anger, we respond in the fruit of the Spirit which takes control of our flesh.

> ***"If your sinful nature controls your mind, there is death. But if the Holy Spirit controls your mind, there is life and peace."***
> ***Romans 8:6 NLT***

When we "give it up" we get so much more in return we will wonder why it took us so long to do it in the first place.

**Father, help me to "give it up" so that you can "give it out." Amen.**

**Read Jude 1:21, 23, Psalm 128** **July 9**

# *Are You Blessable?*

**"I will bless those who have humble and contrite hearts, who tremble at my word. But those who choose their own ways, delighting in their sins, are cursed. Their offerings will not be accepted." Isaiah 66:2**

You would think that we would learn from the history of the children of Israel. Time and time again God rescued, delivered, restored and blessed them, and every time they fell back into idol worship and ignoring God to their peril.

> ***"Blessed is every one who fears the LORD, who walks in His ways." Psalm 128:1***

Today, we expect God to bless us in spite of our indifference and disobedience....in spite of our putting other gods before him, and willfully ignoring Him.

Thankfully, God is longsuffering, patient, and kind. He longs to bring us into that abiding relationship where He can be our friend, answer our prayers, make us fruitful, give us joy, and let us know His love and be aware of the love of others. God really does long to bless us!

We don't have to be rocket scientists to figure out some simple keys to being blessable.

First of all, obedience brings blessings. All of the old covenants were based on this principle, and this principle holds true today.

Think of the consequences of some of the disobedience in your life and the lives of those around you. We will never know the blessings of God to their fullest if we insist on willfully disobeying God and ignoring the calls of the Holy Spirit to contrition and repentance.

We learn from Scripture that we are blessable when we are meek, when we mourn, when we hunger and thirst for righteousness, when we are persecuted for the cause of Christ, when we are merciful, when we seek to promote peace, and when we have a clean heart.

We are blessable when we endure temptation and persevere through times of testing, when we are generous, compassionate, and kind.

> ***"Live in such a way that God's love can bless you as you wait for the eternal life that our Lord Jesus Christ in his mercy is going to give you" Jude 1:21 NLT***

**Father, by the power of Your Spirit, help me to be blessable. Amen.**

**July 10** **Read Romans 15:1-13, Ecclesiastes 4:7-12**

## *Encourage!*

**"Think of ways to encourage one another to outbursts of love and good deeds." Hebrews 10:24 NLT**

There is a power too often ignored and too little used in the lives of believers. This power can change lives, strengthen relationships, and accomplish miracles. This power is available for everyone to generate, and for everyone to receive. It is the power of positive reinforcement, or of edification which means "building up."

> **"A person standing alone can be attacked and defeated, but two can stand back-to-back and conquer. Three are even better, for a triple-braided cord is not easily broken."**
> ***Ecclesiastes 4:12***

The formula is not all that complicated. We start by demonstrating love and being sensitive to the weaknesses of others so that we do not become stumbling blocks.

We add participation in edifying corporate worship and fellowship with other believers where we can grow with each other in unity of faith, knowledge, and spiritual maturity into the fullness of Christ.

The bond that is built through encouraging others is a bond that is not easily broken. Knowing that someone cares and believes in us makes it much more difficult to fall into a sin trap that would betray that trust.

God continues to supply manna from heaven to His children to feed and nourish us in His love, so that we can nourish and love others. He often chooses to nourish us through His Word. Sometimes He uses us to nourish others, and others to nourish us through the power of positive reinforcement.

> **"May God, who gives this patience and encouragement, help you live in complete harmony with each other—each with the attitude of Christ Jesus toward the other."**
> ***Romans 15:5 NLT***

Who can you bless through an encouraging word, an act of kindness, or a demonstration of love or concern today?

**Father, help me to use the power of edification to bless others. Amen.**

Read 2 Corinthians 3:1-6

July 11

# *Self Sufficiency*

**"So now I am glad to boast about my weaknesses, so that the power of Christ may work through me." 2 Corinthians 12:9b NLT**

Among one of the most desirable character traits in the world today is self sufficiency. We admire people who seem to have it all together and who don't need help from anyone. We tend to look down upon the welfare recipients and less fortunate as not being self sufficient.

***"I will not tolerate people who slander their neighbors. I will not endure conceit and pride." Psalm 101:5 NLT***

There is certainly nothing wrong with being responsible and able to succeed in any endeavor. The danger comes when we get so egocentric that we begin to worship ourselves and our abilities, and fail to give God the Glory, and to acknowledge our dependency on Him.

Before we get too proud and cocky, it is good to ask ourselves what talent, what ability, what resource we have that has not been God-given. When we realize that every breath we take comes from God, and that we are totally dependent upon Him for even life itself we begin to get the idea that we are not as self sufficient as we would like to think.

If, in our self sufficiency, we fail to allow God's strength to be made perfect in our weakness, we are going to miss out on mega blessings. Self sufficiency goes hand in hand with self centeredness, and neither of these is listed among the fruit of the Spirit.

People who are self sufficient need no help. It is only when they come to the realization that they have a problem, and humble themselves and confess their sins and their need for a Savior that God can even enter into the sanctuary of their soul.

Would you really rather trust in your self and your power rather than in the power of the One who calmed the water, divided the sea, healed the sick and overcame death and the grave?

***"It is not that we think we can do anything of lasting value by ourselves. Our only power and success come from God. 1 Corinthians 3:5 NLT***

**Father, thank you for letting me find my real sufficiency in You and Your all sufficient grace. Amen.**

# *Tolerate?*

**"If the godly compromise with the wicked, it is like polluting a fountain or muddying a spring." Proverbs 25:26**

We seem to be living in the age of toleration. We are asked to tolerate life styles that the Lord calls abominations. We are asked to compromise and give up some of our strongly held beliefs in the name of tolerance. Our tolerance and apparent indifference has eroded our family values and made homosexuality and abortion respectable.

> ***"O God, You take no pleasure in wickedness; You cannot tolerate the slightest sin." Psalm 5:4 NLT***

While longsuffering and patience are evidence of the fruit of the Spirit, compromising our beliefs by letting false teachings and sinful practices go unchallenged are not considered fruits. Does pro-choice not also really mean that a woman has the choice to murder a child? Does freedom of religion mean that we allow secular humanism to become the religion of the state and schools?

Jesus did not tolerate the money changers in the temple or the hypocrisy of the scribes and Pharisees.

Toleration has brought our misery index to an all time high. We are not only breaking our covenant with God, but we are robbing our children and future generations of the blessing of God's covenant of Grace.

We are not commanded to tolerate, but to love. True love does not mean caving in and tolerating sin, or becoming self righteous and judgmental.

We must reach out in love and bring the power of the Word of God into the lives of others. Only God can judge and change hearts and work repentance, and He does this primarily through His Word.

> ***"I know all the things you do, that you are neither hot nor cold. I wish you were one or the other! But since you are like lukewarm water, I will spit you out of my mouth! Revelation 3:15, 16 NLT***

**Father, give me the wisdom, spiritual discernment, and courage to love, but never to tolerate, and know the difference. Amen.**

**Read 1 John 5, Psalm 98** **July 13**

# *Understanding Our Peace*

**"Now we have received, not the spirit of the world, but the Spirit who is from God, that we might know the things that have been freely given to us by God." 1 Corinthians 2:12**

Do you sometimes find yourself wondering what life is all about? Do you often feel that you have more questions than you have answers? Welcome to the Club! This club is as old as the beginning of time, and has millions of members in every country throughout the world.

> ***"The LORD has made known His salvation; His righteousness He has revealed in the sight of the nations.***
> ***Psalm 98:2***

One of the great joys of heaven is going to be in having all of our questions answered, and receiving the "understanding that surpasses all our peace." In the meantime, there is a way that we can get many of our answers. It's called "abiding."

When we abide in God's Word, we can know that God created us in His image. We can also know He placed a longing in our hearts that only a right relationship with Him can satisfy. We can know that free will led to disobedience and we are all born with this inherited weakness which puts us at enmity with God.

> ***"These things I have written to you who believe in the name of the Son of God, that you may know that you have eternal life, and that you may continue to believe in the name of the Son of God.***
> ***1 John 5:13 NLT***

We can know that God, in his infinite wisdom and love came up with a cure for this problem. He came in the flesh and blood of a man and after living a perfect, sin-free life, in perfect obedience allowed Himself to be mocked, humiliated, almost beaten to death, and finally nailed to the cross. As the perfect, unblemished Sacrifice, Christ earned us forgiveness for our every sin and act of disobedience and gave us a new, everlasting life through faith in this truth and the One who made it happen. When we abide in God's Word, we receive that quiet understanding and that perfect love that casts out all fear, and we wonder no more.

**Father, help me to wonder less and trust and believe more as I abide in Your Word. Amen.**

# *Pruning or Punishment*

**"But I know! I, the LORD, search all hearts and examine secret motives. I give all people their due rewards, according to what their actions deserve." Jeremiah 17:9 NLT**

Whether we are being disciplined by God as punishment for our sins, or pruned by God in order that we may become more fruitful, it hurts just the same.

> ***"Every day I call to You, my God, but You do not answer. Every night You hear my voice, but I find no relief."***
> ***Psalm 22:2***

One of the best ways to determine whether we are being disciplined or pruned is through self examination.

While it is presumptuous to think anyone knows the mind of God, there are certain principles that He has laid down in His Word that can offer a lot of insight.

Just as He loved us enough to send His Son to die for us, He loves us enough to chasten us as severely as it takes to correct us and bring us back into a right relationship with Him when we fall into unrepented sin.

If, after serious prayer and self examination, we are not convicted of any sins for which we are suffering chastening; we must consider the probability that we are experiencing the pruning of God. Through this we are being conformed more and more into the image of Christ and being equipped to produce the fruit for which God created us.

We are better equipped to forgive when we have been forgiven much. We are better equipped to comfort and love others when we have been comforted and loved. We are more sensitive to pain and suffering when we have experienced it for ourselves.

As God molds and melds us through the refiners fire, after we have determined that our problem is not an unconfessed or unrepented sin, we need to consider it all joy that God is working in our lives to draw us closer to Him. We must believe that God does work all things for the good of those who love Him and are called according to His purposes. This is much easier said than done, but nevertheless true.

> ***"My brethren, count it all joy when you fall into various trials,"***
> ***James 1:2***

**Father, as You lead me to the green pastures and still waters through the valleys let me remember that You are the Good Shepherd. Amen.**

Read Matthew 3:1-12, Psalm 36 July 15

## *Mandatory Evacuation*

**"Those who live in the shelter of the Most High will find rest in the shadow of the Almighty." Psalm 91:1 NLT**

Weather information has become available as never before.

> ***"How precious is Your unfailing love, O God! All humanity finds shelter in the shadow of Your wings."***
> ***Psalm 36:7 NLT***

We have radar, airplanes, and satellite tracking that will provide us with vital information that can chart the paths of storms very accurately and with great detail.

Although sometimes not 100% accurate, forecasts have been accurate enough to save thousands of lives by ordering mandatory evacuation from low-lying and at risk areas when hurricanes approach.

Many refuse to heed even the mandatory evacuations, often at their own peril.

John the Baptist was probably the best forecaster of all time. He was actually born for the specific task of forecasting the coming of Jesus Christ and the New Covenant that He would bring.

When John ordered the mandatory evacuation from sin through repentance, he was the voice in the wilderness to which the Scribes and Pharisees would not listen.

Jesus ordered the abandonment of living controlled by the flesh in order that we might find fulfillment in being born again, so that we might live the new life in the Spirit, totally free from condemnation.

A judgment worse than any hurricane, typhoon, or tornado is coming. Have you answered God's call to evacuate? Have you left bondage to sin to become free in Christ? Wouldn't you rather be under the shelter of His wings when judgment comes?

> ***"Who warned you to flee God's coming judgment? Prove by the way you live that you have really turned from your sins and turned to God"***
> ***Matthew 3:7b, 8 NLT***

**Father, help me to obey Your commands and seek protection under the shelter of Your wings. Amen.**

July 16 Read Colossians 2:6-23, Deuteronomy 10:12-22

# *Channels of God's Grace*

**"He has shown you, O man, what *is* good; and what does the LORD require of you but to do justly, to love mercy, and to walk humbly with your God?" Micah 6:9**

God's all powerful, all sufficient grace is the birth right of every believer. We can't earn it, because it is the unmerited favor of God. It wouldn't be grace if we could earn it.

> ***"And now, Israel, what does the LORD your God require of you? He requires you to fear him, to live according to His will, to love and worship Him with all your heart and soul, and to obey the LORD'S commands and laws that I am giving you today for your own good." Deuteronomy 10:12:13 NLT***

The key to living the abundant life in Christ is understanding how God's grace is channeled into our lives, so that we are continually being transformed by it into the image of Christ.

God imparts His unmerited favor to us through many channels. In addition to receiving salvation by grace, we have Baptismal grace, the grace imparted when we celebrate the Lord's Supper, and the grace that comes through the hearing or reading of the Word.

All of these and every other grace are offshoots from our faith which "jump starts" the flow of God's grace into every area of our lives through obedience. Scripture time and time again confirms and reaffirms the blessings of obedience.

> ***"And now, just as you accepted Christ Jesus as your Lord, you must continue to live in obedience to Him." Colossians 2:6 NLT***

When we begin appropriating the mind of Christ by abiding and growing in our relationship with Him through getting to know Him through His Word and through the reflection of His love we experience through others, we will enjoy an ever increasing fullness of God's Grace.

When we practice obedience in every area of our lives, we will experience the truth that God "*is able to do exceedingly abundantly above all that we ask or think, according to the power that works in us.*"

**Father, help me to channel the fullness of your grace through obedience. Amen.**

Read John 8, Jeremiah 9:23, 24 July 17

# *How to be Transformed*

**"For the weapons of our warfare *are* not carnal but mighty in God for pulling down strongholds, casting down arguments and every high thing that exalts itself against the knowledge of God, bringing every thought into captivity to the obedience of Christ," 2 Corinthians 10:4,5**

Our transformation into the image of Christ is an on going process. God desires for all of us to grow into the fullness of Christ so that others will see Christ in us; just as God sees Christ in us when we are saved and made righteous in His sight.

> ***"But let him who glories glory in this, That he understands and knows Me," Jeremiah 9:24 NLT***

Transformation involves dying to sin and becoming alive in and through Christ. As the Holy Spirit begins the process of transformation or sanctification, He removes the chains that bind us and gives us the power to walk in freedom from sin. Christ died to free us from this bondage and gives us an abundant life of peace and joy in the Lord.

Becoming the person we would all like to become in Christ is not about doing, but about being. When we grow into a real close and personal relationship with Jesus Christ, the grace of God becomes manifest in our lives and we want to obey instead of have to.

We grow into this relationship through getting to know Jesus better and better through His Word, worship, and fellowship with other believers. As we abide in the Word, God's grace purifies our hearts and fills them so full of Love that there is just no more room for strongholds of sin in our hearts.

The more we abide we will have more and more answered prayers because we will be praying with the mindset of Christ. We will experience Jesus' joy.

We will become not just acquaintances, but close personal friends with Christ. As we become more and more aware of His love and His character we will begin imitating Him more and more and our lives will reflect the truth that Jesus has moved from our heads to our hearts.

> ***"If you abide in My word, you are My disciples indeed. And you shall know the truth, and the truth shall make you free." John 8:31b, 32***

**Father, continue to supply your all sufficient grace until my transformation becomes complete when I see you face to face. Amen.**

July 18 Read 1 Corinthians 3:10-17, Psalm 18

# *Awards Banquets*

**"And you will be blessed, because they cannot repay you; for you shall be repaid at the resurrection of the just." Luke 14:14**

Awards banquets have become a staple of American life.There is an awards dinner or ceremony for every occasion.

> ***"The LORD rewarded me for doing right; He compensated me because of my innocence." Psalm 18:20 NLT***

We have sports award banquets on every level, from little league to high school, from college to regional and national recognition.

There are dinners held to honor outstanding business men, teachers, volunteers, and even parents.

Theatrical and Musical Awards shows still create a lot of interest and draw large audiences. Sometimes the politics and self promotion for these awards is intense and cut throat.

There is nothing wrong with recognizing outstanding accomplishments through awards ceremonies. They should always remind us that believers in Jesus Christ are going to have the opportunity to receive the greatest award of all when we appear before Him at the great resurrection of the righteous.

Our faith will take us into the presence of God and into heaven itself, where we will give an account of our stewardship of the lives we have been given.

As our lives are subjected to the refiners fire, all impurities, trivial pursuits, and wasted efforts are burned away, leaving only the good things that we have done that glorified God and fulfilled the purposes He willed for us will remain. May we all so live that when our time comes, we will receive the greatest award of all…God's "well done thou good and faithful servant."

> ***"But there is going to come a time of testing at the judgment day to see what kind of work each builder has done. Everyone's work will be put through the fire to see whether or not it keeps its value" 1 Corinthians 3:13 NLT***

**Father, by the power of Your Spirit, enable me to store up treasures in heaven that will not burn up when they are tested in the fire. Amen.**

Read Romans 3:9-31, Psalm 31 July 19

## *How's Your Misery Index?*

**"Give us gladness in proportion to our former misery! Replace the evil years with good." Psalm 90:15 NLT**

The "Misery Index" was devised by an economist in the 1970's to define the bad effects of unemployment and inflation on the economy.

> ***"Misery has drained my strength; I am wasting away from within."***
> ***Psalm 31:10b NLT***

A noted psychiatrist devised a stress index to determine point at which a nervous breakdown would occur.

Miseries like death of a loved one, divorce, financial problems, health problems, etc, were all given scores depending on the severity of the problem, and when the combined score went above 300, a nervous breakdown was imminent.

We all have our share of shortcomings and problems that will send our misery index over the breaking point if we are not anchored deep in the peace and security of a love relationship with God that comes through faith in, and a personal relationship with, Jesus Christ.

There is a misery index brought on by the consequences of our inherited and actual sins that can sometimes seem to soar through the roof and rob us of our health, happiness, joy and peace.

The sin of unbelief can doom us into an eternity of misery in hell. Pride, envy, jealousy, anger, and lust can pile misery upon us.

The lost live with their misery through developing a hardened heart and dull conscience. It is only when the Holy Spirit breaks through these barriers that anyone lost can receive the gift of eternal life.

A believer's conscience is designed to make us so miserable that we will acknowledge our sin before God and receive not only forgiveness, but the power to repent and die to sin and come alive in Christ.

> ***"Wherever they go, destruction and misery follow them. They do not know what true peace is."***
> ***Romans 3:16, 17 NLT***

It's good to know that God provides a safety valve for our misery. We can unload all our sins, sorrows, and griefs at the cross and let Jesus free us from the bondage of burdens and fill us with the peace that surpasses all understanding.

**Father, help me to overcome misery and find true joy in You. Amen.**

**July 20** **Read James 1:9-18, Psalm 119:72-77**

# *True Prosperity*

**"Then He said to them, "Watch out! Be on your guard against all kinds of greed; a man's life does not consist in the abundance of his possessions." Luke 12:14 NIV**

Prosperity has long been the goal of individuals, companies, cities, states, nations and countries. We pray for prosperity for ourselves and for others.

> ***"Your law is more valuable to me than millions in gold and silver!"***
> ***Psalm 119:72 NLT***

There is a prosperity that transcends the world's concepts, and is much greater than any other prosperity the mind can conceive. We are talking about the prosperity of the soul.

This prosperity is all around us. In some areas in deepest, darkest Africa we will find some of the poorest, but richest people alive today. Jesus is literally all they have, but they have found all they need in Him for true prosperity.

The prosperity of the soul provides the riches of God's grace that supplies every need through every circumstance of this life. When the world has turned you down and not a true friend can be found, God's grace can and will sustain all who have the prosperity of the soul.

The prosperity of the soul overcomes the greed of the flesh which is never satisfied and always wanting more. Jesus' warning to be on guard against all kinds of greed goes unheeded in our worldly pursuit of possessions, power, and pleasure.

When anyone bases their security on the abundance of their possessions, what peace will they have when the time comes to leave them all behind?

Godly contentment and peace produce the security and joy of living a life of abundance that overcomes the sting of our financial poverty and the despair of adverse circumstances.

> ***"Christians who are poor should be glad, for God has honored them."***
> ***James 1:9 NLT***

Our salvation is our "pearl of great price" which gives us the unconditional love, forgiveness, and significance from God which empowers us to live lives of true prosperity in Christ.

**Father, help my soul abide under the shelter of your wings and in the prosperity of your grace. Amen.**

**Read Luke 14:25-34, Psalm 119:58-64** **July 21**

# *Significant Others*

**""Come, be my disciple," Jesus said to him. So Matthew got up and followed him." Matthew 9:9 NLT**

In the culture of today, "significant other" is usually described to refer to a live-in companion or lover of the same or opposite sex.

> ***"I entreated Your favor with my whole heart; Be merciful to me according to Your word."***
> ***Psalm 119:58***

It should be used more often to describe a person whose close relationship with an individual affects that individual's behavior and attitudes, who serves as a role model, and whose approval is sought.

We can all think of someone and sometimes many who have been "significant others" in our lives. In addition to my wife, I think of two or three teachers, a brother and a sister, some preachers, and a few very close friends who are and have been "significant others" in my life.

Jesus should be our ultimate "significant other!" He invites each of us to become His disciple. We should daily seek to grow in that close personal relationship with him that will mold us into His image.

When we make Jesus our role model great things will happen in our lives. As we get to know and imitate Him through growing in His Word, we will want do the things that He did to please His Father, and will receive the grace and resurrection power of the Holy Spirit.

When Jesus really is our "significant other" we pray with His mindset and get these prayers answered. As our relationship with Him grows from Savior to Friend to Teacher, Jesus reveals everything to us that His Father revealed to Him.

God's plan and desire for every believer is that they grow into the fullness of Christ and reflect His love and glory in every area of our lives. He wants others to see Jesus when they see us. We will often be the only Jesus someone may ever see.

> ***"If you want to be my follower you must love Me more than your own father and mother, wife and children, brothers and sisters—yes, more than your own life."***
> ***Matthew 17:26 NLT***

The power to be the children of God can be ours when we make Jesus our "Significant Other."

**Father, help me to live a life of significance in Christ. Amen.**

July 22 2 Thessalonians 1, Genesis 15:14-21

# *The Best Intentions*

**"I am the one who searches out the thoughts and intentions of every person. And I will give to each of you whatever you deserve" Revelation 2:23b NLT**

Most people are full of good intentions. No one gets up in the morning intending to have a wreck, seeking to suffer, or trying to be miserable. No one goes into a marriage intending to make their mate miserable. No business intends to alienate customers or disappoint with their products or services. No doctor intends to kill a patient.

***"As far as I am concerned, God turned into good what you meant for evil." Genesis 50:20a***

It is very hard to imagine any believer consciously intending to do evil, or any unbeliever consciously intending to go to hell.

"The road to hell is paved with good intentions" is defined in one dictionary as: "merely intending to do good without actually doing it is of no value." This saying sounds a whole lot like James' assertion that "faith without works is dead."

God has been known to often turn the worst of intentions into good, as evidenced by Joseph's brothers selling him into slavery.

Every believer needs to be constantly aware of their need to follow through with their good intentions. "Talking the talk" without "walking the walk" is a big problem for many believers. As Jesus reminds us, *"the spirit is willing, but the body is weak."(Matthew 26:38)*

When things go wrong in spite of our best intentions, it is so good to know that God judges our hearts and knows that our intentions were good. He even stands ready to forgive even when our intentions were bad if we confess with godly sorrow and repentance.

Jesus carried out His good intention to save us by dying on the cross for our sins. We can show our appreciation by not only intending to become like Christ, but by also cooperating with the Holy Spirit in being transformed by the renewing of our minds. This is the good intention for which God created us.

"And we pray that God, by his power, will fulfill all your good intentions and faithful deeds." 2 Thessalonians 1:11b NLT

**Father, by the power of your Spirit, give me the strength to turn my good intentions into good actions with good results. Amen.**

**Read Hebrews 10:19-39, Isaiah 1:16-20** **July 23**

# How Often Do You Bathe?

**"Blind Pharisees! First wash the inside of the cup, and then the outside will become clean, too." Matthew 23:26 NLT**

According to a recent survey, 85 out of 100 people bathe once a day, and around 25 of these bathe twice a day. About 12 out of 100 bathe 2 or 3 times a week, and 3 out of a hundred once a week or less.

> ***"Wash yourselves, make yourselves clean; Put away the evil of your doings from before My eyes."***
> ***Isaiah 1:16***

Bathing and physical hygiene has come a long way in this country with the advent of indoor plumbing. Unfortunately, our spiritual hygiene does not seem to have fared as well.

We probably have less than 20 out of 100 people who bathe daily in the waters of confession, godly sorrow, repentance, or daily Bible reading or meditations and maybe 40 out of 100 who bathe weekly in God's grace through corporate worship and the fellowship and encouragement of fellow believers.

Many only bathe once or twice a year on Easter and Christmas. Others see their friends not bathing, so they quit themselves. Some don't like the soap and just quit bathing instead of trying a different soap.

When we received Jesus Christ as our Savior, we washed our filthy robes of sin in the blood of the Lamb, and were made clean in God's eyes. Receiving salvation is not the end of anything, but the beginning of everything.

God's grace bathes us when we confess and repent in prayer. This grace becomes manifest in our lives when we feed upon His written and preached Word, encourage and serve fellow believers, and share the Good News with unbelievers.

> ***"Let us go right into the presence of God, with true hearts fully trusting him. For our evil consciences have been sprinkled with Christ's blood to make us clean, and our bodies have been washed with pure water."***
> ***Hebrews 10:22 NLT***

We will never receive all of the blessings of growing into the cleanliness and fullness of Christ until we start bathing daily.

**Father, create in me a clean heart and renew a right spirit in me daily as I abide in you. Amen.**

**July 24** **Read Revelation 22:12-21, Psalm 90:12-17**

## *Only Time Will Tell*

**"The Lord isn't really being slow about his promise to return, as some people think. No, he is being patient for your sake. He does not want anyone to perish, so he is giving more time for everyone to repent." 2 Peter 3:9 NLT**

From how long marriages will last to how successful our children will become to how successful a medical treatment – we often hear: "only time will tell."

> ***"Teach us to make the most of our time, so that we may grow in wisdom."***
> ***Psalm 90:12 NLT***

It is a good thing to remember that God already knows what only time will tell. God knew us before we were born. He knows everything about our past, present, and future.

What comfort there is in knowing that in spite of this, God loves us unconditionally, forgives us forever, and accepts us just as we are when we open the door when Christ comes knocking through the Holy Spirit.

God knows whose going to receive His wonderful gift of salvation, and whose going to reject it.  He is keeping this door open until the right number of sinners comes to Christ.

From the promise of a land flowing with milk and honey to the promise of a Savior, time has shown that God keeps His promises.

We don't have to be rocket scientists to figure out the revelations of God.  We can see it in creation all around us, and we have it recorded in the Holy Bible.  We can best use our time to grow in our relationship with God by getting to know Him more completely through His Word.

When we see sin abounding throughout the world, it is good to know that God is all powerful and that He is in control.

> ***"See, I am coming soon, and My reward is with Me to repay all according to their deeds."***
> ***Revelation 22:12 NLT***

As we go through times of doubt and struggles, it's even better to know by faith that God works all things for our good and His glory, and we can be confident that time will tell that this is true.

**Father, thank you for the time you have taken to reveal your love to me in Christ, and let me have the time of my life in sharing this love with others.  Amen.**

**Read Philippians 2:1-13, Psalm 63:1-8** **July 25**

# God's CPR

**"They did not conquer the land with their swords; it was not their own strength that gave them victory. It was by your mighty power that they succeeded; it was because you favored them and smiled on them." Psalm 44:3**

Cardiac Pulmonary Resuscitation has saved the lives of hundreds of thousands of people. It provides a trickle of oxygenated blood to the brain and heart and keeps these organs alive until defibrillation can shock the heart into a normal rhythm. We should all be aware of what it does and how to do it.

> ***"I have seen You in Your sanctuary and gazed upon Your power and glory." Psalm 63:2 NLT***

God has provided a wonderful CPR to act as first aid when we get out of the normal rhythm of life in Christ. We are all cracked pots that often leak profusely. We need our souls refreshed and restored daily through confession, prayer, and repentance.

We can not win our daily battles against sin on our own. If we could, Jesus would not have had to die for us. We can try harder, pursue our own agendas, and make all the promises we want to ourselves and to others, but without the transforming power of God working in us through the Holy Spirit, we are going to most often fail.

I was in bondage to cigarettes for 50 years. I quit a hundred times, but was never able to win the battle until I asked the Lord to take away my desire for cigarettes almost 20 years ago.Since that day I've never smoked or even wanted to smoke another cigarette.

The same power that raised Jesus from the dead is available to all believers to enable us to live transformed lives by the grace of God.

It's not about doing more or trying harder, it's about being in Christ and receiving His all sufficient grace through abiding in Him and His Word, and taking advantage of grace powering confession, prayer, and repentance.

> ***"[13]For God is working in you, giving you the desire to obey him and the power to do what pleases him." Philippians 2:13 NLT***

**Father, thank you for your throne of grace to which I can come for the strength I need to be conformed into the image of Christ.**

**July 26** **Read Romans 8, Psalm 19**

## *Who's Your Designated Driver?*

**"Do not let sin control the way you live; do not give in to its lustful desires." Romans 6:12 NLT**

The use of a designated driver to stay sober and get all of the imbibers home safely after an evening of indulgence in intoxicating drinks has been widely promoted, and probably saved a lot of arrests, tickets, and lives.

> ***"Keep me from deliberate sins! Don't let them control me.Then I will be free of guilt and innocent of great sin."***
> ***Psalm 19:13 NLT***

Since we are all often driven by the flesh, we also need to make The Holy Spirit living within us our designated driver on the highway of life. We need to be overflowing instead of overcome.

As long as we persist in driving in the flesh we are going to encounter all of the problems that come when we forget about seeking the kingdom of God and His righteousness first.

When we are flesh-driven, the sins of the flesh manifest themselves in every area of our lives. We are often overcome by pride, greed, envy, lust, idolatry, and other sin defects manifested in and by our flesh.

When we are Spirit-driven the sin has no more dominion over us and we become free to live in the peace and joy of the Lord.

As we are overflowing with the long suffering, patience, kindness, love, and self control of the Holy Spirit we become transformed by the renewing of our minds and begin a new life as born-again believers in Christ.

We are Spirit-driven to love God and to serve Him and others. God's commands become our desires. As we grow in our relationship with Christ, by the power of the Holy Spirit unleashed through God's Word, self- gratifying desires of the flesh become God glorifying desires of the Spirit. We will develop a passion for living lives fully pleasing to God and fruitful in every good work.

> ***"Those who are dominated by the sinful nature think about sinful things, but those who are controlled by the Holy Spirit think about things that please the Spirit."***
> ***Romans 8:5 NLT***

Have you made the Holy Spirit your designated driver? Is it time that you do?

**Father, help me to allow the Holy Spirit to become my designated driver in every area of my life. Amen.**

**Read Romans 8:15-23, Psalm 91** **July 27**

# *Turning God Loose*

**"For you have been called to live in freedom—not freedom to satisfy your sinful nature, but freedom to serve one another in love." Galatians 5:13 NLT**

We often miss out on much of the joy, beauty, and abundance of our life in Christ because we put God in a box.

> ***'He who dwells in the secret place of the Most High shall abide under the shadow of the Almighty." Psalm 91.1***

We hold on to traditions, misperceptions, and self control instead of celebrating the one who did away with so many traditions and misperceptions.

God created us for His pleasure and for us to enjoy His love, faithfulness, kindness, compassion, grace, mercy, and the beauty and abundance of a new life in Him.

When we turn God loose by surrendering to His will and His purposes for our lives, there is no limit to where He will take us and how He will use us for His glory. As we abide in God's Word and get to know Him better through His Son, God's grace fills us with His truth. God's Spirit fills us with His power, and we become transformed into the likeness of Christ.

Knowing that God loves us unconditionally and has forgiven us of everything we have ever done or will ever do gives us the security we need to flourish in our new life in Christ.

Believing God's truth that we are no longer slaves to sin and that sin no longer has dominion over us gives us the resurrection power of God to begin living out this truth in our lives.

When we let go of the baggage of our sins, our egos, and insecurities, we let God out of our box and turn Him loose to live life to the fullest in us.

> ***"Now you are free from sin, your old master, and you have become slaves to your new master, righteousness." Romans 8:18 NLT***

All of the blessings of abiding, plus all surpassing peace forever, is what Jesus died to set us free for and is our birth right by faith in Jesus Christ as our Savior and Master.

**Father, thank you for breaking the power of sin in my life. Give me your all sufficient grace to live as a slave to your righteousness. Amen.**

# *You are Being Audited*

**"But there is going to come a time of testing at the judgment day to see what kind of work each builder has done." 1 Corinthians 3:12a NLT**

A letter from the Internal Revenue Service notifying you that your tax return is being audited brings a lot of angst regardless of whether or not you've done anything wrong.

> ***"They are a warning to those who hear them; there is great reward for those who obey them." Psalm 19:11 NLT***

We should be a lot more concerned about the audit of our lives at the great throne of judgment at the resurrection of the just.

Heaven is a free gift for all who receive it by faith in Jesus Christ and His death on the cross. The evidence of this faith is the transformed life James is talking about when he says that "faith without works is dead."

Jesus makes it very clear that those who profess Christ with their mouths, but who do not love and forgive others will have no home in heaven. Forgiveness, kindness, and sharing the good news are not options but commands.

Jesus died on the cross to set us free from bondage to sin so that we could become slaves to His righteousness. He gives us the transforming power of the Holy Spirit to live lives pleasing to God. The grace of God is free, but it's not cheap. It cost God His only Son and we dare not abuse God's grace by continuing to wallow in the pig pens of sin.

> ***"And you will be blessed, because they cannot repay you; for you shall be repaid at the resurrection of the just." Luke 14:14***

In addition to our destination being confirmed, our rewards beyond salvation will be handed out. There is a mystery about what these rewards might be, but we need to be aware that they do exist and not be ashamed to seek them.

We need to audit ourselves daily by asking whether we are living as slaves to righteousness by bearing the fruit of the Spirit. Is there any evidence to convict us of being born again Christians?

**Father, by the power of your Spirit, let me be found among the truly redeemed, and let me hear your "well done" on judgment day. Amen.**

Read Colossians 1:15-23, Proverbs 29 July 29

## *Mirror Mirror on the Wall*

**"For whom He foreknew, He also predestined to be conformed to the image of His Son, that He might be the firstborn among many brethren." Romans 8:29 NLT**

We live in an image conscious world. Everyone from politicians to preachers try to project a positive, pleasing image.

> ***"The fear of human opinion disables; trusting in God protects you from that."***
> ***Proverbs 29:25 MSG***

Teenagers seek to build their image among peers through wearing the cool clothes, listening to the cool music, and talking the cool talk.

As we grow older, we go through the hoops of developing or acquiring the image of the upwardly mobile, intellectually challenged, or being jerks, phonies, or genuine people.

We all have image problems in some areas. We struggle with our self image and often like ourselves too much, or not enough. Others see us as saints or sinners, bums or beautiful people, friends or foes, successes or failures, depending on their observations and experiences with us.

It's so good to know that we don't have an image problem with God. He sees us as we are, with all our faults and shortcomings, and loves us and accepts us in spite of them. However, He begins the process of conforming us into the image of Christ through the lives we lead and the witness our lives reflect.

As we grow into the fullness of Christ, we will reflect His character in every area of our lives. We, like the early disciples, will be identified as one of His elect, and people will see the humility, grace, beauty, and love of God and others manifest in us.

> ***"Christ is the visible image of the invisible God. He existed before God made anything at all and is supreme over all creation."***
> ***Colossians 1:15 NLT***

When we look into the mirror, we need to see clearly who we are now and who Christ wants us to be. We need to resolve to cooperate with the Holy Spirit in obedience and submission, as He molds and melds us into being all that God would have us be actually, as well as spiritually.

**Father, let others see the love of Christ in me. Amen.**

# *The Brain Drain*

**"This I say, therefore, and testify in the Lord, that you should no longer walk as the rest of the Gentiles walk, in the futility of their mind," Ephesians 4:17 NLT**

The New Life in Christ is made possible only by the indwelling of the Holy Spirit in the hearts of all who receive Jesus Christ as Savior and the incredible power, strength, and energy this provides.

***"He gives power to those who are tired and worn out; he offers strength to the weak" Isaiah 40:29 NLT***

God's power and the energy He generates are limitless, eternal, and all encompassing. Although God has set our spirits free from the power of sin, there are forces of evil at work on our flesh that will grieve and quench the Holy Spirit within us if we choose to allow it.

We all need to be constantly on guard against the "brain drain." When we waste any of our God-given power and energy on egocentric, unholy, unwholesome, or counter-productive thoughts, we are wasting power and energy that could be better used for the cause of Christ and growing into His fullness.

We can waste a lot of energy in holding on to past hurts and offenses by others instead of forgiving and moving on. We can waste a lot of energy in worrying which does not add one cubit to our stature. We can waste energy in arguing, complaining, pursuing immoral pleasure, and worshipping the idols of our mind.

How much better to use this energy to: *"Fix your thoughts on what is true and honorable and right. Think about things that are pure and lovely and admirable. Think about things that are excellent and worthy of praise."(Philippians 4:8b NLT).*

***"But now you are free from the power of sin and have become slaves of God. Now you do those things that lead to holiness and result in eternal life. Romans 6:22 NLT***

When we stop the "brain drain" we can find the joy of living life to its fullest in the fullness of its love, beauty, peace, and joy.

**Father, give me the power and strength to stop my "brain drains." Amen.**

# The Theology of Suffering

**"And it's trouble ahead if you think life's all fun and games. There's suffering to be met, and you're going to meet it." Luke 6:25 MSG**

It's interesting that the oldest book of the Bible is all about suffering. We can learn all we'll need to know, and more than we'll ever be able to understand, about suffering by studying the Book of Job.

> ***"For I know that my Redeemer lives, And He shall stand at last on the earth;" Job 19:25***

Job learned all about undeserved suffering. Even as the most righteous man living, he found himself getting blindsided by suffering.

Instead of trying to get rid of suffering by getting rid of God, as his wife suggested, he came to respect the mystery of suffering and how it can bring us closer and closer to God.

Job's realization that we should not accept all of the good things from God without accepting the bad echoes Paul's assertion that says "*And since we are his children, we will share his treasures—for everything God gives to his Son, Christ, is ours, too. But if we are to share his glory, we must also share his suffering."(Romans 8:17 NLT)*

The "name it and claim it" proclaimers who teach that we will be healthy, wealthy, and wise are probably the cruelest of all when they ascribe our sufferings to a lack of faith.

We owe it to ourselves and to our children to develop a Biblical perspective on suffering. We all need to understand that suffering is something that we are all going to experience, and usually even more as believers; that life is not fair, but that God is always fair, and that no pain or suffering lasts forever.

As God uses suffering (as He often does) as a tool to inspect, correct, or perfect us as part of His plan to conform us into the image of His Son, we need to respond with thanksgiving, patience, and longsuffering, confident of the joy that is set before us in Christ.

> ***"So if you are suffering according to God's will, keep on doing what is right, and trust yourself to the God who made you, for he will never fail you." 1 Peter 2:21 NLT***

**Father, give me the faith to persevere and the strength to endure whenever suffering comes my way. Amen.**

August 1 Read Revelation 7:9-17, Psalm 33

# *The Winners Circle*

**"All athletes practice strict self-control. They do it to win a prize that will fade away, but we do it for an eternal prize."** ***2 Corinthians 9:25 NLT***

In horse racing, every winner is acknowledged in the winner's circle where a trophy is awarded and the jockey, owners, trainers, and friends get to have their pictures taken with the winner.

> ***"Don't count on your warhorse to give you victory— for all its strength, it cannot save you." Psalm 33:17 NLT***

When a sinner receives Jesus Christ as Savior we are invited into God's winner's circle, where heaven is filled with great joy over us.

We are ushered into the family of God as joint heirs with Christ and receive the crown of eternal life.

As members of the "winner's circle" we join the Saints who have gone on before us to do great things for the the kingdom of God.

As winners in Christ, we are privileged to receive by faith the same supernatural power that raised Christ from the dead, and enabled the heroes of the faith to do mighty deeds in the name of the Lord. We are empowered to do the good deeds for which God created and planned for us to do before we were ever born.

Winning the spiritual victory over sin and death by faith qualifies us for winning the physical and emotional trials of life as we grow into the fullness of Christ and receive every spiritual blessing to help us.

Christ has won the battle over sin for us and set us free to pursue holiness in and through Him. He gives us the Holy Spirit to keep us in the circle of His will to guide and empower us.

There will be no losers in heaven. We are all winners in Christ. Let us therefore believe it, live like it, and rejoice, always seeking to be used by God to bring others into this glorious position.

> ***""These are the ones who come out of the great tribulation, and washed their robes and made them white in the blood of the Lamb" Revelation 7:14b***

**Father, now that you have given me a taste of winning, let us all strive to arrive into your heavenly presence full of good deeds we have done in thanksgiving and praise to you. Amen.**

Read James 1:12-27, Psalm 37

August 2

## *Rave Reviews*

**"For whoever finds me finds life and wins approval from the LORD. But those who miss me have injured themselves. All who hate me love death." Proverbs 8:35, 36 NLT**

The world prospers on rave reviews. Movies and plays thrive on good reviews by professional reviewers and testimonies of those who have seen them.

> ***"He'll validate your life in the clear light of day and stamp you with approval at high noon."***
> ***Psalm 37:6 MSG***

Manufacturers crave rave reviews from satisfied customers who can make the difference between profits or losses.

Scripture is full of rave reviews about God and His compassion, majesty, sovereignty, presence, glory, and love.

Life abounds with rave reviews from sinners saved by grace who have been brought back from the deadness of and slavery to sin, through receiving the new birth through faith in Jesus Christ.

We get a rave review from God when we receive Jesus Christ as our Lord and Savior. His declaration of "righteous" is better than any 5 star rating we could ever receive in this world.

If we truly love God and all that He has done for us through Christ, we will seek the ultimate rave review that comes from living a life of celebration and praise doing the things that honor and glorify God.

"Well done, thou good and faithful servant," is the greatest rave review anyone could ever receive, and it is within reach of all believers.

We need to live every day mindful that we are going to get to give an account of what we have done with the lives we have been given.

> ***"Blessed is the man who endures temptation; for when he has been approved, he will receive the crown of life which the Lord has promised to those who love Him.***
> ***James 1:12***

After all the wood, hay, and stubble of our self-glorifying efforts have been burned away, what will be left to merit a rave review for us?

**Father, help me to show my appreciation for all you have done for me. Amen.**

August 3 **Read 2 Peter 1, Isaiah 40:4-9**

## *Our Big Time God*

**"You didn't have enough faith," Jesus told them. "I assure you, even if you had faith as small as a mustard seed you could say to this mountain, 'Move from here to there,' and it would move. Nothing would be impossible."Matthew 17:20 NLT**

Big-time problems require big-time problem solvers. This is why we need to appropriate by faith the full resources available through our big-time God!

> ***"Every valley shall be exalted and every mountain and hill brought low; the crooked places shall be made straight" Isaiah 40:4***

God showed up big-time to part the waters of the Red Sea to save the children of Israel. He showed up biggest of all as Jesus Christ – Immanuel (God with us)-to break the bondage of sin and to reconcile man to God.

We have a tendency to put limits on God and His ability to empower us to do all things through Christ and His strength. As we grow into the fullness of Christ we will stop limiting God by our unbelief, unforgiveness, ungodly living, and failure to "ask, seek, and knock."

When we get to know God through intimacy with Christ, God shows up big-time in our lives. The faith to move mountains of sin, illness, worry, depression, or doubt, is the birth right of all who receive the new birth in Christ.

> ***"So make every effort to apply the benefits of these promises to your life. Then your faith will produce a life of moral excellence. A life of moral excellence leads to knowing God better." 2 Peter 1:5 NLT***

As we trust and obey God, we receive the promised blessings of answered God-glorifying prayers, friendship with God through Christ, awareness of the love of God and of others, and Jesus' joy.

God is not only big-time; He is always on time to show up in exactly the right place, in the right way, and at the right time.

**Father, thank you for your unfailing love and promises that are mine by faith; give me the faith to enjoy them now and forever. Amen.**

Read 2 Corinthians 13, Psalm 42 August 4

## *Are we there yet?*

**"The promise of "arrival" and "rest" is still there for God's people. God himself is at rest. And at the end of the journey we'll surely rest with God. So let's keep at it and eventually arrive at the place of rest, not drop out through some sort of disobedience." Hebrews 4:8 MSG**

Whether traveling to grandma's or Disney World, probably every parent has heard this question from impatient children on the road.

> ***"I'm thirsty for God-alive. I wonder, "Will I ever make it—arrive and drink in God's presence?"***
> ***Psalm 42:2 MSG***

"Are we there yet" and "how much longer" are questions that we all ask about our life's journey. Sometimes life seems so hard and troubles so great; we long for the bliss of heaven that going home to be with the Lord promises.

Other times as the reality of a terminal illness makes "how much longer," take on new meaning, or the twilight years draw us nearer and nearer to our final destination, we wonder "are we there yet?"

The question of "are we there yet?" is a good one to constantly ask ourselves in terms of growing into the fullness of Christ and being conformed into His image, which is God's desire for each of us.

> ***"Examine yourselves as to whether you are in the faith. Test yourselves. Do you not know yourselves, that Jesus Christ is in you?—unless indeed you are disqualified."***
> ***2 Corinthians 13:5***

Although we may never reach this objective until we receive our glorifed new bodies and eternal life in heaven, we can certainly enjoy the blessings and benefits of this life that growing in our relationship with God through intimacy with His Son promises.

As we abide more and more in Christ by giving Him more and more control over our lives, we have the love, friendship, joy, answered prayers, and pleasure of being fruitful in good works that glorify God's promise.

**Father, thank you for giving me the security of knowing my final destination and that I will get there at exactly the right time. Amen.**

**August 5** **Read Luke 12:35-48, Psalm 57**

# *Raising the Bar*

**"You must crave pure spiritual milk so that you can grow into the fullness of salvation. Cry out of this nourishment as a baby cries for milk, now that you have had a taste of the Lord's kindness." 1 Peter 2:2, 3 NLT**

Pole vaulting and horse show jumping are very exciting events to watch. As the bar is raised round after round, the excitement builds as contestants are eliminated at every level until the one who jumps highest, or highest and fastest, wins.

> ***"The deeper Your love, the higher it goes: every cloud is a flag to Your faithfulness"***
> ***Psalm 57:10 MSG***

God's character development program for us involves raising the bar round after round as we pursue the perfection of Christ.

We have so many obstacles to jump it takes a lot of practice, study, and submission to the will of God to even come close to being conformed to the image of Christ.

God is continually at work in us through the Holy Spirit to grow us into spiritual maturity that will equip us to bear much fruit. God seems to set the bar for us based on the talents and gifts we have been given, and how well we use them for His glory.

The fact that Scripture says "that to whom much is given, much is expected," and that the widow's mite was the greatest gift of all seems to confirm that God expects more from some than from others. The principal of proportionality prevails.

God knows the limits of our endurance and abilities. He will provide a means of escape from temptations too big to handle on our own.

> ***"Much is required from those to whom much is given, and much more is required from those to whom much more is given."***
> ***Luke 12:48b, NLT***

God does not expect us to give money or talents we do not have. He looks at the heart and asks that we love and serve Him with all our hearts. When we give 100% of our being, we have grown into the fullness of Christ.

**Father, help me to persevere over and through all obstacles as I seek to become like Christ. Amen.**

Read 2 Thessalonians 1, Psam 96 **August 6**

# *Worthiness*

**"There is really only one thing worth being concerned about. Mary has discovered it-and I won't take it away from her." Luke 10:42 NLT**

When we think of worth, we usually think of the value or price of something. We think that a house or car is worth going in debt for. We think some things are worth keeping, and throw other things away.

> ***"For great is the LORD and most worthy of praise; He is to be feared above all gods."***
> ***Psalm 96:4 NIV***

Our values tell a lot about us.

The way we spend or hoard our money is a good indicator of how selfish, wasteful, or generous we are.

The way we spend our lives is a good indicator of what our priorities are. When we pursue pleasure, power, applause, or any other ambition apart from God we are never going to find true happiness.

There is an old hymn that asks "what will you give in exchange for your soul?" It is sad to think that so many give up all of the joys of heaven and eternal life in selling out their souls to the world, their flesh, or the devil.

We need to ponder daily how much we are worth to God. When we realize that He thought we were worth having His Son die for, we begin to realize the breadth and depth of God's love. This makes us long to live lives worthy of our calling in Him.

As we grow in this relationship, we will become more and more aware of the truth that since God deemed us worthy of dying for, we can know for sure that He is worth living for.

God is worthy of our praise and our trust. As we learn to trust Him, we experience the incredible peace and joy that only He can give. We experience the truth of Ephesians 3:20, which says, *"Now to him who is able to do immeasurably more than all we ask or imagine, according to his power that is at work within us."*

> ***"With this in mind, we constantly pray for you, that our God may count you worthy of his calling, and that by his power he may fulfill every good purpose of yours and every act prompted by your faith."***
> ***2 Thessalonians 1:11 NIV***

**Father, help me to live a life worthy of your love. Amen.**

August 7 Read Luke 6:27-38, Proverbs 15

## *Watching Out for Those EGR's*

**"The Lord's servants must not quarrel but must be kind to everyone. They must be able to teach effectively and be patient with difficult people." 2 Timothy 2:24 NLT**

I learned this code word for difficult people from Rick Warren. He mentioned that in about every group, you are going to find an EGR, or someone for whom "Extra Grace is Required."

> ***"A wrathful man stirs up strife, But he who is slow to anger allays contention." Proverbs 15:NLT***

Speaking from experience, I would suggest that all of us are EGR's at times when we get our comfort zone squeezed, sometimes take ourselves too seriously, or leave the fruit of the Spirit, back at the fruit stand of grace. We too often lash out in anger, frustration, or caustic comments.

Many times we will find great reward in extending extra grace to those who need it. Since few people will give difficult people the time of day, those who respond to them with the grace required, will often break through the barrier of insecurities that usually cause such conduct. These people can develop some beautiful friendships with these "EGRs" and may even be the conduit of God's love that saves their souls.

I would be very surprised if any pastor did not have a mental EGR list of difficult parishioners.

When we think about it we can all identify with the extra grace we required to come to saving faith, and require to stay there. Sometimes we can barely stand ourselves, and wonder at the amazing grace of God that pours out to us in spite of our less than admirable conduct.

> ***"Do you think you deserve credit merely for loving those who love you? Even the sinners do that!" Luke 6:32 NLT***

When we run across EGR's, we need to remember EPR (extra prayer required) and pray that God will move in and move anger, self-centeredness, bad tempers, and bad attitudes out.

**Father, thank you for extending me the extra grace I required, and help me to extend it to others. Amen.**

**Read Mark 9:17-27, Hebrews 11, Psalm 19** **August 8**

# *Taking God Seriously*

**"“Listen to me and take it to heart. Honor my name,” says the LORD Almighty, “or I will bring a terrible curse against you. I will curse even the blessings you receive. Indeed, I have already cursed them, because you have not taken my warning seriously.” *Malachi 2:2 NLT***

We see a lot of failing to take God seriously all around us, and often times within us, as we journey through life.

> ***“They are a warning to those who hear them; there is great reward for those who obey them.”***
> ***Psalm 19:11 NLT***

When we take ourselves too seriously and lead self-serving, self-centered lives instead of God-serving, Christ-centered lives, we are failing to take God seriously.

How many blessings are we missing out on because we often fail to take God seriously? How many consequences of sin and bad choices do we have to live with because we failed to take God seriously?

Bondage and captivity have been the ongoing consequences of God's children failing to take Him seriously.

We all need to ask ourselves how seriously we have taken God's Word in not only doing the things He has told us not to do, but also in failing to do the things He has told us to do.

When we fail to forgive, to help those in need, to visit the sick and those in prison, and to be God's witness in this sin-sick world we are failing to take God seriously.

> ***“But without faith it is impossible to please Him, for he who comes to God must believe that He is, and that He is a rewarder of those who diligently seek Him.***
> ***Hebrews 11:6***

Hebrews 11 is full of examples of the heroes of the faith who took God seriously and harvested the blessings of taking God seriously.

As we work, while it is day before the night comes, may we take God's purpose for our lives seriously.

**Father, help me to trust, obey, and take you seriously in ever area of my life. Amen.**

August 9 Read Romans 15, Proverbs 11

# *Asset Appreciation*

**"And now, friends, we ask you to honor those leaders who work so hard for you, who have been given the responsibility of urging and guiding you along in your obedience. Overwhelm them with appreciation and love!" 1 Thessalonians 5:12 MSG**

Homes are the biggest material asset many people own and they usually continue to appreciate in value.

> ***"The generous prosper and are satisfied; those who refresh others will themselves be refreshed."***
> ***Proverbs 11:25 NLT***

Financial planners make a living from managing investment portfolios so that they appreciate in value. We are all asset managers of the relationships that God privileges us to have with other people.

These assets appreciate through the simple act of appreciation.

God loves and thrives on our appreciation. Our lives should be a celebration of showing our appreciation to Him.

Many of us struggle to overcome a critical and judgmental spirit. When we start looking for faults, we are sure to find them and never stop to think that when others look for faults in us they are sure to find them.

When we spend our time appreciating people instead of depreciating them our relational portfolio will grow and increase beyond measure. Everyone loves to be appreciated. If we think about it, we will find that most of our best friends are our best friends because they appreciate us and we appreciate them.

Starting with God, our spouses, and spreading to our family, friends, acquaintances, and all those the Lord puts in our path each day - we need to develop the habit of expressing our appreciation by sincere words and deeds.

> ***"So accept each other just as Christ has accepted you; then God will be glorified."***
> ***Romans 15:7 NLT***

Giving appreciation to others will produce dividends that will let our relational asset list grow in both quantity and quality. Wouldn't you like to be an appreciation investor?

**Father, by the power of your Spirit, help me to continually show my appreciation to you and to others. Amen.**

Read Romans 8:1-20, Psalm 16 August 10

# *The Double Standard*

**"The LORD despises double standards of every kind." Proverbs 20:10 NLT**

Although the playing field of life continues to become more level, we are still a world of double standards.

> ***"You will show me the way of life, granting me the joy of your presence and the pleasures of living with you forever."***
> ***Psalm 16:11 NLT***

There is still a double standard in wages and positions between men and women and between the white majority and ethnic minorities.

There is also the double standard between the world and God.

The world says take all you can get - God says share all you have been given. The world says the one with the most toys wins - God says the one with the most faith wins. The world says it's all about you, God says it's all about Him.

Double standards often lead to double mindedness. As we coexist in our corruptible flesh with our incorruptible spirit, we often allow the the flesh to bring out the worst in us, instead of letting the power of the Holy Spirit bring out God's best in us.

There are many even within churches who are trying to lower God's standards in the name of love and inclusion.

Although our God is an equal opportunity God, He does have a double standard between believers and unbelievers.

To those who believe that they are sinners, whose sins have been forgiven, and that they have received a new birth and eternal life through faith in Jesus Christ, God gives the keys to His kingdom for now and forever.

> ***"If your sinful nature controls your mind, there is death. But if the Holy Spirit controls your mind, there is life and peace."***
> ***Romans 8:6 NLT***

To those who reject God's call to salvation and insist on wandering aimlessly lost in a life of unbelief, God gives a one way ticket to a kingdom of darkness and the eternal torment of hell.

May we all cut through the double talk and double standards of the world and believe that Jesus is the only way, truth, and life.

**Father, may I never compromise your standards by buying into the standards of the World. Amen.**

August 11 Read 1 Timothy 4:7-16

# *Conserving Energy*

**"I heard a voice out of Heaven, "Write this: Blessed are those who die in the Master from now on; how blessed to die that way!""Yes," says the Spirit, "and blessed rest from their hard, hard work. None of what they've done is wasted; God blesses them for it all in the end."Revelation 14:13 MSG**

The ever increasing price of energy is disrupting our economy and working financial hardship on a lot of people. The world has become very conscious of conserving energy.

> ***"You don't want to squander your wonderful life, to waste your precious life among the hardhearted." Proverbs 5:9 MSG***

There are other types of energy that we're all guilty of wasting. We waste the energy of our bodies by using them as pleasure palaces instead of as temples of the Holy Spirit. Whether wasting them on substance abuse or immoral activities there is a lot of wasted energy going down the drain that could be better used to glorify God.

We waste the energy of our minds on hours of trivial pursuits and ego building efforts that offer no real and lasting peace or satisfaction. Worst of all, we waste the energy of our souls, by spending so much time worrying, wanting, judging, blaming, being angry, being proud, taking offense or being unforgiving; that we quench the Holy Spirit and all that God is seeking to accomplish through us.

We only have so much oil in our candle. We can conserve and use it wisely for growing into the fullness of Christ and accomplishing the purposes He created us for before we were ever born, or we can waste it on self-centered, destructive attitudes, and practices.

> ***"Do not waste time arguing over godless ideas and old wives' tales. Spend your time and energy in training yourself for spiritual fitness." 1 Timothy 4:7***

When we realize that we are going to have to give an accounting for how well we used the time, talents, and treasures we have been given, it might be beneficial to think about how we can quit wasting them.

**Father, help me to use my energy for seeking You and pursuing the righteousness of Your kind. Amen.**

Read James 3:13-18, Job 28

August 12

## *Living Wisely*

**"I ponder every morsel of wisdom from you, I attentively watch how you've done it. I relish everything you've told me of life, I won't forget a word of it." Psalm 119:15 MSG**

There is a wisdom of the flesh that is all about "looking out for #1" and leading egocentric, self-serving, and self-seeking lives. This is a mentality that feeds the basic instincts of our flesh and eventually reaps a whirlwind of bad consequences and the severe judgment of God.

***"And this is what he says to all humanity: 'the fear of the LORD is true wisdom; to forsake evil is real understanding.' Job 28:28 NLT***

The conventional wisdom of the world is all about "being all that you can be" in your own strength and being wise in the materialistic, secularistic, and hedonistic ways of the world. The wisdom of God rises above and beyond all earthly wisdom. It is powered by the Holy Spirit and energizes all believers to live lives of peace, joy, and beauty as modeled and taught by our Lord and Savior, Jesus Christ.

Reverence and respect for the Lord is the beginning of all true wisdom. Understanding that God's thoughts and God's ways are higher and submitting to this realization will help us to avoid much needless worry and stress.

Wisdom will teach us that there is a way which seems right to man that leads to destruction, and that God has set boundaries not to kill our joy and pleasure, but to insure it.

Living wisely begins and ends with growing in the knowledge and understanding of the Lord as He reveals Himself through Scripture, prayer, worship, circumstances, and other believers.

***"But the wisdom that comes from heaven is first of all pure. It is also peace loving, gentle at all times, and willing to yield to others. It is full of mercy and good deeds. It shows no partiality and is always sincere. And those who are peacemakers will plant seeds of peace and reap a harvest of goodness." James 3:17,18 NLT***

**Father, fill me with all wisdom and spiritual discernment as I seek to live wisely by abiding in You and Your love. Amen.**

**August 13** **Read Matthew 7, Psalm 130**

# *Finding What You Look For*

**"I, even I, am He who blots out your transgressions, for my own sake, and remembers your sins no more. Isaiah 43:25 NIV**

We are always looking for something. Whether it's a bargain, a cure, fun, fellowship, or peace and quiet, we are always looking.

***"LORD, if you kept a record of our sins, who, O Lord, could ever survive? Psalm 130:3 NLT***

In the area of relationships, we need to be mindful that we are most often going to find what we are looking for in people. If we look for the best in people, we are generally going to find it. If we look for the worst, we will also find that.

Much of what we'll find will be determined by how well we manifest the love and kindness of God to others. People have a tendency to respond in kind.

When we look for the best in others and offer the positive encouragement of love and kindness, we will usually find their best. When we bring anger or a critical, judgmental spirit into any relationship, we will most often bring out the worst in others.

People like to be appreciated, not judged. In living out the great commandment as followers of Jesus Christ, we need to be imitators of Him and model His love, compassion, and humility to others as He has modeled it to us.

We have all received an abundance of God's grace manifested in the birth, life, death, and resurrection of Jesus. We are all works in progress and are going to continually need forgiveness, grace, and mercy as we live out our lives being conformed and transformed into the image of Christ.

When our Lord says, *'Assuredly, I say to you, inasmuch as you did it to one of the least of these My brethren, you did it to Me,' (Matthew 25:40);* He is reminding us that everyone is precious in God's sight and for Jesus sake,

***"Therefore, whatever you want men to do to you, do also to them, for this is the Law and the Prophets." Matthew 7:12***

God loves us not for what He sees in us at our worst, but for what He sees in us at our best- when we are clothed in the righteousness of Christ.

**Father, Help me to look for and bring out the best in others. Amen.**

Read 2 Corinthians 2:14-17, Isaiah 5:2-7 **August 14**

# *How Sweet it Is!*

**"My child, eat honey, for it is good, and the honeycomb is sweet to the taste. In the same way, wisdom is sweet to your soul. If you find it, you will have a bright future, and your hopes will not be cut short." Proverbs 24:13, 14 NLT**

Sweet is defined as being pleasant to the taste, fragrant, much loved, or dear, wholesome, fresh, skillful, or proficient. Spiritual sweets are healthy, non-fattening, and something we should all "pig out" on.

***'What more could I have done to cultivate a rich harvest? Why did my vineyard give me wild grapes when I expected sweet ones?***
***Isaiah 5:4***

We need that special sweetness that can only be found in the fruit of the Spirit. When we live out our lives bearing love, joy, peace, longsuffering, kindness, goodness, faithfulness, gentleness, and self-control, we are going to have that sweetness of spirit that is so appealing to others and fragrant acts of worship to God.

When we abide in Christ through worship, fellowship, and getting to know Him intimately through His Word, the sweetness of the grace of God will remove all of the bitterness of unforgiveness, malice, anger, and rebellion, replacing it with the sweet joy of the Lord.

As we become wholesome and proficient in the Word, we discover the sweetness that only comes when we discover the reality of "Christ in us, our hope of glory."

The old, old hymn "'Tis so sweet to trust in Jesus", reminds us of the sweetness of taking God at His word and resting on His promises for cleansing, eternal life, joy, and peace.

***"Now thanks be to God who always leads us in triumph in Christ, and through us diffuses the fragrance of His knowledge in every place.***
***2 Corinthians 2:14***

Your sweetness is a fragrant offering that brings pleasure to everyone, especially to the God who loves you with an everlasting love and created you to be a fragrance of the sweetness of His love to others.

**Father, keep me ever mindful of the sweetness of your love and the joy of passing this sweetness on to others. Amen.**

**August 15** **Read Romans 11:30-36, Psalm 145**

## *Our Overwhelming Generosity*

**"Are any of us strong enough to give God a hand, or smart enough to give him advice?" Job 22:2 MSG**

Our freely given opinions and advice to God is not exactly what Scripture is referring to when it says we can be generous on all occasions.

> ***"Great is the LORD, and greatly to be praised; And His greatness is unsearchable." Psalm 145:3***

The conceit of a duck floating down the river and asking that the drawbridge be raised is nothing compared to our presumption that we have a better plan than God's in many areas of our lives and the lives of others.

Failure to acknowledge the sovereignty of God and to really believe that He *"works all things for the good of those who love Him, and who are called according to His purposes," (Romans 8:28*) can have serious consequences.

How many people do we know who are angry with and have given up on God because of the loss of a loved one or some other hurt or disappointment in life? How many prayers do we offer that are really selfish prayers or attempts to give God advice?

In the Lord's Prayer, and in His prayer in the garden of Gethsemane, our Lord acknowledged the sovereignty of God and unconditional submission to His sovereign will.

There is nothing wrong with asking God for special favors, healing, or blessings upon others. God does hear and answer our prayers, especially if we are abiding in Christ and are praying in submission to the all knowing, ever loving, and ultimately good will of God.

> ***"Is there anyone around who can explain God? Anyone smart enough to tell him what to do? Anyone who has done him such a huge favor that God has to ask his advice?" Romans 11:34 MSG***

We are not here as advisors of God. We are here as advisees, to learn all we can and live holy lives of obedience and cooperation with the one who always has our good and His glory in mind.

**Father, let me never presume upon Your sovereignty or Your good and gracious will. Amen.**

Read Galatians 4:1-11, Psalm 51 August 16

## *Of Human Bondage*

**"For the LORD sees clearly what a man does, examining every path he takes. An evil man is held captive by his own sins; they are ropes that catch and hold him." Proverbs 5:22, 23 NLT**

Like it or not, every child born of woman is born in bondage to sin. It's part of our human nature. Scripture after Scripture confirms this.

> ***"For I was born a sinner—yes, from the moment my mother conceived me."***
> ***Psalm 51:5 NLT***

Secular Humanism and liberal thought to the contrary, people grow in their bondage which is rooted in selfishness, self gratification, and allegiance to the forces of evil which are contending for the souls of men and women.

No one likes to admit that they are slaves to anyone or anything, but the facts speak otherwise. The multi-billion dollar porn industry gets these billions from slaves to sexual stimulation. The drug dealers get billions from slaves to pills or powder. People spend their lives in bondage to seeking power, possessions, and the approval of others.

The worst bondage of all is the bondage of our will. We are all going to choose to worship something. It will either be ourselves, our spouses, our jobs, our pleasures, our treasures, or some other form of idolatry. However, we can, by the power of the Holy Spirit, choose to worship God and be set free from our bondage to sin by His transforming power. Jesus has come to set the captives free. When we are born again through faith in Jesus Christ, we have died to the dominion and condemnation of sin and become alive in the righteousness of Christ.

Through faith in Jesus Christ we are freed from bondage to sin of any kind and receive the perfect love of God that even casts out fear. We are freed to live today and to face tomorrow secure in the unconditional, everlasting love of God that gives us that all sufficient grace, all surpassing peace for today, and our bright and glorious hope for tomorrow.

> ***"Even so we, when we were children, were in bondage under the elements of the world."***
> ***Galatians 4:3 NLT***

**Lord, thank you for setting me free from bondage to sin. Please give me the strength and power of the Holy Spirit to live free. Amen .**

August 17 Read Romans 8:17-25, Psalm 31

# *Levels of Life*

**"Unlike the culture around you, always dragging you down to its level of immaturity, God brings the best out of you, develops well-formed maturity in you." Romans 12:2 MSG**

Life is all about levels. We have levels of maturity, levels of achievement, and levels of prosperity. We go from one grade level to the next in school. We participate in athletics from pick up games to organized competitions on the grade school, high school, college, and sometimes professional level.

> ***"Get down on my level and listen, and please— no procrastination! Your granite cave a hiding place, Your high cliff area a place of safety." Psalm 31:2 MSG***

There are three levels in the lives of every believer. We become saved by the grace of God through faith in Jesus Christ and become temples for the Holy Spirit. By the power of the Holy Spirit, we grow into the fullness and likeness of Christ through sanctification. We begin as little children, feeding on the milk of the Good News and begin a life long journey through level after level of knowledge, spiritual wisdom and discernment, and spiritual maturity as God continues to conform us into the likeness of His Son.

As we advance through these levels of life in Christ, God and His will continue to increase and our self-centered, sinful nature decreases as we discover the peace and joy of abiding in Christ.

All of the work of the Holy Spirit comes to fruition when we reach the level of glorification when we die and share in the Glory of Christ. We will live forever in glorified, incorruptible bodies, in a state of perfect bliss and happiness where there will be no more tears, no more sorrow, and no more pain.

Salvation, sanctification, and glorification. May we all receive the wisdom to understand and the strength to persevere, advance, and look forward to reaching that highest level.

> ***"Yet what we suffer now is nothing compared to the glory he will give us later" Romans 8:18***

**Father, help me to keep my calling sure and my joy complete as I grow higher and higher into your fullness. Amen.**

Read 1 Corinthians 1:17-31, 1 Kings 3:9-12 **August 18**

## *An Understanding Heart*

**"Wisdom is enshrined in an understanding heart; wisdom is not found among fools." Proverbs 14:33 NLT**

> ***"The Lord was pleased with Solomon's reply and was glad that he had asked for wisdom." 1 Kings 3:10 NLT***

In the arrogance of our flesh, we all have the temptation to second guess God on occasion. From our world-centered, human perspective, some of the things God does just don't make sense to us. *To "Trust in the LORD with all your heart, and lean not on your own understanding," (Proverbs 3:5)* is perhaps for many the hardest command we will ever be asked to obey.

Untimely deaths, tragic accidents, broken relationships, ruined lives, and other calamities we see all around us, or experience ourselves, test our faith right down to its very foundation, or hopefully up to its highest level, as we receive the strength and wisdom that comes from on High in times of trouble.

Solomon, the wisest man who ever lived, was at his wisest when he asked God for an understanding heart. It is only with an understanding heart filled with wisdom from on High that we can ever experience the depth of God's love, the riches of His grace, and the fullness of His joy. *"Oh, the depth of the riches both of the wisdom and knowledge of God! How unsearchable are His judgments and His ways past finding out!" (Romans 11:33 NLT)*

Often we do not appreciate the wisdom of God in some of our circumstances, but can later look back and see how God really does work all things for the good of those who love Him and who are called according to His purposes.

> ***"But of Him you are in Christ Jesus, who became for us wisdom from God— and righteousness and sanctification and redemption-" 1 Corinthians 17:30 NLT***

Wisdom is all about living wisely in the nurture and admonition of the Lord. We cannot acquire godly wisdom apart from God, and we can not acquire it by osmosis. We pray for it, seek it in abiding in God's Word, and get to know Him and His Will through it.

**Father, let me seek after godly wisdom all the days of my life. Amen.**

August 19 Read Ecclesiastes 3:1-15, Romans 12

# *The Rhythm of Life*

**"And it will come to pass in that day *That* the mountains shall drip with new wine, The hills shall flow with milk, And all the brooks of Judah shall be flooded with water; A fountain shall flow from the house of the LORD" JOEL 3:18**

There is a rhythm of life all about us. In nature we see the ebb and flow of the tides, the rising and setting of the sun, and the fluctuation of the seasons.

> ***"To everything there is a season, A time for every purpose under heaven:" Ecclesiastes 3:1***

Our lives on this earth reflect the rhythm of life. We experience the seasons of infancy, childhood, adulthood, old age, and the joys and pains of each season.

The question we all have to answer is what rhythm of life will we choose. God gave us all a free will and the freedom to choose our rhythm.

We can choose the rhythm of the flesh and spend lives bent on gratifying the basic instincts of our flesh and end up in the pig pen of the damned, or we can choose to live out the rhythm of life in the blood bought freedom of the Spirit by receiving eternal life through faith in Jesus Christ.

Proverbs 14:12 tells us: *"There is a way that seems right to a man, but its end is the way of death."* Joshua exhorted the Israelites to choose who they would serve, but made it clear He and His house would serve the Lord.

God has the perfect plan for each of us. *"For I know the plans I have for you," says the LORD. "They are plans for good and not for disaster, to give you a future and a hope." (Jeremiah 29:11)*

> ***"I beseech you therefore, brethren, by the mercies of God, that you present your bodies as a living sacrifice, holy, acceptable to God, which is your reasonable service" Romans 12:1***

As we go through the seasons of life, how sweet it is to be in rhythm with the One who promises to work all things for the good of those who love Him and are answering His call to fulfill the purposes for which we were created.

**Father, help me to be ever mindful of the rhythm of life and help me to stay in step with You. Amen.**

**Read Ephesians 2:1-10, Psalm 40** **August 20**

# *Don't Just Do It!*

**"Jesus answered and said to him, "Most assuredly, I say to you, unless one is born again, he cannot see the kingdom of God." John 3:3**

We live in a performance oriented society. We are exhorted to "just do it" in athletics, business, conduct, and practically every other area of life.

> ***"I take joy in doing Your will, my God, for Your law is written on my heart." Psalm 40:8 NLT***

When it comes to "doing it" with regards our salvation we must never forget that Christ has done it all for us on the Cross of Calvary and that our salvation is not a matter of doing, but a matter of believing.

It is sad, but true that many Christians still base their salvation on how well they perform. "I've lived a good life," "I've never hurt anyone," and "I have been a good spouse or parent," are some of the most common reasons given for the hope of heaven.

While it is true that faith without works is dead and there are rewards to be stored up in heaven by doing things that please and glorify God, we need to always remember that "being" is the only thing that makes us acceptable to God.

God says that "apart from me you can do nothing." Until we are born again into a personal relationship with God through faith in Jesus Christ all of the "doing" in the world is not going to amount to a hill of beans in determining our eternal destination. All our "doings" will certainly not store up treasures in heaven if we're not going there in the first place.

> ***"God saved you by his special favor when you believed. And you can't take credit for this; it is a gift from God. Salvation is not a reward for the good things we have done, so none of us can boast about it." Ephesians 2:8, 9 NLT***

Our "being" reflects more and more of who we are in Christ as we grow in our knowledge of God through His Word.

As we receive the power we need to live lives fully pleasing to God by abiding in Christ, our "being" motivates our "doing" the things that please God and accomplish the purposes for which we were created.

**Father, let my "being" bring the fruit of the Spirit and Your holiness into every area of my "doing" in the journey of life. Amen.**

# *Inspections*

**"Eventually there is going to be an inspection. If you use cheap or inferior materials, you'll be found out. The inspection will be thorough and rigorous. You won't get by with a thing." 1 Corinthians 3:13 MSG**

We live in an inspection oriented society. We have inspectors checking food, restaurants, medications, and gasoline pumps.

> ***"Tell all the nations that the LORD is king. The world is firmly established and cannot be shaken. He will judge all peoples fairly."***
> ***Psalm 96:30 NLT***

I especially appreciate that the airplanes I ride in are inspected often. It seems strange that we put such great emphasis on inspecting everything except the most important thing.

Instead of spending so much time inspecting and judging other people, we need to be inspecting ourselves and measuring our progress in how much we're growing in spiritual maturity and into the fullness of Christ.

Daily recognition, confession, and repentance of our sins will halt or slow their progression. When we judge and correct ourselves, God won't have to, and we can escape some of the chastening that our loving heavenly father metes out as needed.

Daily retrospection of our day's activities should not neglect reflecting on what we have learned or how we have grown in our friendship with, and knowledge of, Jesus.

We can never thank God enough for calling us into a saving relationship through faith in His Son, but living a life of celebration, praise, and service to Him will prepare us for the ultimate inspection.

> ***"For no other foundation can anyone lay than that which is laid, which is Jesus Christ"***
> ***1 Corinthians 3:11***

When Jesus inspects what we have done with the time, talents, and treasures God has given us, His "well done thou good and faithful servant," will be the greatest music our ears have ever heard.

**Father, Help me to build wisely on the firm foundation you have provided that I might be ready for the ultimate inspection. Amen.**

**Read 2 Timothy 1, Psalm 136** **August 22**

## *Faithfulness We Can Trust*

**"I am the LORD," He says, "and there is no other. I publicly proclaim bold promises. I do not whisper obscurities in some dark corner so no one can understand what I mean. And I did not tell the people of Israel to ask me for something I did not plan to give. I, the LORD, speak only what is true and right." Isaiah 45:19 NLT**

We seem to live in a world of broken promises. Two out of every three couples break their marriage promises.

> ***"Give thanks to the LORD, for He is good! His faithful love endures forever." Psalm 136:1 NLT***

Politicians continue to break promises they made in order to get elected. Relative truth seems to also mean that promises are no longer relative.

The truth is that we are never going to find any perfect person we can trust to never disappoint or let us down, and we are going to disappoint and let others down in one way or another, as well.

The Good News is that we can trust the faithfulness of God. His love is unconditional and everlasting. His promises are sure.

God's faithfulness is recorded throughout Scripture. Today's Psalm is a litany to His enduring love and faithfulness. He has delivered, forgiven, and restored His chosen ones since the beginning of time.

Jesus Christ is the Living Testament to the faithfulness of God. He is God Incarnate, the living Word, and the promised Redeemer who died for our broken promises so that we wouldn't have to.

> ***"For if we are faithful to the end, trusting God just as firmly as when we first believed, we will share in all that belongs to Christ." Hebrews 3:14 NLT***

In this world of make believe and broken promises, isn't it great to know that we have an all-powerful, all-knowing, and ever-faithful God whose promises are sure and who loves us with an everlasting love no matter what?

**Father, I thank and praise You for your faithfulness. By the power of the Holy Spirit living within me, may I always know that I can trust you in every area of my life. Amen.**

August 23 Read John 15:1-8, Psalm 66

## *Hindered Prayers*

**"Listen! The LORD is not too weak to save you, and He is not becoming deaf. He can hear you when you call. But there is a problem—your sins have cut you off from God. Because of your sin, He has turned away and will not listen anymore." Isaiah 59:1, 2**

One of the greatest privileges we have as children of God and joint heirs with Christ is the privilege of carrying everything to God in prayer, and knowing that He will listen, consider, and answer in His time and in His way.

***"If I had not confessed the sin in my heart, my Lord would not have listened. But God did listen! He paid attention to my prayer. Psalm 66:18, 19 NLT***

When we are abiding in Christ, we can be sure that all of our prayers that glorify God and that are in accordance with His will will be heard and answered.

Scripture tells us that "the prayers of a righteous man availeth much," to "pray without ceasing," and that "God inhabits the praises of His people." We need to be persistent and fervent in prayer.

However, there are character defects and attitudes that will cause God not to listen to our prayers. Willful, unconfessed sins are obvious hindrances to getting God to hear and answer our prayers.

When we are living lives separated from God by our sins, we have no right to expect God to be on call. "*The eyes of the Lord watch over those who do right, and his ears are open to their prayers. But the Lord turns his face against those who do evil."(1 Peter 3:12 NLT)*

An unforgiving spirit and selfish motives will corrupt our prayer channel of communication with God. Failure to be understanding and to honor wives as joint heirs together of the grace of life will hinder any husband's prayers.

***"But if you stay joined to me and my words remain in you, you may ask any request you like, and it will be granted!" John 15:7 NLT***

When we "plug in" to the power of prayer available by faith to all believers, we will discover the incredible joy that answered prayers bring. We dare not let anything hinder our prayer life in Christ.

**Father, thank you for the privilege and blessing of prayer. Amen.**

Read Romans 5:1-12, Psalm 24 August 24

## *How's Your Standing*

**"Stand fast therefore in the liberty by which Christ has made us free ..." (Galatians 5:1)**

Many of the miracles performed by Jesus and the Disciples empowered the crippled, disabled, and even the dead to stand up and walk. This is exactly what happens to all who receive Jesus Christ as their Savior and Lord.

> ***"Who may climb the mountain of the LORD? Who may stand in His holy place?***
> ***Psalm 24:3 NLT***

We are empowered to stand up and walk in freedom from bondage to sin and in the liberty of our new life in Christ.

By the enabling power of the Holy Spirit who comes to live within all believers, we are given the strength to stand up, stand fast, stand on, and stand forever in the all sufficient grace of the Lord.

Jesus told the Apostle Paul: *"Now stand up! For I have appeared to you to appoint you as my servant and my witness. You are to tell the world about this experience and about other times I will appear to you." (Acts 26:16)* He tells us to do the same today.

We are all called to "stand up, stand up for Jesus"! When the storms of life come, we are told to "stand fast" and are given the supernatural strength and power of the Holy Spirit to persevere through even the worst of circumstances.

What comfort there is in knowing that God is working everything for our good and His glory, that these problems are not going to last forever, and that a glorious crown awaits all who "stand fast" in their faith and their walk. The only thing that is going to last forever is the wonderful gift of eternal life which is ours to enjoy now and forever.

> ***"Because of our faith, Christ has brought us into this place of highest privilege where we now stand, and we confidently and joyfully look forward to sharing God's glory."***
> ***Romans 5:2 NLT***

Nothing should ever separate us from the love of God that is ours through faith in Jesus Christ or rob us of our joy in knowing that we are going to dwell in His heavenly home with Him forever.

**Father, thank You for the blessed assurance I have in standing on your promises. Amen.**

August 25 Read 1 Peter 2:1-12, Proverbs 1:20-33

## *Finding the Right Outlet*

**"Present yourselves as building stones for the construction of a sanctuary vibrant with life, in which you'll serve as holy priests offering Christ-approved lives up to God." 1 Peter 2:4b MSG**

The key to a fulfilling life in Christ is to find the right outlet for your energy, talents, drives, and emotions.

> ***"But whoever listens to me will dwell safely, And will be secure, without fear of evil." Proverbs 1:33 NLT***

We all have a lot of excess energy that we can either expend on trivial pursuits or self-centered agendas, or we could use this energy to grow in our relationship with the Lord through growing in His Word.

God has provided the right outlet for our sexual drives. It is one man and one woman in a God-ordained spiritual and physical union called marriage. Any deviation from what God has ordained leads to dysfunctional lives and robs us of the greatest pleasure God wants us to have through the gift of sexuality.

God provides us with plenty of outlets to be salt and light in a sin-sick world. We are called to be Ambassadors for Jesus Christ with the command to love and serve others.

The best outlet for all of the basic instincts and evils of our old sin nature that satan may use to destroy us is the Cross of Calvary

> ***"But you are not like that, for you are a chosen people. You are a kingdom of priests, God's holy nation, His very own possession. This is so you can show others the goodness of God, for he called you out of the darkness into his wonderful light." 1 Peter 2:9 NLT***

When we learn to let out our anger, disappointments, lust, envy, pride, and other cardinal sins that often creep in as we co-exist with our flesh and our spirit, the Holy Spirit will fill us with the fruit of His Spirit.

We not only find the right outlet, but we become the right outlet of God's love, grace, and mercy that He can use to build up His kingdom.

**Father, by the power of Your Spirit, make me the right outlet for others to see Jesus. Amen.**

Read Galatians 6, Psalm 63 August 26

## *A Most Important Principle*

**"Remember this—a farmer who plants only a few seeds will get a small crop. But the one who plants generously will get a generous crop." 2 Corinthians 9:6 NLT**

God's grace that gives us our free gift of salvation through faith in Jesus Christ is the foundation of our faith. God loves us unconditionally, sets us free from all condemnation, and forgives us for every sin we have ever committed or will ever commit.

> ***"The rivers of God will not run dry; they provide a bountiful harvest of grain, for you have ordered it so" Psalm 93:9b NT***

As wonderful and amazing as the grace of God is it cannot and will not always insulate us and free us from the consequences of our bad choices and sinful actions.

Scripture after scripture reminds us of the fact that we will reap what we sow. When we give cheerfully and generously of our time, talents, or treasures, we will harvest an abundance of blessings.

When we sow seeds of love, kindness, and compassion we will harvest blessings of love, kindness, and compassion. When we forgive, we will be forgiven. When we are faithful stewards of the lives God has given us, we will reap a harvest of blessings in this life and the next.

The consequences of sin and bad choices are often severe and painful. When we sow seeds of anger and bitterness we will reap thorns of anger and bitterness. When we sow in the pride of the flesh we will find out what Scripture means when it says that *"God resists the proud but gives grace to the humble."(Proverbs 3:34)*

> ***"So don't get tired of doing what is good. Don't get discouraged and give up, for we will reap a harvest of blessing at the appropriate time" Galatians 6:9 NLT***

We need to always remember that there is a reaction for every action and to act accordingly to make sure that the reactions to our actions bring glory to God, harvests of blessings to others, and to ourselves. The principle "What goes around comes around" and the golden rule should be guiding lights for the way we live our lives.

**Father, by the power of Your Spirit, help me to sow the good seed that's brings a harvest of blessings. Amen.**

 **Read Matthew 5:3-11, Ecclesiastes 2**

# *The Pursuit of Happiness*

**"How happy are those who fear the LORD—all who follow his ways! You will enjoy the fruit of your labor. How happy you will be! How rich your life!" Psalm 128:1, 2 NLT**

We live in a world driven by the pursuit of pleasure. TV ads are often instruction manuals for finding pleasure in booze, cars, events, and sex. The great American dream has turned into the great American nightmare as we pursue getting great careers, great marriages, great kids, great homes, and great cars.

> ***"Then I realized that this pleasure is from the hand of God.[2]For who can eat or enjoy anything apart from Him?" Ecclesiastes 2:24B, 25 NLT***

Failing to bring our children up in the nurture and admonition of the Lord, so that they might find true happiness is a forgotten command in most households. We choose to bring them up wanting them to have it better than we had it and teaching them that happiness comes from material things and self-gratification, instead of from a right relationship with God.

Our upward mobility should not be focused on accumulating wealth, approval, and position. It should be focused on looking upward and keeping our eye on the prize that God has for us for now and forever. There is no greater state of well-being and contentment than having the peace of God that surpasses all understanding. There is no more pleasurable or satisfying experience than living the good life in Christ. Best of all, this good life lasts forever!

Happiness sought through wickedness is limited to this life, is short, vain, and uncertain. When we try to find it through wealth, power, or vain pleasure, we are never going to experience true happiness.

> ***"You're blessed when you're content with just who you are—no more, no less.That's the moment you find yourselves proud owners of everything that can't be bought." Mstthew 5:3 MSG***

God has set boundaries for our good pleasure. No good thing will He withhold from those who love Him.

**Father, help me to pursue happiness and godly contentment in you. Amen.**

Read 1 Corinthians 15:55-58, Psalm 140:1-8 **August 28**

# *Beware of the Killer Bees*

**"And I have given you authority over all the power of the enemy, and you can walk among snakes and scorpions and crush them. Nothing will injure you." Luke 10:19**

A strain of Africanized bees, also known as "killer bees" is spreading rapidly throughout the world. They are aggressive, attack in large groups, hate high pitched sounds, swarm more often, and produce much less honey than honey bees.

> ***"Their tongues sting like a snake; the poison of a viper drips from their lips." Psalm 140:3 NLT***

Any bee sting can cause often fatal shock in someone who is allergic to them. It is a good idea for anyone to keep an antidote for the allergic reaction caused by bee venom. As bad as bee stings may be, we have to deal with the deadly venom of sin much more often. The venom of evil is all around us. When we are stung we are often overcome by shock, which can cripple and eventually kill us.

Thanks be to God that He has provided us with the perfect antidote that will fight off our allergic reaction and restore us. The blood of Jesus Christ, shed on the cross of Calvary, not only removes the sting of death, but also regenerates us into temples where the Holy Spirit indwells and transforms us into new creatures in Christ. This antidote frees us from bondage to sin and gives us not only the power to overcome death and the grave, but to persevere through the storms and temptations of life.

A daily dose of confession and repentance will bring the resurrection power of the Holy Spirit to strengthen us through our moral lapses, failures, pains, and sufferings. When we add the full armor of God, we will be vaccinated against the attacks of the real killer bees.

> ***"For sin is the sting that results in death, and the law gives sin its power." 1 Corinthians 15:56***

**Father, help me to keep my immunizations up to date by abiding in your Word and coming to your throne of grace daily. Amen.**

August 29 Read Luke 15:11-31, Psalm 69

# *Doing the Limbo*

**"Repent therefore of this your wickedness, and pray God if perhaps the thought of your heart may be forgiven you. For I see that you are poisoned by bitterness and bound by iniquity." Acts 8:22, 23**

> ***"Deeper and deeper I sink into the mire; I can't find a foothold to stand on." Psalm 69:2 NLT***

You have probably been to a party or watched a movie where people did the limbo. People dance under a bar usually held by two other people and the bar is lowered each time everyone dances under it, until only one person has danced under without touching the bar. Although this is a terrible and destructive way to live life, many people seem to be doing the limbo in seeing how low they can go before bottoming out.

Every addiction is like a limbo dance where the participant sinks lower and lower as the addiction gets stronger and stronger. The prodigal son is a good example of someone doing the limbo. He took an early inheritance and left the love, security, and comfort of his home and family for the bright lights and big city. After he wasted his inheritance on cigarettes, whiskey, and wild, wild women (or whatever the vices of the day were), He sank so low that he was hungering for slop with the pigs in a pig sty.

God has given everyone a free will and permission to do the limbo if that's what they choose. Many sink so low and never recover. Others finally come to their senses and repent and turn to God whose outstretched arms are always ready to receive those who bring a broken spirit and contrite heart to Him. In Catholic theology, limbo is an abode for souls banned from heaven because they have not received Christian Baptism.

> ***"A few days later this younger son packed all his belongings and took a trip to a distant land, and there he wasted all his money on wild living." Luke 13:13 NLT***

Whether sinking in sin or unbelief, no one should want to do the limbo.

**Father, guide me and guard me that I never dance the limbo of a depraved life of bondage. Amen.**

Read Ephesians 4:30-32, Proverbs 3 August 30

## *Costs So Little, Means So Much*

**"This is what the LORD Almighty says: Judge fairly and honestly, and show mercy and kindness to one another. Zechariah 7:9 NLT**

There seems to be a lack of kindness in every aspect of life these days.

> ***"Never let loyalty and kindness get away from you! Wear them like a necklace; write them deep within your heart." Proverbs 3:3 NLT***

We need to remember that we need to show mercy if we expect to receive it, and that kindness begets kindness.

Rude and obnoxious behavior often denotes the insecurity of living in a "dog eat dog" world where any show of kindness or courtesy might be viewed as weakness.

We are created and commanded to love others. Paul's great definition of love in 1 Corinthians 13 reminds us that love is not only patient, but kind. A cup of kindness costs so little and yet can mean so much to others, and it can even bring a smile to God's face.

From the simple courtesy of opening a door for someone to responding to anger with longsuffering and patience, we can find opportunities to show the love of God through kindness every day in many ways.

We see kindness demonstrated at its best during disasters. 9/11, hurricanes, and tornadoes seem to bring out the best in people. The observance of Christmas seems to bring out kindness that lays dormant the rest of the year in many people.

It costs nothing to be kind to our servers at restaurants and stores, to yield the right of way in traffic, to give someone our seat on a bus or in a crowded waiting room, and to take advantage to perform random acts of kindness to others in many situations.

> ***"Instead, be kind to each other, tenderhearted, forgiving one another, just as God through Christ has forgiven you. Ephesians 4:32 NLT***

We can reach out and touch someone today with a cup of kindness that will mean so much to them.

Let's make that hospital or shut in visit, send that card of encouragement or remembrance, or reflect God's love through our kindness to others in some other way this day.

**Father, May I glorify You through my kindness to others. Amen.**

August 31 Read Philippians 2:1-18, Psalm 147

# Unbridled

**"I will remove all the proud and arrogant people from among you. There will be no pride on my holy mountain. Those who are left will be the lowly and the humble, for it is they who trust in the name of the LORD." Zephaniah 3:11b, 12 NLT**

Among the worst character defects anyone can have, an unbridled tongue is probably exceeded only by an unbridled ego. When we remain self-centered instead of Christ-centered, we are going to have problems in every area of our lives. As Rick Warren so aptly starts in his book, "Purpose Driven Life," "It's not about You!"

***"The LORD lifts up the humble; He casts the wicked down to the ground." Psalm 147:6 NLT***

We see spoiled children who think that the world revolves around them and that everyone should be subservient to their whims and desires. Although adults are more subtle, the same mind-set prevails in the hearts of many people.

Whether we call it pride or ego, it keeps many from receiving the wonderful gift of eternal life through faith in Jesus Christ because they cannot humble themselves enough to submit to His Lordship.

As bad and as prevalent as sexual immorality is in today's world, pride and arrogance are probably five times as prevalent, and top God's hate list.

Scripture affirms time and time again that: *"True humility and fear of the LORD lead to riches, honor, and long life." (Proverbs 22:4)*

When we persist in pride, arrogance, or pretentiousness we can be sure that God will do whatever it takes to humble us, so that we can be conformed to the image of Christ.

How much better to dump our self-centered pride at the cross, and develop humility as we submit to the Lordship of Jesus Christ.

***"Don't be selfish; don't live to make a good impression on others. Be humble, thinking of others as better than yourself." Philippians 2:3 NLT***

**Father, let all of my glorying be in the joy of my salvation and glorifying the One who gave it to me. Amen.**

Read Hebrews 6:19, Psalm 40 September 1

## *Lord, Teach Me Patience & Please Hurry*

**"Since God chose you to be the holy people whom he loves, you must clothe yourselves with tenderhearted mercy, kindness, humility, gentleness, and patience." Colossians 3:12 NLT**

Patience is a virtue many of us seem to struggle with even in our new life in Christ. We live in an age of instant gratification, communication, and self-centeredness.

> ***"I waited patiently for the LORD to help me, and He turned to me and heard my cry." Psalm 40:1 NLT***

Impatience is a major cause of almost all accidents. When we get impatient, oftentimes bad things happen and we often find ourselves ending up spending twice as much time and energy as if we had just been patient and taken our time in the first place.

How many relationships have we had go sour because we were too quick too speak and get angry?

God's character development program for us involves teaching us to be patient and steadfast despite opposition, difficulty, or adversity. Time and time again Scripture reminds us to patiently endure.

God tells us in James 5:11, *"My brethren, take the prophets, who spoke in the name of the Lord, as an example of suffering and patience. Indeed we count them blessed who endure. You have heard of the perseverance of Job and seen the end intended by the Lord—that the Lord is very compassionate and merciful."*

Impatience can not only lead us into bad marriages, but is often the underlying cause of conflict in even the best of marriages. When we are impatient with our spouses or our children, we are not modeling the love of Christ which we are all commanded to reflect.

> ***"That you do not become sluggish, but imitate those who through faith and patience inherit the promises." Hebrews 6:12***

If God was not longsuffering and patient with us, we would all be doomed. Should we not also be longsuffering and patient with others?

**Father, help me to be patient in every area of my life. Amen.**

September 2 Read John 17, Psalm 23

# *Practical Christianity*

**"I am overwhelmed with joy in the LORD my God! For He has dressed me with the clothing of salvation and draped me in a robe of righteousness. I am like a bridegroom in his wedding suit or a bride with her jewels." Isaiah 61:10 NLT**

We are made holy in God's sight the minute we receive Jesus Christ as our Savior. This is our position spiritually, and this is the holiness which makes it possible for us to see the Lord in heaven.

> ***"He restores my soul; He leads me in the paths of righteousness For His name's sake."***
> ***Psalm 23:3***

Becoming holy in the sight of those around us is the essence of practical Christianity. The Holy Spirit comes to live inside of us to begin the ongoing transformation from sinner to saint, as God conforms us into the image of Christ by the incredible power and strength of the Holy Spirit.

In God's sight we are instantly sanctified and being made holy day by day, month by month, and year by year as evidenced of the lives we lead as professing Christians growing into the fullness of Christ. Practical Christianity is not only "talking the talk," but "walking the walk" of faith, obedience, humility, and purity.

Practical Christianity is proven by our reflecting the Love of God to others. We will bear the fruit of the Spirit - love, joy, peace, patience, kindness, goodness, faithfulness, gentleness, and self-control. As temples of the Holy Spirit we need to keep our temples clean through the daily cleansing of confession and repentance.

> ***"Make them pure and holy by teaching them your words of truth."***
> ***John 17:17 NLT***

The good news is that we don't have to become practical Christians in our own strength. This is the work of the Holy Spirit, who will guide us into all truth, and give us the power to live holy lives as ones set apart for the glory of God.

**Father, lead me along the paths of righteousness. Amen.**

**Read Matthew 13:13-30, Psalm 51** **September 3**

## *Bring Back the Romance!*

**"Nevertheless I have this against you, that you have left your first love. Remember therefore from where you have fallen; repent and do the first works, or else I will come to you quickly and remove your lampstand from its place—unless you repent." Revelation 2:4, 5**

When you fell in love with your spouse you were filled with passion, thought about him or her day and night, and would look for ways to please him or her.

> ***"Restore to me again the joy of your salvation, and make me willing to obey You.***
> ***Psalm 51:12 NLT***

Sometimes the ravages of living in a sin-sick world cause betrayal, anger, or unmet expectations. When selfishness, greed, unforgiveness, or a critical spirit move in, love often moves out.

When we first fell in love with Jesus, we experienced the peace and joy of our salvation and the assurance of everlasting life. We thought about, and prayed to, Him, were on fire to tell others about Him, and looked for ways to please Him.

Unfortunately for many of us, our passion and romance with Jesus was put on the back burner as we got caught up in living life our way and by the world's standards, instead of living God's way and for His glory.

Instead of keeping God first, we relegated him to a distant second, or worse, in our overall love list. We neglected corporate and personal worship and got out of His Word, preferring the vast wasteland of TV and other sinful distractions.

In His longsuffering and patience, God will put up with a lot more rebellion and playing second fiddle than we would, and the Holy Spirit will continue to work mightily to bring us prodigals out of the pig sty and back into the sheepfold.

> ***"'An enemy has done it!' the farmer exclaimed. 'Shall we pull out the weeds?' they asked."He replied, 'No, you'll hurt the wheat if you do. Let both grow together until the harvest. Then I will tell the harvesters to sort out the weeds and burn them and to put the wheat in the barn.'"***
> ***Matthew 13:28-30 NLT***

**Father, keep the Romance with you in my life by power of your Holy Spirit. Amen.**

# *When Troubles Come*

**"For our present troubles are quite small and won't last very long. Yet they produce for us an immeasurably great glory that will last forever." (2 Corinthians 4:17) NLT**

It's not a question of if, but when. When troubles come to God's Saints, (and this is what all we who believe are) we need to understand that they are to be expected even in the lives of believers. Jesus said we would have many sorrows.

> ***"His anger lasts for a moment, but his favor lasts a lifetime! Weeping may go on all night, but joy comes with the morning." Psalm 30:5***

First of all, we need to judge ourselves to determine the cause of our troubles. If they are the consequence of our sin, we need to confess and repent. Otherwise, we need to rejoice and submit to the refining that God is putting us through for our ultimate good and His glory.

We can take comfort that these troubles are relatively weightless in the light of the Glory that is to come. It's really good to know that no matter how bad our troubles are, they are only temporary and will not last forever.

When we realize that God is going to do whatever it takes to conform us into the image of His Son, we should count it all joy that our troubles are part of God's character development program for us.

Why should we think ourselves above the Apostles, who all suffered much more than we will ever suffer?

The key to dealing with troubles is in choosing how we will respond. We can choose to respond with self-pity which will lead us to doubt and depression, or we can respond with the joy of knowing that these troubles are going to end in joy and blessedness as God works all things for our good and His glory.

> ***"So be truly glad! There is wonderful joy ahead, even though it is necessary for you to endure many trials for a while." 1 Peter 1:6 NLT***

May God grant us all the longsuffering and patience required as He supplies His all sufficient grace and strength to see us through our troubles and into the joy and blessings that endurance and perseverance bring.

**Father, help me to be faithful and strong in times of trouble. Amen.**

**Read Mark 12:28-34, Psalm 40** **September 5**

## *One Well Done Deserves Another*

**"What can I offer the LORD for all he has done for me?" Psalm 116:12 NLT**

Jesus did everything His father told Him to do, was obedient unto death, and as a result God has marked our sin debt "paid in full," if we have received Jesus Christ as our Savior.

> ***"Now that you have made me listen, I finally understand—you don't require burnt offerings or sin offerings." Psalm 40:6 NLT***

Every other religion in the world is based on doing something that has already been done. All others seek to win right standing with God by what they do instead of what God has already done for all who will believe it. Jesus' motive in living a life of perfect obedience and righteousness was not to earn anything for Himself….He already had everything. He came to overcome sin and death for us as the incarnation of God's love.

We would not think of going to someone's home for dinner, and then asking how much we owed them for it. To think we can do anything to add to the perfect sacrifice of Jesus to earn our salvation, we are deluding ourselves and denigrating the gift of God and suffering of Christ.

The only meaningful response to God's love is love. Because He first loved us, we seek to love Him by loving others and by living lives pleasing to Him.

> ***The religion scholar said, "A wonderful answer, Teacher! So lucid and accurate—that God is one and there is no other. And loving Him with all passion and intelligence and energy, and loving others as well as you love yourself. Why, that's better than all offerings and sacrifices put together!" Mark 12:32 MSG***

We cannot earn our salvation, but we can earn God's thanks by being conduits of His love, grace, mercy, comfort and forgiveness to others. Will we hear Jesus say: "Well done, thou good and faithful servant?"

We should begin each day seeking God's will for our lives and end each day with the joy of having done something that pleased God.

**Father, let seeking your "well done" encourage me in my daily walk. Amen.**

## *Sponge Bob Theology*

**"Let the word of Christ dwell in you richly in all wisdom, teaching and admonishing one another in psalms and hymns and spiritual songs, singing with grace in your hearts to the Lord." Colossians 3:16**

There's nothing fishy about being a sponge. We need to be more like one. When we absorb the Word of God into our minds and hearts like a sponge, we are going to become bigger and stronger in every area of our lives.

> ***"No one who trusts in You will ever be disgraced, but disgrace comes to those who try to deceive others." Psalm 25:3 NLT***

The problem is that we often soak up the wrong things that can destroy us. When we become self-absorbed, we will be controlled by our own sinful, selfish nature, and seek the gratification of our flesh and our pleasure above everything. We will be filled with lust, greed, envy, jealousy, pride, anger, and other sins.

When we let the Word of God dwell richly within us, we become transformed through the renewing of our minds. We become Christ-centered and absorbed with learning everything we can about Him, so that we can become more and more like Him.

The Fire of the Holy Spirit will fill us with an insatiable desire to soak up everything we can to grow in our knowledge of God, know His will for our lives, and ultimately grow into the fullness of Christ.

We can't sponge off of someone else's salvation. God may use the faith of our fathers, mothers, or friends to help us receive saving faith, but we must enter into that personal relationship with Jesus Christ of our own free will and in our own identity.

> ***"Fix your thoughts on what is true and honorable and right. Think about things that are pure and lovely and admirable." Philippians 4:8b NLT***

Life is full of choices. We can choose to soak up trashy movies, trashy TV, and live trashy lives producing the garbage of the flesh, or we can soak up the good things of God and produce the fruits of righteousness worthy of our calling in Him.

**Father let me soak up the living water of your Word that I might lead a life pleasing to You and fruitful in every good work. Amen.**

**Read 2 Corinthians 4:7-17, Job 5:7-27** **September 7**

# *The Salvage Business*

**"Cling tightly to your faith in Christ, and always keep your conscience clear. For some people have deliberately violated their consciences; as a result, their faith has been shipwrecked." 1 Timothy 1:18 NLT**

Whether an auto junk yard, stripping buildings before demolition, **or** salvaging treasures from sunken ships, salvaging is big business.

> ***"He will rescue you again and again so that no evil can touch you." Job 5:19 NLY***

Many can attest to the fact that they had reached the bottom of their flesh-driven lives before God called them through the power of the Holy Spirit into a new life through faith in Jesus Christ. The holy transformation that takes place is proof positive that Jesus does "make all things new!"

Time and time again the Holy Spirit comes to salvage our salvation as we stumble and fall into sins of every kind that would doom us to everlasting death and destruction were it not for the amazing grace of God.

It has been widely reported that Thomas Edison had almost a thousand failures before he invented the light bulb.

We are going to experience a lot of failures in our relationships with others, our carrying out of the great commission, and in health and financial issues.

On a good day, we might get by with only 3 sins of commission or omission which would total over 1,000 sins a year or 70 to 100 thousand sins in our lifetime.

> ***"We are hunted down, but God never abandons us. We get knocked down, but we get up again and keep going." 2 Corinthians 4:9 NLT***

God gave each of His children the indwelling presence and power of the Holy Spirit to salvage our precious gift of salvation from the shipwrecks of life. The Spirit will pick us up and put us back on solid ground no matter what and when we confess and repent.

**Father, thank you for saving me from drowning in my sins. Amen.**

# *Join The Family!*

**"Because of our faith, Christ has brought us into this place of highest privilege where we now stand, and we confidently and joyfully look forward to sharing God's glory." Romans 5:2 NLT**

When we join the family of God through receiving Jesus Christ as Savior and Lord by faith, we become not only brothers and sisters, but also joint heirs with Him of all the blessings and privileges of this life and the everlasting life in heaven.

> ***"Let me share in the prosperity of your chosen ones. Let me rejoice in the joy of your people;" Psalm 106:5a NLT***

We have the blessing of the Holy Spirit living within us to effect a holy transformation that conforms us into the likeness of Christ. We have every spiritual blessing, including the wonder-working resurrection power of God and His all sufficient grace.

We have the privilege of casting all of our burdens upon the Lord. There is no higher purpose or greater joy in life than the privilege of doing the good works that glorify God and which He purposed for us before we were even born.

When we are filled to overflowing with God's love through our personal relationship and friendship with Jesus, we are going to be conduits of God's love to others.As we continue to die to self and become more and more alive in the fullness of Christ, we are going to be privileged to have God do great things through us that we could never do on our own. The idea of giving carries bad connotations to our self-centered nature, but becomes our greatest privilege when we are transformed and controlled by the Holy Spirit.

The One who counted it all joy to give His life for us, will give us this joy as we exercise our great privilege of giving our time, talents, and treasures to honor Him and proclaim His glory.

> ***"They begged us again and again for the gracious privilege of sharing in the gift for the Christians in Jerusalem." 2 Corinthians 8:4 NLT***

**Father, help me to "count it all joy" and be ever mindful of the privileges of giving. Amen.**

**Read Romans 13:8-14, Psalm 19** **September 9**

## *Virtue or Vice?*

**"If your sinful nature controls your mind, there is death. But if the Holy Spirit controls your mind, there is life and peace. For the sinful nature is always hostile to God." Romans 8:6, 7 NLT**

Self control is either one of the best or one of the worst character qualities a person can have.

> ***"Keep me from deliberate sins! Don't let them control me. Then I will be free of guilt and innocent of great sin." Psalm 19:13 NLT***

It is most often used in the context of being a fruit of the Spirit that brings discipline to discipleship, strength in fighting temptation, and containing anger, pride, envy, and other sins.

Self control can also be a fatal vice in this life. It is probably the number one cause of atheism and continued separation from God.

A lot of people are simply not willing to give up control of their lives to God. They do this without realizing they are actually giving up all hope of eternal life and dooming themselves to the everlasting torment of hell.

Even among believers, the desire for self control is probably the biggest root of evil that stunts our growth in Christ and growing into His fullness. When we insist on living controlled by our flesh, we will never fully know the peace and joy of living the new life in Christ that is controlled by the Holy Spirit and obedient to God.

When we bring our self-serving agenda's into our marriages, our relationships, and especially into our service in the church, we are often going to find that we have brought bad consequences for ourselves and for those around us.

> ***"But let the Lord Jesus Christ take control of you, and don't think of ways to indulge your evil desires." Romans 13:14 NLT***

The fruits of love, joy, peace, longsuffering, kindness, goodness, faithfulness, gentleness, and the good self-control are Spirit borne and evidence of our new life in Christ.

We will never be able to fulfill our calling to be imitators of Christ and to grow into His fullness, unless we are willing to give up self control for God control and the power for living that this gives.

**Father, by the power of Your Spirit give me the right kind of self control. Amen.**

September 10 Read John 4:12-36, Psalm 80

# *We're all Recovering*

**"If death got the upper hand through one man's wrongdoing, can you imagine the breathtaking recovery life makes, sovereign life, in those who grasp with both hands this wildly extravagant life-gift, this grand setting-everything right, that the one man Jesus Christ provides?" Romans 5:15 MSG**

> ***"Restore us, O God; Cause Your face to shine, And we shall be saved!" Psalm 80:3***

We hear a lot about recovering alcoholics and addicts. As widespread and common these problems, we need to realize that these are not the only problems from which people are recovering.

Millions of people are recovering from some sort of physical illness. Recovery is sometimes never complete and often involves learning to live with a physical disability. Millions of people are struggling to recover from financial woes that have made them slaves to their creditors. Recovery often involves a major change in lifestyles and spending habits. Millions more are recovering from emotional problems or distress of some kind. The emotional scars of the past are often just swept under the rug where they fester and break out over and over again.

Many are often in recovery from the consequences of sin or other spiritual problems. Whether we call it recovery, restoration, or healing, we are all going to need a lot of it as we live life in an imperfect world as imperfect people born with consequences of inherited sin.

The greatest recovery of all comes from dying to the power of sin and death and becoming alive forever in Christ through receiving Jesus Christ as our Savior and Lord by faith. We become the redeemed children of God, brothers and sisters of Christ, and recover all the rights and privileges as joint heirs to the eternal riches of God's favor and grace in this life on earth and in heaven.

> ***"Therefore if the Son makes you free, you shall be free indeed." John 8:36***

We receive the incredible strength and power of the Holy Spirit that will sustain us through our recovery from the effects of a broken body or a broken heart.

**Father, let my recovery be complete in You. Amen.**

Read 2 Corinthians 3:16-21, Psalm 63 September 11

## *Glimpses of Glory*

**"The heavens tell of the glory of God. The skies display his marvelous craftsmanship." Psalm 19:1 NLT**

> ***"So I have looked for You in the sanctuary, To see Your power and Your glory."***
> ***Psalm 63:2***

The overwhelming power and magnificence of the Lord is manifested all around us. The more we look for it, the more we will see it. The righter of "Battle Hymn of the Republic" saw the glory of the Lord manifest in the conflct to free the slaves.

We often sense the glory of the Lord in the wonders of His creation. Sunsets, majestic mountains, and new born babies give us glimpses of God's glory.

I have often glimpsed the glory of the Lord in the presence of 50,000 men coming together in worship and praise at Promise Keepers gatherings.

Most recently, I glimpsed the glory of the Lord in seeing the largest crowd ever gathered for the Pope's funeral. I believe that only God could gather together so many people filled with such love and order.

If we look, we will glimpse the glory of the Lord in the everyday lives of other believers. We see the glory of God in the lives of those who receive Jesus Christ. We see it in us as He conforms us into the image of Christ. Miraculous physical and emotional healings, forgiving of the unforgivable, and extraordinary feats by ordinary people all give us glimpses of the Glory of God.

> ***"And all of us have had that veil removed so that we can be mirrors that brightly reflect the glory of the Lord. And as the Spirit of the Lord works within us, we become more and more like him and reflect his glory even more."***
> ***2 Corinthians 3:18 NLT***

God continues to show up to calm the storms of life, remove the mountains of doubt, and to bless us more than we could ever dare ask or hope.

There are many things that only God can do, and when we see or experience them we are glimpsing the Glory of God. May we never cease to give Him the praise, honor, and glory that He deserves.

**Father, May I always behold Your glory around me. Amen.**

# *The Beat Goes On*

**"But the time is coming and is already here when true worshipers will worship the Father in spirit and in truth. The Father is looking for anyone who will worship him that way." John 4:23 NLT**

Today many churches are caught up in the worship culture wars of what is and what is not Christian music, and what kind of hymns should be sung at worship. Everyone seems bent on preserving the traditional hymns of their heritage, and give little thought to the importance of music in reaching and keeping the young.

> ***"Those who lead blameless lives and do what is right, speaking the truth from sincere hearts." Psalm 15:2 NLT***

The Billy Graham organization has been at the cutting edge of using music to touch the hearts of old and young alike for years. Their youth nights use contemporary Christian artists to fill the stadiums with young people. Their nightly crusades include old favorites, contemporary, country, and western beats by secular artists.

The truth is that God has given us hearts for different types of music with different beats. Music has a universal appeal and is important to every culture. Within everybody, we will find those who love classical music, country & western, swing, jazz, rock and roll, and everything in between.

When we understand that the music itself is just a conduit for delivering the Word and that the Word never returns void, we can be more understanding and tolerant of those singing a different tune and using a different beat to encourage a different generation that responds to a different type of music.

> ***"Jesus replied, "And why do you, by your traditions, violate the direct commandments of God?" Matthew 15:3 NLT***

We should all let the beat go on in any manner that delivers the Word and offers praise and glory to God. It's not how you worship, but WHO you worship that counts!

**Father, never let my personal preferences impede the spreading of Your Word through musical styles and beats that bless others. Amen.**

**Read 1 John 4:15-21, Psalm 16** **September 13**

## *Jesus is Alive!*

**"For it has pleased God to tell his people that the riches and glory of Christ are for you Gentiles, too. For this is the secret: Christ lives in you, and this is your assurance that you will share in his glory." Colossians 1:27 NLT**

Knowing that Christ is alive in us through the power of the Holy Spirit is the key to having a real and personal relationship with Him.

> ***"You will show me the way of life, granting me the joy of Your presence and the pleasures of living with You forever."***
> ***Psalm 16:11 NLT***

When the Holy Spirit discloses the reality of Christ living in us and through us, we reach a level of intimacy that brings all of the blessings of abiding.

We experience the joy of the Lord, the love of God and others, answered prayers, fruitfulness, and friendship with Christ.

As the great hymn says: "He walks with me and He talks with me, and tells me I am His own.... the joys we share as we tarry there, none other has ever known." These words are a powerful reminder that we need to daily "go to the garden alone" in prayer and meditation on His Word if we want the fullness of His joy.

The more we appropriate the presence of Jesus alive in us, the less tolerant we will be of our sinfulness, and the more inspired we will be to live lives worthy of our calling as brothers and sisters of Christ.

We will experience Christ living in us more and more as we learn more about Him through His Word. We will experience Christ living through us as we reach out in love to those around us and find ourselves loving, serving, and forgiving others as we have been loved, served and forgiven.

> ***"All who proclaim that Jesus is the Son of God have God living in them, and they live in God."***
> ***1 John 4:15 NLT***

All other religions are worshipping dead prophets. We alone have the privilege of worshipping our living Lord through a real and personal relationship of faith that makes Him real and alive in our lives.

**Father, thank you for revealing this secret to me. Amen.**

September 14 Read Ephesians 6:10-19m Psalm 3

# *Fighting the Good Fight*

**"Train me, GOD, to walk straight; then I'll follow your true path." Psalm 86:11a NLT**

The US armed forces stunning success in the Iraqi war is a tribute to the training and equipment given to our troops. High-tech weapons require high-tech skills that can only be developed through intensive training. If it takes 3 months of basic training and many more months of specialized training to become a good soldier in the US Army, how long do you think it will take to become effective soldiers of the Cross?

> ***"But You, O LORD, are a shield for me, My glory and the One who lifts up my head." Psalm 3:3 NLT***

We are all living on a battleground where the powers and principalities of evil and darkness are doing everything they can to keep us in the darkness of unbelief and doubt that leads to death and destruction.

Praise God! He gives us the finest training manual ever written and provides the equipment we need to fight the good fight against the flesh, the world, and the devil.

When we buckle the truth of God's Word around us and put on the peace of our salvation as sandals to keep us walking in this truth, we are putting on God's equipment that will cause us to stand firm.

Just as Jesus used God's Word as the sword of the Spirit to overcome the wiles and temptations of the evil one, we can do the same thing when we have successfully completed our basic training in the Word. As we persevere in persevering in the Word, we will be equipped with the breastplate of righteousness to protect our hearts from evil, the helmet of salvation to protect our minds from doubt and despair, and our faith will grow so strong that it will shield us from the satanic attacks that come our way.

> ***"Put on all of God's armor so that you will be able to stand firm against all strategies and tricks of the Devil" Ephesians 6:11 NLT***

When we couple the protection of our armor with the power of prayer, we will be able to stand firm and overcome the World for Christ.

**Father, help me to continue my training daily so that I can better use the equipment You provide for fighting the good fight. Amen.**

Read Galatians 5:16-24, Proverbs 4:5-13 September 15

## *God's Character Development Program*

**"And then take on an entirely new way of life—a God-fashioned life, a life renewed from the inside and working itself into your conduct as God accurately reproduces his character in you. Ephesians 4:20 MSG**

We are all works in progress. God's plan is to sanctify and make us holy in His sight by calling us into a saving relationship through faith where we receive the righteousness of Christ in God's eyes.

> ***"Learn to be wise, and develop good judgment. Don't forget or turn away from My words." Proverbs 4:5 NLT***

Like any good coach, the Holy Spirit uses training, discipline, reward, punishment, and encouragement to help us win. The Holy Spirit knows each of us better than we know ourselves, and has the incredible power and strength of Almighty God to accomplish the task of holy transformation.

God's character development program involves not only hearing and studying the Word, but also living in the "laboratory of life" where we can grow in spiritual wisdom and discernment.

We find ourselves receiving the exact amount of chastisement or discipline we need to turn away from our sinful behavior through godly sorrow and repentance. We will find the truth of reaping what we sow when we struggle through the consequences of our sins, and experience the blessings of obedience when we put God first in all things.

> ***"If we are living now by the Holy Spirit, let us follow the Holy Spirit's leading in every part of our lives." Galatians 5:25 NLT***

The Holy Spirit brings us the comfort of God's love and the security of His promises to encourage our character development.

Best of all we receive the grace of God sufficient to persevere through our trials until we are safely home in the everlasting arms of our Savior.

**Father, thank you for loving me not only to die for, but also enough to do whatever it takes to make my eternal destination secure. Amen.**

September 16 Read Romans 6:1-23, Psalm 134

# *Our Call to Holiness*

**"Pursue peace with all *people,* and holiness, without which no one will see the Lord:" Hebrews 12:14**

> ***"Lift your hands in holiness, and bless the LORD."***
> ***Psalm 134:2 NLT***

Holiness is sometimes a hard virtue to comprehend. We often confuse it with piety or religiosity, rather than being "set apart" and living in spiritual purity.

Holy also has to do with the presence of God. We hear of standing on holy ground or entering the Holy of Holies. We seldom stop to think that when two or more of us are gathered in the name of Christ, His promised presence makes it a holy place no matter where we are.

The reality that our bodies are holy places also seems to escape our attention when we think about holiness. The truth that they are temples of the Holy Spirit should inspire us all to keep our temples clean and healthy. Everything we do with them should be done to honor and praise God.

Our call to holiness is our call to grow into the fullness of Christ by imitating Him. We do this by loving God and loving and serving others as Christ has loved and served us. By appropriating the character of Christ in our everyday walk of faith, is also a response of our call to holiness.

We became Holy in the sight of God when we received the holiness of Christ by answering God's call to salvation through faith in Jesus Christ. We should become more holy daily through the incredible transforming power of the Holy Spirit who comes to live within us when we answer the call to salvation.

> ***"But now having been set free from sin, and having become slaves of God, you have your fruit to holiness, and the end, everlasting life"***
> ***Romans 6:22 NLT***

Our new birth involves taking off the filthy rags of our own righteousness and putting on the righteousness of Christ in every area of our lives.

This is an ongoing process that we live through and grow in day by day. It will not be completed until we see God face to face in heaven.

Personal holiness is the evidence of the transformation and regeneration of every believer.

**Father, help me to heed your call to holiness and to submit to the Holy Spirit in making holiness an actuality in my life of faith. Amen.**

Read Romans 5, Psalm 86 September 17

# *A Common Misperception*

**"The LORD *is* gracious and full of compassion, slow to anger and great in mercy. The LORD *is* good to all, and His tender mercies *are* over all His works." Psalm 145:8, 9**

I never cease to be amazed at the number of people who have a totally wrong perception of God.

***"You, O Lord, are a God full of compassion, and gracious, Longsuffering and abundant in mercy and truth."***
***Psalm 86:15***

Whether it's from controlling, abusive parents, or from fear-mongering preachers or Sunday School teachers, the idea that God is a God of wrath just waiting for us to get out of line so that He can zap us is far too common and totally unfaithful to Scripture.

God Himself said: *"I am the LORD, I am the LORD, the merciful and gracious God. I am slow to anger and rich in unfailing love and faithfulness. I show this unfailing love to many thousands by forgiving every kind of sin and rebellion." (Exodus 34:6)*

While it is true that God hates sin and we often suffer consequences for it, God is Love, and He loves us in spite of our sins. He loved us enough to come die for us and He loves us enough to chasten and discipline us as He conforms us into the image of Christ. God's chastening is not done out of wrath, but out of love.

God also declares: *"For I know the plans I have for you," says the LORD. "They are plans for good and not for disaster, to give you a future and a hope." (Jeremiah 29:11)*

Our father knows best. He has established boundaries for us not because He is a kill joy, but because He wants the very best for us and and that is to have the fullness of joy that comes only from living within the parameters of His will and in a right relationship with Him.

If we are believers, we will never have to worry about the wrath of God.

***"But God demonstrates His own love toward us, in that while we were still sinners, Christ died for us."***
***Romans 5:8***

**Father, never let me doubt for a minute that you are a God of Love, mercy, and compassion. Amen.**

September 18 Read Acts 4:7-42, Isaiah 63:7-16

# *The "Big Bang" Theory*

**"In the beginning God created the heavens and the earth. The earth was empty, a formless mass cloaked in darkness. And the Spirit of God was hovering over its surface." Genesis 1:1 NLT**

Some scientists seem to prefer the unbelievable to the unthinkable.That we are products of random chance evolution without a creator is unbelievable and remains an unproven theory.

***" Where is He who put His Holy Spirit within them, Who led them by the right hand of Moses, With His glorious arm," Isaiah 63:11b,12a***

To those who do not believe in God and prefer to believe in the sovereignty of man, it is unthinkable for them to think God created the universe and everything in it.

There are mysteries about the creation of the universe and life that we are not going to fully understand this side of heaven, where all things shall be revealed. There is one "big bang" theory that all believers can attest to by experience and observation. It is what happens when the incredible transforming power of God becomes manifest in the life of a believer.

Sinners become saints, the lost become found, and the evidence of a new life in Christ is there for all to see. Everyone noticed the change in the disciples after they were filled with the Holy Spirit.

The persecutor Saul became the Apostle Paul, the Christian faith spread like wildfire throughout the world as a result of this "big bang." It takes the "big bang" to enter into the family of God. As God tells us through Paul in 1 Corinthians 12:3b: *"and no one can say that Jesus is Lord except by the Holy Spirit."*

***"They brought in the two disciples and demanded, "By what power, or in whose name, have you done this?" Acts 4:7 NLT***

The Holy Spirit calls, works faith to believe and receive, and fills us with His indwelling presence and power to live our abundant new life of freedom from sin and death.

May we all appropriate this "big bang" truth and forget about the theory.

**Father, thank you for giving me the "big bang" of eternal life through faith in Jesus Christ. Amen.**

Read Luke 8:3-18, Malachi 3:9-18 September 19

## *The Sting of Stinginess*

**"The world of the generous gets larger and larger; the world of the stingy gets smaller and smaller." Proverbs 11:24 MSG**

God's economy makes it very unwise and unprofitable to be stingy in any area of our lives. In the area of money, God calls us robbers or cheaters when we fail to be generous with our tithes to Him and even pronounces a curse on those who are stingy with Him financially.

> ***"You have cheated Me of the tithes and offerings due to Me. You are under a curse, for your whole nation has been cheating Me." Malachi 3:8b, 9 NLT***

Although we seldom think of it in the sense of being stingy, when we fail to serve the Lord with all our hearts, our minds, and our strength, God says that we are speaking against Him.

When we think of all of the blessings we receive from God, and how we continually need to go to His throne of grace to ask for more, it is inconceivable that we would risk being stingy with God with our treasures, talents, time, or our praise and adoration.

Jesus makes it very clear through His parables that there is a cause and effect relationship between forgiving and not forgiving, giving and not giving, and loving and not loving.

The effects of stinginess in any of these areas are consequences that we can avoid by being generous in giving these things in abundance to all those in need when the opportunity comes.

> **"So be careful that you don't become misers of what you hear. Generosity begets generosity. Stinginess impoverishes." Luke 8:18 MSG**

Stinginess goes with self-centeredness. When we put our wants, needs, and agendas first, we are relegating God to playing second fiddle, which is a position He will not tolerate. May the power of the Holy Spirit grant us all the grace to rid ourselves of self-centeredness and stinginess.

**Father, help me the experience to joys and blessings of generosity. Amen.**

# *Attitude Adjustment Hour*

**"Therefore do not be unwise, but understand what the will of the Lord *is.* And do not be drunk with wine, in which is dissipation; but be filled with the Spirit," Ephesians 5:17, 18**

Many bars and lounges seem to fill up every day around 5 for attitude adjustment hour, a/k/a "happy hour."

> ***"We were filled with laughter, and we sang for joy.And the other nations said, "What amazing things the LORD has done for them." Psalm 146:2 NLT***

We all most certainly need a daily attitude adjustment hour, and if we are wise and understand what the will of the Lord is, we will seek the refreshing filling of the Holy Spirit and the grace that is imparted through prayer, meditation, and getting into the Word of God.

Our "happy hour" should be spent getting high on Jesus and His joy.

Sunday worship should be the greatest attitude adjustment hour of our week. We should go with great enthusiasm and joy, knowing that we are going to meet with the Lord and His body of believers and ultimately be encouraged, comforted, and strengthened for living the abundant life in Christ.

Unfortunately, the world, our flesh, and the devil are not working on a once a week basis and some old habits and attitudes die hard. We need to "ask, seek, and find" on a daily basis if we are to grow into the fullness of Christ.

Satan will often try to bring back old attitudes of pride, rebellion, doubt, anger, envy, lust, or self-centeredness. We need to put on the full armor of God to withstand these attacks and to adjust our attitudes so that we can bear the fruit of the Spirit which is love, joy, peace, longsuffering, kindness, goodness, faithfulness, gentleness, and self-control.

Our daily attitude adjustment hour should be an hour of abiding in Christ and celebrating the indwelling presence of the Holy Spirit. God promises great rewards and blessings for those who do this.

> ***"Instead, there must be a spiritual renewal of your thoughts and attitudes." Ephesians 4:23 NLT***

**Father, help me to adjust my attitudes so that they reflect the fullness of your Spirit living within me. Amen.**

Read Matthew 5, Isaiah 26:1-19 September 21

## Perfection Does Exist

**"till we all come to the unity of the faith and of the knowledge of the Son of God, to a perfect man, to the measure of the stature of the fullness of Christ;" Ephesians 4:13**

> ***"You will keep in perfect peace all who trust in You, whose thoughts are fixed on You!" Isaiah 26:3***

The reality of our sinfulness and the truth that "all have sinned and fall short of the glory of God," often causes us to come up short in pursuing perfection by growing into the fullness of Christ.

First of all, we need to believe and understand that we have been made perfect in God's sight by having the righteousness of Christ imputed to us when we received Him as our Savior. Not only does God see us as perfect because of Christ spiritually, He comes to live in us as the Holy Spirit to inspect, correct, and perfect us through His incredible power day by day, week by week, and year by year, as we are transformed by the renewing of our minds into becoming more and more like Christ in this earthly life.

Scripture tells us: *"But let patience have its perfect work, that you may be perfect and complete, lacking nothing." (James 1:4)* God commands us to be perfect and tells us about many elements of perfection in Matthew 5.

Being conformed into the image of Christ means being transformed and becoming like Christ by imitating the way he lived and loved others during His life on earth. James 1:2-5 tells us*: "My brethren, count it all joy when you fall into various trials, knowing that the testing of your faith produces patience. But let patience have its perfect work, that you may be perfect and complete, lacking nothing."*

> ***"Be perfect, therefore, as your heavenly Father is perfect." Matthew 5:48***

Not by our own strength, but by the power of Christ living in us through the Holy Spirit, we can know the "perfect" peace of a mind stayed on Christ, the "perfect' love that casts out all fear, the "perfect" will of God, and the strength of God made "perfect" in our weaknesses, as we grow into the fullness of Christ and Christian maturity.

**Father, help me to pursue the perfection of Your Son in every area of my life, by the perfecting power of Your Spirit living in me. Amen.**

# *Learning to Walk*

**"Who among you fears the LORD and obeys his servant? If you are walking in darkness, without a ray of light, trust in the LORD and rely on your God." Isaiah 50:10 NLT**

Learning to walk takes time and often involves a lot of painful falls and stumbles. Positive reinforcement seems to speed up the process and make it easier.

> ***"I will behave wisely in a perfect way. Oh, when will You come to me? I will walk within my house with a perfect heart." Psalm 101:2***

Learning to "walk in love" also often takes time and involves a lot of painful falls and stumbles. The truth is that we can't do it without the power of the Holy Spirit and the positive reinforcement of God's Word.

Some seem to prefer to "walk in spite" and enjoy the temporary satisfaction revenge or vengeance seems to bring. "Don't get mad, get even" becomes a springboard for walking in spite. This seems especially prevalent in the aftermath of divorce, and children often pay a terrible price for the spiteful behavior of their parents.

Walking in shame is another means of travel for many people who carry such a burden of guilt over failures or sins that they will not, or cannot, let go of at the cross.

Walking in sin often seems a whole lot easier and a lot more fun than walking in love. This is the natural walk of the natural man living in the flesh of a sin-sick world doomed for destruction.

Walking in love is all about walking in the supernatural power of the Holy Spirit instead of walking in the bondage of the flesh. Walking in love starts when we receive the love of God and a new birth through faith in Jesus Christ as our Savior. We obviously can't walk in something we don't have.

> ***"And walk in love, as Christ also has loved us and given Himself for us, an offering and a sacrifice to God as a sweet-smelling aroma." Ephesians 5:2***

Once our vertical relationship of love is established, the Holy Spirit begins the ongoing work of holy transformation.

As we surrender more and more control from our flesh to our spirit, we learn to walk longer and stronger in love and receive the peace and joy that it affords.

**Father, help my walk to reflect your love, grace, and mercy so that all around me can know that I am yours. Amen.**

**Read Matthew 23, Psalm 50** **September 23**

## *Am I The Great Pretender?*

**"Therefore, laying aside all malice, all deceit, hypocrisy, envy, and all evil speaking, as newborn babes, desire the pure milk of the word, that you may grow thereby, if indeed you have tasted that the Lord *is* gracious." 1 Peter 2:1 NLT**

There is perhaps some pretension in all of us. The root word of hypocrisy and hypocrite traces back to the Greek word meaning actor. Many times we find ourselves acting out roles based on our self image, a desire to please, or to meet the expectations of others. Paul says that he has become all things to all men so that by all means he may save some.

> ***"But God says to the wicked: "Recite my laws no longer, and don't pretend that you obey Me."***
> ***Psalm 50:16 NLT***

This may have worked well for Paul, but it has been a disaster in many churches where the truth has been compromised in the name of love or numbers, and people are told what they want to hear instead of what they need to hear. We often have a performance gap between who we are at church on Sundays and who we are the rest of the week.

There is often such a difference between "talking the talk" and "walking the walk," that we become stumbling blocks instead of building blocks for the cause of Christ among our family, friends, and acquaintances. The Scribes and Pharisees were the great pretenders of Christ's day. He did not mince words in showing what he thought of their hypocrisy and self righteousness. He called them snakes and a brood of vipers. We need to be ever mindful that we cannot pretend with God. He knows our every thought, and what's really in our heart. We must continually guard our hearts and cleanse them daily of all pretense and hypocrisy through confession and repentance.

> ***"You try to look like upright people outwardly, but inside your hearts are filled with hypocrisy and lawlessness."***
> ***Matthew 23:28 NLT***

**Father, by the power of Your Spirit, help me to live inside out as one of your redeemed. Amen.**

September 24 Read 2 Corinthians 4:7-18, Psalm 147

# *Walking Wounded*

***"I have told you these things, so that in me you may have peace. In this world you will have trouble. But take heart! I have overcome the world." John 16:33 NIV***

The walking-wounded survivors of the battles of life are all around us. Each of us to some degree can be counted among them. There are physical, emotional, financial, relational, and spiritual wounds that we sometimes feel will never heal.

> ***"He heals the brokenhearted, binding up their wounds." Psalm 147:3 NLT***

All too often, our wounds are self-inflicted. When we go into battle filled with pride and arrogance, we are inviting disaster. When we pursue self-centered lives, we are going to focus on satisfying the desires of our flesh and miss out on fulfilling the purposes for which God created us. We need to understand that we are involved in spiritual warfare against the flesh, the world, and the devil. Evil is all around us.

The war against sin and death was won by the death and resurrection of Jesus Christ. The devil has been mortally wounded, but still prowls around seeking who he may devour. We must protect ourselves with the full armor of God that he has provided for all believers to appropriate by faith.

We can find healing for our wounds through the blood of Jesus. By His stripes we were healed relationally with God and receive the assurance of eternal life.

Just as the Master gave sight to the blind, healed the lame, and cast out demons in Scripture, He can heal our broken hearts and whatever wounds that need healing. When we take our wounds to the Cross we will find the "balm of Gilead" that will take away our sorrows and replace them with the incredible peace and joy of the Lord.

> ***"We are pressed on every side by troubles, but we are not crushed and broken. We are perplexed, but we don't give up and quit." 2 Corinthians 4:8 NLT***

**Father, just as you died on the Cross so that I wouldn't have to, you live to love me with your all sufficient grace and strength that will heal my wounds. Thank You! Amen.**

**Read Luke 7:23-25, Psalm 68** **September 25**

# *Daily Resurrection*

**"*Through* the LORD'S mercies we are not consumed, because His compassions fail not. *They are* new every morning; great *is* Your faithfulness." Lamentations 3:21, 22 NLT**

cannot hold the living water from the well of life very long. Our strength to live the good life of faith is non-existent. We are totally dependent on the strength and grace of God.

> ***"Blessed is the Lord, Who daily loads us with benefits, The God of our Salvation!" Psalm 68:19 NLT***

Just as God gave just enough manna for one day to the children of Israel, He gives just enough strength and grace sufficient for our needs of the day only, and we need to go to the well daily to be renewed and refreshed.

When we confess and turn away from our sin on a daily basis, we find the mercy and grace of God renewed daily and experience the resurrection power of God anew every day. Just as we died to sin and became alive in Christ when we first believed, we need to die to sin and become alive in Christ on a daily basis. The holy transformation that began when we first believed can continue to conform us into the very image of Christ.

As we grow in spiritual maturity, we will discover that becoming a disciple is all about the daily discipline of daily confession, repentance, and resurrection.

David's prayer that God create a clean heart and renew a right spirit within him should be in our daily prayers that we might receive the daily filling that we all need in order to grow into the fullness of Christ.

> ***"Then He said to the crowd, "If any of you wants to be my follower, you must put aside your selfish ambition, shoulder your cross daily, and follow Me." Luke 7:23 NLT***

**Hear my prayer, O Lord, and renew your grace and mercy to me every day that I might become an imitator of Christ. Amen.**

**September 26** **Read 1 Peter 2:1-11, Psalm 119:103-112**

## *Proof of the Pudding*

**"Taste and see that the LORD is good. Oh, the joys of those who trust in him!" Psalm 34:8 NLT**

> ***"How sweet are Your words to my taste, Sweeter than honey to my mouth!" Psalm 119:103 NLR***

Don Quixote wasn't too smart when it came to differentiating between dragons and windmills, but He was smart enough to figure out that the "proof of the pudding is in the eating," or that the actual use of something is the best test.

We can come up with all the brilliant ideas in the world, and talk until we're blue in the face, but "The proof of the pudding is in the eating!"

When it comes to our relationship with God, we can be encouraged by the testimony of family and friends or by the wonderful examples found in Scripture, but salvation is a unique experience to every person who receives Jesus Christ as Lord and Savior.

When we hear Jesus talk about being the bread of life, "the proof of the pudding is in the eating." Once we appropriate the riches of God's love and mercy in Christ and let the Lover of Our Soul become the ruler of our life, we are free to eat at the "Royal Buffet," and even enjoy the fruit from the tree of life.

As our personal relationship with Christ grows from Savior and brother to best friend, we start tasting the wonderful fruit of the Spirit being made manifest in us. We start enjoying the sacred delights of answered prayers, loving others, and the awareness of the love of others.

When the resurrection power of the Holy Spirit comes to live within us the transformation process begins. We receive the power and desire to become slaves to righteousness. God's "don'ts" become our "don't want too's," "our can'ts" become "cans," and the love of Christ becomes manifest in us.

> ***"Cry out for this nourishment as a baby cries for milk, now that you have had a taste of the Lord's kindness." 1 Peter 2:2b, 3 NLT***

The sweetness of God's grace fills us and pours out through us, as we taste the incredible joy and peace of being in a right relationship with God through becoming brothers, friends, and followers of Christ.

**Lord, let me taste the sweetness of a life of abiding in You. Amen.**

**Read John 15:9-17, Job 23:10-17,** **September 27**

## *Divine Appointments*

**"And as it is appointed for men to die once, but after this the judgment, so Christ was offered once to bear the sins of many. To those who eagerly wait for Him He will appear a second time, apart from sin, for salvation." Hebrews 9:27, 28 NLT**

We all live lives with divine appointments orchestrated by God for His glory and our good.

> ***"For He performs what is appointed for me, And many such things are with Him." Job 23:14 NLT***

God's call to salvation is a divine appointment that we dare not let anyone or anything keep us from answering.

The more we grow in spiritual maturity by abiding in the Word, the better able we will be to recognize and take advantage of the appointments when they come.

This is especially important in the area of fulfilling our highest purpose, which is to lead others into a saving relationship with Jesus Christ. We are all encouraged to always be ready to explain the hope that is within us if asked. *(1 Peter 3:15b)*

Like it or not, we all have divine appointments for disappointment, pain, suffering, and other troubles. Many of these divine appointments are going to be missed if we remain self-centered instead of Christ-centered, and do not exercise good stewardship of our time, treasures, and talents.

We all have an appointment with death that was determined by God before we were ever born. We need to show up for this suitably attired in the white robe of righteousness, which we receive by faith in Jesus Christ.
As believers, we have our divine appointment to meet Jesus face to face and give an account of our lives at the resurrection of the just. We will be welcomed into heaven where there is no more pain and suffering, no more sorrow, no more sin, and no more tears.

> ***"You did not choose Me, but I chose you and appointed you that you should go and bear fruit, and that your fruit should remain, that whatever you ask the Father in My name He may give you." John 15:16 NLT***

**Father, make me ever sensitive and discerning that I might recognize my divine appointments in life. Amen.**

# *Are You Disabled?*

**"Don't copy the behavior and customs of this world, but let God transform you into a new person by changing the way you think." Romans 12:2 NLT**

When we think about disabilities, we naturally zero in on physical and mental handicaps, without even thinking of spiritual disabilities.

> ***"The Lord upholds all who fall, and raises up all who are bowed down."***
> ***Psalm 145:14 NLT***

Spiritual disabilities in the lives of believers make it impossible to grow into the fullness of Christ, which is God's desire for us.

An unforgiving spirit makes it impossible to receive the forgiveness we all need. Greed disables us and makes it impossible to live in the fullness of Christ.

We cannot serve two masters and when we make money and possessions our god, we lose the peace of the Lord and the security of our right relationship with Him. Fear can overcome us like a thief in the night and rob us of our strength and witness.

The disabilities of pride, anger, envy, or sexual immorality can not only cause harm to others, but will stunt our growth in holiness and keep us from ever becoming spiritually mature.

Unbelief is the worst disability of all. Without faith it is not only impossible to please God, but it dooms us to eternal damnation instead of eternal life and our hope of glory in Christ.

When we received Jesus Christ as our Lord and Savior, all of our spiritual disabilities were covered with the righteousness of Christ and made righteous in God's sight.

Best of all, we received the indwelling presence of the Holy Spirit and His incredible resurrection power and strength that enables us to overcome our disabilities. The Holy Spirit sanctifies us day by day and year by year as we become more and more like Christ in every aspect of our lives.

> ***"A final word: Be strong with the Lord's mighty power.***
> ***Ephesians 6:10 NLT***

**Father, enable me to overcome my spiritual disabilities by the power of Your Spirit. Amen.**

Read Hebrews 6:9-20, Psalm 31 September 29

## *Living in the Valleys*

**"Let us hold fast the confession of *our* hope without wavering, for He who promised *is* faithful." Herews 10:22**

The life of every believer is marked by highs and lows as we live through the ebb tides of life. Scripture is full of examples of the highs and lows of Job, Abraham, David, Joseph, and even our Lord.

> ***"So be strong and take courage, all you who put your hope in the LORD!***
> ***Psalm 31:24 NLT***

Those who have experienced the incredible high of being set on fire for the Lord by the transforming power of the Holy Spirit have never known such joy or peace.

When God makes all things new in the life of the believer, all those around will notice the changes that take place, just as those around the disciples noticed the change that came when they received the resurrection power of God through the indwelling of the Holy Spirit.

When our faith in God moves the 18 inches from our Heads to our hearts we will experience the love, joy, and peace of the Lord like we have never experienced it before.

As great as these feelings are and as much as we should treasure them and strive to keep the fire of the Spirit burning brightly within us, we should always remember that our assurance of salvation and our right standing with God through faith in Jesus Christ are not based on feelings, but on Truth as revealed in God's Word.

Our feelings will often run low as we go through valleys of doubt, disappointment, failure, pain, and suffering. It is only when our faith is anchored deep in the Word of God and His promises that we can persevere through life in the valleys.

Feelings may change, but God's gift of salvation for all who believe never changes. Our foundation needs to be on this truth rather than on feelings, no matter how wonderful and powerful they may seem.

> ***"that by two immutable things, in which it is impossible for God to lie, we might have strong consolation, who have fled for refuge to lay hold of the hope set before us."***
> ***Hebrews 6:19 NLT***

**Father, help me to persevere through the valleys of life anchored deep in the assurances of Your Word. Amen.**

# *Co-Existing*

**"No servant can serve two masters; for either he will hate the one and love the other, or else he will be loyal to the one and despise the other. You cannot serve God and mammon." Luke 16:13**

The sooner we realize that we are co-exisiting with our sinful flesh during our life the better prepared we will be to know how to respond when our sinful, self-centered nature tries to take control.

> ***"How lovely is Your tabernacle, O LORD of hosts! My soul longs, yes, even faints for the courts of the LORD; My heart and my flesh cry out for the living God." Psalm 84***

Once that temptation to sin takes root in the mind, we often cooperate by justifying, rationalizing, or denying that we have a problem.

We justify by saying that everyone's doing it or that God wants us to be happy. We rationalize by saying we're only human and can't help it, or that the devil made us do it. We deny it by refusing to admit that we are sinning against God by ignoring or disobeying His commandments.

When we learn to cooperate with the Holy Spirit, we will be well on our way to being transformed and controlled by the Holy Spirit.

We will be convicted that everyone doing it doesn't make it right and that there is no happiness to be found in disobeying God.

We will believe that God has set us free from the bondage of sin and will provide the strength and power to resist and escape.

> ***"But now we have been released from the law, for we died with Christ, and we are no longer captive to its power. Now we can really serve God, not in the old way by obeying the letter of the law, but in the new way, by the Spirit." Romans 7:6 NLT***

We may have to co-exist, but we cannot and do not have to serve two masters.

When we appropriate this truth by faith, we will harness the resurrection power of the Holy Spirit and overcome the power of our flesh, the world, and the devil to control us.

**Father, guard my heart and let no unwholesome thought or unholy desire take root in it. Amen.**

Read Isaiah 29:13-24 October 1

## *Where's Our Passion?*

**"These people make a big show of saying the right thing, but their heart isn't in it. They act like they're worshiping me, but they don't mean it. They just use me as a cover for teaching whatever suits their fancy." Matthew 15:8 MSG**

There is a danger lurking within every church and every believer. It has caused wars, the killing of many innocent people, and generations of conflict between professing Christians.

> ***"They honor me with their lips, but their hearts are far away." Isaiah 29:13b NLT***

When we become devoted to doctrine and causes instead of Jesus, we have become members of "The Church of the Latter Day Scribes and Pharisees."

As noble as defending the faith may seem, it should never become a higher agenda than the Greatest Commandment or Great Commission.

Jesus' displeasure with the hypocrisy and legalism of the scribes and Pharisees of the day serves as a constant reminder that it's not about doing or saying, but about being.

When churches define themselves as being sanctuaries for saints instead of hospitals for sinners, Jesus will not be found among them.

How many man-made agendas for building bigger sanctuaries or pointing out the faults of other denominations become the main thing instead of kingdom-building through evangelism and discipleship?

"*The heart is deceitful above all things.*" *(Jeremiah 17:9).* We must always guard our hearts so that religion does not become our God. We need to pray continually for the spiritual wisdom to know the difference between God's purposes and man's agendas.

> ***"By this we know that we are in Him. He who says he abides in Him ought himself also to walk just as He walked." 1 John 2:6***

May our passions always be Christ-centered rather than self-centered.

**Father, help me to take You and Your Word more seriously and myself and the doctrines of men less seriously. Amen.**

October 2 Read James 1:1-17, Psalm 24

## *Unconditional Love - Conditional Blessings*

**"May God bless you with his special favor and wonderful peace as you come to know Jesus, our God and Lord, better and better." 2 Peter 1:2 NLT**

God's love is unconditional. He loves, forgives and accepts us just the way we are. But God's blessings are both unconditional and conditional. He makes the sun to shine on the just as well as the unjust. He has given man dominion over every living thing on earth without any conditions whatsoever.

> ***"They will receive the Lord's blessing and have right standing with God their savior." Psalm 24:5 NLT***

However, there are many other blessings that are based on our obedience. *"Now if you will obey me and keep my covenant, you will be my own special treasure from among all the nations of the earth; for all the earth belongs to me." (Exodus 19:5)* All of the Old Testament covenants promise blessings for obedience.

There is the blessing of our salvation which is based on faith. *"For God so loved the world that he gave his only Son, so that everyone who believes in him will not perish but have eternal life." (John 3:16)*

There will be blessings in heaven based on what we have done with the life we have been given on this earth. Whether there are degrees of glory or whether we will be given the privilege of serving more is not clear, but the fact remains that Scripture after Scripture makes it abundantly clear that we can earn blessings in heaven. *"Then at the resurrection of the godly, God will reward you for inviting those who could not repay you." (Luke 14:14)*

Finally, we should never forget that there are blessings given on the condition that we ask for them. *" Yet you do not have because you do not ask. You ask and do not receive, because you ask amiss, that you may spend it on your pleasures." (James 4:2b,3 NLT)* God answers unselfish God-honoring prayers!

> ***"But when you ask him, be sure that you really expect him to answer, for a doubtful mind is as unsettled as a wave of the sea that is driven and tossed by the wind." James 1:6***

**Father by the power of your Spirit teach me to ask for those blessings that will glorify you! Amen**

**Read Romans 4, Psalm 32** **October 3**

## *Grading on the Curve*

**"Be perfect, therefore, as your heavenly Father is perfect." Matthew 5:48 NIV**

Grading on the curve is a wonderful system in school and out. I have even made an "A" on a test with a score of 60 when it was compared to the scores of the others in the class. Grading on the standard would have required me to score at least 93 to make an "A," and I would have gotten an "F" for 60.

> ***"Blessed is he whose transgressions are forgiven, whose sins are covered." Psalm 32:2 NIV***

We are continually grading ourselves on a curve when we compare ourselves scholastically, athletically, physically and financially.

Grading on a standard is another story. Your grade doesn't depend on how others did, but how well you measured up to perfection. I love the practice of rating bands "superior" as the highest rating in band competitions.

Unfortunately, many sincere and lifelong followers of Christ refuse to accept the fact that God does not grade on the curve. When you ask many about their hope for heaven, they will say: "I've been a good person," "I've attended church regularly," "I have been faithful to my spouse," "I have paid my tithes," etc.

As admirable as these attributes are, they offer no real basis for a hope of heaven.

Thank God that we are not going to heaven because of our performance, but because of the superior performance of Jesus Christ, who met God's standard of perfect holiness and righteousness and imputed all of this to us by faith, so that God will give us His superior rating.

> ***"He was delivered over to death for our sins and was raised to life for our justification." Romans 4:25 NIV***

**Lord, let me always anchor my hope in the righteousness of Jesus, and not my own. Amen**

October 4 Read Philippians 4:4-8, Psalm 4

## *The Grace of Graciousness*

**"Let the word of Christ dwell in you richly in all wisdom, teaching and admonishing one another in psalms and hymns and spiritual songs, singing with grace in your hearts to the Lord." Colossians 3:16**

There seems to be a growing shortage of kindness and courtesy in every area of life. Tactfulness, charm, and generosity of spirit have become rare qualities seldom seen.

> ***"You are fairer than the sons of men;***
> ***Grace is poured upon Your lips;***
> ***Therefore God has blessed You forever."***
> ***Psalm 45:2***

Politicians from both parties bemoan the lack of civility and graciousness in political campaigns and legislative processes. The art of disagreeing without being disagreeable has become a lost art. Fender-benders bring out the worst instead of the best in people. Many seem to be looking for any excuse to vent their rage and pent-up frustrations.

Even disagreements between believers boil over into name-calling and character assassinations that divide the body and bring shame to the namesake of those who call themselves Christians.

Generosity of spirit should be the defining characteristic of every believer. Whether carrying our duty to the Great Commandment or Great Commission, when we are generous in bearing the fruit of the Spirit we are giving a sweet offering to the Lord that will always be pleasing to Him.

Jesus should be our role model for learning and living our lives in graciousness. This should be the goal of all who would call themselves His disciples.

> ***"Finally, brethren, whatever things are true, whatever things are noble, whatever things are just, whatever things are pure, whatever things are lovely, whatever things are of good report, if there is any virtue and if there is anything praiseworthy—meditate on these things."***
> ***Philippians 4:8***

**Father, by the power and strength of the Holy Spirit living within me, help me to excel in the grace of graciousness. Amen**

Read 1 Corinthians 1, Psalm 27 October 5

## *Don't be Exploited!*

**"Although He died on the cross in weakness, He now lives by the mighty power of God. We, too, are weak, but we live in Him and have God's power—the power we use in dealing with you.**
**2 Corinthians 13:4 NLT**

In business, sports, and warfare, exploiting weaknesses is often the key to winning. Businesses look for weaknesses in their competitor's products or services to exploit. Coaches and players study game tapes carefully looking for weaknesses of other teams that they might take advantage of.

> ***"Wait on the LORD; Be of good courage, And He shall strengthen your heart; Wait, I say, on the LORD!"***
> ***Psalm 27:14 NLT***

Many a war has been won by identifying and taking advantage of the weaknesses of enemies.

There are two people who know our weaknesses better than we know them ourselves. One is seeking to use them to devour us, and the other is continually covering them with His strength.

Satan is a master of finding and attacking the areas of our lives where we are most vulnerable. Whether it's our pride, fear, lust, greed, or envy, the evil one is continually attacking and seeking to defeat us through exploiting our weaknesses.

The fact that Jesus knows our every weakness and still loves us and provides the incredible resurrection power of the Holy Spirit to cover our weaknesses with His strength.

Instead of exploiting our weaknesses, God uses them for His glory and our good. When the Holy Spirit comes and makes us aware of our sin and our need for a Savior, He gives us the strength to call upon the name of the Lord to be saved. He also equips us with His full armor so that we can stand against the forces of evil that are seeking to devour us.

> ***"God is far wiser than the wisest of human plans, and God's weakness is far stronger than the greatest of human strength."***
> ***1 Corinthians 1:25 NLT***

**Father, thank you for covering my weaknesses with Your strength and giving me the power to overcome. Amen**

**October 6** **Read Titus 2:11-15, Psalm 80**

## *Watch Those Turnovers!*

> ***"Turn us again to yourself, O God. Make your face shine down upon us. Only then will we be saved."***
> ***Psalm 80:3 NLT***

In basketball and football the ability to cause the opposing team to make turnovers and to avoid making turnovers is the key to most victories. Turnovers are the key to receiving and living transformed lives in Christ. When we turn over control of our lives from our flesh to God's Spirit, God's mighty power is unleashed in our lives and we become new, born-again believers.

As the Holy Spirit takes up residence within us, the ongoing process of being conformed into the image of Christ and growing into His fullness begins.

Our daily walk often takes us into spiritual war zones where the battle between the world, the flesh, and the devil rages, we sometimes lose and turn over control of our passions, our time and talents, or our treasures to worldly agendas that grieve the Holy Spirit and impede our progress in Christian growth.

Thanks be to God, these lost battles are not a lost war, and God can and will turn these losses into our good and His glory when we turn them over to Him through daily confession and repentance. As we grow into the fullness of Christ, we grow in the realization that we are totally dependent on the grace and mercy of God and the mighty power of His Spirit. Then we begin surrendering more and more of our will and agendas by turning them over to the control of God and seeking His will and His purposes for our lives.

> ***"And we are instructed to turn from godless living and sinful pleasures. We should live in this evil world with self-control, right conduct, and devotion to God,***
> ***Titus 2:12 NLT***

It is so good to know that our failures are never final and that if God loved us enough to send His Son to die for us, He certainly loves us enough to keep us in the fold of His all-sufficient sustaining grace.

**Father, help me to avoid the turnovers of sin and its consequences by turning over control of my life to You. Amen**

**Read 1 Corinthians 15:40-54, Isaiah 26:1-19** **October 7**

## *Who's Your Landlord?*

**"For we know that when this earthly tent we live in is taken down—when we die and leave these bodies—we will have a home in heaven, an eternal body made for us by God himself and not by human hands." 2 Corinthians 5:1 NLT**

We are all tenants living in corruptible bodies that begin dying the moment we are born. We are all given a free will to choose how we live during the term of our lease.

> ***"Yet we have this assurance: Those who belong to God will live; their bodies will rise again!"***
> ***Isaiah 26:19 NLT***

We can choose to live a life in the flesh controlled by our sinful nature, blinded and separated from the love of God, or we can receive the power of the Holy Spirit to open the door when Jesus knocks and receive a new lease on life that extends the terms beyond this life into all eternity.

Jesus Christ came to live and die to give us a new lease on life in the Spirit and paid our rent in full by dying on the cross so that we could be transformed by the renewing of our minds in Christ.

Our new lease on life is unconditional and non-cancelable. We are given the Holy Spirit as our security deposit, guaranteeing that this lease will be in effect forever with no more payments required.

Under the terms of this lease we are set free from the condemnation and domination of sin so that we can live lives fully pleasing to our lord and fruitful in every good work.

When we take out this lease by faith, our bodies become temples of the Holy Spirit who comes to live in us as our resident building superintendent.

> ***"When this happens—when our perishable earthly bodies have been transformed into heavenly bodies that will never die—then at last the Scriptures will come true:***
> ***1 Corinthians 15:54 NLT***

The Spirit guides us into all truth, cleanses and restores from all storm and damage, and covers our weaknesses with His strength.

Have you taken out your new lease on life?

**Father, thank You for giving me a new lease on life filled with the joy and peace of a forever life with and in You. Amen**

October 8 Read Mark 9:17-27, Psalm 63:1-8

## *Why Limit God?*

**"I pray that you will begin to understand the incredible greatness of his power for us who believe him. This is the same mighty power that raised Christ from the dead and seated him in the place of honor at God's right hand in the heavenly realms." Ephesians 1:19-20**

As joint heirs with Christ, we who believe have been given every spiritual blessing along with the incredible greatness of God's power. We can do all things through Christ, who strengthens us.

> ***"I have seen you in your sanctuary and gazed upon your power and glory."***
> ***Psalm 63:2 NLT***

With the unlimited blessings and the grace and power of God at our disposal, why do we often limit God's blessings and power?

We limit God's power in our lives by unbelief. When we fail to believe that God has given us what He says He has given us, we clog up the pipeline of power and never grow into the fullness of Christ.

Disobedience is another power-breaker that impedes God's perfect plan for our living the abundant life in Christ. When we insist on going our way instead of God's way in any area of our lives, we are going to experience a major power outage.

Lack of perseverance can often serve as a circuit breaker, interrupting the flow of God's power into our lives. We too often get discouraged and give up too soon and too easily instead of hanging tough and appropriating the promises and power of God by faith.

Unforgiveness and allowing persistent and unrepented sins to fester grieve the Holy Spirit and keep us from living in the fullness of God's Power.

As born again believers being grown into the fullness of Christ by the sanctifying power of the Holy Spirit, we need to avoid limiting the unlimited power of God available to us. Instead of being controlled by the flesh, we need to be transformed by the Spirit. We need to believe and ask God continually to help our unbelief.

> ***"Jesus said to him, "If you can believe, all things are possible to him who believes."***
> ***Mark 9:23***

**Father, do not let unbelief, disobedience or doubt separate me from your power. Amen**

**Read 1 Corinthians 3:10-15, Psalm 56** **October 9**

# *We Are All Authors*

**"I saw the dead, both great and small, standing before God's throne. And the books were opened, including the Book of Life. And the dead were judged according to the things written in the books, according to what they had done." Revelation 20:12**

We are all authors of our own "book of life." It is comforting to know that our names have already been written in this book and that we have been judged righteous by our faith in Jesus Christ.

> ***"You keep track of all my sorrows. You have collected all my tears in your bottle. You have recorded each one in your book."***
> ***Psalm 56:5 NLT***

In addition to our names, it seems clear that rewards, in proportion to what we have done that honored and glorified God and reflected our love for Him, will be bestowed. We can be sure that our perseverance in our faith through hardships and persecutions are being recorded.

We are writing new entries in our book of life on a daily basis. When we consider which activities we spend our time on, it should make us more mindful that only the time spent with and for God will count for anything.

We are writing our own book of life through our checkbooks. When our giving is in proportion to what we have been given and is done cheerfully and not under compulsion, our heavenly bank account will become a real storehouse of blessings.

Our book of life will also contain the record of how well we have used the talents God has given us for His glory and for the building of His kingdom. Our greatest record that will shine brighter than the stars after all our works have been tested in the fire will be those whose names are also in the book of life because God has used us to help make them His disciples.

> ***"But there is going to come a time of testing at the judgment day to see what kind of work each builder has done"***
> ***1 Corinthians 3:13 NLT***

**Father, while there is still time, give me the power of Your Spirit to improve my book of life in ways that pleases and glorifies You. Amen**

October 10 Read 1 Timothy 6:11-21, Psalm 128

## *Incredible Pursuits*

**"And My elect shall long enjoy the work of their hands. They shall not labor in vain, Nor bring forth children for trouble; For they *shall be* the descendants of the blessed of the LORD, And their offspring with them." Isaiah 65:22b, 23**

We often lose sight of the tremendous blessings that God's favor upon America and almost all its people have brought over the past century. As a nation, we have gone from working from daylight to dusk to eke out a meager living to a people abounding in leisure time and sufficient resources to enjoy so many of the good things God has provided.

> *"You will enjoy the fruit of your labor. How happy you will be! How rich your life!" Psalm 128:2 NLT*

On any given day in any given community we find young and old alike pursuing their interest in and enjoying sports of all kind: spectator sports, hunting, fishing, crafts, photography, collecting, traveling, camping, animals, etc.

By and large, these benefits of a higher standard of living are a good thing and things that we should enjoy and be thankful for.

While too much leisure time often does become the devil's playhouse and our advances in education have too often taken God out of the equation, we can still enjoy a lot of positive outlets for our interests and talents without being corrupted by the sin and evil all around us.

For believers, pursuing our interests and expressing our talents through the incredible number of opportunities available can and should be great outreach opportunities for reaching lost people who we are never going to reach in church or other channels. Whenever we pursue other interests as ambassadors of Christ, we will find how really incredible these pursuits can be.

> ***"Command those who are rich in this present age not to be haughty, nor to trust in uncertain riches but in the living God, who gives us richly all things to enjoy." 1 Timothy 6:17***

**Father, let my recreational pursuits and leisure time become mission fields for glorifying You and advancing Your kingdom. Amen**

**Read John 6:35-58, Psalm 44:1-8** **October 11**

# *Let's Go Soaring!*

**"But those who wait on the LORD will find new strength. They will fly high on wings like eagles. They will run and not grow weary. They will walk and not faint."   Isaiah 40:31 NLT**

The incredible power that raised Christ from the dead, that changed Paul from a murderer and persecutor of Christians into an Apostle that God used to change the world, and the power that changed defeated disciples into bold and courageous proclaimers of the Gospel resides within every one of us who claim Jesus Christ as Lord and Savior.

> ***"It was by your mighty power that they succeeded; it was because you favored them and smiled on them"***
> ***Psalm 44:3b NLT***

When we exchange our lives of sin in the flesh for a new birth in the Spirit, we receive the enabling strength and power to overcome besetting sins, and to rise above our circumstances, shortcomings and failures. We can actually be transformed into the fullness of Christ and be reflectors and conduits of God's glory.

Just as the disciples obeyed the Lord and waited for the promised power of the Holy Spirit, we need to trust in the Lord with all our hearts and acknowledge His Lordship over us so that He can make straight our paths and continue to make us more like Him until we see Him face to face.

As long as we hold back and hold out in any area of our lives and persist in trying to soar in our own strength in these areas, we are never going to leave enough room to grow into the fullness of Christ and experience the incredible joy and strength that this brings. When we miss out on the strength and power of being all that we can be in Christ by trying to be all that we can be in our selves, we are not only short changing ourselves, but we are stiff-arming God and falling short of glorifying Him to the utmost.

> ***"I live by the power of the living Father who sent me; in the same way, those who partake of me will live because of me."***
> ***John 6:57 NLT***

**Father, let me soar with You under the shelter of Your wings of grace and glorify You in every area of my life.  Amen**

October 12 Read 2 Corinthians 12:1-9, Psalm 84

## *It's All About Grace*

**"God is sheer mercy and grace; not easily angered, he's rich in love." Psalm 103:8 MSG**

Grace can perhaps be best understood as being the special favor and power of God bestowed on those who believe. It starts with the free gift of salvation through the power of faith given by the Holy Spirit to receive Jesus Christ as our Savior.

> ***"For the LORD God is our light and protector. He gives us grace and glory. No good thing will the LORD withhold from those who do what is right." Psalm 84:11 NLT***

From the minute we are born again by faith in Christ, we are sheltered under the wings of God's amazing grace and the mighty resurrection power of the Holy Spirit dwelling within us. Grace allows us to live the sanctified life that we can never live by our own strength or reason.

Some of the treasures of God's grace we enjoy are the grace of forgiveness and cleansing and the grace of giving and forgiving. We receive the special favor and power of God to grow into the fullness of Christ and become more like Him day-by-day.

Grace is the all-sufficient special favor and power of God that carries us through the failures and sufferings of life. We receive the grace to endure, to persevere, and to "keep on keeping on."

The story of Job is probably the greatest testimony to the all-sufficient grace of God that can be found in all of Scripture. Job persevered through every imaginable tragedy and suffering, only by the special favor and power of God, and emerged through it all restored and blessed beyond all measure.

> ***"Three different times I begged the Lord to take it away. 9Each time he said, "My gracious favor is all you need. My power works best in your weakness." 2 Corinthians 12:8 NLT***

Paul's prayers for removal of his thorn in the flesh was answered not by the removal of the thorn, but by the promise of God's special favor and power sufficient to perfect God's strength in Paul's weakness.

**Father, let your strength be made perfect in my weaknesses as you pour out your favor and power in every area of my life. Amen**

**Read Romans 7:4-25, Psalm 18** **October 13**

# Watch Out for Those Propensities

**"But remember that the temptations that come into your life are no different from what others experience. And God is faithful. He will keep the temptation from becoming so strong that you can't stand up against it. When you are tempted, he will show you a way out so that you will not give in to it. 1 Corinthians 10:13 NLT**

Propensity means "often intense natural inclination or preference or leaning." Satan is aware of our propensities and is continually pushing our hot buttons to exploit them. We can avoid a lot of grief, pain, and consequences if we can identity our propensities and consciously seek to avoid or overcome them.

> ***"For I have kept the ways of the LORD; I have not turned from my God to follow evil."***
> ***Psalm 18:21 NLT***

Even as born-again believers who have been set free from domination and condemnation of sin, we co-exist in the flesh with those old natural inclinations or propensities.

We have propensities for pleasure, for power, and for approval. We have leanings toward anger, envy, pride, idolatry, and lust.

When these propensities surface, we need to know how to recognize them and deal with them with the full armor of God and His marvelous power and strength. We don't need to feed our propensity for alcohol by going to a bar or beer party. We don't need to feed our leanings for lust by going to the wrong movies, TV or internet porn sites.

God is aware of our propensities to sin and has not left us unprotected and unequipped to overcome them. He has given us the shield of faith, the sword of the Spirit, the breastplate of righteousness, the helmet of salvation, the belt of truth, and the shoes of peace.

Best of all, when we stumble and fall, He is always there to forgive, to pick us up, and give us the strength to repent when we confess and cry, "Holy to the Lord!"

> ***"Oh, what a miserable person I am! Who will free me from this life that is dominated by sin? Thank God! The answer is in Jesus Christ our Lord."***
> ***Romans 7:24,25a NLT***

**Father, help me to guard against my propensities and to stand firm in the mighty resurrection power of Your Spirit. Amen**

October 14 Read John 1, Psalm 85

## *We Are Blessed!*

**"Blessed be the God and Father of our Lord Jesus Christ, who has blessed us with every spiritual blessing in the heavenly places in Christ." Ephesians 1:3 NLT**

This verse should be one of the most encouraging in all of Scripture for believers. It is filled with promise and power. It should set our hearts on fire for the love of God that is ours in Christ.

> ***"Yes, the LORD pours down his blessings." Psalm 85:12a NLT***

When we begin to inventory the spiritual blessings and privileges we enjoy as believers and let the reality of this truth sink in, we will never be the same.

God has bestowed all spiritual blessings that prepare us for heaven. He has given us pardon, adoption as sons and daughters, and the enlightenment and power of the indwelling presence of the Holy Spirit. We receive the blessings of wisdom and spiritual discernment that we might know how to properly respond to our calling.

It is God's purpose and will to bestow spiritual blessings upon those He has chosen to receive the saving grace of God through faith in Jesus Christ. His favor is upon us in this life and in the next.

The peace and joy of our salvation, happiness through holiness by the wonderful blessing of sanctification, and the blessed graces of God's empowering love are the birthright of every born-again believer. Although temporal blessings vary from believer to believer, spiritual blessings are imparted in abundance to every believer. We are given the graces of loving, giving, and forgiving.

We are given the blessing of being set free from condemnation and domination by sin and the privilege of being transformed into the image of Christ by being born again.

> ***"We have all benefited from the rich blessings he brought to us—one gracious blessing after another" John 1:16 NLT***

God truly is our fount of every blessing, and we have the joy of knowing this and the thrill of appropriating His blessings and His incomparable power into our every day life.

**Father, keep me ever mindful and ever thankful for every spiritual blessing you have bestowed upon me in Christ. Amen**

Read James 1:4-8, Psalm 103 **October 15**

## *Do We Wobble?*

**"This is what God says: 'Why do you disobey the Lord's commands? You will not prosper. Because you have forsaken the Lord, He has forsaken you.'" 2 Chronicles 24:20 NIV**

Wobbling in order to get around God's clear teachings is part of the rebellion package with which we are all born.

> ***"The Lord's love is with those who fear Him, and His righteousness with their children's children- with those who keep his covenant and remember to obey his precepts.***
> ***Psalm 103:17b, 18 NIV***

Just as children are continually testing the boundaries of behavior and conduct with their parents, we seem to have this idea that we can wobble with God and get away with it.

Satan started the wobbling process by questioning Eve as to whether God really said what He said about eating the fruit.

We wobble by rationalizing that everyone's doing it so it must be ok, that God wants me to be happy and this would make me happy, and even that God understands and somehow gives us special dispensation.

We are probably more wobble-prone in the area of giving to the Lord than any other area. Whether it be in the area of giving treasures, talents, or time, we often try to get by with giving as little as possible instead of trying to figure out how to give as much as possible.

As new born babes, it is easy to stumble and wobble a lot as we learn to walk in the Lord and His ways. As we grow into spiritual maturity we should replace wobbling with walking straight in the holiness of Christ to which we have been called, using the power and strength of the Holy Spirit to do what we are unable to do on our own.

> ***"But when he asks, he must believe and not doubt, because he who doubts is like a wave of the sea, blown and tossed by the wind."***
> ***James 1:6 NIV***

When it comes to sin, we need to confess it and repent and never wobble about whether it is really sin or look for excuses for continuing in it.

**Father, help we to walk on the solid ground of your will instead of wobbling in the quicksand of my own. Amen**

October 16 Read 1 John 4:7-20, Psalm 97

# Open Our Eyes Lord

**"Be imitators of God, therefore, as dearly loved children and live a life of love, just as Christ loved us and gave himself up for us as a fragrant offering and sacrifice to God." Ephesians 5:1 NIV**

How many people do you know who remind you of Jesus? One of the sacred delights of all believers should be those we know who remind us that Jesus is alive and well, and living and loving among us and through us.

> ***"Light is shed upon the righteous and joy on the upright in heart"***
> ***Psalm 97:11 NIV***

Millions of people have seen Jesus in the life and love of Billy Graham. Many have seen it in the life and love of Mother Teresa. We can all see Him in the lives of those around us if we will just open our eyes.

If we open our eyes and look, we can see Jesus living and at work all around us. The common characteristics of those who remind us of Jesus are humility, a sweet spirit, and the love of God shining through to bless and encourage others.

Through all of the sin and evil that abounds, the grace of God continues to abound even more through the transformed lives of love and compassion of His disciples.

There are random acts of kindness and generosity going on throughout the World that light up the dark corners through people and ministries that are living some of the best sermons ever preached as they live out the Great Commandment and Great Commission.

And how about us? Who do people see when they see us? Do they see humility or pride? Do they see joy or do they see abrasiveness and irritability? Do they see the love of God or the love of self? Do they hear the talk but never see the walk?

> ***"God is love. Whoever lives in love lives in God, and God in him. In this way, love is made complete among us so that we will have confidence on the day of judgment, because in this world we are like him"***
> ***1 John 4:16b, 17 NIV***

. When we open our eyes to seeing and learning what He did and what He taught, and applying it to our lives, others will see Jesus in us.

**Father, open my eyes that I might see you in others; and that I might grow into your fullness so that others see You in me. Amen**

**Read Luke 14:15-34, Psalm 86** **October 17**

# *The Great Exchange*

**"What good will it be for a man if he gains the whole world, yet forfeits his soul? Or what can a man give in exchange for his soul?" Matthew 16:26 NIV**

> ***"For great is Your mercy toward me, And You have delivered my soul from the depths of Sheol." Psalm 86:13 NIV***

Once we have tasted that the Lord is good, it becomes hard to believe that we waited so long to answer our call to salvation and eternal life in Christ.

We often have become so concerned about what we might have to give up that we became blinded by the enormity of what we receive. Often, we have just not been willing to give up the world and all of its pleasures for a hope of heaven that seems so distant.

We cling to our pride and our distorted fleshly view of what we think will make us happy, and sometimes spend years wandering aimlessly lost clinging to the futility of our sins through which we willfully stay separated from God.

We all need to daily think about the grace of God which has allowed us to trade our sorrows for Jesus' joy, our worries for Jesus' peace, our guilt for God's forgiveness, and our sin-dominated lives for the freedom of living forever in the strength and power of the Holy Spirit in a new life in Christ.

When we consider what Jesus gave up in exchange for our souls, we should be ashamed to even have thought that we might have to give up. He gave up the kingdom of the World and all of its pleasures and His own life in exchange for our sins, so that we could live forever in Him.

> ***"So likewise, whoever of you does not forsake all that he has cannot be My disciple." Luke 14:33 NIV***

As we cling to the false hope and false security of living in our strength and for our purposes, we will never know the true happiness and fulfillment of exchanging our old life in the flesh for a new life controlled and transformed by the Spirit.

**Father, thank You for leading me to accept the best trade ever offered. Amen**

## *Do You Double Dribble?*

**"Do not conform any longer to the pattern of this world, but be transformed by the renewing of your mind. Then you will be able to test and approve what God's will is–his good, pleasing and perfect will." Romans 12:1-3 NIV**

Double-dribbling is a no-no in basketball. You can't dribble with both hands, and you can't start dribbling again after you stop.

> **"Since you are my rock and my fortress, for the sake of your name lead and guide me."**
> **Psalm 31:3 NIV**

We all at some time or another try to get by with "double-dribbling" on God. We want to control the ball of life by our flesh and by our Spirit at the same time, and it just won't work. We often stop and repent of what we are doing, and then start it all over again.

When we dribble through life in the flesh, we are going to be controlled by the lust and pride of the flesh and will never grow into the fullness of Christ. When we dribble in the Spirit, we are going to be transformed and become more Christ-like day-by-day.

The turnovers caused by our double-dribbling can be disastrous. Every time we dribble in the flesh, we commit a turnover and give up control of our bright future and hope in Christ from God's hands and take control of our destinies for ourselves.

Even after we are born again and begin living a new life of freedom and victory in Jesus, our "turnover" into everlasting life and our joy in the Lord is going to be constantly attacked by the forces of evil that are all about us.

> ***"You, however, are controlled not by the sinful nature but by the Spirit, if the Spirit of God lives in you. And if anyone does not have the Spirit of Christ, he does not belong to Christ."***
> ***Romans 8:8-10 NIV***

Instead of committing a costly turnover, we should pass the ball to the Holy Spirit and let His strength cover our weaknesses, letting Him armor us so that we can get the ball back and get a fresh dribble to take to the basket of eternal life that awaits all who believe.

**Father, help me to avoid those costly turnovers of life by turning to You. Amen**

**Read Matthew 6:19-34, Psalm 4** **October 19**

# Who's Our Almighty?

It is a fact of life that people are created to worship. Every society has tribal customs of worship and manmade gods to worship.

> ***"How long, O men, will you turn my glory into shame [How long will you love delusions and seek false gods"***
> ***Psalm 4:2 NLT***

The history of the Old Testament and the world today bears out the fact that everyone is going to worship someone or something. We hear about worshipping "the almighty dollar," pleasure, fame, and ourselves. From God's perspective, any person or thing that we put above Him has become our almighty.

Time after time, in spite of having God's presence, provision, and blessings in so many ways, the children of Israel were ready to worship a golden calf or some other idol instead of God at the slightest whim.

Our God is a jealous God who commands that we worship Him and Him alone with all our hearts, souls and beings. He will not tolerate our hearts' affection and minds' attention being taken from Him and His glory, and wasted on our own vain pursuits and agendas.

The world is constantly and continually teaching that we are children of a god of chance and that we should trust the wisdom of man and man's abilities. God reminds us that all of the knowledge and wisdom of man is foolishness to God. We are exhorted to *"Trust in the Lord with all your heart; do not depend on your own understanding. Seek his will in all you do, and he will direct your paths."* *(Proverbs 3:5-6 NLT)*

> ***"No one can serve two masters. Either he will hate the one and love the other, or he will be devoted to the one and despise the other. You cannot serve both God and Money."***
> ***Matthew 6:24 NIV***

When our relationship with God is based on putting Him first and seeking His kingdom and His righteousness, He has promised to supply all our needs and to give us the joy of our salvation. Why would we jeopardize this by making anything else our almighty?

**Father, help me to rid myself of any other "almighties" that would offend and diminish my relationship with You. Amen**

## *Where's Your Hope?*

**"But those who hope in the Lord will renew their strength. They will soar on wings like eagles; they will run and not grow weary, they will walk and not be faint." Isaiah 40:30-32**

There seems to be a lot of wishing going on without much hoping. We wish or desire for what we perceive are good things for ourselves and others but somehow seem to become very doubtful about our wishes coming true.

> ***"But the eyes of the Lord are on those who fear him, on those whose hope is in his unfailing love."***
> ***Psalm 33:18***

"I wish I could lose ten pounds." "I wish I could get a new car," "I wish I would win the lottery," are just a few of the desires expressed that are common to many people.

There is often a large gap between our wish and our hope with regard to salvation. When asked about being sure of going to heaven, even many professing believers become hesitant and unsure. "I think I am," "I hope that I am," and often "how can anyone be sure of this." We must understand the facts: *"I write these things to you who believe in the name of the Son of God so that you may know that you have eternal life." (1 John 5:12-14)*

It is so good to know that our hope is a living hope based on the incredible power of God, where it becomes not only a desire but an expectation and confirmed fact of faith.

When our hope is confirmed by faith and trust in the incredible promises of God, we are no longer tossed about by conflict and doubt, but stand strong in the security of God's love and the blessed assurance of the hope we have in Him.

> ***"Let us hold unswervingly to the hope we profess, for he who promised is faithful."***
> ***Hebrews 10:23 NIV***

We can not only hope but, like Job, know that *"our redeemer lives and that He will again stand upon the earth."* (Job 19:25 NIV)

**Father, give me that hope that cannot disappoint in a God who cannot fail. Amen**

**Read Romans 6, Psalm 130** **October 21**

## *Forgiveness Easier Than Permission*

**"Do not be deceived. God cannot be mocked. A man reaps what he sows." Galatians 6:6-8**

Children are quick to learn that it is often a whole lot easier to get forgiveness than receive permission. We adults often have the same idea.

> ***"If you, O Lord, kept a record of sins, who could stand? But with you there is forgiveness; therefore you are feared. Psalm 130:3, 4 NIV***

If we don't ask, we can proceed without the guilt of disobedience and proceed to ask for and receive forgiveness. This is often a rationale for spending money we should not be spending while out shopping.

God has given the law that we might know what He permits and what He prohibits. He has even written it into our hearts. It convicts us of our sin and our need for a Savior, curbs our sinful conduct, and is a guide for righteous living.

God's covenant of Grace that has come upon us and has made forgiveness available to us all for everything should be never be construed as license to sin or permission to go through life sinning. Rather, we should treasure this freedom from the condemnation of sin so that we might pursue holiness and live lives fully pleasing to God.

Our relationship with Christ should become so real and intimate that we know what He expects and requires of us. We should love and want to please Him so much that we never think of doing anything that He would not approve or give permission to do, even though we know that His grace abounds over and above all our sins.

> ***"And do not present your members as instruments of unrighteousness to sin, but present yourselves to God as being alive from the dead, and your members as instruments of righteousness to God." Romans 6:13 NIV***

**Father, keep me seeking to please you instead of my self, and help me to learn more and more about pleasing you. Amen**

# *The Highway of Holiness*

**"And a main road will go through that once deserted land. It will be named the Highway of Holiness. Evil-hearted people will never travel on it. It will be only for those who walk in God's ways; fools will never walk there." Isaiah 35:8 NLT**

God hates sin. When we see the power, majesty, and holiness of God revealed through Scripture, we see the wrath of God poured out against all who rebel against His holiness and revel in the deeds of darkness.

> ***"Go out! Prepare the highway for my people to return! Smooth out the road; pull out the boulders; raise a flag for all the nations to see." Isaiah 62:10 NIV***

But as much as God hates sin, He loves sinners even more. God's justice has been satisfied and we are all now able to walk on the Highway of Holiness by virtue that we have been made holy in sight of God because of the sinless perfection and holiness of Christ.

Thank God that He loves us beyond His hatred of our sin. Unlike the Scribes and Pharisees of the day who condemned not only sins but also sinners, God came in the person of Jesus Christ to condemn sin but save sinners and put us on the Highway of Holiness through His resurrection.

Just as the sins of the disciples and Apostle Paul were buried at the cross when they died to sin and became alive in Christ, we who receive Jesus Christ as Lord and Savior by faith have all our guilt, condemnation, and control by our sins forgotten, removed, and covered by our New Birth in the Spirit

God will establish our right to walk on the highway of holiness through faith and give us the power to stay on this road by the resurrection power of Christ in us, which is our hope of glory.

> ***"You can enter God's Kingdom only through the narrow gate. The highway to hell is broad, and its gate is wide for the many who choose the easy way. " Matthew 7:13, 14 NLT***

**Father, help me to walk on the highway of holiness all the days of my life, in Jesus name. Amen**

Read Romans 3:9-31, Psalm 40 October 23

## *Spiritual Security*

**"Those who know your name trust in you, for you, O LORD, have never abandoned anyone who searches for you." Psalm 9:10 NIV**

Back in the 1930's, the idea that the Federal Government should start retirement and disability benefits for all workers was not warmly received among many people. Many saw social security as social welfare which they believed would lead to the demise of the American Way.

> ***"But may all who search for you be filled with joy and gladness. May those who love your salvation repeatedly shout, "The Lord is great!"***
> ***Psalm 40:16 NIV***

The sense of social security we live out daily at school, at work, at play, and within the family is going to a large degree determine the quality of our every day lives. In school and on the playground we seek the social security of being accepted by others.

We often find ourselves in socially insecure situations. A party may become too rowdy; a sporting event may turn into a free-for-all. We can find ourselves watching movies so bad we try to slip out unnoticed.

. Perhaps the real social security concern should be about receiving real security through the life changing power of the Gospel of Jesus Christ. This is a social security based on a close and personal relationship with God through faith and friendship with His Son, Jesus Christ. His death on the cross has made us righteous in the sight of God. The gift of the transforming power of the Holy Spirit gives us the power to become like Christ.

We receive unconditional love, total forgiveness for our past, present, and future sins, and total acceptance as joint heirs with Christ. We become dead to the dominion and condemnation of sin and alive in Christ. We receive the ultimate "social security" for now and forever.

> ***"We are made right in God's sight when we trust in Jesus Christ to take away our sins. And we all can be saved in this same way, no matter who we are or what we have done."***
> ***Romans 3:22***

**Father, keep me ever mindful that my real social security benefit is in you. Amen**

**October 24** **Read James 1:19-25, Psalm 81**

# *Good Listeners*

**"God blesses the one who reads this prophecy to the church, and he blesses all who listen to it and obey what it says. For the time is near when these things will happen." Revelation 1:3 NLT**

One of the biggest problems in the world today is the absence of good listeners. A constant complaint most often heard by marriage counselors is the fact that many spouses just don't listen.

> ***"Listen to me, O my people, while I give you stern warnings. O Israel, if you would only listen!"***
> ***Psalm 81:8 NLT***

Students tune out teachers, children tune out parents and vice versa. It is interesting to note that most of the people we admire are good listeners who listen to us.

Scripture is filled with examples of believers who chose to ignore God's calls to repentance and persisted in living a futile life apart from God.

God continues to speak to us through His Word, His Sprit, and other believers as He reveals Himself to us and opens the eyes of our heart so that we not only listen, but hear and obey.

Our good shepherd has called us by name and will in no way cast out those who have listened, learned, and obeyed the master's voice.

How many tsunamis, earthquakes and other natural disasters must we experience before we learn the truth that God allows tragedies to fall on the just and the unjust? How many people are going to die today into an eternity of torment because they chose not to listen, not to obey, and not to enter?

Disasters should serve to remind us that there is a day of judgment coming for all, and that it is earlier than we think. God's window of opportunity for answering His call to saving faith and eternal life has already closed for millions who have ignored His call and died into eternal death.

> ***"And remember, it is a message to obey, not just to listen to. If you don't obey, you are only fooling yourself."***
> ***James 1:22 NLT***

Obeying God's call to repentance is the greatest comfort we can know as we persevere through the evil that abounds all around us in this sin-sick world.

**Father, teach me to listen carefully and obey You so that Your blessing will surround me. Amen**

Read Ephesians 3, Psalm 71 October 25

## *The Original Supercharger*

**"For the Kingdom of God is not just fancy talk; it is living by God's power." 1 Corinthians 4:20 NLT**

We live in a supercharged world. There is an obsession for more power, more speed, and more strength for about anything. Supercharged engines can harness exhaust gasses to provide incredible extra speed when needed for cars, boats, and planes.

> ***"My life is an example to many, because you have been my strength and protection. That is why I can never stop praising you; I declare your glory all day long."***
> ***Psalm 71:7-8 NIV***

Many athletes seem to have supercharged strength through steroids. Many people seem to trust in alcohol or drugs as superchargers for living and surviving through the many perplexities of life.

The Holy Spirit has always been and always will be God's means of supercharging the lives of His believers.

The disciples were immediately transformed with more power and strength and ability that they ever dreamed possible when they received the supercharging of the Holy Spirit. They lead the way for a revolution that overcame the forces of evil and darkness in the World.

Throughout history ordinary people have been "supercharged" to do extraordinary things for God as they brought the Good News of salvation through faith in Jesus Christ and made disciples throughout the world. The apostle Paul went from tormentor and persecutor of Christians to champion proclaimer of the Good News when he received the transforming super power of a New Birth in Christ.

> ***"May you experience the love of Christ, though it is so great you will never fully understand it. Then you will be filled with the fullness of life and power that comes from God."***
> ***Ephesians 3:19 NLT***

We should never forget that we have been "supercharged" with the resurrection power of Christ living in us, and appropriate this power by faith that never doubts in a Christ who never fails so that we can live supercharged lives, fully pleasing to God and fruitful in every good work.

**Father, give me the supernatural power of the Holy Spirit that I might glorify You in every area of my life. Amen**

# *Our "Throw Away" World*

**"For the LORD will not cast off His people,Nor will He forsake His inheritance." Psalm 94:14**

Landfills and garbage dumps are filling up faster than they can be built thanks to the "throw away" culture of our times.

> ***"Cast your cares on the Lord and he will sustain you; he will never let the righteous fall."***
> ***Psalm 55:21-23 NIV***

We have "throw away" bottles, diapers, and cameras. It is almost cheaper to throw away a computer printer instead of buying a replacement cartridge.

"Clean plate clubs" are a thing of the past as we probably throw away enough food everyday to feed a third world country.

The real tragedy of our "throw away world" is the millions of babies being murdered each year through abortion. We throw away spouses, friends, and sometimes even pastors without even a twinge of regret.

Many people throw away God when tragedy strikes or temptation wins out.

What joy there is in knowing that we do not have a "throw away" God. He has promised to be with us always, even to the ends of the earth. He will never leave us or forsake us.

The only thing that God wants us to throw away is our sinful nature. He died to save us from bondage and the condemnation of sin. Sin can no longer have any dominion over us when we experience the new birth in Christ.

We are going to continually sin and fall short of the glory of God even though we have been redeemed and made holy in His sight. But as the Holy Spirit takes up residence in our hearts and begins the ongoing work of making us as holy, we will grow into the fullness of Christ.

> ***"I give them eternal life, and they will never perish. No one will snatch them away from me."***
> ***John 10:28***

**Father thank You for Your assurance that whoever calls upon your name will be saved and that you will never throw us away. Amen**

# Check Out Time

**"Jesus told her, "I am the resurrection and the life. Those who believe in me, even though they die like everyone else, will live again." John 11:25 NLT**

Every hotel, motel, or resort has a check out time. Unless you are able to make special arrangements, you have to be checked out by this time in order to avoid paying another day's rent.

> ***"But as for me, God will redeem my life. He will snatch me from the power of death." Psalm 49:15***

We each have a check out time from life on this earth. This was set by God before we were ever born and whether we are allowed to check out early or live a long life, our times are in God's hands.

God does promise a long life to those who honor their fathers and mothers. *(Exodus 20:12, Deuteronomy 5:16)*

We know that suicide is abhorrent because all hope of forgiveness through repentance is gone with it. We can commit spiritual suicide by checking out of a relationship with God and pursuing the perceived pleasures of sin.

God is absolutely sovereign. He is in control of everything. In His sovereignty, He allows a lot of bad things to happen even to good people from our perspective.

God is also absolute love and goodness. Although we may never see it from our perspective, He does make all things new, and He does work all things, including our sins and their consequences for our good and His glory.

The important thing is not only that there is a check out time, but that we need to be ready when it comes. We need to be dressed in the white robe of righteousness that is ours only by faith in Jesus Christ. This is the only proper attire assuring a royal transport to eternal life in heaven, where we will never check out.

> ***"That is why I said that you will die in your sins; for unless you believe that I am who I say I am, you will die in your sins." John 8:24 NLT***

**Father, don't let me check out without confirmed reservations for my next destination. Amen**

October 28 — Read Luke 15:11-32, Proverbs 17:9-17

# *Timeless Friends*

**"A man of many companions may come to ruin, but there is a friend who sticks closer than a brother." Proverbs 18:23-25**

One of the sacred delights of life is the timeless quality of special friendships. If we are very blessed, we will have a few special people who we can go years without seeing, and then see and enjoy just as if it had just been a few days since we saw them.

> ***"A friend is always loyal, and a brother is born to help in time of need." Proverbs 17:17 NIV***

These friendships transcend time, distance, circumstances and neglect. We can run into an old childhood friend, classmate, cousin, or church friend and have shared experiences come to mind and be greatly blessed. This is probably why reunions of any kind are so enjoyable for so many people.

In this transient society where we move around a lot, it is sometimes very difficult to go home again because there have been so many of them that we haven't been able to establish any roots anywhere. When we do go back, those special people who are on our "must see" list will be the ones we seek out and enjoy seeing and visiting.

It is good to know that people are universal. We find the good, bad, and ugly wherever we go, and might even meet someone today who will become a special friend for life.

It's even better to know that we have a timeless friend in our Lord Jesus Christ, who will stick closer to us than a biological brother. He will never leave us or forsake us. Although we may sometimes move away from Him, He will always be our friend and brother and give us a glad welcome back when we come back home to Him.

> ***"The son said to him, 'Father, I have sinned against heaven and against you. I am no longer worthy to be called your son." Luke 15:21 NIV***

The parable of the prodigal son teaches that our wise, kind, Heavenly Friend is delighted to welcome us back and renew our friendship just as if we had never left. This eternal truth makes this timeless Friend even more special.

**Father, thank You for the blessing of my timeless friends but even more for the blessing of my friendship with Jesus. Amen**

Read Matthew 6, Psalm 118 October 29

# *Opening the Eyes of Our Heart*

**"I pray also that the eyes of your heart may be enlightened in order that you may know the hope to which He has called you, the riches of His glorious inheritance in the saints." Ephesians 1:18 NIV**

Every child born of woman is born with spiritual blindness. The gene of inherited sin comes with every birth. This spiritual darkness can only be cured by the Holy Spirit, who comes to open the eyes of our hearts so that we can see and receive Jesus by faith.

> ***"The stone the builders rejected has become the capstone; the Lord has done this, and it is marvelous in our eyes." Psalm 118:22-23 NIV***

When the Holy Spirit opens the eyes of our heart, He opens the door to a brand new life in the Spirit, which is freed to grow into the fullness of Christ. We will see everything more clearly.

The eyes of our heart will let us see the glory of the Lord in all creation. We will see the heavens, land and sea, and all of God's creatures as evidence of God's handiwork.

When our belief in Jesus moves from our head to our heart, the eyes of our heart will open and we will see the resurrection power of our risen Lord transforming us into the likeness of Christ day-by-day, right up until we see Him face-to-face.

We will see God at work around us and through us. The things of God that are spiritually discerned will be seen at last and we will never be the same. Old things will pass away and all things will be made new as we focus the eyes of our heart on the wonderful truths of the kingdom of God and His righteousness.

We will see the love of God abound in the love of others and we will see the real peace and joy of the Lord. We will see the reality of Christ living in us and living through us, as we live lives of celebrations and praise, when we see what great things God has done and is going to do through the eyes of our heart.

> ***""The eye is the lamp of the body. If your eyes are good, your whole body will be full of light. But if your eyes are bad, your whole body will be full of darkness. If then the light within you is darkness, how great is that darkness!" Matthew 6:22, 23 NIV***

**Father, open the eyes of my heart that I might see Jesus. Amen**

**October 30** **Read Revelation 21, Isaiah 60**

# *Bright Lights of the City*

**"However, as it is written: "No eye has seen, no ear has heard, no mind has conceived what God has prepared for those who love him." 1 Corinthians 2:9 NIV**

People seem drawn by the bright lights of the big city. Novel after novel and movie after movie have portrayed the lives of those who have been attracted to the bight lights of the city and gone to seek their fame and fortune.

> ***Your sun will never set again, and your moon will wane no more; the Lord will be your everlasting light, and your days of sorrow will end."***
> ***Isaiah 60:20 NIV***

For every success, there are probably dozens of failures or shattered dreams, unfulfilled expectations and devastating disappointments as thousands have found that all that glitters is not gold and that life in the big city is not all that they had hoped for.

The Bible tells about one who went to the big city and blew his inheritance on wild living. The home he had left never looked so good as when he was reduced to eating slop with the hogs just to survive.

There is a little bit of the prodigal son in all of us. We often get caught up in self-seeking the bright lights of popularity, pleasure and treasure, as portrayed by the world only to find that they are not that great after all.

There are the real bright lights of the city awaiting all who call upon the name of Jesus. Nothing could shine brighter than the New Jerusalem of heaven, where the streets shine as only gold can, where all those who have won souls for Christ will shine like stars, and where Jesus, the lamp and the glory of the Lord, shines brighter than the sun.

> ***"The city does not need the sun or the moon to shine on it, for the glory of God gives it light, and the Lamb is its lamp."***
> ***Revelation 21:23 NIV***

Our minds cannot comprehend the future glory that awaits us. Knowing that every tear will be wiped away, that there will be no more sickness, no more troubles, and no more sin are just appetizers to the foretaste of glory awaiting all those who die in the Lord.

**Father, help me to walk in the light of your grace as I journey to the bright light of Your city called heaven. Amen**

1 Corinthians 6:9-20, Proverbs 14:12:35 **October 31**

# *Trick or Treat*

**"Then the LORD God asked the woman, "How could you do such a thing?" "The serpent tricked me," she replied. "That's why I ate it." Genesis 3:13**

Satan is the biggest con man who ever lived. When he comes knocking we'd best just lock the door. He's not coming for treats - he is coming to give us the treatment.

> ***"There is a way that seems right to a man, but its end is the way of death." Proverbs 14:12***

This master of the bait and switch promises pleasure and delivers scrambled brains, guilt, disease and death.

If we just leave the door slightly ajar, he comes in through the smallest of openings and, once in, can trick us into trading our birth right of the abundant new life we received when we received Jesus Christ for the wages of sin.

How many people do you know who have ridiculed the weaknesses of others who have become addicted slaves to alcohol, tobacco, pornography, adultery, or drugs, only to become addicted them selves.

Satan promised Eve the treat of knowing as much as God and tricked her into disobeying God and partaking of the forbidden fruit. Humanity has been in a mess ever since.

"God didn't really mean that", "everyone's doing it", "God wants me to be happy"," I can enjoy this without becoming addicted:" are not thoughts that come from God, but tricks that Satan uses to plant thoughts into our hearts that can speed our descent into the downward spiral of moral decay and disaster.

> ***"Do you not know that the unrighteous will not inherit the kingdom of God? Do not be deceived." 1 Corinthians 6:9***

The good news is that we have not been left defenseless by our Savior. He has freed us from bondage to sin.

He has also given us the armor to withstand the tricks of the evil one if we will only put it on.

**Father, give me the wisdom and spiritual discernment to recognize and not fall for the tricks of the great deceiver. Amen**

**November 1** **Read Galatians 6:1-10, Psalm 37**

# *Cutting Off Your Nose*

**"He who sows iniquity will reap sorrow, and the rod of his anger will fail." Proverbs 22:8 NLT**

There is a lot of profound truth passed down from generation to generation through old sayings like, "Don't cut off your nose to spite your face," which means that anger, vengeance, or unforgiveness causes you a lot more harm than it does the one you are angry with, trying to get even with, or refusing to forgive.

> ***"For evildoers shall be cut off; But those who wait on the LORD, They shall inherit the earth."***
> ***Psalm 37:9***

Time after time, satan has used taking offense at something someone said or did at church to fuel anger and a falling away from God by breaking off from His body and losing all of the grace that God wants to give us through the hearing of His Word and fellowship of other members of the body.

How many people do you know who have become angry at God and turned their backs on Him and the incredible blessings that only come from living in a close and personal relationship with Jesus Christ?

God reminds us time and time again that vengeance belongs to Him, and that He will take care of repaying evil and doesn't need our help. There are a lot of people in jail who took meting out justice and vengeance in their own flesh, and suffering severe consequences.

No one wants to bring misery and destruction upon themselves, and yet some will let roots of bitterness actually destroy them and even make them physically ill. When we think of all the forgiveness we need and receive from God and how He makes it abundantly clear that we cannot be forgiven unless we forgive others, it is inconceivable that we persist in this dead end pursuit with deadly consequences.

> ***"Don't be misled. Remember that you can't ignore God and get away with it. You will always reap what you sow!"***
> ***Galatians 6:7 NLT***

We often are our worst enemies. When we waste our time and energy cutting off our nose to spite our face, satan doesn't have to waste his time on us. He already owns us.

**Father, by the power of Your Spirit, help me bear the fruit of Your Spirit in every area of my life. Amen**

# *Not What but Who*

**"Jesus answered her, "If you knew the gift of God and who it is that asks you for a drink, you would have asked him and he would have given you living water." John 4:10 NIV**

There are many who believe that success in life depends not so much on what you know but on who you know. It seems that those who know the right people can get things done where others fail. Lobbyists and public relations firms are paid big bucks not for what they know but for who they know.

***"Continue your love to those who know you, your righteousness to the upright in heart." Psalm 36:10 NIV***

This is also a fundamental truth for followers of Jesus Christ. Our very salvation really depends not on what we know, but on knowing Jesus as our living Savior and Lord of our life.

We can have all of the biblical knowledge in the world, but unless it Is received in our hearts by faith through the power of the Holy Spirit, it is not going to get us anywhere.

The Scribes and Pharisees spent a lifetime studying and undergoing religious training, but they did now know Jesus. James reminds us that even demons know God and shudder.

Unless we know Jesus as our risen Lord who lives and gives us the Holy Spirit to daily walk with us and talk with us through His Word, prayer, and other people, we do not really know Jesus.

We can know that Jesus was a good man who lived a good life, healed people, was crucified died and buried, but not know Jesus.

When we really know Jesus, we will know that He really is the way, the truth, and the life, and longs for us to get to know Him not only as our Savior, but as our friend and brother who fills us with His joy, who answers our prayers, and who has restored our relationship with God.

***"If you really knew me, you would know my Father as well. From now on, you do know him and have seen him." John 14:7 NIV***

When we really know Jesus, we will learn what obedience and fruitful faith is all about as we get to know Him and become more like Him day-by-day, year-by-year, until we see Him face-to-face.

**Father, help me to know you better. Amen**

# *Chips off the Old Block*

**"Jesus turned and said to Peter, "Get behind me, Satan! You are a stumbling block to me; you do not have in mind the things of God, but the things of men." Matthew 16:22-24 NIV**

We sometimes still hear this old expression used to note similarities in looks or personalities of children in relation to their parents. It can also be used to sum up who we are in Adam. We are chips off the old block of sin passed on to every child born of woman since the fall of Adam and Eve in the Garden of Eden.

> ***"The stone the builders rejected has become the capstone; the Lord has done this, and it is marvelous in our eyes." Psalm 118:22 NIV***

If we have come to saving faith and persist in focusing on the cares and enticements of this world, we are going to be stumbling blocks to others. Our constant prayer should be that we would not give any one cause to stumble and fall away or stay away from a right relationship with God.

Instead of stumbling blocks, we should be ever mindful of who we are to be in Christ. We are to be building blocks. When we build our lives on faith, love and obedience, we are going to grow into the fullness of Christ.

We are put on this earth to glorify God and to build up His kingdom. When we begin to live like we believe this, great things will happen in our lives and the lives of those God chooses to bless through us.

There is the biggest block party ever thrown going on thousand of times daily in heaven as the angels rejoice over each lost sinner being saved.

What joy there is when others will see Jesus in us as we become imitators of Him! We are all called to be chips off the block of faith that generates a new birth and new identity in Christ for others, just as it has done for us.

> ***"You also, like living stones, are being built into a spiritual house to be a holy priesthood, offering spiritual sacrifices acceptable to God through Jesus Christ" 1 Peter 2:5 NIV***

**Father, help me to be a building block. Amen**

**Read James 4:1-10, Psalm 51** **November 4**

## *Car Wash Blues*

**"Blessed are those who wash their robes, that they may have the right to the tree of life and may go through the gates into the city." Revelation 22:14**

An old Jim Croce 70's song was the lament of a young drop-out who applied for an executive position and was told they had all those they could use, and found himself with the steadily depressing "working in a car wash blues.

> ***"Wash away all my iniquity and cleanse me from my sin. Psalm 51:1-3***

If you think about it, car washes are a great illustration of the life of the believer.

Even though most new cars are delivered spotlessly clean and with some sort of protective finish, they don't stay that way very long.

We see all of the muddy, bug-infested cars pull into the car wash and then pull out clean and shiny, looking like new. They have vacuums and carpet shampoos for the inside, engine degreasers, etc.

When we receive Jesus Christ as our Savior, we are delivered from sin and death and given a spotlessly clean white robe of righteousness, and we become alive with a new birth and new identity in Christ.

As travelers through life in a sin-sick world, we are going to run into and through a lot of road dirt of flesh, the world, and the devil. No matter how hard we try, some of it is going to stick to us. We need to go to God's car wash to get cleansed of the road dirt and road kill of life through godly sorrow, confession, and true repentance.

God not only operates the best car wash imaginable, He even provides armor-all for our souls. He gives us the Holy Spirit to guide us into all truth, convict us of our sins, and to be our sword of the Spirit and give us the full armor of God.

Have you been to the car wash of grace lately? Just as many believe that a clean car seems to run better, millions know that we run the race of life better with a clean temple.

> ***"Come near to God and he will come near to you. Wash your hands, you sinners, and purify your hearts, you double minded." James 4:8 NIV***

**Father, thank you for giving me a way to stay clean. Amen**

# *Be an Enabler!*

**"Who, by the power that enables Him to bring everything under his control, will transform our lowly bodies so that they will be like his glorious body?" Philippians 3:20-22 NIV**

"Enabler" is a term widely used in substance abuse and mental health studies to refer to those who enable emotionally troubled or addicted people to continue their destructive life styles. Parents who allow their children to grow up disrespectful and disobedient to them are enabling them to grow up as problem adults. Any one that enables an able-bodied person to get through life without working is enabling someone to go against the clear teaching of Scripture.

> ***"It is God who arms me with strength and makes my way perfect. He makes my feet like the feet of a deer; He enables me to stand on the heights." Psalm 18:32-33 NIV***

We don't hear as much about good enablers who might allow someone to go to college, to minister in foreign mission fields, or to pursue a worthwhile but economically worthless calling.

As believers in Jesus Christ, we are called to be imitators of Christ, who is the greatest enabler of all time.

By the power of the Holy Spirit, we are enabled to die to sin and become alive in Christ. We are enabled to love God and love others, even the unlovable. We are enabled to live a new life in Christ free from condemnation and bondage to sin, and to live lives fully pleasing to God. We are enabled to endure the troubles of life, and to experience the sufficiency of God's grace and mercy. We are enabled to experience the surpassing peace and incredible joy of Jesus.

We are commanded to be enablers as we have been enabled. We need to enable our children and others to grow into a right relationship with God through faith in Jesus Christ by not only teaching, but by also modeling our love for God and for others in our lives.

> ***"[4]to rescue us from the hand of our enemies, and to enable us to serve him without fear in holiness and righteousness before him all our days. Luke 1:74, 75 NIV***

**Father, help me to be a good enabler. Amen**

Read Luke 19:1-9, Psalm 1 November 6

## On Blueberry Hill

**"With that kind of hope to excite us, nothing holds us back." 2 Corinthians 3:12 MSG**

This is an ever-popular song, but terrible theology. We have trouble enough seeking our thrills in all the wrong activities and wrong places.

> ***"Instead you thrill to God's word; you chew on Scripture day and night." Psalm 1:2 MSG***

The thrills of life, where we experience an exciting emotion and sometimes even a tingly or numbing feeling, are special moments in the lives of everyone. Thrills can be actual like being an active recipient or vicarious as in thriller movies or sporting contests.

We talk about the thrill of romance, the thrill of winning, the thrilling roller coaster ride, the thrilling first date, thrill of receiving marriage proposals or having them accepted, etc. For better or worse, we are all blessed with a lot of thrills in life.

The problem comes when we become thrill seekers for all the wrong things and in all the wrong places. We can easily slip into idolatry as we pursue sinful and harmful thrills.

For the true believer, there will come a time when we experience the thrill of being in love with Jesus. We will begin each day rejoicing in the Lord and the great things He has done and is going to do for us and through us. We will experience the thrills of helping others and doing great things for God.

We will daily know the thrill of God's presence and the wonders of His love as He fills us with both. We will look back on the thrill of being called by God into saving faith and being used for His purposes We will look forward to the thrill of seeing Him face-to-face in heaven and living with Him in that heavenly mansion He has prepared for those who believe.

> ***"Zacchaeus quickly climbed down and took Jesus to his house in great excitement and joy." Luke 19:6 NLT***

When we find our thrill on Calvary's hill, we will begin an exciting adventure of a brand new life with a brand new identity, and this should be the biggest thrill of all in the life of every believer.

**Father, thank you for allowing me to grow into spiritual maturity where I will know the true thrills of my life in You. Amen**

# *How Much is Enough?*

**"You are under a curse-the whole nation of you-because you are robbing me." Malachi 3:9 NIV**

Greed can be a bottomless pit of emptiness. Those obsessed by it are never satisfied. It is usually used in terms of wealth, but can also be applied to power, applause, and pleasures. When asked how much is enough, the answer is usually,"just a little bit more."

> ***"How can I repay the Lord for all his goodness to me? Psalm 116:12 NIV***

There is another very important aspect of this question that is all too often misunderstood even by believers. When we ask "how much is enough" to give to God, we often think in terms of how little we can get by with instead of how much more we can give.

We need to understand that we are just tenant farmers and sharecroppers in the kingdom of God. God owns everything and just allows us the privilege of living on His land and producing fruits of righteousness that will glorify Him and build up His domain. All we have to do is read the daily paper and we will see that God can foreclose on us at any time.

In light of God's love for us, it might be well to ask how much of our time, talents are treasures are enough for God. We know from Scripture that we should give proportionately. We know that when we give under compulsion or grudgingly, God is not pleased. We know that God has been generous with us so that we can be generous on all occasions. Only the security of knowing who we are and where we are going because of Jesus Christ can give that godly contentment and peace that can take away our insatiable desire for more of the things of this world.

Only when we survey the passion of the Cross can we understand that we can never give enough to thank God for the great things He has done for us; but we can be looking for opportunities for giving Him more of everything instead of looking for excuses for giving Him less.

> ***"Remember this: Whoever sows sparingly will also reap sparingly, and whoever sows generously will also reap generously." 2 Corinthians 9:6 NIV***

**Father, give me the passion to give You more instead of less of all that I am and have. Amen**

**Read 2 Peter 1:1-10. Isaiah 25** **November 8**

# *Pest Control*

**"...to make her holy, cleansing her by the washing with water through the word." Ephesians 5:26 NIV**

In my part of the country, pest control service is a necessity. All houses being sold are required to be inspected for termite damage. The friendly climate of Florida for people also makes it a friendly climate for all kinds of roaches, spiders, ants, and other insects.

> ***"On this mountain he will destroy the shroud that enfolds all peoples, the sheet that covers all nations; he will swallow up death forever."***
> ***Isaiah 25:7. 8 NIV***

Life is often a reflection of nature. When we view sins as pests living in the friendly climate of the world, we can easily see the need for sin control.

Jesus promised and has sent the Holy Spirit to deal with our sin infestations. A one-time treatment triggered by faith wipes out the power of sin to kill us. Our Sin-Exterminator takes up residence within us to keep sin out and to exterminate any that slips in on a daily basis.

We need to hate sin more than the pests that will take up residence in our homes if we let them. When we can squash the off button on our TV remote control as eagerly and automatically as a bug that dares invade our home, and swat temptations as eagerly as we swat the occasional fly that dares bug us, we will be on our way to growing into the fullness of Christ.

Just as we are instructed to keep our houses clean and not leave anything around for the pests to feed on, we are instructed to keep our new temples of the Holy Spirit clean through daily cleansing by confession and repentance.

> ***'His divine power has given us everything we need for life and godliness through our knowledge of him who called us by his own glory and goodness."***
> ***2 Peter 1:1-10 NIV***

Our victory over sin was won for us by the blood of Jesus on the cross of Calvary. Satan has been defeated and mortally wounded. His attacks can no longer kill the believer and can have absolutely no dominion over us when we put on the full armor of God on a daily basis.

**Father, help me to remember to call upon You and Your resurrection power that no infestation of sin lives within me. Amen**

**November 9** **Read Jeremiah 31:33-36, Psalm 4**

# *The Perfect Sleeper*

**"Come to me, all you who are weary and burdened, and I will give you rest." Matthew 11:28 NIV**

The mattress wars are raging and about every storefront in any town is now selling them. Mattresses too pretty to cover up are going for several thousand dollars a set and selling like popcorn.

> ***I will lie down and sleep in peace, for you alone, O Lord, make me dwell in safety.***
> ***Psalm 4:8 NIV***

The new space age material is quite a sensation. The old standbys like Beauty Rest, Sealy "Posturepedic," and Serta "Perfect Sleeper" promise to have you sleeping like a kitten with no backaches.

The best mattress ever made cannot guarantee a good night's sleep. The agonies of broken hearts, guilty consciences, and pillow cases of worry can leave us tossing and turning all night long, no matter what kind of mattress we have.

Life can be a bed of roses, but even these are accompanied by thorns that can rob us of our joy and lead to long nights of agonizing sleeplessness.

There is no better aid to sleep than a conscience cleaned of guilt by the blood of Jesus Christ and a life filled with the peace that surpasses all our understanding.

We have the God of all comfort who will mend our broken hearts, cleanse our consciences of all guilt, and give us His peace.

He invites us all to cast our burdens on Him and enter into that perfect rest that we find only in the sanctuary of His grace which He has promised to supply, sufficient for all our needs every day of our lives.

> ***"I have given rest to the weary and joy to the sorrowing."***
> ***Jeremiah 31:25 NLT***

May our relationship grow so close and personal that our "pillow talk" of prayer will lead us into perfect sleep and renewed grace and mercy every morning thanks to the faithfulness of God.

**Father, instead of counting sheep, teach me to count my blessings until I receive the blessing of perfect sleep. Amen**

**Read Acts 17:16-31, Psalm 97** **November 10**

## *Spectator Sports*

**"Do you see what we've got? An unshakable kingdom! And do you see how thankful we must be? Not only thankful, but brimming with worship, deeply reverent before God. For God is not an indifferent bystander." Hebrews 12:28 MSG**

Spectator sports attendance is staggering. On the professional label, over 67 million attend major league baseball games, 20 million at basketball, and 18 million for pro football and 7 million for NASCAR races each year.

> ***"Rejoice in the Lord, you who are righteous, and praise his holy name."***
> ***Psalm 97:12 NIV***

Annual attendance at United States Churches is estimated to be a little over 600 million people. When the radio and TV audience is added, it probably still does not match total sporting event attendance.

The real question, which only God knows, is how many of us view church attendance as a spectator sport? How many of us go to be inspired and entertained by gifted performances by the Choir or Praise Team, and by an eloquent and entertaining preacher?

We need to stay mindful that this is not what going to church is about. We need to stay mindful that we go to worship, not to be spectators. When we participate with our mind's attention and our hearts affection, we are going to celebrate our joy in the Lord and what He has done and is doing in our lives and the lives of those around us.

We are going to receive the grace of God through praising Him, listening for Him to speak His Word through our pastor, by sharing His love with others, by remembering His broken body and shed blood, and proclaiming His coming again through the Lord's Supper.

Our God is a personal God. He invites us to come into His presence at corporate worship personally and with great joy and eager anticipation. He will be pleased and we will be strengthened and encouraged.

> ***"While Paul was waiting for them in Athens, he was greatly distressed to see that the city was full of idols."***
> ***Acts 17:16 NIV***

**Father, Help me to go to church "brimming" with worship. Amen**

**November 11** **Read Acts 6:1-7, Psalm 25**

# *Satan's Playground*

**"I appeal to you, brothers, in the name of our Lord Jesus Christ, that all of you agree with one another so that there may be no divisions among you and that you may be perfectly united in mind and thought." 1 Corinthians 1:9-11 NIV**

There is a danger lurking wherever two or more are gathered to do the Lord's business. Too many times self-centered agendas of the flesh take precedence over Christ-centered agendas of the Spirit.

> ***"Show me your ways, O Lord teach me your paths; guide me in your truth and teach me."***
> ***Psalm 25:3,4b NIV***

The Lord gets credit for a lot of leadings that are really the pet project or agenda of some individual. Pride produces the desire to control and impose self will in the name of God's will too often. This turns the church into satan's playground.

We have heard of churches arguing over the choice of carpet or choir robes, styles of worship, and support of pastors or choir leaders. Terrible wars have been started within congregations and even denominations that must surely bring tears to Jesus' eyes.

It is a blessing to have successful businessmen and professionals give their time, talents and resources to the Lord. They can use their experiences and successes to glorify God and build up His body, but we all need to always remember that the Church is not a business, but the Bride of Christ charged to proclaim the Good News and Great Commandment.

. There is a fine line between leading from the flesh and from the Spirit, and it is well to always remember the first requirement for leaders is that they be filled with the Holy Spirit, and that all decisions should be based on Scriptural wisdom and discernment from on high.

> ***"Brothers, choose seven men from among you who are known to be full of the Spirit and wisdom. We will turn this responsibility over to them."***
> ***Acts 6:3***

**Father, help me to check my ego at the cross when I set out to conduct your business. Amen**

**Read 1 Corinthians 4:1-5, Psalm 119:1-13** **November 12**

# *The Tip of the Ice Berg*

**"He tunnels through the rock; his eyes see all its treasures. He searches the sources of the rivers and brings hidden things to light." Job 28:11 NIV**

We can often only see a few outward manifestations of some real problems within. As with ice bergs, there is usually a whole lot more below that we will never see.

> ***"I have hidden your word in my heart that I might not sin against you."***
> ***Psalm 119:11 NIV***

None of us can know what's really in another's heart. Sometimes we don't even know what's in our own heart. *"The human heart is most deceitful and desperately wicked. Who really knows how bad it is?" (Jeremiah 17:9)*

Who we are when nobody's looking is a much better barometer of who we really are. We can all put on a happy face (or be hypocrites which is derived from the Greek word for actors.) with true feelings and sinful thoughts and deeds submerged below the water line hidden from sight.

Does our Christianity only come out in church on Sundays while it is overcome by our flesh the rest of the week?

It is comforting to know how God sees us. He knows all and sees all both above and below the water line, and still loves us never because of our sins, but because of Jesus.

God loves us better than we love ourselves. He forgives us for things we have a hard time forgiving ourselves. He didn't even let His love for His Son keep him from allowing Him to die so that we wouldn't have to.

God's love is deeper than the ocean. We need to anchor deep in His Word so that our lives that can reflect the true love and faith that reaches deep below our water line.

> ***"He will bring to light what is hidden in darkness and will expose the motives of men's hearts. At that time each will receive his praise from God."***
> ***1 Corinthians 4:5b NIV***

**Father, cleanse my heart of any sin lurking below. Amen**

November 13 Read Romans 1:16-32, Psalm 79

# Court of Last Resort

**"He declared us not guilty because of his great kindness. And now we know that we will inherit eternal life." Titus 3:7**

The wheels of justice sometimes turn slow. There are legal remedies for every occasion, right up to the Supreme Court of the United States.

> ***"Oh, do not hold us guilty for our former sins! Let your tenderhearted mercies quickly meet our needs, for we are brought low to the dust."***
> ***Psalm 79:9 NLT***

In addition to courts of last resort, our justice system also provides for pardons by governors and the president. Our great country and system of government has sometimes seemingly gone overboard in providing ample opportunity for wrongdoers to have their convictions set aside or be pardoned.

Most of our criminal and civil justice systems are based on the Judeo-Christian laws and commandments of the Old Testament.

We all, for our own sakes, and for the sake of those we love, need to be aware that Jesus Christ is our "court of last resort." Today's Scripture plainly states that all are "without excuse" for not knowing God and receiving a pardon for our sins by receiving Jesus Christ as our Lord and Savior.

> ***"From the time the world was created, people have seen the earth and sky and all that God made. They can clearly see his invisible qualities--his eternal power and divine nature. So they have no excuse whatsoever for not knowing God.***
> ***Romans 1:30 NLT***

God's justice system decrees that sins are punishable by death, and that the sins of the guilty will not go unpunished. It is an amazing testimony to the love, grace, and mercy of God that He would send His own Son to suffer the punishment and death our sins deserved so that we would not have to.

Before we go to the court of last resort to receive the judgment of God, we should all make sure that we are going with a full pardon with our sin debt marked "paid in full" by the blood of Jesus.

**Father, thank You for the pardon I have received at the cross. Amen**

Read 2 Timothy 1:5-14, Psalm 119:49-56 November 14

## *Dead Skunk in the Middle of the Road*

**"Then Jesus said to the disciples, "If any of you wants to be my follower, you must put aside your selfish ambition, shoulder your cross, and follow me." Matthew 16:24 NLT**

When we approach a dead skunk on the highway, we are going to know it. The smell is pungent and penetrating. There is something worse than a dead skunk on our road of life. This one can do a lot of damage and even be deadly. It's also known as our comfort zone.

> ***"I meditate on your age-old laws; O Lord, they comfort me." Psalm 119:52 NLT***

The rich young ruler missed out on eternal life because it squeezed his comfort zone.

We hold onto control in many areas of our life because surrendering them to God squeezes our comfort zone.

When we travel through the valleys of fear, doubt, rejection, envy or pride, the border bullies seem to take control and we retreat into our comfort zone, often to where we have no area of comfort left.

We miss opportunities for witnessing, strengthening, and growing in our relationship with the Lord and with others because we don't expand our comfort zone by trusting God and walking by faith one step at a time. We expand our comfort zone as we experience the love, peace, and security of God and His promises.

As we see God's faithfulness in supplying our needs, answering our prayers, and giving us the encouragement of other believers, we become strengthened to expand our comfort zone for serving Him more and more and better and better.

> ***"For God has not given us a spirit of fear and timidity, but of power, love, and self-discipline." 1 Timothy 1:7 NLT***

When we respond to God's truth with a Christ-centered perspective instead of our comfort-centered flesh, we will find greater joy in the journey of life.

**Father, help me to overcome the border bullies that are squeezing my comfort zone and keeping me from being all that I can be and doing all that I want to do for You. Amen**

**November 15** **Read 1 Peter 2, Psalm 34**

# *I Can See Clearly Now*

**"He replied, "Whether he is a sinner or not, I don't know. One thing I do know. I was blind but now I see!" John 9:25 NIV**

As one of the millions who have been blessed by the modern day miracle of cataract surgery, "I can see clearly now" takes on a very real and exciting meaning in the physical sense. "I can see clearly now" takes on an even more exciting meaning in the life of the believer as we are called out of darkness into the wonderful light of God's love, grace, and mercy.

> ***"Those who look to him are radiant; their faces are never covered with shame." Psalm 34:5 NIV***

As we grow up in our salvation by feeding on God's Word, we see God at work in every area of our lives as God, through the Holy Spirit, begins the lifelong process of making us more like Christ.

We will see more clearly that God's way is always the best way and that God has established boundaries and guides for living, not to kill our joy and pleasure, but to enhance it.

We will see more and more of God's promises coming true as we experience answered prayers, the power of His all sustaining grace and presence in time of trouble, and see what it means to have friendship with God through our personal and intimate relationship with His Son.

We will find all surpassing peace that will surpass our sorrows, our pains, and our failures. We will find the supernatural strength to carry us when ours runs out.

The life of the believer should be one of seeing God's purposes and plans, His unconditional love, and our future more clearly day-by-day, year-by-year, until we see Him face-to-face.

> ***"This is so you can show others the goodness of God, for he called you out of the darkness into his wonderful light." 1 Peter 2:9b NIV***

**Father, help me to see more clearly through Christ centered lenses instead of myopic, self centered lenses, and rejoice and be glad in what I see. Amen**

Read Hebrews 10:11-35, Psalm 51 November 16

## *If We Catch, He'll Clean!*

**"Come, follow me," Jesus said, "and I will make you fishers of men." Mark 1:17**

This favorite bulletin board message delivers a powerful truth in a short sentence we all need to understand.

> ***"Wash away all my iniquity and cleanse me from my sin."***
> ***Psalm 51:1-3 NIV***

We are called to be fishers of men, not cleaners. Behavior modification is something the Holy Spirit does. When we try to change people's behavior through our flesh, it is not going to work.

When God uses us to lead someone to receive Jesus Christ, He also removes the veil that separates them from His presence, and the Holy Spirit indwells and begins the life-changing work of Holy Transformation.

God accepts all who call upon His name just as they are, but He loves us all too much to let us stay that way. Day-by-day, the Holy Spirit is living and working within us to conform us into the image of Christ.

The law makes us live and perform under compulsion. God's grace inspires us to live under the conviction that we have been redeemed by the blood of the Lamb.

It is the supernatural power of the Holy Spirit that makes us realize that we don't have to do anything, but makes us want to do everything that will show our love to God for what He has done for us.

God not only cleanses us through the washing and regeneration of baptism, but He cleanses us daily when we take the road dirt of our sin to His throne of grace through daily confession and repentance.

God may well use us to mentor and encourage the fish He has used us to catch, and we should pray continually for them; but we can find great comfort and joy in knowing that He will do the cleaning.

> ***"let us draw near to God with a sincere heart in full assurance of faith, having our hearts sprinkled to cleanse us from a guilty conscience and having our bodies washed with pure water."***
> ***Hebrews 10:22 NIV***

**Father, help me to be a fisher of men and bait my hook by being a "sermon in shoes" that will draw the unsaved. Amen**

November 17 Read Luke 17:20-37, Psalm 22:22-31

# *He is no fool...*

**"Yes, a person is a fool to store up earthly wealth but not have a rich relationship with God." Luke 12:21 NLT**

Through all the ages and continuing up to this very day, heroes of the faith are being born and dying all over the world. We thank God for Billy Graham, Mother Teresa, and millions of others who spent their lives for the cause of Christ.

> ***"All the rich of the earth will feast and worship; all who go down to the dust will kneel before him those who cannot keep themselves alive."***
> ***Psalm 22:29 NLT***

Jim Elliott, one of the missionaries savagely killed by the Indians in the Amazon Basin years ago, wrote before his death: "He is no fool who gives what he cannot keep to gain what he cannot lose."

This is a profound truth worth pondering. For the unbeliever, it brings out the danger of regarding the Gospel as foolishness. None of us can keep anything that we accumulate, worship, or live for in this world, except God. There are no storage vaults, investment portfolios, or pleasure palaces in hell.

To realize that we have gained and cannot lose this right standing (if we really received it) gives us not only cause to rejoice but the desire to respond by living lives worthy of our calling as sons and daughters of the living God.

In the exchanged life, what we are asked to give up pales by comparison to what we are given. We exchange guilt for grace and self-centered seeking for Christ-centered security within and without. We receive a future and a hope for today, tomorrow, and forever.

When we consider the promises of God's presence, protection, power, and favor that we receive, it should become a no-brainer to give up the selfishness, pride, anger, envy, lust, and other sins we are asked to surrender.

> ***"Whoever tries to keep his life will lose it and whoever loses his life will preserve it."***
> ***Luke 17:33 NLT***

**Father, help me to survey the wondrous cross and give You honor, praise and glory for the exchanged life You have given me. Amen**

**Read 1 Corinthians 4:1-5, Psalm 62** **November 18**

# *Are You Well Spent?*

**"Let us not become weary in doing good, for at the proper time we will reap a harvest if we do not give up." Galatians 6:9 NIV**

Almost everyone is value conscious and strives to see that their money, time and talents are well spent. To some, anything spent in pursuit of pleasure and gratification of any kind is well spent. Many find the time spent in developing their talents is too demanding and they find other things that they would rather be doing, much to their sorrow later.

> ***"...and that you, O Lord, are loving. Surely you will reward each person according to what he has done."***
> ***Psalm 62:12 NIV***

Almost everyone will agree that time spent with family is time well spent. When we invest in our children's future by spending time with them when they are young, we will most likely be rewarded with their love and good character when they are older.

Time spent studying is time well spent at exam time, or, as in the case of studying the Word of God, when testing comes.

Salvation is a free gift of God's grace through faith in Jesus Christ. Our heavenly home is assured. But there is coming a day when we are going to be called to give an account of how we have spent our lives.

The idea that we will be rewarded beyond salvation for well spent lives is an idea full of conjecture; but Scripture does mention rewards and blessings that we will receive at the resurrection of the just.

> ***When the Lord comes, he will bring our deepest secrets to light and will reveal our private motives. And then God will give to everyone whatever praise is due.***
> ***1 Corinthians 4:5b NLT***

When it's furnace stoking time in glory we are all going to find out how well spent our lives have been. When all of the trivial pursuits and chasing after the wind endeavors have burned away, what's left is going to define whether we have lived well spent lives. May we all seek to live lives well spent and fully pleasing to God.

**Father, keep me ever mindful that my life is not my own, that You created me for Your good purposes and for Your glory. Amen**

November 19 Read 1 Peter 3:14-16, Psalm 34

# A Career in Modeling

**"Whoever acknowledges me before men, I will also acknowledge him before my Father in heaven." Matthew 10:32 NIV**

The world of high fashion offers good paying high-profile modeling jobs for men, women, and children. The use of attractive models has long been used to attract buyers to products.

> *"Let the Lord's people show him reverence, for those who honor him will have all they need."*
> *Psalm 34:9 NLT*

We have all been called to careers in modeling the love of God. There is no more effective evangelism tool than a life modeling the change through a personal relationship with Jesus Christ.

One of the greatest compliments a believer can receive is to be asked why they are always so kind, cheerful, compassionate, happy, etc. What a great opportunity to give God the glory through our testimony of the life changing power of God.

Jesus Christ came to model authentic Christianity by living without sinning in a sin sick world, by loving others, especially the unlovable others, and by doing the Will of the Father Who sent Him. He modeled ultimate forgiveness and perfect righteousness.

We are commanded to be imitators of Christ. We will never model the sinless perfection and perfect righteousness of Christ in the flesh. Knowing by faith that we have these qualities in the eyes of God, because of our faith in Jesus Christ, should inspire us to model the fruit of the Spirit we do have.

> *"Instead, you must worship Christ as Lord of your life. And if you are asked about your Christian hope, always be ready to explain it."*
> *1 Peter 3:15 NLT*

When we are modeling the fruit of love, joy, peace, patience, kindness, goodness, faithfulness, and self control in our everyday lives, we are being true to our calling in Christ.

**Father, help me to reflect the love, peace, and joy I have in you to others, that they might be save. Amen**

Read Luke 19:11-26, Psalm 94 November 20

# *Interior Decorating 101*

**"No eye has seen, no ear has heard, and no mind has imagined what God has prepared for those who love him."**
**1 Corinthians 2:9b NIV**

When we receive Jesus Christ as Savior, we receive the keys to the kingdom of eternal life in heaven in a brand new home. Actually, we are promised a mansion. This is our gift by the grace of God, through faith. We do nothing to earn it.

> ***"Judgment will come again for the righteous, and those who are upright will have a reward."***
> ***Psalm 94:15 NIV***

As wonderful as heaven will be, it is not the end of anything except sin. It is the beginning of everything in a new life for all eternity.

Since the sins of pride, envy and jealousy will be banished, there will be no concept of rank or anyone being any better than any one else.

There is much Scripture referring to rewards in heaven, treasures in heaven, and even ruler-ship in heaven. The faithful stewards who managed the lives they had been given were promised the responsibility managing cities in heaven.

We receive a great deal of love and satisfaction in responding to God's love on this earth by loving God and others and glorifying Him. What joy there will be when Jesus says, "well done, good and faithful servant," and proceeds to reward us with the privilege and joy of serving and glorifying Him in His heavenly kingdom!

Thank God we are not going to have to move into our new mansions with the baggage of our sins. Thank God we are going to have the rewards of our good works decorating our mansions in heaven with even greater opportunities to show our love for Him by serving Him and enjoying Him forever.

> ***"The next servant also reported a good gain--five times the original amount. `Well done!' the king said. `You can be governor over five cities."***
> ***Luke 19:18 NIV***

**Father, help me to decorate my life with the good works you created me for here, that I might enjoy serving and glorifying You to the fullest in heaven. Amen**

November 21 Read Acts 10:34-36, Psalm 143

# *Words We Love to Hear*

**"Do not let any unwholesome talk come out of your mouths, but only what is helpful for building others up according to their needs, that it may benefit those who listen." Ephesians 4:9 NIV**

Of all the words we love to hear, words of love top the list. "I love you," "God loves you," "I forgive you," and "Jesus loves me" are terms of affirmation that we need on a daily basis.

> ***"Let the morning bring me word of your unfailing love, for I have put my trust in you. Show me the way I should go, for to you I lift up my soul." Psalm 143:8 NIV***

We can't tell our spouses that we love them often enough. Letting God tell of His love for us through His Word is music to our ears. It literally sets our hearts to dancing as we respond by praising God and telling Him how much we love Him.

We all love to hear words of good news and appreciation. "Thank you," "great job," "your application has been approved," and "you're invited" are music to our ears.

We don't always like to hear a lot of words spoken in love, but in time, we usually will recognize how helpful, important and necessary these have been as God uses His Word and the words of others to help us confront our sins and deal with them with confession and repentance.

We need always to make sure we are hearing truth, and not just what we want to hear. We need the gift of spiritual discernment as we filter what we hear through God's Word to make sure we are not hearing something that merely pleases our vanity and egos, without any validation from God's Word.

> ***"You know the message God sent to the people of Israel, telling the good news of peace through Jesus Christ, who is Lord of all." Acts 10:36 NIV***

I personally can think of no sweeter words that we should love to hear more than "well done, good and faithful servant," when we meet our Savior face to face and give an account of our stewardship of life.

**Father, by the power of the Holy Spirit, help us to lead lives fully pleasing to You and fruitful in every good work. Amen**

**Read Colossians 3:12-17, 1 Chronicles 16:7-36** **November 22**

# *The Way of Thanksgiving*

**"There, in the presence of the LORD your God, you and your families shall eat and shall rejoice in everything you have put your hand to, because the LORD your God has blessed you." Deuteronomy 12:7 NIV**

Long before Thanksgiving Day was proclaimed a national holiday in 1941, God had ordained a thank offering as a means of worship for His people.

> ***"Give thanks to the Lord, for he is good; His love endures forever."***
> ***1 Chronicles 16:34 NIV***

Among the many things for which people of the Old Testament were exhorted to give thanks, "His love endures forever" is one of the most oft mentioned and repeated reasons for thanksgiving.

Scripture also encourages thanking God for salvation, His goodness, His unfailing love, wonderful deeds, righteousness, and for being our strength and our shield.

The thanksgiving "way" is the daily "thanks living" of our lives in response to God's love in sending Jesus Christ to die that we might live, and to show us how to live life to the fullest in Him.

One day is not enough time to count all of the physical, material, relational and spiritual blessings of our past, present, and future lives.

Our Lord realized the importance of giving thanks. Before the feeding of the 5,000, at the last supper before partaking of both the bread and the wine, and for God answering His prayer for raising Lazarus as they took away the stone, Jesus gave thanks to the Father.

> ***"And whatever you do, whether in word or deed, do it all in the name of the Lord Jesus, giving thanks to God the Father through him."***
> ***Colossians 3:17 NIV***

Thanksgiving is a holiday for the heart. May Thanksgiving Day be just one of 365 opportunities for living the thanksgiving way as we grow into the fullness of Christ.

**Father, thank You! Amen**

November 23 Read Philippians 4:1-9, Psalm 28

## *God's Thanksgiving Love*

**"Be joyful always; pray continually; give thanks in all circumstances, for this is God's will for you in Christ Jesus." 1 John 1:12**

It is very easy to be filled with overflowing joy and thankfulness at Thanksgiving when we are surrounded by loved ones enjoying a bountiful feast and thinking about all the good things we have to enjoy.

> ***"The Lord is my strength and my shield; my heart trusts in him, and I am helped. My heart leaps for joy and I will give thanks to him in song."***
> ***Psalm 28:7 NIV***

This is a good thing and a wonderful feeling, especially when we realize that God is the source of every good thing and of all our blessings.

There are millions of people who find it very hard if not impossible to find any thing to be thankful for on Thanksgiving or any other day. The overwhelming grief over departed loved ones, health issues, divorce, relational strife, and financial problems make depression the main course of the holiday meal for many.

The absence of problems like these should give all great cause to rejoice and praise God that they have been spared such sorrows.

On the other hand, all who are hurting in any way can experience the thanksgiving love of God when they rejoice and give thanks to God in their distress.

> ***"Do not be anxious about anything, but in everything, by prayer and petition, with thanksgiving, present your requests to God. And the peace of God, which transcends all understanding, will guard your hearts and your minds in Christ Jesus."***
> ***Philippians 4:6-7***

When we see Paul and Silas rejoicing and praising God when they were imprisoned, we see why Paul can say with all certainty that God's peace will guard our minds and our hearts, and that His all sufficient grace will supply our every need.

**God, thank You for the special blessings you promise when we go through the hard times with thanksgiving and praise to You. Amen**

**Read Romans 10:5-13, Genesis 28:10-20** **November 24**

# *Ladder to Success*

**"Then you will have success if you are careful to observe the decrees and laws that the LORD gave Moses for Israel. Be strong and courageous. Do not be afraid or discouraged."**
**1 Chronicles 22:13 NIV**

When we think of success, we often apply the world's standards of achieving wealth, fame, or position in life.

*"What's more, I will be with you, and I will protect you wherever you go. I will someday bring you safely back to this land. I will be with you constantly until I have finished giving you everything I have promised."*
*Genesis 28:15 NIV*

Most often achieving success in this sense involves climbing the steps of education, experience, discipline, tenacity, and performance.

Success is also defined as "the favorable or prosperous termination of projects or endeavors."

God's exciting promise to Jacob is one that we need to bank on as we climb the ladder of life and reach a favorable and prosperous termination in heaven that will never end.

God not only calls us to salvation. He calls us to obedience, holiness, and service as we grow into the fullness of Christ through our relationship with Him.

Once we come under His umbrella of grace by receiving Jesus Christ as Savior, the Holy Spirit comes to convict, comfort, and empower us to climb every mountain, persevere through every hardship, and mirror the image of Christ in every aspect of our lives as we climb closer and closer to Him.

*"As the Scripture says, "Anyone who trusts in him will never be put to shame." For there is no difference between Jew and Gentile–the same Lord is Lord of all and richly blesses all who call on him,"*
*Romans 10:11-12 NIV*

Our real success will come in hearing, "well done thou good and faithful servant," when we stand before Him and give an account of the lives He has given us.

**Father, Help me to climb higher and higher on your ladder. Amen.**

## *Soaring with the Eagle*

**"You have seen what I did to the Egyptians, and how I bore you on eagles' wings and brought you to Myself." Exodus 19:4**

The dictionary defines turkey as a dud, loser, naïve, inept, or stupid person. It might be well that all of us remember on Thanksgiving Day and every day that turkeys are for eating, not for being.

> ***"He shall cover you with His feathers, and under His wings you shall take refuge."***
> ***Psalm 91:4***

It is interesting to note that most elections come in the same month as Thanksgiving. By this time we have had our fill of the human turkeys. From time to time, even the disciples seemed act more like turkeys than ones called to soar with The Eagle.

The Scribes and Pharisees were perhaps the biggest turkeys of all time. They loved to strut around in fancy plumage being pious and holy on the outside as they strutted like the turkeys they really were.

Before we get too filled with hypocritical glory, we best remember that we will not have to think very far back to when we have been a turkey in some area of our lives. We often probably are carrying some of our left over turkey of life as excess baggage that we will carry to our graves.

Sometimes we find it very difficult to soar with The Eagle when we find that we are flying with turkeys. We are to live in the world and be the salt and light of it, but we are never to let it overcome us.

Satan often uses the troubles of life that can also be called turkeys to try to ground us and keeping us from being all that we have been created and called to be in Christ.

When God calls us into a personal relationship with Him through faith in Jesus Christ, He calls us to soar with Him under the shelter of the wings of the Holy Spirit, who will keep us safe in the everlasting arms of God.

> ***"And they heard a loud voice from heaven saying to them, "Come up here." And they ascended to heaven in a cloud."***
> ***Revelation 11:12***

May every Thanksgiving Day remind us that we can eat all the turkey we want, but we don't have to be one.

**Father, teach me how to fly under the shelter of your wings. Amen**

**Read Matthew 16:13-15, Psalm 43** **November 26**

# *The No Spin Zone*

**"But there were also false prophets among the people, just as there will be false teachers among you. They will secretly introduce destructive heresies, even denying the sovereign Lord who bought them–bringing swift destruction on themselves." 2 Peter 2:1-3 NIV**

Spinning has become a multi-million-dollar business. We see and hear the political spin being put out daily as hired guns for a particular point of view scurry to get their perspective put on everything from politician's misconduct to special interest agendas on everything from minimum wage to health care.

> ***"Send forth your light and your truth, let them guide me; let them bring me to your holy mountain, to the place where you dwell."***
> ***Psalm 43:3 NIV***

Satan was the original spin master, and unfortunately, is alive and perhaps more active than ever within individuals, congregations, and denominations that comprise the household of faith.

From the serpent questioning whether God really said what He said to Eve to the scribes and Pharisees who tried to discredit Jesus, every word and every miracle throughout His life, to the present day adulterers and waterers down of God's truth, spinning has become one of the most advanced arts of sinning.

Whether we call it public relations, propaganda, or spinning, the battle for our mind's opinions to be swayed or influenced is intense, ongoing, and often too successful.

> ***"When Jesus came to the region of Caesarea Philippi, he asked his disciples, "Who do people say the Son of Man is?"***
> ***Matthew 16:13 NIV***

Thank God that He has given us all spiritual wisdom and discernment of His Word, if we will only use it to get to know Him and His clear revelations of which He is and what He says so that we will not fall for the false spinning going on all around us.

**Father, protect me from the deceitful spinning of the world, the flesh, and the devil and let me seek Your perspective from Your Word. Amen**

November 27 Read 2 Corinthians 5:18-21, Psalm 119:73-80

## *Alienation of Affections*

**"So if you are standing before the altar in the Temple, offering a sacrifice to God, and you suddenly remember that someone has something against you, leave your sacrifice there beside the altar. Go and be reconciled to that person. Then come and offer your sacrifice to God." Matthew 5:24 NLT**

It is against the law for a third person to cause estrangement between a husband and wife, and injured spouses have received some big judgments in courts of law against an offender.

> ***"Let me be reconciled with all who fear you and know your decrees."***
> ***Psalm 119:79 NLT***

Beyond the bond and sanctity of marriage, alienation of affection causing estrangement between us and God is one of the devil's favorite tools for trying to bring us down.

At some time or another, people are going to disappoint us and cause alienation. We need to realize that we are sometimes going to disappoint and cause alienation, often without even knowing it.

Pride, greed, envy, unforgiveness, anger, lust, and selfishness are some of the biggest causes of the alienation of affections with others and with God.

Marriages falling apart, family feuds over inheritances and other issues, broken relationships with friends all involve some element of alienation of affections.

The steps we take in becoming reconciled to God (confession and apology, asking forgiveness, and resolving to end the conflict) are also the steps we need to take in restoring relationships with others.

> ***"Now all things are of God, who has reconciled us to Himself through Jesus Christ, and has given us the ministry of reconciliation,"***
> ***2 Corinthians 5:18***

It is painful and humbling and will not always work, but will often result in not only restoring, but in building even stronger relationships. Do you have an alienation that needs to end?

**Father, let me give the grace and forgiveness you have so freely given to me to others to prevent any alienation of affection. Amen**

Read 1 John 4:7-20, Psalm 23

November 28

## *God's Love is Real*

**"Whether we are high above the sky or in the deepest ocean, nothing in all creation will ever be able to separate us from the love of God that is revealed in Christ Jesus our Lord. Romans 8:39 NLT**

It is impossible to fully comprehend or try to put God's love in a container, since there's nothing big enough to contain it.

> ***"Surely your goodness and unfailing love will pursue me all the days of my life, and I will live in the house of the Lord forever". Psalm 23:6 NLT***

He pours it out through the heavens and earth that declare His glory. He reveals it through His Word and through His living Word, Jesus Christ. We experience God's love through the love and kindness of others.

God's love provides and sustains us. His love comforts and encourages us when we need it, and disciplines us when we deserve it.

God not only loved us enough to send Jesus to die for us, but He loves enough to send the Holy Spirit to live in us and transform us into the image of Christ. God's love is available to all who will receive it by believing in Jesus Christ as their personal Lord and Savior and allowing the Holy Spirit to fill them with God's love and the desire to share God's love with others.

We should never let any circumstance or satanic power cause us to doubt God's unconditional love. We should never let anything keep us from loving God with all our hearts.

> ***"Dear friends, let us continue to love one another, for love comes from God. Anyone who loves is born of God and knows God" 1 John 4:7 NLT***

Knowing that God really loves us, that He is with us, and that He will see us through the worst of times so that we can appreciate and enjoy Him in the best of times will give us the strength and joy we need to carry us through.

**Father, thank you for the blessed assurance of Your love and Your working all things for my good. Amen**

**November 29** **Read Romans 6:15-23, Psalm 25**

## *Our Pro Choice God*

**"Today I have given you the choice between life and death, between blessings and curses. I call on heaven and earth to witness the choice you make. Oh, that you would choose life, that you and your descendants might live!" Deuteronomy 30:19 NLT**

Freedom of choice is probably one of the least understood and most profound articles in God's "Bill of Rights." Although God has put a longing for Him into our hearts and would have all men to be saved by receiving Jesus as Savior, He is not going to force Himself on anyone.

***"Who are those who fear the Lord? He will show them the path they should choose." Psalm 25:12 NLT***

If we choose to reject God's wonderful gift of salvation and live life in the trivial pursuits of living life controlled by our flesh, the world, or the devil, God respects our choice and even provides a place where we can live lives forever -- tormented and separated from Him.

Nobody goes to hell by God's choice, but by their own choice to reject and continue to live lives separated from God.

Although God makes it perfectly clear that He wants us to seek Him and His righteousness first so that He can add all that we need for living life to the fullest in a love relationship with Him through His Son, God is not going to force His righteousness or His goodness on anyone.

God has made His existence perfectly clear through nature, through His Word, and through His Son. No one is going to have ignorance of God as an excuse for choosing to reject Him.

***"Don't you realize that whatever you choose to obey becomes your master? You can choose sin, which leads to death, or you can choose to obey God and receive his approval." Romans 6:9 NLT***

Our freedom of choice to receive or reject Jesus will stay with us up to the very end of our lives on earth. The thief on the cross validates this truth. When it comes to being "pro choice," it is hard to fathom why anyone would choose being pro death over pro life in Christ.

**Father, help me to make the right choices. Amen**

**Read 2 Timothy 4:15-16, Psalm 28** **November 30**

## *Safety Net*

**"But all who listen to me will live in peace and safety, unafraid of harm." Proverbs 1:33**

How could there be a circus without nets. The high wire aerialists and trapeze artists would all be dead were it not for the nets that catch them and cushion the falls.

> ***"O Lord, You are my rock of safety. Please help me; don't refuse to answer me." Psalm 28.1***

Unemployment, hospitalization and Social Security programs are safety nets that have proven effective in avoiding the devastating effects as experienced during the great depression for millions of people.

We should remember to praise God that because of Medicaid, every one can receive the nursing home care they need but could never afford without this safety net.

Wise stewards seek to store up rainy day nest eggs to provide for a better standard of living during retirement and a safety net for the contingencies of illness, accidents, and unexpected expenses.

How fortunate for us that God sent Jesus Christ to cushion our fall and restore our right standing with Him through faith in His Son. Jesus not only cushions our fall and saves us from the death penalty because of our sins, He cushions our falls with His safety net of grace.

He is our safe harbor where we can persevere through the storms of life raging all around us and often threatening to wash us away.

> ***"I was snatched from the jaws of the lion! God's looking after me, keeping me safe in the kingdom of heaven." 2 Timothy 4:16 MSG***

Once we receive this safety net by faith, we are commanded to use it to become fishers of men. We do this by telling how we were free falling in a life without a future or a hope until the love of God caught us and set us on a firm foundation of faith.

**Father, thank you for giving me the security of your unconditional love and forever forgiveness. Amen**

December 1 Read Matthew 18:6-7, Psalm 103

# *The Fall Out*

**"I show this unfailing love to many thousands by forgiving every kind of sin and rebellion. Even so I do not leave sin unpunished, but I punish the children for the sins of their parents to the third and fourth generations." Exodus 34:7 NLT**

Adam and Eve sinned and got not only themselves, but all who would come after them kicked out of paradise.

> ***"His salvation extends to the children's children of those who are faithful to his covenant," Psalm 103:17 NLT***

The bad choice of rejecting God's wonderful gift of salvation and relationship breaks the covenant of Grace which has been promised to the children and children's children of believers.

The bad choice of walking out instead of working it out often scars children and robs them of the security of being loved.

The bad self-serving choices we make almost always cause a fall out and harm to others.

Satan has used the moral failures of believers to discourage and cause millions of others to stumble and fall away over the centuries. Prisons are full of professing Christians who in a bad moment have made a bad choice and are suffering lingering and painful consequences.

God sent Jesus Christ to die on the cross to set the captives free. We are no longer in bondage to sin. We are free to be all that we can be in Christ.

When temptations come (as they will) we are free to claim God's promise that He will provide a means of escape, and His strength to make the right choices when confronted by evil.

> ***"Jesus said: "But if anyone causes one of these little ones who trusts in me to lose faith, it would be better for that person to be thrown into the sea with a large millstone tied around the neck." Matthew 18:6***

The Holy Spirit will often give us the awareness of what harm our bad choices will do to others in order to help us make the right choice in fleeing, standing firm, and overcoming temptation.

**Father, let me live in the freedom to make wise choices. Amen**

**Read Romans 1:16-22, Psalm 107** **December 2**

## *Feed the Hungry*

**"When they had finished eating, Jesus said to Simon Peter, "Simon son of John, do you truly love me more than these?" "Yes, Lord," he said, "you know that I love you." Jesus said, "Feed my lambs." John 21:15 NIV**

> ***"For he satisfies the thirsty and fills the hungry with good things."***
> ***Psalm 107:9 NIV***

The world is full of starvation and hunger. The plight of so many millions of people going hungry is sad indeed.

The world is also full of spiritual hunger and starvation. Millions of people throughout the world have an inborn hunger for meaning and purpose in their lives that is being either fed poison or not being fed at all and left wandering aimlessly seeking to satisfy their hunger in ways that will never fulfill.

Spiritual hunger can only be fed by Jesus, who is the bread of life. It is only when we find security and significance in Him that we can find the peace that satisfies our every longing and makes us hunger and thirst after righteousness in a celebration of joy and thanksgiving over knowing God and what He has done for us through the life, death, and resurrection of Jesus Christ.

When we have our hunger for God replaced by our hunger for seeking His righteousness, we become free to feed the hungry among us who are starving for the Good News that God loves us, that He wants a close and personal relationship with us through Jesus, and to satisfy our every longing for the peace and joy that only He can give.

> ***"For I am not ashamed of this Good News about Christ. It is the power of God at work, saving everyone who believes— Jews first and also Gentiles.***
> ***Romans 1:16 NIV***

When we share God's love and the Good News of salvation through faith in Jesus Christ with others, we are truly feeding the hungry.

**Father, keep me ever mindful of the hunger for You that you have put in the heart of everyone, and use me to feed that hunger with those around me. Amen**

**December 3** **Read John 6:38-40, Isaiah 7:13-15**

## *He's Arrived!*

**"On that day the announcement to Jerusalem will be, "Cheer up, Zion! Don't be afraid! For the LORD your God has arrived to live among you. He is a mighty savior. He will rejoice over you with great gladness. With his love, he will calm all your fears. He will exult over you by singing a happy song." Zephaniah 3:16-17 NLT**

Christmas should be a spiritual marker for all believers. It marks God's coming down to lift us up. He has arrived to live among us. He is a mighty Savior. He has come to calm all our fears with His love.

> ***"All right then, the Lord himself will choose the sign. Look! The virgin will conceive a child! She will give birth to a son and will call him Immanuel— 'God is with us." Isaiah 7:14 NLT***

There are distractions all around us that satan would use to rob us of our peace and joy in Christmas. We overspend and overeat. We become depressed over the absence of loved ones who have gone on before us or from other physical, financial, emotional, or relational problems.

Through all of the distractions the babe of the manger comes to rejoice over us and to bring joy to others through us as His birthday continues to remind us of the new life and new hope that we have in Him. The one who hates and will not tolerate sin came down and suffered the pain of so much sin by so many sinners.

He modeled God's love so that we might learn how to love and live in the peace and joy of God's love every day of our lives on this earth and in the next.

> ***"For I have come down from heaven, not to do My own will, but the will of Him who sent Me" John 6:38 NLT***

He continues to exult over us with great gladness as He sits at the right hand of the Father and shields us from God's wrath as His robe of righteousness covers our sins. May we never lose sight of the tidings of great joy that are ours for now and forever through receiving the arrival of Christ as our personal Savior.

**Father, may I always give you cause to sing a happy song over me. Amen.**

# *Spiritual Malnutrition*

**"For the weapons of our warfare *are* not carnal but mighty in God for pulling down strongholds, casting down arguments and every high thing that exalts itself against the knowledge of God," 1 Corinthians 10:4,5a NLT**

I don't know where this illustration originated, but I believe that it sums up our daily battle against sin as well as anything I have ever heard. The idea is that our flesh and our spirit are like two dogs fighting, with the best fed dog winning.

> ***"Bless the LORD, who is my rock .He gives me strength for war and skill for battle." Psalm 144:1 NLT***

Along with secular humanism, children are fed condoms, birth control, and abortion options in our schools instead of Bibles, prayer, and the moral absolutes of the Ten Commandments.

Our spiritual growth is stunted and our lights go dim as we spend by far the biggest part of our time slopping with the pigs in the vast wasteland of TV, pornography, and selling out to the world's standards instead of God's.

When we think that we can maintain our spiritual health by going to church on Sunday and receiving spiritual nourishment one hour a week, we are thinking exactly the way satan would have us think.

When we constantly drink of the polluted water of sin instead of the living water of the Savior, we are going to find that we are going to lose the battle raging within us.

When we stand before Christ at the resurrection of the just and give an account of how we spent our time that we were given on this earth, are we going to have anything left after the wood, hay, and stubble of our lives has been burned?

> ***"I have written to you who are young because you are strong with God's word living in your hearts, and you have won your battle with Satan." 1 John 2:14b NLT***

**Father, Let me feast daily and richly on the riches of your love, your grace, and your salvation as I abide in Your Word and grow strong in You. Amen**

**December 5** **Read Matthew 7:7-11, Psalm 69**

## *Giving God a Buffet of Prayer*

**"Devote yourselves to prayer with an alert mind and a thankful heart." Colossians 4:2 NLT**

God loves, hears, and answers our prayers. We learn from Scripture that he inhabits the praises of His people, that He delights in giving what we ask that will glorify Him and be in accordance with His good and gracious will and perfect plan for our lives.

> ***"Then I will praise God's name with singing, and I will honor him with thanksgiving." Psalm 69:30 NLT***

He is a rewarder of those who seek Him, and He will even grant the desires of our heart. He is able to do *"far more abundantly than all we ask or think." (Ephesians 3:20 NASB)* He even tells us through James that we have not because we ask not, and that the fervent prayer of a righteous man (or woman) avails much.

This all being true, and it is because God says so, we need to take prayer more seriously. One way to do this is to develop a prayer buffet.

When we worship the power, majesty, and goodness of God in prayer, we worship a bigger God. When we humble ourselves and confess our sins with godly sorrow and true repentance, we receive grace and mercy to cover all our sins.

Scripture records that God will honor our faith and trust in extraordinary ways when we rejoice and give thanks for answered prayers and not only the good things but also what we perceive to be the bad things of life.

After we have done all this, we are ready to ask God for whatever we think we need and for the needs of others. Our prayers will become less self-centered and more Christ-centered. Best of all, we will approach the throne of grace more boldly and expectantly, anchored by the confidence that answered prayers bring.

> ***"If you then, being evil, know how to give good gifts to your children, how much more will your Father who is in heaven give good things to those who ask Him!" Matthew 7:11***

Prayer should not be offered as a snack, but a full course buffet.

**Father, strengthen my prayer base as you strengthen my faith base in your Word. Amen**

**Read Hebrews 7:15-28, Psalm 31** **December 6**

# Our "Pro Bono" Attorney

**"And He bore the sin of many, and made intercession for the transgressors." Isaiah 53:12b NLT**

Whether we like to think about it or not, we are all awaiting trial. Some are even in bondage awaiting trial, and, worst of all, we are all as guilty as sin. In fact, we are all guilty of sin!

> ***"Love the Lord, all you faithful ones! For the Lord protects those who are loyal to him, but he harshly punishes all who are arrogant." Psalm 31:23 NLT***

If we are honest and compare our thoughts, words, and things we've done and failed to do with God's standard of perfection, we have more than enough entries in our sin record to qualify for a lifetime sentence with no hope of parole.

We often get outraged at some of the famous defense attorneys who manage to get really bad and really guilty people off free. To see the guilty set free on some of the tricks and technicalities used sometimes seems to make a mockery of our justice system.

The reality of death is that we are all going to die. God's Word clearly tells us that we are all going to stand trial and be held accountable for all of our sins when we die, and that "the wages of sin is death."

There is an old saying, "He who has himself as his lawyer has a fool for a client." When it comes to standing before God at the great judgment, this is most certainly true.

If we enter God's court thinking that we have been good enough or refusing to believe that there is a judgment day, we are going to have a rude awakening even after death.

How good it is to know and believe Jesus Christ's death on the cross has been credited to our sin account and made us righteous in God's sight. Jesus is not only the best defense attorney we could ever have, but He is working pro bono. He is pleading our case for free.

> ***"Therefore he is able, once and forever, to save everyone who comes to God through him. He lives forever to plead with God on their behalf." Hebrews 7:25 NLT***

**Father, thank you for the assurance of knowing that Jesus has never lost a case in your throne of judgment and justice. Amen**

December 7 Read John 15:9-14, Psalm 103:13-18

# *Fatherly Love*

**"The Father loves the Son and has placed everything in His hands." John 3:37**

A common thread among a large majority of the ever-increasing prison population is the absence of a father or the presence of an abusive dysfunctional father. It is hard for these prisoners to relate to the concept of fatherly love.

> ***"As a father pities his children, so the LORD pities those who fear Him."***
> ***Psalm 103:13***

A lot of other people get a distorted view of God as a stern and demanding father just waiting for us to get out of line so that He can pour out His wrath upon us. We must never forget that God is love and we should view Him as such.

If you have been blessed with an earthly father who loves you and who has been there for you and reflected the love of the heavenly father to you, take time to thank God for him, and to thank him for his love.

If you are a father, think about the responsibilities you have to be the spiritual head of your family, and to love your children enough to bring them up in the nurture and admonition of the Lord.

.Fathers and mothers should never lose sight of the fact that we are to model Christ in our lives so that our children will learn to do the same.

Thanks be to God that we all can know the love of our heavenly father through the Son whom he has sent.

He constantly reveals His love to us through His Word, and the overflowing cup of physical, material, relational, and spiritual blessings which are ours in Christ.

May we seek to imitate the love of our heavenly father by learning and living the teachings and examples He set when He lived among us as Jesus Christ!

> ***"I have loved you even as the Father has loved me. Remain in my love."***
> ***John 15:9 NLT***

Our mission in life should be to grow up to be just like our heavenly father!

**Lord, I thank you for loving me with a perfect fatherly love that will never fail, never leave me, and will continue to supply my every need. Amen.**

**Read Colossians 3, Psalm 42** **December 8**

## *Seeking the Living*

**"Then, as they were afraid and bowed *their* faces to the earth, they said to them, "Why do you seek the living among the dead?" Luke 24:5**

The resurrection of our Lord and Savior Jesus Christ is the greatest happening in the history of the World. Because He is risen, we who believe can have confidence that we too have risen to live in the power, presence and victory of the living Lord.

> ***"I thirst for God, the living God. When can I come and stand before him?"***
> ***Psalm 42:2 NLT***

By the resurrection power of the Holy Spirit which is given to all true believers we can die to living in the power of the flesh, the world and the devil, and live in the newness of the fullness of life in the Spirit of the living Lord.

As we die to self and become alive in Christ and seek Him, we will grow in all of the blessings promised to those who abide in Him. We will have Jesus' friendship, His Joy, the awareness of His love and the love of others, and answered prayers. We can lead lives pleasing to Him and fruitful in every good work.

There is absolutely no excuse for continuing to live in the dead end road of sin and death. We have been redeemed by the blood of the Lamb. We have been crucified with Christ and resurrected into the newness of life in Him and with Him, and our lives will reflect the transformation that has taken place.

As we seek the living Lord and to be conformed to His image by the life changing power of the Holy Spirit, the fear and terror of death is replaced by the certainty of living forever under the shelter of God's wings of grace and promises of an even better and more glorious life to come.

> ***"If then you were raised with Christ, seek those things which are above, where Christ is, sitting at the right hand of God."***
> ***Colossians 3:1***

Let us never again live in sin among the dead, but always in the power and presence of the living Lord.

**Father, help me to stay out of living in bondage to death and to live in the fullness of my living Lord. Amen**

December 9 Read Galatians 6, Psalm 40

## *A "Person of Interest"*

**"But the very hairs of your head are all numbered. Do not fear therefore; you are of more value than many sparrows."**

**Matthew 10:30-31**

"Person of interest" has come to enjoy wide usage to describe suspects or potential suspects in crime investigations.

> ***"But I am poor and needy; Yet the LORD thinks upon me. Psalm 40:17 NLT***

Beyond crime investigations we all have, are, or will become "persons of interest."

We all have or have had parents, spouses, family, friends, preachers, teachers, and stars of TV, movies, or sports who are "persons of interest" to us. When we are attracted to someone of the opposite sex, they become "persons of interest."

When someone becomes a "person of interest," we are interested in everything about them. As we grow in our relationship with them, we get to know them better by learning more about them.

We need to know that we became a "person of interest" to God long before we were ever born. God knew our name before we were ever conceived. He is interested in everything we do in this life He has given us and has made great plans for us if we will only receive His gracious gift of eternal life, and trust and obey Him.

The key to a happy life now and forever is in making Jesus Christ the "person of interest" around who we build and live our lives. He is the Way, the Truth, and the Life, and no good thing will God withhold from those who make Him their "person of interest."

> ***". Because of that cross, my interest in this world died long ago, and the world's interest in me is also long dead." Galatians 6:14bNLT***

When we become interested enough to learn what he did and said, we will learn what we should be doing and saying.

Our first lesson should be to love God as He did. Secondly we should love others and make everyone God puts across our path a "person of interest" as we reflect God's love to them.

**Father, thank You for making me a "person of interest" to You. By the power of Your Spirit, help me to make Jesus the primary "person of interest" in my life. Amen**

**Read Luke 11:1-9, Ecclesiastes 12** **December 10**

# *Everyone's a Seeker*

**"So, you see, it is impossible to please God without faith. Anyone who wants to come to him must believe that there is a God and that he rewards those who sincerely seek him." Hebrews 11:6**

There is a lot of talk and attention given to conducting "seeker friendly" worship services as a means of connecting with the unsaved or unchurched. Some churches have seeker services on Sundays and believer services on Wednesday.

> ***"Here is my final conclusion: Fear God and obey his commands, for this is the duty of every person. God will judge us for everything we do, including every secret thing, whether good or bad.***
> ***Ecclesiastes 12:13-14 NLT***

The truth is that the world is full of seekers. Unfortunately, too many are seeking in the wrong places.

In addition to the basic physical needs for food, clothing, and shelter, everyone has the basic emotional or spiritual need for security and significance. Everyone wants to matter to themselves and others.

The book of Ecclesiastes is probably the best book on seeking ever written. Solomon, the wisest man who ever lived up until the coming of Christ, was the ultimate seeker.

He sought security and significance in sensual pleasure of every kind, power, possession and work, which is exactly what much of the world is doing today. He found that none of these things provided that "peace that surpasses all understanding."

We can be wiser than Solomon by realizing that only a right relationship with God through faith in Jesus Christ will satisfy our longing for the security and significance that only. He can satisfy.

Only when we find the unconditional love, forever forgiveness, and security and significance of who God has made us to be in Christ, will we find what's really worth seeking.

> ***"For everyone who asks, receives. Everyone who seeks, finds. And the door is opened to everyone who knocks."***
> ***Luke 11:10 NLT***

**Father, let me be a seeker of souls with whom I can share what I have found in You. Amen**

**December 11** **Read 1 Corinthians 1, Psalm 37**

## *Have You Been Validated?*

**"So, friends, confirm God's invitation to you, his choice of you. Don't put it off; do it now." 2 Peter 1:10 MSG**

A lot of stores and restaurants offer free parking in commercial parking garages, but you have to get your ticket validated.

> ***"He'll validate your life in the clear light of day and stamp you with approval at high noon."***
> ***Psalm 37:6 MSG***

God offers a free parking space in heaven, but you have to get validated by faith in Jesus Christ who paid for your ticket with His blood on the Cross.

Jesus not only stands at the door and knocks, inviting us all into a personal relationship with Him, but He is seated at the right hand of God holding the spot open for us.

Jesus gives us all the validation we need in this world and all eternity. By his stripes we have been healed. By rising from the dead He has validated that we too will rise from the grave into eternal life.

We too often seek to validate ourselves by the world's standards instead of God's. All over the world, there are people who have nothing, but have everything in Christ. There are people who have everything but have nothing because they are separated from God.

When we find Christ, we find unconditional love, forever forgiveness, and the security and validation of God as His grace erases guilt, and sustains us daily no matter what.

The standards of the world and the approval of other people may validate us for a short time in this world; be we must always be mindful that this world is not our home and that our validation in Christ is the only one that will last forever.

> ***"who will also confirm you to the end, that you may be blameless in the day of our Lord Jesus Christ."***
> ***1 Corinthians 1:8***

There should be evidence of our validation in the lives we live. If our lives don't fit who we are in Christ, we had best seek the transforming power of the Holy Spirit and God's grace by abiding in Him through His Word, prayer, and the fellowship of other believers.

**Thank you for confirming me through your righteousness. Amen**

**Read 2 Peter 1, Psalm 59** **December 12**

## *Never Under Estimate God*

**"Jesus said to him, "If you can believe, all things *are* possible to him who believes." Mark 9:23**

Scripture after Scripture validates the incredible power, presence, all-knowing knowledge, foreknowledge, wisdom, holiness, justice, and love of God, which comprise the character of God.

> ***"But as for me, I will sing about your power. I will shout with joy each morning because of your unfailing love." Psalm 59:16 NLT***

God created the world and everything in it, but many fail to give Him the praise and glory He deserves for this, preferring to credit to random chance evolution instead.

God's power to tame or unleash the forces of nature is still under estimated. The same God who destroyed life by water, who parted the Red Sea to deliver the children of Israel from bondage, who raised Jesus from the dead, is our God today and alive and well, still exercising this power whenever He decides the timing is right to fulfill His purposes.

God's presence has gone from a burning bush, to a mountain top, to the Ark of the Covenant, to life on this earth as Jesus Christ, to presence in the heart of all believers through the indwelling of the Holy Spirit.

God's wisdom is so much higher than our own. His holiness is sinless perfection and something we can obtain only through receiving the righteousness of Christ by faith in Him and what He did on the cross.

Knowing that God's judgment will be tempered only by His mercy that is ours to appropriate through faith in the blood of Jesus Christ is the most important knowledge we can ever appropriate by faith.

> ***"And by that same mighty power, he has given us all of his rich and wonderful promises." 2 Peter 1:4 NLT***

We grow in our faith through our personal relationship with Jesus Christ and the power of the Holy Spirit. We must never miss out on the fullness of God's love for every area of life by under estimating any aspect of His character or power.

**Father, keep me ever mindful of your strength and power that is mine to appropriate by faith. Amen**

**December 13** **Read 1 Peter 1, Psalm 107**

# *Don't Lose Your Claim Check*

**"But as for me, I know that my Redeemer lives, and that he will stand upon the earth at last. And after my body has decayed, yet in my body I will see God" Job 19:25-26 NLT**

Claim Checks have long been the means for redeeming baggage and hocked items from pawn shops, cloak rooms, and laundries. The old saying "no ticket, no laundry" became a watchword for safeguarding your claim checks.

> ***"Let the redeemed of the LORD say so, whom He has redeemed from the hand of the enemy," Psalm 107:2***

When it comes to redeeming our souls, it takes more than a cardboard ticket. It takes the washing away of sin and death by faith in the blood of Jesus, which is evidenced by a new birth through the transforming power of the Holy Spirit.

When Jesus told Nicodemus that he must be born again, He was in effect saying "no laundry, no ticket!" Unless we wash away our sins in the blood of the Lamb, we will never know the peace and joy of eternal life now and forever.

In addition to being made clean in God's sight, the Holy Spirit begins the life long process of cleansing, sustaining, and empowering us to become more like Christ in our everyday life.

The transformed life is the outward evidence that we have been redeemed and born again into the freedom and new life in Christ. Our conduct should reflect the inward cleansing of our hearts that only happens when our belief moves from our heads to our hearts. Scripture makes it very clear that all who profess faith are saved. If we are merely hearers of the Word who only "talk the talk" without "walking the walk," Jesus will say He never knew us.

> ***"...knowing that you were not redeemed with corruptible things, like silver or gold, from your aimless conduct received by tradition from your fathers," 1 Peter 1:18 NLT***

When we carry our claim check in our heart we can be sure that a glad welcome awaits our eternal home in heaven which Christ has gone ahead to prepare for all of His redeemed.

**Father, may you never be ashamed to call me one of your redeemed. Amen**

Read James 3, Isaiah 35

December 14

# *How to Tame the Savage Beast*

**"Don't sin by letting anger gain control over you. Think about it overnight and remain silent." Psalm 4:4 NLT**

There is a lesson to be learned from the power of water being harnessed into enough electricity to power an entire city or region.

*" "No lion shall be there, Nor shall any ravenous beast go up on it; It shall not be found there. But the redeemed shall walk there, Isaiah 35.9*

The lesson is that we can, by faith, harness the incredible power of the Holy Spirit to tame the savage beast of sin that dwells within the heart of every child born of woman.

When we submit to the yoke of allegiance to God by surrendering our lives to the Lordship of Jesus Christ, we are promised the "power from on High," which is the indwelling of the Holy Spirit.

Just as God's power saves us and makes us holy in His sight by imputing the righteousness of Christ, God's power destroys the power of sin to rage within us and through us by supplying His all sustaining and all sufficient grace on demand to supply our every need.

We see this incredible grace at work throughout Scripture. It empowered Joseph to flourish through the worst of circumstances. It transformed Paul from persecutor to proclaimer, from murderer to magnifier.

God's grace empowered a rag tag bunch of disciples to proclaim the Good News with power and boldness and start its spread throughout the world.

God's grace can and will transform all believers who will channel the power of God's grace into their every day lives through growing in the knowledge of God's clear commands and directions and obedience to them.

*"People can tame all kinds of animals and birds and reptiles and fish, but no one can tame the tongue." James 3:7*

The power of God's grace is not only the birthright of every born again believer but also the evidence and confirmation of our new birth in Christ.

**Father, by the power of Your Spirit, help me to control the savage beast that sometimes rages for control within me. Amen**

December 15 Read 1 Peter 5:6-10, Psalm 119:25-40

# *Revivals We Don't Need*

**"In just a short time, he will restore us so we can live in his presence. Oh, that we might know the Lord! Let us press on to know him! Then he will respond to us as surely as the arrival of dawn or the coming of rains in early spring." Hosea 6:2 NLT**

We usually think of revival in terms of reviving people from death to sin and life in Christ by the power of the Holy Spirit through the preaching of the Word.

> ***"Behold, I long for Your precepts. Revive me in Your righteousness." Psalm 119:40***

Unfortunately, we often seem to do a better job of reviving our sinful habits and bad attitudes daily instead of seeking a clean heart and right spirit on a daily basis.

Time after time we bury our sins at the foot of the cross and then revive them and all the guilt associated with them time and time again. Even though God says that He has forgiven our sins and remembers them no more, satan keeps throwing darts of doubt our way to undermine this wonderful testimony to God's love and mercy.

All too often, we revive our old self-centered hearts and attitudes in spite of the fact that God has given us a new heart based on a Christ-centered relationship of mutual love for God and for others.

Perhaps worst of all, the great deceiver revives doubts about our salvation when we stumble or succumb to the temptations he throws our way in order to undermine our faith and the security we have through our relationship with God through faith in Jesus.

Jesus Christ ransomed us from the dominion and death of sin once and for all by His death on the cross. We did nothing to earn this and can do nothing to keep it except abide in God's love by abiding in His Word.

> ***"In his kindness God called you to his eternal glory by means of Jesus Christ. After you have suffered a little while, he will restore, support, and strengthen you, and he will place you on a firm foundation." 1 Peter 5:10 NLT***

We should never again return to the captivity and domination of sin in our lives but rather remember our baptism through which we became dead to sin and alive in Christ.

**Father, help me to leave my sins and my doubts at the cross and live in the fullness of your joy. Amen**

Read Ephesians 1:3-14, Psalm 94 December 16

## *God's Life Support Systems*

**"Be strong and of good courage, do not fear nor be afraid of them; for the LORD your God, He *is* the One who goes with you. He will not leave you nor forsake you." Deuteronomy 31:6**

There has been a debate raging over when to pull the plug on brain dead people who cannot live without being connected to life support systems for breathing and taking nourishment.

> ***"In the multitude of my anxieties within me, Your comforts delight my soul." Psalm 94:14***

Thanks be to God that he never pulls the plug on the life support systems He provides for unbelievers. Although actually dead men walking in darkness and despair; God keeps His life support system and the offer of salvation plugged in until the very last breath is drawn. This is the lesson of the thief on the cross and the workers in the vineyard.

For the believer who receives God's wonderful gift of eternal life through faith in Jesus Christ, God provides a built-in, unpluggable life support system in the person and presence of the Holy Spirit.

He has also been given as a guarantee that God's eternal life support will never be unplugged from any true believer.

The true believer may stumble and fall in the flesh from time to time, but the Holy Spirit is at work making intercession to God for us, and convicting us of our need for confession and repentance, and imparting God's grace to us through prayer, the Word, Baptism, Lord's Supper, circumstances, and the encouragement and fellowship of other believers.

The Holy Spirit will do whatever it takes to complete the task that He has begun in our lives. He will provide the chastening we need to bring us back, the scourging we might need to develop the humility, long suffering, love, and obedience of Christ within us, which is our hope of glory.

> ***"The Spirit is God's guarantee that he will give us everything he promised and that he has purchased us to be his own people. This is just one more reason for us to praise our glorious God." Ephesians 1:14 NLT***

We may "pull the plug" on God but He will never forsake or "pull the plug" on us. There is eternal life support for all believers!

**Father, thank you for the assurance of your forever and unconditional love, forgiveness, and acceptance in Christ. Amen**

# *Vanity of Vanities*

**"I live in that high and holy place with those whose spirits are contrite and humble. I refresh the humble and give new courage to those with repentant hearts." Isaiah 57:15b NLT**

Scripture warns us not to think too highly of ourselves, yet we continually try to build ourselves up with inflated pride in our image, our knowledge, our possessions, and even our righteousness.

> ***"Arise, O judge of the earth. Sentence the proud to the penalties they deserve." Psalm 94:2 NLT***

If we think about those people who most remind us of Jesus, we will notice that they almost always project the quality of humility, and reflect the love of Jesus.

Conceit is the vanity of vanities that will destroy a close and personal relationship with God through faith in Jesus Christ, and keep many from getting to know Jesus.

When we persist in self-centered pursuits instead of Christ-honoring conduct in any area of our lives, we are worshipping ourselves or the idols of our minds instead of Christ.

There is nothing wrong with wealth or possessions unless they possess us. There is nothing wrong with the approval of others unless we worship this approval more than God's and go against God's clear commands in order to gain the approval of men.

It is great to increase our knowledge if we always remember that there is a big difference between wisdom and knowledge and we do not try to replace the wisdom of God with the knowledge of men.

> ***"When you bow down before the Lord and admit your dependence on him, he will lift you up and give you honor." James 4:10 NLT***

Our call to salvation is a call to righteousness. It is a good thing to imitate Christ and glorify God by our good deeds as evidence of our faith.

When we believe that we are going to heaven because of our righteousness instead of Christ's, and think that we are better than others we become guilty of the vanity of vanities.

**Father, take away my self pride and let my pride be in You. Amen**

# *Changing Message*

**"Dear friends, I am not writing a new commandment, for it is an old one you have always had, right from the beginning. This commandment—to love one another—is the same message you heard before." 1 John 2:7 NLT**

It is utterly amazing how so many people for so many reasons have tried and continue to try to change or ignore the clear messages of Scripture. We are cherry pickers and nit pickers.

> ***"Keep my message in plain view at all times. Concentrate! Learn it by heart! Those who discover these words live, really live; body and soul, they're bursting with health." Proverbs 4:21 MSG***

The cherry pickers seem to think that the Bible is a salad bar where they can go in and pick what they want to believe and discard the rest. They will most always say that the Bible contains the Word of God instead of that the Bible is the Word of God. The nit pickers will get so hung up on rules and regulations and the defense of them that they lose sight of the fact that our purpose is to spread the Gospel and not defend the traditions of a particular denomination.

God clearly tells us that He is the same yesterday, today, and tomorrow. He does not change.

The centrality of the Gospel is the Good News that God loves us so much that He sent His Son to die on the cross for us as the perfect sacrifice for our sins, and that all who believe this will have eternal life.

We have those who add a litany of things that we must believe and do to receive His wonderful gift.

> ***"For the message of the cross is foolishness to those who are perishing, but to us who are being saved it is the power of God." 1 Corinthians 1:18***

Those who say we don't have to do anything are absolutely right. When we are born again believers, we will want to do everything that God wants us to do as we grow in Christ.

The most important thing to remember about God's message is that it has never and will never change; but that it will change us when we answer His call to salvation by the power of the Holy Spirit.

**Father, let your message never change but always change the hearts of all who hear it. Amen**

December 19 Read John 10, Psalm 1

## *Why Not Now?*

**"For He says, "In an acceptable time I have heard you, and in the day of salvation I have helped you." Behold, now is the accepted time; behold, now is the day of salvation." 2 Corinthians 6:2 NLT**

Life forever doesn't begin when we die and go to heaven. It begins when we receive Jesus Christ as Lord and Savior and are born again. When Jesus stands knocking at our door, we had better listen and be ready to open our hearts to Him so that we can start living life to the fullest by growing into the fullness of Christ here on earth.

> ***"Oh, the joys of those who do not follow the advice of the wicked, or stand around with sinners, or join in with scoffers."***
> ***Psalm 1:1 NLT***

Jesus makes it very clear that we are to let nothing stand in the way of his call to follow Him.

A lot of people ignore God's call to salvation because they don't want to give up some of the perceived pleasures they think they are enjoying apart from God. They think that there is plenty of time after they sew their wild oats and enjoy their life in the flesh to the fullest.

When Jesus sends the Holy Spirit to let us die to sin and we become alive in Christ we begin enjoying the real treasures and pleasures that only a right relationship with God through faith in Jesus Christ can bring.

According to many of those who have put off God's call in favor of doing their own thing, every aspect of doing life God's way is so superior to living life the world's way they can't believe what they missed out on for so long.

There is absolutely no reason for going through wasted years piling up guilt and consequences of being separated from God when God promises that we will have life to the fullest in Him now and forever whenever we answer Jesus' call to follow Him. God promises to make all things new, and to work all things for our good. Dare we put off His call any longer?

> ***"My sheep recognize my voice; I know them, and they follow me. I give them eternal life, and they will never perish. No one will snatch them away from me"***
> ***John 10:27, 28 NLT***

**Father, you do make all things new and renew your love, grace and mercy every day to those who call upon Your name. Amen**

Read 1 Corinthians 13, Psalm 5 December 20

## *How's Your Love Life?*

**"If you love me, show it by doing what I've told you. I will talk to the Father, and he'll provide you another Friend so that you will always have someone with you. This Friend is the Spirit of Truth." John 14:15 MSG**

Although this question often carries romantic implications, it is much more meaningful to ask in connection with our love affair with Jesus.

> ***"For you bless the godly, O Lord, surrounding them with your shield of love." Psalm 5:22 NLT***

When we think about it, our lives should be all about our love life with God. This is why we were created, and this should be our main purpose in living.

We were created in God's love for the purpose of being conduits of God's love to others that they might be encouraged in their love life with God, or hopefully that those who do not know the love of God may come to know Him through us.

When we paraphrase 1 Corinthians 1:13 1-8 and substitute "Jesus" for the word love, we see the character and personality of Christ that bears out the truth that "God is love."

When we substitute our names for the word love in verses 4 through 7, we can see how close we have come and how far we have to go in growing into the fullness of Christ.

These verses should be the target we strive for as we place our minds attention and hearts affection to being conformed into the image of Christ. It should be the hearts desire of every believer that our love life with the Lord could be identified by this definition.

> ***"Love suffers long and is kind; love does not envy; love does not parade itself, is not puffed up; does not behave rudely, does not seek its own, is not provoked, thinks no evil; does not rejoice in iniquity, but rejoices in the truth; bears all things, believes all things, hopes all things, endures all things." 1 Corinthians 13:4-7 NLT***

Although we may often fail and disappoint God, how comforting it is to know that God's love is unfailing and will never disappoint. Oh, what a Savior!

**Father, keep my love life burning with passion for You and all the love You give to me daily. Amen**

December 21 — Read Matthew 13:1-23, Psalm 15

## *Upon Further Review*

**"Every day I review the ways He works; I try not to miss a trick. I feel put back together, and I'm watching my step." Psalm 18:22 MSG**

Judges, committees, appeals courts, etc. are often asked to review their findings or the findings of others in order to confirm or reverse their recommendations or decisions. Death row inmates go through review after review until the "court of last resort" has issued the order to proceed with an execution.

> ***"Who may worship in your sanctuary, Lord? Who may enter your presence on your holy hill?***
>
> ***Psalm 15:1 NLT***

As believers, we really need to further review our lives in Christ on a daily basis. It is so easy to get distracted and take our eyes off of Jesus and back onto ourselves and our agendas. We often forget to keep the "main thing" the "main thing."

Upon further review, do we find seeking the Kingdom of God and His righteousness first on our list of priorities?

Everything we do and say should reflect our new birth in Christ, and who He has made us to be. As we have been given unconditional love, forever forgiveness, and total acceptance by God, we should be giving these gifts of God's grace to others.

There is coming a time when the stewardship of our lives will come up for further review by Christ. After the wood, hay, and straw of all our wasted efforts and trivial pursuits have been burned away, will there be anything left to confirm that we really are true believers, or ones whose faith is rooted in the rocky or thorny ground gives no evidence of the transforming power of Christ in us?

> ***"The good soil represents the hearts of those who truly accept God's message and produce a huge harvest—thirty, sixty, or even a hundred times as much as had been planted." Matthew 13:23 NLT***

As ones who have the blessed assurance of eternal life in the here and now and in the home in heaven that Christ has gone to prepare for us, we should earnestly seek to honor Him and what He has done for us by bearing the fruit of the Spirit, and living lives fully pleasing to Him.

**Father, may my life reflect your Glory and have abundant fruit remaining after your further review. Amen**

Read Romans 5, Psalm 40 December 22

# The Great Compromiser

**"So leave the corruption and compromise; leave it for good," says God. "Don't link up with those who will pollute you. I want you all for myself." 2 Corinthians 6:16-18 MSG**

Kentucky's greatest son, Henry Clay, has gone down in history as the great compromiser. He was a compromiser in the very best sense in that he was able to be a peace maker among differing interests, and our country is much better for it.

***"I do not hide your righteousness in my heart; I speak of your faithfulness and salvation. I do not conceal your love and your truth from the great assembly." Psalm 40:9-11 NIV***

We are urged to be peacemakers but never compromisers in the bad sense. In spite of being encouraged to compromise what should be our core values as Christians on a daily basis, we are told to "stand firm," to "resist the devil and he will flee."

When we partake of or participate in any form of evil, we are compromising our new life in and who we are in Christ. The battle against: pride, envy, anger, laziness, greed, gluttony, and lust is a daily battle, and the temptation to compromise in any of these areas is a real and constant danger in the life of every believer.

We should never confuse the forgiveness of God with compromise. God has and always will hate sin, and what He has called abominations will always be abominations in His sight.

As much as good hates sin, the Good News is that He loves us even more -- so much more that He sent His only begotten Son to die on the cross so that we will not have to die and live in bondage to sin.

God's forgiveness is not a compromise. It is amazing grace freely given to all who call upon the name of the Lord.

***"The law was added so that the trespass might increase. But where sin increased, grace increased all the more." Romans 5:19-21 NIV***

When we survey the wondrous cross, we would do well to remember that it is wiser to cooperate with God who wants only the best for us than to compromise with the one who is out to destroy our souls.

**Father, help me to be a cooperator instead of a compromiser. Amen**

**December 23** **Read 2 Peter 2:14-25, Psalm 6**

## *Unholy Presumption*

**"But those who obey God's word really do love him. That is the way to know whether or not we live in him." 1 John 2:1 NLT**

> ***"O God, you take no pleasure in wickedness; you cannot tolerate the slightest sin."***
> ***Psalm 5:4 NLT***

The world takes its toll on all of us. Day after day, week after week, month after month, year after year we are barraged by sinful thoughts, sinful acts and sinful practices until we become callous and the power of these outrages against God to shock us becomes weaker and weaker.

We make unholy presumptions that maybe these things are not so bad after all. We rationalize that every one's doing it. That it's only a movie, so it really doesn't matter. We appropriate low standards of conduct and morality so that we are no longer set apart as salt and light. We compromise our witness and give aid and comfort to the enemy and great sadness to God.

We always want to think about the love, grace, and mercy of God, without thinking about the fact that God still hates sin and is angered by it. In His love, His wrath still falls and His chastening still occurs. Jesus' reaction to the money changers and the hypocrites show that God's righteous indignation is real.

> ***"And when people escape from the wicked ways of the world by learning about our Lord and Savior Jesus Christ and then get tangled up with sin and become its slave again, they are worse off than before."***
> ***2 Peter 2:16 NLT***

He loves us as His dear children in whom He delights and wants to take pleasure. He gives us growth pills of prayer, Word and Sacrament so that we grow strong in Him. He didn't make us to be willows bending and yielding with every breeze. He wants us to be mighty oaks standing firm against the storms.

When we see the stripes that were inflicted on Christ, the pain he suffered because of our sins, there is nothing trivial or casual about them. We should never fall into unholy presumption about sin.

**Father, keep me ever mindful of the price Jesus had to pay for me, and let me live accordingly. Amen**

Read Ephesians 3:17-20, Psalm 90 December 24

## *Going Home for Christmas?*

**"But God removed him from the kingship and replaced him with David, a man about whom God said, 'David son of Jesse is a man after my own heart, for he will do everything I want him to.'" Acts 13:22**

Christmas is the busiest travel season of the year. Busses, trains, airplanes and highways are jammed with travelers scurrying to get home in time to spend Christmas with family loved ones.

> ***"Lord, through all the generations you have been our home!" Psalm 90:1 NLT***

Christmas is a time for shared blessings and shared joys. For too short a period of time, there is sort of coming together among friends and strangers alike and there is a sweet savor of peace and good will.

Christmas can and should be the greatest time of all when we let it remind us of our coming home to God.

God came down from all of the perfection of heaven to show us how to come home to the heart of God through a personal relationship restored by faith in Jesus Christ, who came to show us God's heart manifested by His love, His Grace, His Mercy, and the wonder working power of His Spirit.

We all like sheep have gone astray, and even after we enter the sheep fold of the Good Shepherd that assures us of the joy of heaven when we die, we still need to come home to the heart of God through daily confession and repentance so that we can know the blessings of obedience and fulfillment in accomplishing God's purposes for us in this life on earth.

As we prepare to go home this Christmas, let's make sure that we prepare our hearts anew for going home to the heart of God from whom all blessings flow and be sure to ponder what Christmas is really all about.

> ***"And I pray that Christ will be more and more at home in your hearts as you trust in him." Ephesians 3:17a NLT***

**Father, let me daily come home to your heart through obedience. Amen**

December 25 Read Philippians 3:14-20, Proverbs 3

# *Keep Your Eye on the Prize*

**"What has captured your reason? What has weakened your vision, that you turn against God and say all these evil things?" Job 15:12 NLT**

Our lives are fueled by visions. We fantasize, visualize, and are motivated by visions.

> ***"Wise living gets rewarded with honor; stupid living gets the booby prize." Proverbs 3:5 MSG***

Visions have resulted in all of the great inventions of the world being conceived in someone's imagination and being birthed through the relentless pursuit of this vision.

Visionary leaders have birthed great ideas and worked to make them happen in government, business, and industry.

God has spoken through visions given to His Prophets down through the ages. Scripture itself has been written by the inspiration of the Holy Spirit by those God chose.

From a self centered perspective, our visions of what will make us happy lead us to pursue them relentlessly.

Whether it's possessions, sex, power, prestige, athletic prowess, or approval of peers, we seek to do whatever we can to find this happiness we think that these things will bring. And herein lies a big problem for many believers and nonbelievers alike.

When we let any other vision take priority in our lives over Jesus Christ as our hope of Glory, we are setting ourselves up for a big disappointment.

Christ alone can satisfy the longing God has placed in our hearts for Him, and Christ alone is the source of every real blessing in this life and the forever life to come. Our happiness should be based on who we are in Him and what we have through our relationship with Him. All other ground is sinking sand.

> ***"I strain to reach the end of the race and receive the prize for which God, through Christ Jesus, is calling us up to heaven" Philippians 3:14 NLT***

**Father, help me to keep my eye on who I am and what I have in You. Amen**

Read 1 Corinthians 3:16-20, Psalm 39 December 26

## *When it Doesn't Make Sense*

**"'My thoughts are completely different from yours,'" says the Lord. 'And my ways are far beyond anything you could imagine. For just as the heavens are higher than the earth, so are my ways higher than your ways and my thoughts higher than your thoughts.'" Isaiah 55:8-9**

Sometimes things just don't make sense from our human perspective. The good die young, the evil prosper, and wickedness seems to have the upper hand.

> ***"My mouth shall speak wisdom, And the meditation of my heart shall give understanding. Psalm 39:2***

*Scripture is full of paradoxes that only the enlightenment of the Holy Spirit by the grace of God allows to make any sense. "If you try to keep your life for yourself, you will lose it. But if you give up your life for my sake and for the sake of the Good News, you will find true life."(Mark 8:35) "Our hearts ache, but we always have joy. We are poor, but we give spiritual riches to others. We own nothing, and yet we have everything." (2 Corinthians 2:10) "Since I know it is all for Christ's good, I am quite content with my weaknesses and with insults, hardships, persecutions, and calamities. For when I am weak, then I am strong." (2 Corinthians 12:10)* – are just a few of many paradoxes that just don't make sense to the human mind.

It is only when we grow into the fullness of Christ and become mature in God's Word that we can accept that He does work all things for our good no matter what our human understanding.

> ***"Stop fooling yourselves. If you think you are wise by this world's standards, you will have to become a fool so you can become wise by God's standards." 1 Corinthians 3:18 NLT***

What does make sense is that God's Word is true, His promises are sure, and that He has plans to bless all who call upon the name of Jesus for the salvation of their souls and the blessing of eternal life. When we learn to walk by faith and not by sight everything we need to know will be perfectly clear to us and we can look forward to all the things we do not understand being made perfectly clear when we get to heaven.

**Father, when things don't make sense, let me commit my ways to you in full confidence of your good purposes being fulfilled. Amen**

**December 27** **Read Hebrews 10:30-39, Psalm 94**

## *God's Justice Will not be Denied*

**"Do not be overcome by evil, but overcome evil with good." Romans 12:19b NLT**

What should be our means of retribution and retaliation for people who hurt us? Should we retaliate in kind on the spot? Should we follow the conventional wisdom of the world and "don't get mad -- get even," and begin plotting as to how we will pay back with interest the hurt received?

> ***"God will make the sins of evil people fall back upon them. He will destroy them for their sins." Psalm 94:23a NLT***

Before we do any of the above, we should ask, what would Jesus do? Jesus forgave and asked God to forgive those who humiliated and mocked Him. He tells us, *"Love your enemies, do good to those who hate you, bless those who curse you, pray for those who mistreat you. " (Luke 6:27 NIV)*

We might also consider what God would do.

We don't need to worry about wrongdoers getting their just desserts. God says that vengeance belongs to Him. Our all powerful, all knowing God has said that the sins of the wicked will not go unpunished. We may never see God's punishment of the wicked, but we can be sure from God's infallible Word that He will mete it out in the time and manner He deems appropriate.

Knowing that God is much better at avenging than we could ever hope to be, we might better use all of the energy and emotion that getting even entails by spending it on something more positive, like loving and forgiving others as God has loved and forgiven us.

We need to realize that our only hope for escaping the consequences of our sins is confessing and receiving God's forgiveness through the blood of Jesus. God also says our sins will not be forgiven unless we forgive others. Dare we presume to try to get even?

> ***"Do not throw away this confident trust in the Lord, no matter what happens. Remember the great reward it brings you!" Hebrews 10:35 NLT***

**Father, help me respond with love and forgiveness to those who cause me harm. Amen**

Read 2 Timothy 2:14-22, Psalm 118 December 28

## *Would You Mind Repeating That?*

**"For by grace you have been saved through faith, and that not of yourselves; *it is* the gift of God, not of works, lest anyone should boast." Ephesians 2:8**

> ***"Let all who fear the Lord repeat: "His faithful love endures forever." Psalm 118:4***

Repetition is one of the key's to learning. When it comes to hearing the Good News, some people seem to have a big Attention Deficit Disorder attack. Others have become spiritually hearing impaired.

Even the best of believers need the positive reinforcement of hearing that God loves us unconditionally, forgives us forever, and accepts us just as we are and clothes us in the righteousness of Christ.

We will often hear and see testimonies about how the seeds of the gospel are planted by one and harvested by another. We can never underestimate the power of the Holy Spirit working through God's Word. God says His Word will never return void.

Being born again gives us instant holiness in God's eyes, and we become works in progress as we grow in spiritual maturity and into the likeness of Christ through our new life in Him. We all need the constant repetition of not only the milk of the Good News, but also a healthy daily diet of the solid food of the Word that will assure our spiritual growth.

. We do not need to hit someone over the head with the Good News, but we do need to take advantage of the divine appointments the Holy Spirit provides. We need to be ready to share the Good News by repeating it and by being sermons in shoes as we reflect God's love to others in our every day life.

> ***"Repeat these basic essentials over and over to God's people. Warn them before God against pious nitpicking, which chips away at the faith. It just wears everyone out." 2 Timothy 2:14 MSG***

Since a large majority of professing Christians answer the question of why God should let them in heaven by talking about the good life they've lead; it bears constant repeating to us all that we are going to heaven because of what Christ did on the cross, not because of any personal goodness.

**Father, keep me ever mindful of my need to hear your Word repeated for my nourishment and edification and to repeat it for the nourishment and edification of others. Amen**

December 29 Read 2 Corinthians 12:7-10, Lamentations 3

# *How to Cure Self Pity*

**"No temptation has overtaken you except such as is common to man; but God *is* faithful, who will not allow you to be tempted beyond what you are able, but with the temptation will also make the way of escape, that you may be able to bear it." 1 Corinthians 10:13**

We usually think of temptations in terms of breaking commandments like stealing, committing adultery, bearing false witness, or coveting what some one else has.

> ***"Yet I still dare to hope when I remember this: The unfailing love of the Lord never ends! By his mercies we have been kept from complete destruction. Great is his faithfulness; his mercies begin afresh each day. I say to myself, "The Lord is my inheritance; therefore, I will hope in him!"***
>
> ***Lamentations 3:22-24 NLT***

There are other temptations that are just as bad, if not worse. Worry, doubt, and especially pity parties are a few examples.

We are often so self-absorbed that we never even stop to consider that we are not the only ones who have ever had a problem and never even consider that it could be worse.

Some of the best therapy for self pity available is to look for someone worse off than you. The classic old saying, "I cried because I had no shoes until I saw a man who had no feet," says a lot about how we can get over it.

Even we who experience what we often perceive to be the worst of troubles are so blessed compared to what others we know are going through, instead of falling into self pity; we should fall into the ever loving arms of God with thanksgiving on our lips and joy in our hearts.

Read the book of Job, visit a homeless shelter, a nursing home, a leper colony, and or just look around and you will find all kinds of reasons to rejoice in your circumstances, knowing that they could be worse and that God has promised they will not last forever. Don't ever lose faith in the fact that He can and will work the worst of circumstances into something good for those who love Him.

> ***"Therefore I take pleasure in infirmities, in reproaches, in needs, in persecutions, in distresses, for Christ's sake. For when I am weak, then I am strong."***
>
> ***2 Corinthians 12:10***

**Father, help me to maintain a good attitude in all situations. Amen**

**Read Luke 6, Psalm 17** **December 30**

## *Who's the Apple of Your Eye?*

**"Keep my commands and live, and my law as the apple of your eye." Proverbs 7:2**

Talk about fatal attraction! Eve's attraction to the forbidden fruit (commonly referred to as an apple) brought sin and death into the world.

> ***"Keep me as the apple of Your eye; hide me under the shadow of Your wings," Psalm 17:8***

We often find ourselves attracted to things and people belonging to others, and we can bring a lot of misery and pain to ourselves and to others when we act on this attraction.

When lust, envy, or covetousness becomes the apple of our eyes, as the tree of knowledge of good and evil was for Eve, bad things are bound to happen unless we follow God's admonition to flee. When we stand firm against the temptations of the flesh, the world, or the devil, we are promised that satan will do the fleeing. We stand firm by putting on the full armor of God daily.

When Jesus Christ becomes the apple of our eye, great things begin to happen. When He becomes not only the Lord of our Salvation, but the Lord of our Life, we become the apple of His eye that He created us to be.

God created us in His own image for His pleasure and for fellowship with Him. We are the highest of creation and the only creatures given a soul for worship, fellowship, and relationship with God.

Because of the fall of man in the garden, we have all been born as "bad apples" that will rot with sin and corruption unless we realize our impurity and our need for a Savior.

> ***"You don't get wormy apples off a healthy tree, nor good apples off a diseased tree. The health of the apple tells the health of the tree." Luke 6:43 MSG***

When we receive Jesus Christ as Savior and Lord, we become the "apples of God's eye" and the "good apples" that will bear the good fruit for which God created us.

Who knows, by the grace of God, we might even plant orchards of gift-quality apples as we live out our lives under the shelter of His wings being faithful to the Great Commandment and Great Commission.

**Father, help me to be a faithful attraction and the apple of Your eye. Amen.**

**Read Hebrews 11:12-40, Psalm 92** **December 31**

# *There's Gold in Them Thar Years*

The age of retirement has long been termed the golden years. Visions of all the golf we want to play, all the traveling we want to do, all of the leisure time we will have sometimes seem to be too good to be true and often are.

> ***"Even in old age they will still produce fruit; they will remain vital and green." Psalm 92:14 NLT***

For many people, after a few weeks or few years in retirement, boredom and depression set in and the visions of pleasure have turned into worry and despair.

From God's perspective, retire is what we do when we die, and the golden years are for storing up more gold in the first national bank of heaven as we use all of our accumulated wisdom, extra time and any left over resources in doing many of the things for which we were created and equipped to do by our life's experiences.

By far, the happiest older people I know are those who still have passion for Jesus and are actively involved in ministry to others in faithfulness to the great commission and great commandment.

For men and women alike, opportunities abound in mentoring or even taking in foster children, counseling and sharing problems with people going through some of our "been there – done that's."

Love of travel can take on new meaning when it is combined with taking mission trips to share the gospel in different parts of the world. Time for writing, visiting the sick and the prisoners, comforting and encouraging, doing "honey do" jobs for those with no honeys to do them anymore are all just a few of the retirement year pursuits which can be real gold mine.

> ***"For God had far better things in mind for us that would also benefit them, for they can't receive the prize at the end of the race until we finish the race." Hebrews 11:40 NLT***

Using the extra time and energy to get deeper and learn more about God's Word, and to put our faith sharing skills to greater use bring added assurance and joy to our hearts and a smile on God's face.

When we think about it, there's no sense in waiting for golden years to begin our gold mining operation. We can start right now!

**Father, thank you for letting me discover the real gold of my golden years. Amen**

# Alphabetical Index (A-H)

## Alphabeticl Index H-T

# Alphabetical Index T-Z